PROPHETIC WATERS

Reader, I call these things *prophecy;*
but I wish I be not all this
while writing *history.*

COTTON MATHER

Magnalia Christi Americana; Or,
The Ecclesiastical History of New-England

John Seelye

PROPHETIC
WATERS

The River

in Early American Life and Literature

New York

Oxford University Press

1977

N.B.

This book has taken nearly four years to write and would have taken much longer had it not been for the patronage of the National Endowment for the Humanities and the John Simon Guggenheim Memorial Foundation, public and private funds that freed me from academic responsibilities for two of the four years. Much of that time was spent at the American Antiquarian Society, Worcester, Mass., whose Director, Marcus A. McCorison, extended both working space and services during a period when he was sorely pressed for the same, and I am particularly grateful for the patient help of Mary Brown and her staff.

While working with the Society's collections, I made the acquaintance of Mason I. Lowance, Jr., whose dedication to early American literature changed my original plans, which were then further altered by several suggestions made by Everett Emerson, his colleague at the University of Massachusetts. I am indebted to both men also for the reading which they gave this book in its final stages, and am grateful in this respect as well to Giles Gunn, C. Hugh Holman, and Lewis Leary, my colleagues at the University of North Carolina. Other debts, though outstanding, are for the most part indirect, being to a number of scholars whose writings have established a tradition to which I should like to think my own book belongs, in terms of subject if not approach, an account of which I attempt to render in the "Ex Libris" essay at the end.

There too will be found the scholarly apparatus provided here, an alphabetical list of primary sources cited within, to which page references are made parenthetically, with some occasional help from the abbreviations which appear at the head of the bibliography. Readers who check quotations against the original will find alterations in spelling, syntax, and punctuation—modernizations which, with an occasional elision or minor addition, are intended not to distort the meaning of the text, but to clarify it and synchronize it with the surrounding prose. Antique spellings and conventions add a certain charm to writings of the colonists, but quaintness was not their intention, and we do them a disservice when we preserve their archaic usages.

Curiously, modernization produces one distorting effect, for nowhere in the texts quoted do the ancients, Cavalier or Puritan, use capital "H" when referring to deity by means of the pronoun. That "slight dash of flunkeyism" (to borrow Melville's phrase) is our own.

J.S.

Hillsborough, N.C.
July 1976

Contents

Contents

LIST OF MAPS

Prologue
i. Imperial Design

If we wish to comprehend the imperialistic thrust of American history then we must widen the limits of our literary domain, acknowledging the informing power of our colonial womb, the contingent, even conterminous English empire. But for a number of well-known reasons, there is a scarcity of seventeenth- and early eighteenth-century writing in the South, an absence which makes the establishment of a counterpoise to the sheer mass of New England production difficult. Perry Miller was able to demonstrate that Samuel Danforth's *Errand into the Wilderness* is a segment of a vector that ends at Walden Pond, but to what does William Byrd's Dividing Line point? And from whence? It is one purpose of the book which follows to answer that question, to demonstrate that the twin trajectories of Puritan and Cavalier are convergent legs of a compass defining empire and epic in America.

We can, without diminishing the accomplishment of Perry Miller, do him one better, honoring his thesis concerning the genesis of the *genus* Yankee while reinforcing the "Virginian priority" he early defined and later neglected. We can do so, however, only by ignoring the provincial rule which has hitherto defined as "American" those writers who either had the good fortune to be born in this country or the good sense to die here, a distinction which has in effect guaranteed the preeminence of Puritan writing in studies of colonial literature. We can thereby establish both a newer and an older point of origin, a beginning somewhat further back in time than the Pilgrim advent, a coherence with a clearer narrative outline than the doctrinal wrangles of Boston divines. It is a design which does justice both to the intelligence of Governor John Winthrop and the energy of Captain John Smith, giving as much weight to Byrd's occasional, fractious flights as to the fructuous Matherine matter.

By starting at the original point of English tenancy we can establish

3

a continuity of experience which unites sectional encounters with the American landscape, demonstrating that apparent differences are parts of an uneasy whole, a discursive concordance given unity by an imperial dialectic set in motion by primal events. The aesthetics of imperialism in America, like our institutions, is an eclectic mix of Old World traditions and New World occasions, in organic terms an amoebic genesis, being at first an extension of British empire, but becoming by a gradual process of transference a detached, nuclear empire in itself, ready for further expansion west. The critical struggle in this regard was not the conflict which resulted in political independence, but the half-century of border battles known in this country as the French and Indian Wars, reflections of greater business in Europe but gaining cumulative impact and a certain uniformity of definition here.

What follows, however, does not deal with the French and Indian Wars at length, the conduct and conclusion of which lie beyond the limits which decorum has decreed. The succeeding chapters should be read as an anticipatory exercise, a selection of people, places, and events—literal and literary, mainstream and marginal—which prefigure in the manner of prophecy (and prelude) the apocalypse to come. This book covers, roughly, the first 150 years of England in America, commencing with the ventures launched by Sir Walter Raleigh and ending with William Byrd's terminal demarcation of Virginia's drastically diminished terrain. By beginning and ending in the South, a certain emphasis is given to the Virginian priority, but the intervening bulk is mostly, once again, the matter of (and with) the Puritans. Still, the material in question is not the theological literature with which Perry Miller was largely involved—the sermons and doctrinal tracts reflecting the drift of Puritan thought—but rather the narratives, histories, and poetry with which New England writers gained metaphoric mastery over the landscape, shaping it to suit the changing dimensions of their errand.

That literature will be shown, finally, as forming a complement to the works engendered by Captain Smith and Planter Byrd, the writings of Puritans and Cavaliers falling into place as sequential chapters in one long literary work, an emerging action that is the premier American epic. Less a neoclassic arrangement of unities than an impromptu, organic evolution, an often discordant concord of parts, the American epic is the kind of action that begins as a comedy but darkens toward a tragic end. If America was promises, few were kept, but like promissory notes they were met by extending indebtedness at ruinous rates. America was, more than anything, space, which as *tabula rasa* or blank check provided a relativistic zone, a white world in which men became the monsters they sought to destroy. As space, America was amazement, less a new than a novel world, commencing as that mystery Columbus stumbled upon when he inscribed his diagonal westward in a mistaken passage to India. An interrupted voyage that provided the perspective for a continuing, discontinuous design, it ends as the Dividing Line driven by William Byrd into the Allegheny Mountains, named for a river that would carry the tide of empire into a farther West.

ii. Typick Stream

It is a self-evident truth that fiction mirrors reality, but it is equally true though perhaps not so obvious that fiction is reflected in reality, that historical episodes have a tendency to assume the terminations of Freytag's pyramid. The oldest fictions were presumed to have a basis in real events, however legendary or mythic, and from the American experience there emerge equivalent stories, not oral but written accounts which often approximate because they inspired what would become dominant American genres. Moreover, since so many of the early narratives, reports, and histories were written to encourage colonization or the expansion of colonial enterprise, they are heavy with hope, anticipation being couched in a rhetoric that is pointed toward a glorious yet obscure future, whose reality was often an ironic reversal of expectations. These incipient fictional qualities are reinforced by the literariness of the authors, who even in their ephemeral productions mixed heroic allusions with predictive statistics and who in their more ambitious projects tended toward epic expression.

Whether mercantile, military, or millennial in strategy, the earliest American literature reaches out from record toward revelation, fusing fact with the future, a visionary blend often identified with divine purpose, a transcendent cartography that resulted in the transformation

5

of the landscape on the one hand and in the eventual modification of expectations on the other. So parameters of encounter became the perimeters of definition, for where the unknown provides a certain but unmeasurable quantity of unexpected event, there error abounds, evolving slowly into acknowledged reality but in the meantime adding an element of equivalent fiction to accounts of the New World. Thus, according to George Stewart, the first explorers of the North American continent, putting in at some river's mouth in search of a harbor or the Northwest Passage, would take the name of the stream from the mouth of some Indian, who, having no concept of a river as a connected whole, would supply the name of one aspect of the region touched by the waters thereabout. Another Indian might have supplied another word, and indeed different explorers gave the same river different names, but of the many, chance and occasion selected the one which endured, a name extended thenceforth along the length of the watercourse, becoming fact through usage, though a mistake at the start.

By reason of this mixture of error and emerging actuality, the nature of the gigantic tale that is America, like the Conradian fable it resembles, is defined by a determining degree of inadvertency, of plans gone awry, vectors tilted in an unforeseen direction, chance opportunities seized and warped into circumstantial patterns of event—an improvisatory quality that begins with the accidental discovery by Columbus of an island that became a continent. Comic at one extreme, tragic at the other, the story is disjunctive throughout, a structure in which intention and execution seldom match. George Sandys spent his scarce spare time in Virginia translating Ovid's *Metamorphoses,* the first book (as opposed to pamphlet) written in what would become the continental United States, and if Sandys was something less than an ideal administrator, he provides a certain poetic prescience at the beginning of things. For America as a literary creation is a series of Ovidian transformations, shapes shifting before our eyes as differences are resolved by new possibilities, a unity of continuous change fed by antithetical conceptions, promoting the disjunctiveness that characterizes the Puritan and Cavalier experience.

Because of the primacy of rivers in the exploration and settlement of the Atlantic seaboard, waterways in the North and South play dominant (though dissimilar) roles, as in the matter of their names providing Ovidian shapes that determine the unfolding plot. A protean quantity

and a transfiguring threshold, the river is a defining agent in the metamorphosis of colonies to republic, serving as entrance or border but
always as a symbol of what might be obtained beyond, whether a more
fertile land or a water route to India. "The thing you're after / may lie
around the bend," writes Charles Olson at the start of an epic informed
by the heroics of colonization, and as in his metaphor, the bend in the
river becomes a bight, one in a series of the meanders that lend serpentine shape to both rivers and progress in America. Conrad reminds us
that before there was a Belgian Congo there was a Roman Thames, an
imperial genesis giving forth the fiery seeds that became the brood born
along America's Indian streams, those wilderness confluencies that
nursed a new notion of mankind. Again, as with their Indian names,
America's rivers in terms of epic continuities have their sources in
their mouths, a hermeneutic serpent of mythic and oracular origins ex
pressing the alchemic union of the Old World and the New. So the
Atlantic marries the virgin land, as in European atlases reaching inland by means of open-ended blue latitudes, ocean transformed into
avenues that extend dominion—and illusion—into infinity. Rivers of
darkness or rivers of light, they are above all else prophetic waters, in
which America's future may be read.

I

DIVERSE VOYAGES

Columbus, Cartier,
and the Conradian Shape
of Adventure in America.

i. Myth

Sailing west for the East, Columbus encountered paradisiac islands, one of which he mistook for the mainland of Cathay. On his second voyage, also, continents persisted in becoming islands, but on his third and final journey what the Admiral assumed was yet another island proved to be mainland at last. Sailing into the Gulf of Paria, he was met by a terrific tide of fresh water rushing out of the multitudinous mouths of the Orinoco, the Great River of the South, unmistakable evidence of a continental presence where no land was supposed to be. Struggling toward an acknowledgment of that incredible fact, a gathering awareness of the awesomeness of possibility, Columbus charted the outer margins of America's myth, determining the coast toward which all other captains would sail.

Crazed by adversity, believing himself a vessel of God's will, his very name a signature of prophecy, Columbus decided that he had discovered the ultimate West, that the Great River of the South was one of the mythic quaternity flowing out of the heart of Eden, milk from a primal green breast. At the very start, then, the New World was a mad fiction, an apocryphal text between known worlds, a book which would continue to expand as new chapters were added. As literature, America was the greatest creation of the Renaissance, an eclectic epic in which the imposition of expectations shaped and was shaped by reality, a continuing dialectic of encounter, an action at times heroic, tragic, comic, but above all else a westward-moving line, or rather a convergence of lines at a vanishing point, vectors aligned with the Thirtieth Parallel, along which Columbus set sail for India. *"Indios"* he called the red men who greeted him on the shores of what he assumed was the land he sought, an accident that became a fact and a symbol too. For as George Stewart tells us, "India" itself was a misnomer, taken by invading Persians from the great river Indus (Sanscrit *sindhuh* means simply "river") and applied by the Greeks to the land and its people. Thus the conquerers from the Old World repeated the errors of a world even more ancient, and in so doing they asserted the primacy of rivers to the imperial process. A confluency of voyages, the westward course of European empire continued by means of watercourses that flowed out of and thereby provided entrance into the unknown continent, dark veins from a savage heart.

Rio de la Plata the Spaniards named their imperial stream but *Plomo* would have been a more accurate word, as glorious expectations faded into dreary, deadly reality. For it was up the dragon-mouth Orinoco that the Spanish dream finally disappeared, symbolized by the elusive golden man, El Dorado, a gilded myth who cast off his skin in the jungle, becoming an Indian once again. America, anagrammatized, becomes "a chimera," monster of illusions, and if her rivers proved to be Ovidian streams, capable of manifold metamorphoses, they were personified in the red men who lived along their banks. The Old World provided several epic models for New World adventurers, but Hercules' labors and travels furnish the mythic archetype, identifying gold with the heroic burden, the imperial quest, and in his hunt for the Hesperidean Apples, Hercules first wrestled with Nereus, the Old Man of the Sea, whom he found on the bank of the Great River of the North, and next he wrestled for answers from Antaeus, Son of Ocean and Earth. So with white men and red in the New World, for if America was a mystery symbolized by its rivers, then its wonder was a problem to be solved by grappling with it and questioning it in the form of that fluid, slippery, elusive incarnation, the Indian.

As the river opening inland provides the epic route for the New World hero, so the Indian becomes his chief ally and his most treacherous opponent, an indisputable necessity and a ubiquitous threat. Confronting the red man, the American Janus, questing heroes from the East demanded the secret of the West and were rewarded with ceaseless transformations, fluid fictions mingled with fact which led to dark and violent conclusions. Christopher Columbus again proves the point, for the mystic Christ-bearing dove in his name provided a cruel irony when his quest for Cathay became a holy mission which ended in the bloody Iliums of Incan and Aztec citadels. His mercantile adventure turned into an imperial scheme that was graced by Christian zeal, a mixture of motives which was met by the similarly ambivalent mood of Carib

Indians, greed and ingenuousness which heated into anger, then ex-
ploded, licensing the massacres which followed. And those terrible
twins, Pizarro and Cortez, were themselves transformed into Coronado
and De Soto, whose deluded quests signaled the decline of Spanish
empire in America and gave warrant for Cervantes's burlesque con-
quistadore, Quixote a quietus to the chivalric ideal. Led on by Indians,
Coronado's search for golden cities took him into the dead level of
Kansas, while De Soto's quest ended in the great river which he discovered but which he did not seek to find.

De Soto's monumental mischance puts a double seal on the Spanish
experience, in which rivers were for the most part incidental. Spain in
America was largely a matter of plateaus, mountain strongholds, great
cities to be sacked, a mirror image which holds true for subsequent
New World epics. Thus Portugal, despite her primacy in exploration,
settled on and for a marginal, coastal section of South America, while
New France took shape from a long-armed river, a western Seine, empire which would be stretched to epic length by La Salle's exploration
of the river De Soto had discovered. More than any other colonial presence, New France was river-borne, her experience transforming still
further the Ovidian pattern of encounter with illusion. Columbus in
Canada is Jacques Cartier, his quest also a compound search for gold
and the Northwest Passage, his name yet another prophetic cluster:
Jacques is Jacob, the supplanter, symbol of the Pauline mystery of
iniquity, and Cartier, the man of maps, charting not the coast but the
interior route for those who would follow him to North America, his
great River of the North a line along the Fiftieth Parallel, a waterway
holding steady into the west toward *La Chine*. Columbus provides the
drama of entrance, of first encounter, but it is Cartier's adventure which
lays down the water-borne heroic line in North America, myth becoming mode, events transformed into the stuff of literature, the premier
river epic in the New World.

Straight and broad lay the Hochelaga, the St. Lawrence, peopled
like the Caribbean islands with wild men happy to trade precious
things for trinkets, jubilant over the presence of generous white gods,
hospitable and willing to tell wonderful stories about what was to be
found farther on up the great river. Like Columbus's three voyages,
Cartier's progress along his fabulous line was in stages, each holding
some meaning, not only for himself and the Indians he encountered,

13

but for the future, a long prospect involving France and the natives of Canada, and an even longer one, a far distant future concerning the fate of empires, a balance of power which turned on the fact of the red man and the rivers along which he lived. From our vantage point, determined by a future that Cartier could hardly have imagined, we can understand better the meaning of what he was told by Indians in signs and signals concerning the western regions, discerning between reality and illusion. More important, perhaps, we can perceive other meanings, dark prophecies implicit in gestures, unfolding destiny in fetal event, chance encounters which have been given a symbolic luster with the passage of time and the massive weight of history, geopolitical strata equivalent to geological layers. So pine pitch turns to amber, imprisoning chance ephemera, granting casual immortality.

Once again it is the Indian who is the catalytic conjunction, his hospitality and eagerness to trade furs for falcon bells changing to a more equivocal mood, often erupting in sudden, seemingly inexplicable hostility. Though, as with Columbus, we have only the white man's side of the story, it is obvious that the Indians, being human, had motives like those of the Europeans, and sought to get the better part of any bargain. It was from the start a confidence game, the great American sport, and as the white strangers grew more confident, the red natives grew less so, an uneasiness which increased as the Indian puzzled out the strangers' errand and saw that it was not merely a trading visit. So the Indian emerges once again as a personification of treachery, merging with the familiar outlines of the archetypal betrayer and liar, becoming thereby a suitable antagonist in the unfolding action. The result, as literature, is an epic which, like Tasso's *Jerusalem Delivered,* mingles classical formulas with elements from medieval romance, an eclectic mix endemic to the American mode, a new ordering of forms resulting from the struggle of the Old World to fabricate an artifact capable of encompassing, and thereby conquering, an overwhelming novelty.

ii. Mode

In America the Virgilian epic undergoes a sea change, yet another metamorphosis testifying to the power of new space to transform, for when men move, their works expand, sloughing off boundaries once thought absolute. Camoens celebrated da Gama's exploits by shaping his epic passage to India along Virgilian lines, thus confirming the classical dimension of the Renaissance imperial design, but by so doing he failed to give expression to the grim realities of his own colonial experience which violated the clean line and elevation of his model. In terms of generic unity, the true poets of the New World epic were either chroniclers like Peter Martyr or the captains like Columbus whose reports contain the raw stuff of adventure, often vague and incomplete, shrouded intentionally in secrecy and darkened further by ignorance and misinformation. Unlike the Virgilian model, these heroic forms are fragmentary, lacking the neat finials of classical architectonics, and they are hortatory, like Columbus's reports and letters to Ferdinand and Isabella urging further exploration, calling for more men and money, promising immense profits to come. Virgil dignifies Augustus Caesar by celebrating the mythical Aeneas, but New World writers glorify kings and queens by describing a fabulous future rather than a legendary past, and are concerned with what *will*, not what *has*, happened. That is an important difference, and gives definition to America.

The errands of Greek heroes always bring them home again, even the Hesperides—the definitive West for Greece—lying only so far as the farthest end of the Mediterranean. That central sea, that azure circle, bends all voyages back to the homeland, a geographical expression of classical unity. The epic of the Jews is likewise a story of perpetual return and renewal, commencing with Exodus and culminating in the heroic rise of David, forever retaking the Canaan promised to Abraham and Jacob. The story of Aeneas as told by Virgil contains an analogous motif, the hero's voyage to Italy being a return to ancestral domain, a fulfilment of prophecy. Only with the advent of Christ is a new horizon introduced, the Acts of Paul—a Roman Jew who is also the first Christian hero in the classical mold—reversing the direction and implication of Greek and Roman voyages. St. Paul promises a transcendental, not an earthly goal, an empire of God, not man, and his millennialism tinctures all subsequent Christian adventures, his mission becoming the Crusades, in which the pacific spirit of the Gospels was transformed by northern mists into a barbaric equivalent of the Homeric *élan*. In the Crusader, Christ was shaped to the dimensions of Odin, that Saxon god who combines the qualities of Mercury and Mars, being a god of war and voyages, madness and cunning, conquest and commerce, providing a perfect model for New World enterprise, the Knight-errant.

Columbus, despite his southern origins, is an avatar of Odin, as his little fleet set sail along a line parallel to that of Viking voyagers, and with Columbus the epic voyage for the first time breaks out of the mystic circle, his search for a shorter way to a world ancient as time taking him to a land new as Eden, thereby shattering all notions of limitation and duration, revealing not only heaven but eternity on earth. Still, what Columbus found—or thought he had found—was shaped by what he knew—or thought he knew—and the future he proposed was a version, a magnification, of Europe's past. And those captains who followed the Spaniards to America had their own expectations colored by the Spanish experience, no more so than in the case of Cartier. In his adventures we can detect a new form emerging, endemic to New World conditions and imbued with a sense of the future, yet Cartier's narrative is laden with Old World attitudes, an organic manifestation of expectations and realities that is the dialectic of encounter.

In distinguishing between a literary artifact and a factual report, we often forget that literature begins as experience—as record—that the roots of epic are deep in impacted layers of historic event. In extrapolating from Cartier's adventure an epic line we are performing the function of the poet, who abstracts design from unordered circumstance. Moreover, what was reality for Cartier is fiction—romance—for us because so remote from us. Further, what the Captain took for reality was often an illusion, whether a golden mirage cast by him on a blank horizon or suspicion of treachery darkening untoward actions into agents of mystery and suspense. It is precisely in this penumbraic

16

area that the uniqueness—the Americanness—of Cartier's experience is found, producing a literature which is not a conscious invention but a mixture nonetheless of fact and fiction, giving the shape of wonder to his American adventure. Taking its thrust from commercial and nationalistic motives, Cartier's narrative takes its set from an imperial aesthetic, and though later manifestations of heroics in America will evince a more self-consciously literary form, they are in effect imitations of Cartier's adventure. His river is an incursion of ocean leading the way into a wilderness toward the western sea, an inland extension of the Fiftieth Parallel, a navigational line equivalent to Columbus's Thirtieth, the both mythic ligatures binding a new world to the old. Cartier's line of advance halts, finally, but imagination continues the trajectory into an infinite Beyond.

iii. Matter

Jacques Cartier sailed to America in the sparkling wake of Giovanni da Verrazzano, who had in 1524 explored the Atlantic coast from Cape Fear to Cape Small, looking for signs of gold and northwest passage, and who had caught a glimpse through the North Carolina banks of what appeared to be an inland sea, which he assumed would open to the Pacific Ocean and hence to Cathay. As Verrazzano's name suggests, his assumption was truly crazy, but it contains a certain crazy truth, inspiring three centuries of westering exploration that resulted in what must surely be the greatest example of self-fulfilling prophecy. Verrazzano's was a magnificent illusion, as his map was a broad and open-ended design, and Cartier had the distinction of being the first to go in quest of that great, geopolitical grail. The St. Malo pilot set sail just ten years after the Florentine navigator, and like Verrazzano, Cartier was in the service of Francis I of France, but his version of America provides emphatic contrast to that of his predecessor, an alternative stress which Verrazzano himself had anticipated.

The burden of Verrazzano's "Relation" describes the southeastern coast, which he portrays in glowing terms, but the paradisiac imagery fades as the navigator trends toward the northern shore, and the inhabitants of the New World likewise change, from a handsome, "courteous and gentle" people to men "full of rudeness and ill manners, and so barbarous, that by no signs that ever we could make, we could have any kind of traffic with them" (70). Cartier first touched where Verrazzano departed America, along the Labrador and Newfoundland coasts, and the natives he encountered in Gaspé Bay corresponded to Verrazzano's Yahoos, being so poor that they had nothing worth bartering save the furs they were dressed in, and after they had stripped themselves they began stealing what they could no longer buy. "Wild men," Cartier called them, "truly called wild" (23). He was more optimistic, however, about the wealth to be taken from the seas he found the Indians fishing in, and the land looked fertile too, level as a plain and summertime green. Before departing, the Captain erected a traditional cross, sign of Christian possession and a navigational mark, and he observed the usual custom of capturing a couple of Indians so as to learn more about the interior. At the end of the account of his first voyage to Canadian waters there is a brief glossary of Indian words, a *vade mecum* of empire: In that little dictionary the first word is "God" (for which the Hurons had no term), the last is "Sword" (for which they did), and at the heart of the list, at the absolute center of Cartier's testament, is the fatal word, "Gold" (30-31).

When Cartier recorded Indian words it was in the colonial process of teaching his captives French, by means of which he learned what he wanted to know about their country, including stories of copper ornaments and a large Indian town called Hochelaga at the head of navigation on the great river of the same name. For Europeans who saw America through lenses tinted by the Spanish precedent, "copper" was a metal with alchemical properties, news of which always held out the certain hope of gold, and stories of great Indian towns likewise had a promising Spanish resonance. So Cartier returned to Canada in 1535, his Indian informants serving as pilots up the Great River of the North, but when they reached their own village—called "Canada"— they refused to guide the French any farther, nor would they come back aboard Cartier's ships. Despite this recalcitrant attitude on the part of his guides, Cartier found the "Lord of Canada" to be a friendly old man, who kissed the Captain in approved French fashion and then draped the white man's arm around his red neck, a gesture of trust embued with considerable irony by subsequent events. For in years to come that French arm then resting lightly on the Indian would grow long and heavy, reaching far into his country, past his little town (then a French fortress called Quebec), past the greater town of Hochelaga (Montreal), past the great falls and the greater lakes to the west. Then, bending south, it would reach to the Gulf of Mexico, holding the entire Five Nations within its ambitious angle, defining the meaning of empire in New France.

Despite the hospitable reception given Cartier by the Lord of Canada, which included the gift of an Indian maiden as a gesture of good will, the Captain's translators insisted that the French should not proceed to the up-river town. This mixture of friendliness and stubbornness suggests that the Indians of Canada wished to keep the white man's trade to themselves, but Cartier was convinced that wicked motives were involved, that a plot of some sort was brewing, and nothing that happened afterward removed his distrust. Adding dramatic tension to the events which followed, Cartier's suspicions provide a definitive complexity to his encounter with the men of the New World, darkening his relations with them thenceforth. It was, therefore, without their help that he began the next stage of his journey up the great river, sailing in his pinnace through "as goodly a country as possibly can with eye be seen, all replenished with very goodly trees, and vines laden as full of grapes as could be all along the river, which rather seemed to have been planted by man's hand than otherwise" (54). This pastoral landscape was inhabited by a friendly people, who gave the Captain gifts of food (and more children), demonstrating great joy at his coming.

When Cartier at last put ashore near the great inland town, he was greeted even more effusively, the Indians dancing and singing all night long before escorting him to their city. In imitation of Columbus, Cartier dressed in his finery for the occasion, and like Pizarro he was treated with reverence and awe by the inhabitants of Hochelaga, which was hardly a Cuzco, but a fortified village surrounded by long palisades. Cartier's entrance was accompanied by great jubilation, an opportunity which the pious Captain was quick to seize. As Columbus bore Christ's name to the New World, Jacques Cartier shared the Savior's initials, and was willing to share His gospel, also, beginning with a most appropriate text, the Word as preached in the wilderness by John the Baptist. Then, having pointed the way to heaven for the heathen, Cartier (whose initials were also Caesar's) gained a terrestrial prospect for himself from a near-by mountain, which he called Mount Royal.

Upon this imperial height the Captain struck a Spanish pose, and though his peak in Canada gave him no view of a western ocean, it commanded a fair and level plain, and the Indians described not only great lakes but an inland sea beyond the falls, verifying Verrazzano's map. Cartier's vantage point took in a symbolic terrain, for it would be the locus some two centuries hence of an epical battle for empire, the scene of a terminal Iliad. Symbolic too were the Indian stories of gold and silver and of waterways stretching into an infinite west toward India, information conveyed by means of "signs" and tokens, imperfect communication typical of the ambiguities which define heroic action in America. Such reports tended to gain, not lose, in translation, and in reading them we must always take into account the Indian's propensity for telling strangers what they wanted to hear as much as what they wanted to know.

Cartier, for his part, was so eager for news of gold and westward passage that he lay aside his distrust of Indians in order to believe them, including the down-river inhabitants of Canada who described the fabulous wealth of Saguenay. But he continued to fear treachery, and the suffering and deprivation of a long winter only increased his suspicions. Yet in the end it was the French who proved most treacherous. When spring arrived, they lured their Indian guides once more back on ship, once more to take them back to France. This time Cartier took with him also the friendly old Lord of Canada, who "even from his childhood had never left off nor ceased from traveling into strange countries, as well by water and rivers as by land" (79). But the ancient Indian's unasked-for journey was his last, his life as well as his travels ending in what must have seemed to him a very strange country indeed, and when Cartier returned to Canada in 1541 the Wise Old Man of Earth and Waters was not with him.

Still, his ghost seems to have led the Captain up the Great River of the North, for Cartier's third voyage was an ironic fulfillment of the stories he had been told about the riches of Canada. Along the winding course of the Cap Rouge he found "leaves of fine gold as thick as a man's nail" and black stones sensuously veined with gold and silver threads, and another kind of stone, "like diamonds, the most fair, polished, and excellently cut that it is possible for a man to see" (98-99). This was in the *annus mirabilis,* 1542, the year in which Coronado was tacking across the dusty reality of Verrazzano's Sea in search of Quivera as De Soto was heading in the opposite direction on a similar quest under the same hot, brassy sun. Coronado returned in disgust to Mexico and De Soto, on his way back to Florida, was in death committed to the great river which was to him in life an incidental discovery. Cartier's diamonds, likewise, turned out to be crystals of quartz, his gold and silver the kind found by fools, but in 1542 he thought he had gathered a great fortune, and celebrated the fiftieth anniversary of America's discovery by leaving the continent, never to return.

Encounters with the New World by the Old tended to bring out the beast in men, white as well as red, for survival and prevalence are matters of animal courage, of cunning and superior strength. These are barbaric, not civilized virtues, and beneath the silken finery in which Cartier paraded through the wilderness a wild shadow moved, a silhouette resembling the naked men who walked beside him. Still, barbaric virtues are heroic, even Homeric, and the epic voyage initiated by Cartier on the St. Lawrence would be continued westward by a daring breed of men, half-white, half-red, hybrids symbolic of a mercantile marriage of necessity, *voyageurs* and *coureurs de bois,* names redolent of adventure. The brave explorers who succeeded Cartier in New France, Champlain and La Salle being the greatest among them, extended his trajectory and cemented alliances with Indian tribes along the way, a play of power which made enemies of the Iroquois, thereby aligning aboriginal rivalries with the struggle between France and England for dominance in North America. Two centuries after Cartier's last voyage those complex, combined forces heaved toward their epic conclusion, by which time it was no longer easy to distinguish white men from red as shadows slipped silently through the darker woods.

In 1680 Robert Cavelier La Salle ended his hazardous, solitary trek across the Canadian wilderness from Fort Frontenac to Fort Crèvecoeur, on the Illinois River. By descending to the Mississippi, and then following the great river to the Gulf, La Salle intended to complete an imperial diagram begun by Cartier and Champlain, and he succeeded in doing so two years later. But in 1680 he found his fort deserted and in ruins, having been abandoned by his men, and across the remains of the boat which was to have carried France down the Mississippi, the deserters had scrawled *"Nous sommes tous sauvages,"* a Conradian graffito as Parkman's La Salle is surely an American Kurtz, a reminder of the precedence of the St. Lawrence and the Mississippi over the Congo as an inland pathway of imperialism. That crazy scrawl, La Salle's mad scheme, Verrazzano's nonexistent sea, Cartier's mistaken diamonds and gold, these Conradian touches emphasize the ludicrous dimension of the unfolding American epic. Often abominable, always fascinating, it is a gargantuan story of questing knights who resemble picaresque as much as romantic heroes, for a long, lean, quixotic shadow dogs them through the American woods: knights erroneous, they are the chivalric impulse gone mad, imposing rehearsed but impossible expectations on the vast white shape of the New World.

II

DIVINE
TOBACCO

Hakluyt and the Virginia Business.

i. Trumpet Shrill Thrice Sounded

Where Cervantes mocked the chivalric impulse for a fraud, his great book like the Great Armada a closing chapter in the epic of imperial Spain, Edmund Spenser drew on the same body of materials to provide a pattern for English gentlemen-adventurers, adding hugely to the literature that signaled England's entrance into the contest for empire, instilling a growing mood of nationalism with chivalric idealism. His choice of St. George for the hero of the first and prototypical book of *The Faerie Queene* was a patriotic necessity, but it gave an archetypal significance to the emerging action, for like Langland's crusading Piers Plowman, Spenser's savior-hero has rustic virtues, a celebration of the English yeoman who was the economic (and martial) mainstay of Elizabeth's queendom, in whose honor the book was written.

Elizabeth likewise loaned her name to the English adventure in America, a creation resembling Spenser's poem in that it was an heroic action with a pastoral cast. A knightly errand, interweaving the epic impulse with Christian idealism, Virginia was a romance wherein the wilderness provided space and opportunity for the elevation of simple, country folk to heroic stature. Colin Clout set loose in the American forest, the transplanted Englishman emerges at the far end of the woods as saintly George the Founding Father, a Farmer-General to match the patron Farmer-Knight of the mother country. These pastoral colors should remind us that Virgil celebrated Augustus and empire in other than epic form, and as his *Eclogues* are an Arcadian testimony to the Augustan peace, so his *Georgics* were written in praise of the orderly, hard-working round of peasant life—the agrarian subsoil of empire— the both serving as witness to the pastoral necessity, alternatives to epic, indeed, its complement, adding a green to the golden thread.

The classical agrarian epic is Hesiod's *Works and Days,* and the emerging American action evinces a distinctly Hesiodic strain, being

25

less a tale of arms and the man than man and the plow, the regnant hero a version of Cincinnatus. The symbol of Spain in America is gold, while Canada is represented by the beaver, but English empire in Virginia was chiefly sustained by tobacco. All three are exploitive commodities, obtained by mining, trapping, or exhausting the land, but it was England that put the agrarian stamp on imperialism, realizing the prophecy in Columbus's other name, *Colon,* and giving a new turn to the meaning of the word "colony." It was under the Red Cross of Saint George that America became a true plantation, projecting westward the pastoral myth that provides the bright conceit of Spenser's epic, a voyage sponsored by Sir Walter Raleigh, Spenser's Shepherd of the Ocean. And it was down Spenser's (and Elizabeth's) softly flowing Thames that Raleigh's captains sailed for America, Philip Amadas and Arthur Barlowe bearing names resonant with chivalric romance.

The English epic line was the Fortieth Parallel, a Via Media between the latitudes chosen by Spain and France, mingling elements from those earlier adventures. And like France and Spain, England found a mirror geography in the New World, a region dominated not by one but by a multitude of rivers, a system of relatively short but useful waterways much like those at home, running slowly through fruitful lands. What the English explorers found, however, was not what they sought, for like the French they came looking for gold and a passage to India. In Virginia, as in Canada, the white strangers were told stories by friendly Indians of mines and great cities beyond the coast, of seas not far to the west, inland lures that seemed to remain on a retreating horizon. The Indians of Virginia were also willing to trade furs for trinkets, but they gave freely of their tobacco, and it would be a generation before the English themselves realized the mercantile value of the Indian weed with a Spanish name. Virginia, like the whole of America, was a process of definition, a blundering sequence often darkening into tragedy, yet as literature it has from the beginning a comic and a pastoral shape, bearing a distinctly Elizabethan impress.

ii. Child of Glorious Great Intent

A Renaissance Man, Sir Walter Raleigh was an avatar of those kinds of actions which the opening stage of Elizabeth's England made possible. An author only when kept from more muscular (and more profitable) activities, Raleigh was chiefly an actor, self-cast in a series of dramas of his own making, not the least of which was the Virginia adventure. Like many actors, Raleigh was something of a personal cipher, borrowing identity from event, yet in much that he essayed we can see an essential duality at work, a scheming cunning animated by a brave soul, less flaw than alloy. Ironically, it was his courage, his flights of imaginative daring, which destroyed him, Icarian reaching beyond grasp, the soaring flight toward the sun that is the pathway of poetry and empire and Faustian doom.

The chief mover of Raleigh's fortunes, Queen Elizabeth, preferred that her darling adventurer stay at home. So it was that Virginia, as action, unfolded without him, a necessity resulting in an equivalent to authorial distance. As his friend Sir Edmund Spenser wrote the greatest Elizabethan epic poem, so Raleigh was the creator of Virginia, the geopolitical adventure conceived in the spirit of the *Aeneid* and given its name by Elizabeth herself. Like Sir Walter's most ambitious literary project, his history of the world, it was a grandiose scheme, and like his history (and Spenser's poem) it remained incomplete, cut short not by mortal, but financial necessity. Finally, as Spenser's poem has its literary sources, so too of paramount influence on Raleigh's Virginia was Richard Hakluyt's *Divers Voyages Touching the Discovery of America* (1582). A compendium of errors erupting into myth, Hakluyt's little book resembles Raleigh in being an epitome of fierce nationalism touched by folly, a product of the shadowy motives and occasional sunbursts of nobility and courage which characterized Elizabethan merchant-adventuring. Of a lesser order than Shakespeare's plays, the

27

Divers Voyages is a similar amalgam of borrowed materials, transmuted and unified by a controlling intelligence.

Richard Hakluyt the Younger was an Anglican priest, but he was first and foremost a geographer and editor, a collector-compiler of other men's writings and records, and his favorite form of expression was the dedicatory preface, obligatory in the days of princes and patrons. Hakluyt's longest and most ambitious work survived his death only in manuscript, some of his important shorter writings likewise did not see print during his lifetime, and his monument is a three-volume collection of translations and transcriptions, the *Principal Navigations, Voyages, Traffiques and Discoveries of the English Nation* (1600). Self-effacing, Hakluyt's public pose was also strategic, for he seems to have preferred to promulgate his ideas indirectly, through the careful selection of documents which lent their weight to his argument. His prefaces and dedications are literally pivotal, being versions of fulcrum, bits of matter placed so as to direct the thrust of his great levers.

Hakluyt is a classic example of Isaiah Berlin's hedgehog, his life and works dictated by one great idea, the certainty that a passage to India could be found somewhere in the vicinity of the Fortieth Parallel, and to this grand notion were all his other arguments for exploration and colonization bent. As a proud Englishman ambitious for national glory, Hakluyt called on Queen and country to defeat Spain through emulation, thus beating her at her own game; as protégé and pupil of Richard Hakluyt the Elder, a lawyer and mercantile theorist, he was loyal to his cousin's prophetic vision of America as the solution to England's economic problems, a dumping ground for her manufactured and human surpluses; and as a clergyman he evoked the Macedonian call to Apostle Paul, pointing to the conversion of the Indians as a most worthy and pious errand. But from first to last, Richard Hakluyt was held fast by the same *idée fixe* that motivated so many of the captains whose journals and charts he collected, an obsession which time and the repeated disappointments of the captains who followed his advice (and thereby contributed to his collection) did nothing to diminish.

Hakluyt's *Divers Voyages* provided the model for all his work to follow, being a geopolitician's version of a lawyer's brief, a compilation of authorities which established England's rights in America, which described the attractiveness and fertility of the zone covered by those rights, and finally (though hardly last), which contained evidence of a northwest passage to be found there. His book is dressed out in a patriotic Dedication to Sir Philip Sidney, a nationalistic gage tossed at the feet of Spenser's perfect model of a courtly gentleman and a prime candidate for a New World Aeneas. But his book was actually written in the service of quite a different kind of Elizabethan—though one perhaps more typical—Sir Humphrey Gilbert, for whose ambitious projects Hakluyt served (in Sidney's phrase) "for a very good trumpet." Grossly flawed, an overreacher, yet a genius for enterprise, Sir Humphrey represents the reality of Elizabethan schemes for America, common denominator beneath the courtly bows, flowery dedications, golden poetry, and myth animating the surface manner and means, a man of glorious projects, devious methods, fated conclusions.

At home in the shadowy world of capitalist enterprise in Elizabeth's England—where merchants mingled with magicians and courtly gentlemen held counsel with cutthroats—Sir Humphrey was a moral amphibian who gathered conflicting qualities within himself as at the center of a mystic circle, symbolic of the contrasting hopes placed in him as the Adventurer, profit-seeking version of the questing Knight. Bearing the requisite title, Sir Humphrey was moved by a version of knightly faith, and no man had a greater certainty of finding a "New Passage to Cataia" than he. In 1576, Sir Humphrey had proved the existence of that passage by "authority," "reason," "experience," and "circumstance," empirical evidence given concrete shape by a map in his possession, on which several wide avenues cut their way like the canals of Mars across the blank face of North America, a wonderful chart attributed to the magician, John Dee. Hakluyt's *Divers Voyages* contains a similar work of art, one drawn by Michael Lok, which verified the possibility that the English might "in short space by God's grace find out that short and easy passage by the Northwest" (10). On that map much of what is now the continental United States is occupied by the Sea of Verrazzano, as Verrazzano's *Relation* is by far the longest of the *Divers Voyages,* geography and description hopelessly out of date by 1582 but perfectly suited to Hakluyt's purpose.

Reaching out toward Verrazzano's Sea is Jacques Cartier's River, and though the narratives of Cartier's voyages are not included in Hakluyt's book (perhaps because he published them separately in 1580),

Humphrey Gilbert's Map. The ascription from which this map takes its title is not in Gilbert's hand, but evidence suggests that it was drawn for him by John Dee, the astrologer, mathematician, and necromancer, to promote colonization in North America by "proving" that lands Gilbert intended to settle were adjacent to a water route to India. The contingency of Verrazzano's Sea and Cartier's estuary-like "Hochelaga" (St. Lawrence River) are potent myths here given concrete, if wishful, expression. See R. P. Bishop, "Lessons of the Gilbert Map," *Geographical Journal,* LXXII (1928), 237-43, and D. B. Quinn, "Introduction," *The Voyages and Colonising Enterprises of Sir Humphrey Gilbert,* I (1940), 67-71. On Dee as a map-maker, see G. S. Parks, *Richard Hakluyt and the English Voyages* (1928), 47-50.

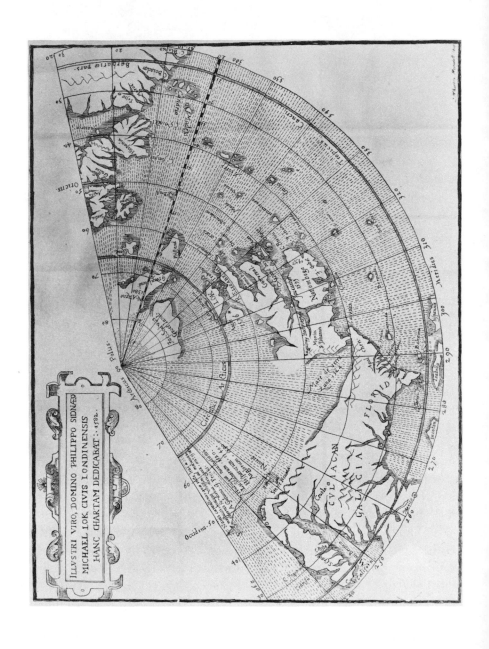

ILLVSTRI VIRO, DOMINO PHILIPPO SIDNÆO
MICHAEL LOK CIVIS LONDINENSIS
HANC CHARTAM DEDICABAT: 1582.

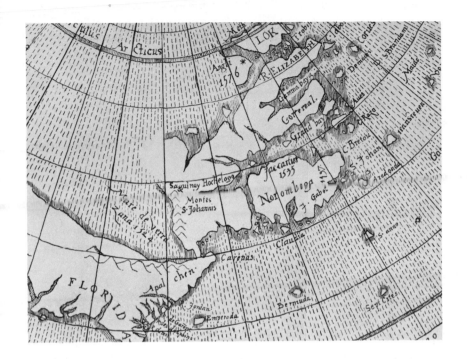

Michael Lok's Map of North America. From Hakluyt's *Divers Voyages* (1582). Courtesy Louis Round Wilson Library, University of North Carolina.

Michael Lok's Map. Like Dee's imaginative draft, Lok's map is a mythic production, encouraging English imperialism by stressing the certainty of finding a water route to India. Cartier's great river stretches inland like a bay, thrusting blade-like branches toward Verrazzano's Sea, a pointedness found in many imperialistic maps during the first century of England in America. See G. B. Parks, *Richard Hakluyt,* 65-66, 184-85.

the editor alludes to them in his Dedication, in an arrangement similar
to the Sea and River on Lok's map. By coupling Cartier's report that
"the people of Saguenay do testify that upon their coasts westward
there is a sea the end whereof is unknown to them" with Indian stories
of a month's "sail to a land where cinnamon and cloves are growing,"
Hakluyt achieved a metaphoric enjambment, intensifying by compressing Cartier's original (H: 11; cf. C: 72, 88). As a sounding trumpet of
enterprise, Hakluyt was willing to arrange his notes for the sake of a
larger harmony, a Horatian *concordia discors,* his *Divers Voyages* a
work in which the line between fact and fiction concerning America is
a conjunctive not disjunctive element. Like the Fortieth Parallel on
Lok's map, which bisects a thin isthmus dividing the Atlantic from
Verrazzano's Sea, it is a creative projection of hope, thus contributing
further to the artifact that was Elizabethan America. *"Geographiam
Esse Historiae Oculum"* was ever Hakluyt's motto, but history's eye for
him was a distorting lens.

Sir Humphrey Gilbert's motto was *Quid Non,* suggesting his courage
and folly: last seen reading aloud from More's *Utopia,* he disappeared
from sight on the high seas in a small ship, the *Squirrel.* Whereupon, in
1583, his patents and privileges, along with his silver-tongued trumpet,
were passed on to his stepbrother, Sir Walter Raleigh. Of finer stuff
and temper than Gilbert, Raleigh was no less an enthusiast for projects
and profits, and in the year following Sir Humphrey's disappearance
into Ocean and Old Night he sent out Barlowe and Amadas to America. For the glory of England and Sir Walter, two clumsy little ships,
slow-moving engines of enterprise, spread their sails like the vanes of a
windmill and headed west along the Fortieth Parallel in quest of a
myth then almost a century old. Hakluyt, meanwhile, was busily employed preparing another line, his "Discourse of Western Planting,"
a master-work of ingenious angling designed to hook the Queen. Bris-
tling with national ferocity toward Spain, Hakluyt's manuscript tracta-
tus amounts to a lengthy fist-shake at the Catholic Carthage, and reads
more like a declaration of war than a prospectus for settlement. Still, it
is a remarkable feat of assemblage, a scrapbook of quotations and putative facts in support of Raleigh's project and Hakluyt's pet ideas, including "those testimonies tending to the proof of the long desired
northwest passage, which with no small care these many years I have

observed in my readings and conferences concerning the same matter," a list of authorities now numbering sixteen (283-84).

The "Discourse" is high-water Hakluyt, his faith of conviction floating a heavy cargo of reasonable argument, logical syllogisms intended, like Drake's treasure-ship, the *Golden Hinde,* to sway Elizabeth. In form and substance it provides stark contrast with the rhapsody which Arthur Barlowe turned in as his report to Sir Walter, a marvel of Golden Age prose also wrought for the eye of the Queen, a conduit of wonder shaped by the same forces, aesthetic and cultural, which influenced Sidney's *Arcadia.* Written to serve Raleigh's cause, it is a companion document to Hakluyt's "Discourse" (and would be included in his *Principal Navigations*), word music rather than rhetorical argument, reminding us that the euphuism of John Lyly was all the mode. As we move from the "Discourse" to Barlowe's report we leave the world of reasoning, however spurious, for the world of description, however specious, a green and golden realm peopled by Golden Age men and women, bravely new but not unlike the world reported by Columbus nearly a century before.

iii. Born to Disastrous End

The dominant influence on Barlowe's report, as on Hakluyt's "Discourse," is Spanish, here figured not as antagonist, but as vision. America is a purely pastoral prospect, commencing with the scent of the New World which greeted the sailors before they sighted land, "as if we had been in the midst of some delicate garden, abounding with all kinds of odoriferous flowers" (94). Beaching on an off-shore island, Barlowe's men found an "incredible abundance" of wild fruits and game and "goodly cedar trees" (96). The soil was "the most plentiful, sweet, fruitful and wholesome of all the world," lending a generous spirit to the people of the New World, who were "most gentle, loving, and faithful, void of all guile, and treason, and such as lived after the manner of the Golden Age . . . as in the first creation, without toil or labor" (106-8).

Docile, hospitable, obedient to authority, the Indians seemed to recommend themselves to a gentle English yoke, and they were eager to acquire English merchandise, thus realizing lawyer Hakluyt's fondest hopes. These American Adams were particularly anxious to obtain "hatchets, axes, and knives," for though they were of the Age of Gold they appreciated the utility of iron artifacts, and Barlowe noted that the "King's brother had a great liking of our armor, a sword, and divers other things which we had" (105). These were not the woolen goods which Hakluyt proposed "venting" in far countries, but it was an encouraging (if to us ominous) sign, and Barlowe refused to exchange good English steel for the pearls offered, lest the Indians put too low a value on his cutlery. Along with pearls, the natives wore ornaments of copper and a gold-like metal (which they in turn refused to barter), and they told stories of "great rivers" inland on which were built "great towns," including a metropolis which "the savages were never at, only they speak of it, by the report of their fathers, and other men, whom they have heard affirm it, to be above one day's journey about" (110).

Barlowe's report combines elements of earlier stories brought back from America, yet the orchestration is Elizabethan, and it served as prelude to the symphony written by Thomas Hariot. Friend to Raleigh, and his scientific adviser, Hariot accompanied the next expedition to Virginia (by then so called) in 1585, where he gathered the information for his *Briefe and True Report of the New Found Land of Virginia* (1588). Hariot shared with John Dee a certain reputation as a magician, and as a writer he had a wizard touch which transformed lead into gold, a mercurial metamorphosis that fulfilled Sir Walter's expectations. Hariot's *Briefe Report* is a mercantile *catalogue raisonné* that substantiated Hakluyt's theories with a list of profitable "commodities," real and imagined. An anatomy of enterprise held together by a lure of profits, it was at least partly intended to discredit those disgruntled colonists who, "by reason of their bad natures, have maliciously not only spoken ill of their Governors, but for their sakes slandered the country itself," a purpose which explains his hyperbolic strategy (322).

Hariot's insistent optimism extended to the inhabitants of the New

World Arcadia, his account agreeing with while expanding upon Barlowe's encouraging news. The Indians, he reported, regarded the Englishmen as gods, and Hariot was sure they could be converted to Christian rule, bring them "through discreet dealing and government to the embracing of the truth, and consequently to honor, obey, fear and love us" (381). The order of priorities is worth noting, for though Hakluyt argued against the Spaniard's barbaric treatment of Indians—the "Black Legend"—recommending instead a strategy of kindness, his charity was in the hope of profit. Hariot was particularly careful to stress the piety of the Indian king, Wingina, who imitated the English at their prayers. This was the same king whose brother had tried to buy English armor, and Wingina seems to have been attracted to the powerful English god for similar reasons, a possibility which time would prove. Wingina's name suggested to Elizabeth the name she gave her new dominion, a pun with no mean dimension, for if Wingina was a personification of the virgin land, he likewise shared the Virgin Queen's cunning, as New World Faery King proving a very Archimago of dark design.

For an account of Wingina's duplicity, we must turn to the report of Ralph Lane, Governor of the Virginia Colony during its first year. Lane was a soldier, not a scholar, and though he was loyal to Raleigh's purpose, and willing to put his preface-imprimatur on Hariot's *Briefe Report*, there are certain strategic discrepancies between Lane's account and the official, published version of affairs. Sir Walter Raleigh, like Coleridge's Hamlet, contained a mixture of Don Quixote's noble idealism and Sancho Panza's peasant realism, and the two men who were his chief agents in Virginia are nearly emblematic of the uneasy marriage which created America. In contrast to Hariot's extended rhetoric of possibilities, an optimistic reticulation of explicit—though putative—commodities, Lane's report is at once forthrightly blunt and evasively obscure, a different style dictated by a different strategy, a covert necessity. For he had failed to find the gold which was Raleigh's greatest hope, and worse, he had fought with the Indians, contrary to his instructions, leaving spilled and therefore bad blood behind him. A justification of his actions, Lane's report was shaped for the most part by events, and, unlike Hariot's, therefore, his account of the first year in Virginia assumes a narrative form. Like Cartier, Lane anchored the future firmly in the recent past, his trajectory of expectation similarly breaking off short of the desired goal, giving way to the vast white space on the imperial map. Where Hakluyt and Hariot were concerned with emphasizing potential profits, Lane sought to explain actual losses, and where the party of hope expressed itself by conjectural assertions, Lane stressed hard realities. Hope assumes the guise of plenitude, the round-ness of inclusiveness, and Hariot's *Briefe Report* is a Boeotian epic, carrying a burden heavy-laden with New World plenty. But reality takes a sparer shape, the knife that slices through the fruit of promise, and Lane's is a lean chronicle of events, the thin line of heroic action.

To Ralph Lane fell the responsibility of governing the little colony and commanding voyages of exploration, not only along the bays and estuaries within the outer banks, but up more than a hundred miles of inland rivers, long voyages which gave his report its definitive shape. Hariot presumably accompanied Lane on these journeys, obtaining thereby the materials of his own report, and something of the difference between them is suggested by Hariot's failure to mention just how it was he managed to get "an hundred and fifty miles into the main" (332). Such vagueness may have been a result of the strategy of colon-ization, for Raleigh hoped to keep the location of his settlement a secret from the Spanish until it was strong enough to defend itself (as well as provide a base for plundering the West Indies). Lane, who was writing for Raleigh's eyes only, could supply facts (and truths) that Hariot had to hide, but such inhibitions only serve to reinforce what is essentially an aesthetic difference, a contrast endemic to the literature emerging from the American experience.

There is, first of all, the pastoral promise, the premise of Barlowe's report and Hariot's little book, a dream of felicitous plenty symbolized by the New World Garden. Second, and conversely, there is the en-counter with the underlying reality of promise, the Voyage, a dark and dangerous passage which nonetheless promotes a final luminous note of hope. Hariot's is a descriptive essay, having anecdotal but no narra-tive potential, while Ralph Lane's report, though occasionally obscure, emphasizes the dramatic nature of a river voyage into the unknown in-terior, a continuation of the genre established by Cartier. Not only is his narrative informed throughout by a soldierly awareness of topogra-phy, a sense of the importance of harbors and waterways to the process of settlement, but these geopolitical considerations are aligned to the essential shape of adventure. His voyage up the Roanoke, a journey into an ever deepening and darkening zone of threat, is quite literally a rising action climaxed by an explosion of violence, followed by the falling action of return and resolution, a *quietus* of death and destruction.

The burden of Lane's narrative is on the treachery of the Indians, in particular "the conspiracy of Pemisapan with the savages of the main," a situation which provides his story the frame of dramatic irony (256). The irony is compounded by the fact that Pemisapan was the Indian whose piety gave Hariot such encouragement, the selfsame Wingina whose people had greeted Arthur Barlowe so warmly. On longer acquaintance, Wingina's attitude toward the English changed—along with his name—into a growing hostility which resulted in his death at their hands. In his plot against the strangers, Pemisapan was assisted by Wanchese, one of two Indians brought by Barlowe back to England to serve as interpreters in the second expedition—another echo of Cartier's narrative. But the other Indian, Manteo, remained loyal to the English, providing an essential division between "good" and "bad" Indians which is further amplified by Menatonon, king of a village on the Chowan river, and Pemisapan's antithesis. Taken prisoner by Lane during an early outbreak of hostility, the old man (like the Lord of Canada) proved to be a cooperative ally under pressure, divulging "more understanding and light of the country than I had received by all the searches and savages that before I or any of my company had had conference with" (259).

Menatonon's river, the Chowan, was similarly accommodating, and promised to be of great use to the English as an avenue of empire. Lane had explored northeast as far as Chesapeake Bay, which he regarded as a better area for settlement than the exposed and shallow harbors of Albemarle Sound. Menatonon told him that the Chowan was navigable to within four days' march of the Bay, a region rich in pearls, and that the confluency of that stream with the Roanoke River likewise provided a waterway from the Chesapeake area into the West, where "a marvelous and most strange mineral" was to be found in a place named "Chaunis Temoatan," a copper-like substance called "wassador," used for ornaments by the Indians (268). And Menatonon also told Lane that the Roanoke's source was a great fountain which stood so near "a sea, that many times in storms (the wind coming outwardly from the sea) the waves thereof are beaten into the said fresh stream, so that the fresh water for a certain space groweth salt and brackish," a remarkable feature of geography that made perfect sense in the days of Richard Hakluyt, suggesting the easy route to Cathay he had predicted (264).

Where the Chowan was a pacific stream, showing "no current in the world in calm weather," the Roanoke had "so violent a current from the west and southwest" that Lane feared "it would scarce be navigable" by boats with oars (263). Still, lured by the possibility of gold, and assured by Hariot that he would undoubtedly find Hakluyt's passage to the Pacific, Lane set out in the Month of Fools with forty men in two rowboats to explore the savage, serpentine river, unaware that the wily Pemisapan had cast a spell before them. Lane had planned to buy provisions from the Indians along the way, but Pemisapan had sent word ahead that the English were coming up the river to wage war, so Lane and his men found only abandoned towns. Despite short rations and hard going, the English persisted, having caught a glimpse of a golden interior, but as with most such quests in America, "it fell out very contrary to all expectation and likelihood" (270). Instead of finding gold or even copper, the English found copper-colored men who fired arrows at them from the trees along the river and then melted away. Discouraged, forced at the last to eat two dogs brought along for other purposes, Lane and his men turned around and headed downstream, back to Roanoke Island and its fortified fragment of England.

Soon after Lane's return, the conspiracy of Pemisapan began to close around the tiny garrison also. Having been forewarned by Menatonon's son, Lane was able to turn the trick, and Pemisapan "had by the mercy of God for our deliverance that which he had purposed for us" (287). God in His mercy also sent Sir Francis Drake with needed supplies, but He next sent a hurricane which smashed the boats and broke the will of the colony. When Drake left for England, so did Lane, Hariot, and all but three Englishmen, who unfortunately tarried too long in the village of Menatonon. This sudden departure, the storm, and the beheading of Pemisapan provide a cathartic ending to Ralph Lane's narrative, a violent fulfillment of a pattern of suspense which corresponds to the tension and release of adventure fiction, the romantic counterpart to the classical epic. Though a thousand miles further south, Lane's is Cartier's (which is to say Cooper's) country, a hazardous terrain in which action is qualified by conspiracy.

Essentially a tale of two Indians, Pemisapan and Menatonon, Lane's narrative also concerns two contrasting rivers, the opulent, easy Chowan and the swift, tricky Roanoke, each associated with an alternative version of savagery. Though Lane's quest for Chaunis Temoatan and the western sea was unsuccessful, he believed it taught a valuable lesson, for the willingness of his men to undergo hardship and danger in the hope of finding gold proved that such a discovery "or a passage to the South Sea, or some way to it, and nothing else can bring this country in request to be inhabited by our nation" (273). Despite Hariot's enthusiasm, not all the sassafras, roots, sweet gums, or cedar to be found in Virginia "would be worth the fetching," and Raleigh's best hope lay in the West, in the direction of Chaunis Temoatan, which "promiseth great things" (273).

Lane recommended therefore that forts be built along the Chowan and Roanoke, a line of defense to be continued overland to Chesapeake Bay so as to permit safe travel from east to west, thus formulating a military, not missionary presence for England in America. Still, though he did not share Hariot's charitable notions about Indians, Lane refused to abandon his faith in Indian stories, and as a result his Virginia is a typically Elizabethan microcosm, bisected by a line that zigs and then zags along the Fortieth Parallel on Michael Lok's map, moving from the pearls and pastoral fruitfulness of the Chesapeake into the heroic, gold-bearing and epical zone of western wilderness. His is a route, a passage into the heart of darkness, which would provide an essential diagram for the American experience during succeeding centuries, the confluence of two rivers a symbolic backdrop for the encounter between white men and a savage land.

iv. Reasons for Rhyme

Neither Lane nor Hariot wrote the final chapter of Raleigh's Virginia, a story terminating in darkness and mystery. Lacking the time and money to benefit from Lane's advice or to mount the detailed scheme for settlement provided by Hakluyt, Raleigh hastily assembled a second fleet of colonists, who sailed off to Virginia in the month of May 1587, their fate adding further shadows to the golden myth. One alone escaped the doom of the Lost Colony: its governor, John White, whose watercolors capture the paradisiac splendors of America as the fate of his daughter and her child suggests its gloom and danger. Returning with the immigrant fleet in order to get further support for his people, White found his countrymen busy pursuing a number of profitable avenues opened up by the defeat of the Armada. No one seemed interested in the dubious investment offered by Virginia, and all ships were heading for the Indies, so it was only after much delay and vexation that the Governor was able to return to America, again alone.

It was late in the season, and in peril of hurricanes, when White put ashore at Hatteras, then crossed over the bar to Roanoke in a boat. He reached the island after nightfall, and seeing a great fire burning in the woods, he had the sailors row toward it, sounding "with a trumpet a call, then afterwards many familiar English tunes of songs, and called to them friendly; but we had no answer," nor did their echo ring (613). So the courtly dream of "this paradise of this world" was allowed to fade with a dying fall, the Spenserian romance ending darkly, with no consummation. White's account of his last voyage to America was added to Hakluyt's collection, one more chapter in his projected magnum opus, the *Principal Navigations,* not a conclusion but a continuation, the failure of the Roanoke venture only an episode in an incomplete, ongoing action, the national epic of empire.

In 1587, as preparations for the second colony were hurried to their imperfect, multilated conclusion, Hakluyt saw Raleigh as the hero of the imperial drama, an identification cemented by his Dedication to that *"illustri et magnanimo viro"* in his edition of Peter Martyr's *De Orbe Novo,* the epic account of Spain's achievement in "the vast regions of the New World" (363). As always for Hakluyt, the Spanish precedent served chiefly as a goad for English activity, and in dedicating his book to Raleigh he urges him to "reveal to us the courts of China and the unknown straits which still lie hid: throw back the portals which have been closed since the world's beginning at the dawn of time" (367). Then, carried on his own tide of enthusiasm, blown by the winds of inspiration, Hakluyt lifts himself to a level of expression which he seldom attained, moving from stock analogies to Homer and Alexander to a most remarkable figure, a metaphor with a long reach into the literature of America.

Realizing the futility, even the silliness, perhaps, of urging a voyage on a man who had no intention of making it, Hakluyt suddenly converted his seafaring hero to Aeneas dallying with Dido, an abrupt change with amazing consequences:

To what end do I exhort you or admonish you to persist in your project, when only recently you sent me letters from Court in which you freely swore that no terrors, no personal losses or misfortunes could or would ever tear you from the sweet embraces of your own Virginia, that fairest of nymphs—though to many insufficiently well known,— whom our most generous sovereign has given you to be your bride? If you preserve only a little longer in your constancy, your bride will shortly bring forth new and most abundant offspring, such as will delight you and yours, and cover with disgrace and shame those who have so often dared rashly and impudently to charge her with barrenness. For who has the just title to attach such a stigma to your Elizabeth's Virginia, when no one has yet probed the depths of her hidden resources and wealth, or her beauty hitherto concealed from our sight? Let them go where they deserve, foolish drones, mindful only of their bellies and gullets, who fresh from that place, like those whom Moses sent to spy out the promised land flowing with milk and honey, have treacherously published ill reports about it (367-68).

So Raleigh's constancy to Elizabeth, his loyalty to his colony, the Queen's barrenness, and Virginia's ill repute are all spun into an ambiguous fabric of allusion, ending by associating the New World with the paradisiac promised land of the Mosaic epic.

Prophetic as literature, as contemporary vision it was seen darkly, as through the eye of geography. Not only would the virgin land prove savagely immaculate, remaining barren as the Queen who assigned it her own putative state, but that selfsame Queen would soon withdraw her favor from Raleigh, punishment for taking a bride not of her giving. Persist, promised Hakluyt, "and you will find at length if not a Homer, yet some Martyr—by whom I mean some happy genius—to rescue your heroic enterprises from the vasty maw of oblivion" (369). Raleigh, that unhappy genius, soon suffered the martyrdom he most abhorred, the consignment to life-in-death, an imposed oblivion in the Tower. There he dreamed of yet another golden river, not Lane's Roanoke or the Chowan, but the great dragon River of the South, the Orinoco, up whose winding channels he later pursued the glimmering shadow of El Dorado, the glorious grail of so many Spanish dons. During the trial which put him in the Tower for his second and longest stay, Raleigh was reviled for a moral monster by Sir Edward Coke: "Thou hast," he jeered, "an English face but a Spanish heart." In a sense not intended by the speaker, his words could serve for Raleigh's epitaph, and in a way they did.

v. Flights upon the Banks of Thames

Virginia, like America, was a territory of the mind, which during the early years of exploration and settlement underwent a progressive particularization and diminution, not only in terms of geography, but in the ratio of promise to fulfillment. "Virginia," during Elizabeth's reign and for a period afterward, referred to the entire eastern seaboard between French Canada and Spanish Florida, a vast tract presumed to extend to the Pacific Ocean, then located somewhere west of the Appalachians. This gigantic uniformity, when compared to the eventual difference of names, purpose, and growth which came to exist between the northern and southern arms of England in America, is another reminder that the New World, at the outset, took its shape from Old World expectations. The process of definition was a form of sculpture, a creative but reductive encounter which, by imposing expectations on the resistant stuff of reality, resulted in a dialectic transformation of subject and object.

The chipping-away process began almost immediately upon actual occupation of the land itself by Raleigh's colony, the experience of possession (however imperfect) acting to dispel the pastoral myth promulgated by Arthur Barlowe. But as "Virginia" over the years became subdivided, first into "Northern" and "Southern," and then into several colonies, the green idea persisted, Hariot's hyperbole in the face of fact establishing a repetitive process of renewal with each succeeding wave of exploration, settlement, and expansion. Ideas seldom die with monarchs, though fortunes often fade, and Elizabethan America had a certain reach into the reign of King James. The renewed cycle of exploration and trade is symbolized by a voyage to Northern Virginia undertaken in 1605 and backed by the Earl of Southampton, who, with his brother-in-law Thomas Arundel, hoped to settle a plantation where Roman Catholics could find refuge. Captain of the voyage was George Waymouth, who, as his name suggests, was looking for a watery entrance to the New World, not in hopes of passage to India (for which he had searched in 1602), but in expectation of the less glorious profit to be made from "habitation and planting." A narrative of Waymouth's voyage was written by a pious passenger, James Rosier, supposedly a priest, whose *Brief Relation* has (not surprisingly) rosy hues. Rosier gave a blessing to all that he saw, but the holiest of his holys was reserved for a great river, which he claimed was (after the Thames) "the most rich, beautiful, large and secure harboring river that the world affordeth" (384). Because of the intentional mystery which usually surrounds initial sorties to America, Rosier does not identify this American "Severne," but it was, apparently, St. George's, in Maine, a symbolic stream whose name provides a Spenserian gloss on his description of the "good ground, pleasant and fertile, fit for pasture" through which it flowed (384).

For Rosier, as for Cartier and Hariot, the encounter with the New World is a matter of pastoral hyperbole, but in Rosier's account the utilitarian note is likewise sounded. Though the country along the river reminds him of "a stately park," with groves of oak "like stands left in our pastures in England, good and great, fit timber for any use," the emphasis on fitness, in terms of pasture or lumber, sets the tone. "High timber trees" on near-by hills become converted to "masts for ships of 400 ton," a metamorphosis sped along by the discovery of a stream running out of those same hills with sufficient force "to drive a mill," and Rosier likewise describes the diversity of "branching streams . . . whereby is afforded an unspeakable profit by the conveniency of transportation from place to place" (384-86). For Rosier, rivers are less avenues of adventure than conduits of trade, "by shipping to bring in all traffic of merchandise, a benefit always accounted the richest treasury to any land," and he compares the St. George's in this regard not only to "our Thames," but to the Seine, the Bordeaux, and the Loire, all "great and goodly rivers, yet it is no detraction from them to be accounted inferior to this, which not only yieldeth all the foresaid pleasant profits, but also appeared infallibly to us free from all inconveniences" (383).

This last, apparently, did not include Indians, with whom Waymouth's party had the usual difficulties attending trade in America, and even as he explored the glorious St. George's he had locked in the hold of his ship (the *Archangel*) five unwilling passengers, along with "two canoes and all their bows and arrows," wild cargo which was "a matter of great importance for the full accomplishment of our voyage" (379). Like the furs bought from the same Indians and the fish taken from their sea, they were to be used in arousing interest in the venture, not for the sake of "a little present public profit," but for "a public good, and true zeal of promulgating God's holy Church, by planting Christianity" (388). The effectiveness of Rosier's pamphlet in promoting this pious end is difficult to assess, but Waymouth's Indians made a great stir in England. Though Southampton's plans came to nothing, his Indians were taken over by Sir Ferdinando Gorges, an English soldier with a Spanish name who for the next thirty years and more would continue the grandiose tradition of his cousins Gilbert and Raleigh in America, a futile, feudal scheme of New World empire on the baronial plan.

But Sir Ferdinando needed middle-class money to launch his colony, and was therefore one of the prime movers of the Plymouth (Northern Virginia) and London (Southern Virginia) Companies, joint-stock arrangements which gathered together the ambitions and capital of adventurers and projectors long associated with New World enterprise—including Richard Hakluyt. Gorges identified his own fortunes with the Plymouth Company, which took the northern half of Raleigh's patent, and along with Sir John Popham he set about settling the coast of Maine, of whose fertility his well-trained Indians had convinced him. Like Raleigh, Sir Ferdinando worked by proxy, and under the leadership of George Popham a company of soldier-settlers in 1607 built a fort on another "very gallant river, very deep and of a good breadth . . . with many goodly islands in it": this was the Kennebeck, or "Sagadahoc" as it was called, a word soon synonymous with failure in *The Historie of Travell into Virginia Britania* (167).

Though an admirable stronghold, Popham's fort was not able to withstand the assault of a Maine winter, and like William Strachey's brief account of its history, the venture came to an abrupt close: "And this was the end of that northern colony upon the river of Sagadahoc" (173). Yet the abandoned fort represented a commitment, however mistaken, and for the next three decades the shadow of quixotism in Northern Virginia bears the unmistakable profile of Sir Ferdinando Gorges, a man whose faith in the potential of America held firm, though he never had occasion to visit the regions to which he lay claim. Perhaps, as in most matters of belief—and creation—a certain distance between subject and object is helpful, as a slight myopia increases erotic passion. In any event, Sir Walter's blurred vision and his version of Virginia became the province of Sir Ferdinando thenceforth, that fairest—and most elusive—of nymphs now a second-hand bride.

vi. I Have It Here
in Black and White

Richard Hakluyt was another who never visited the great object of his infatuation, although in 1606 he at one point intended to sail with the London Company's fleet when it set out for its patent in Southern Virginia. Had he done so, considering his age and sedentary calling, the result would have probably been fatal, thereby putting a fitting period to his career. As it was, Hakluyt lived on to die in the same year as his fellow cosmographer, William Shakespeare, and where the playwright made poetry out of the Virginia adventure, his *Tempest* drawing myth and symbol from Strachey's chronic of misery, Hakluyt reversed the process, providing the fable which became the very hard facts of a starveling, near tragic event. If Sir Ferdinando Gorges inherited the large views of Elizabethan imperialism, Hakluyt preserved incarnate its epical geopolitics and mercantile opportunism, both men behaving as though the disasters at Roanoke and on the Kennebeck had never occurred.

It was, in short, to Hariot's Virginia that the London Company ships set sail, though Hariot himself made only a brief entry in his journal concerning the event—the rest of the page being filled with notations on the rainbow effect of prisms on light. For literary accompaniment the departing fleet had to depend on Michael Drayton's celebratory ode, whose language is reminiscent of Arthur Barlowe's lyrical report, describing "Earth's only Paradise," to whose inhabitants "the golden age / Still nature's laws doth give" (161). Raleigh is forgotten, however, and as if to credit the true author of "Virginia," Drayton ends his ode with praise for "industrious Hakluyt, / Whose reading shall inflame / Men to seek fame." Though Hakluyt at the last did not make the journey, he traveled with the fleet in letter as well as spirit, and if the "brave heroic minds" who sailed did not find time to "attend" Hakluyt's inflammatory book of voyages, they perforce paid attention to the "Instructions by Way of Advice" they carried with them, a document in which Hakluyt's hand is clearly evident.

"Get the pearl and gold," wrote Drayton, and the prosaic "Instructions" are no less optimistic, but the larger hope, as always with Hakluyt, concerned the Northwest Passage. He advised the colonists therefore to locate their fort on the most considerable river they could find, not only for the sake of a harbor and protection from Spanish attack, but because by "that way you shall soonest find the other sea" (49). As Drayton's poem preserves in honey the golden pastoral vision of Elizabeth's reign, Hakluyt's "Instructions" give order to the mad certainties which the expanding mood of nationalism produced, for like his earlier plans for America, they are set forth in a tidy, orderly, logical, and reasonable fashion, neat categories which seem absurd, even insane, when compared with the immensity of the unexplored continent—to say nothing of the element of the unexpected, so predictably great in a new world. The "Instructions" must have looked good on paper back there in London, with every presumed contingency provided for, all matters given consideration, due proportion, and stress. Like most civilized men, Hakluyt and his associates took great comfort in numbers, and by parceling out the unknown in a neat arrangement of tens, twenties, and forties, the "Instructions" imposed the sureness of measure, ignoring the potential of west-tending rivers discovered by Ralph

Lane, which tended to change from linear to serpentine configurations once they entered the savage wilderness.

"When you have discovered as far up the river as you mean to plant yourselves and landed your victuals and munitions," Hakluyt instructed, "to the end that every man may know his charge, you shall do well to divide your six score men into three parts: whereof forty of them you may appoint to fortify and build . . . thirty others you may employ in preparing your ground and sowing . . . the other ten of these forty you must leave as sentinel at the haven's mouth" (51). The first eighty men having been put to work creating civilized order out of primeval chaos, the remaining forty were to explore the region around. This party received more explicit instructions than did the first two: "You must observe if you can, whether the river on which you plant doth spring out of mountains or out of lakes. If it be out of any lake the passage to the other sea will be the more easy, and it is like enough that out of the same lake you shall find some spring which runs the contrary way toward the East India Sea." Not that this was to be an idle excursion in search of Cathay, for the explorers were to carry with them picks and shovels, to test any hills they should find for precious minerals. Nor were the Indians forgotten: the colonists were instructed "not to offend the naturals" in any way, "and whensoever any of yours shoots before them, be sure that they may be chosen out of your best marksmen" (52).

Unlike the Roanoke venture, the Jamestown experiment was successful, but not because of Hakluyt's "Instructions." Still, from the start the colonists attempted to obey them—at least the parts concerning the discovery of gold and a northwest passage—and the imposition of expectations aroused by their instructions upon the reality of the New World resulted in a kind of comedy, not a romantic, affirmative version of *The Tempest,* but a continuation of Jonson's *Eastward Ho!* As with the King in whose name the colony was founded, at James Fort cunning passed for craft, and the ensuing drama was in all ways Jacobean, the stage being held by equivalents of Caliban, Trinculo, and Stephanos. It is a satire on mankind's propensity for greed and deceit, culpability from which neither savage nor civilized man is free, and the magnanimity essential to an epic is largely missing from the unfolding action—nor is nobility, natural or otherwise, much in evidence either. Though knights and even a Percy were present, the middle-class spirit reigned—

not the love of hard work, law, and order, but its reverse, a lust for easy riches which perverted authority into the rule of self-interest, resulting in an action from which a Prospero—along with Hariot— is missing.

vii. That Tawney Weed

One of the earliest reports sent back from Jamestown was written by George Percy, and it bears all the marks of a refined, courtly sensibility, an atavistic fragment, like Drayton's poem, of the Elizabethan vision. Percy declared that he "was almost ravished at the first sight" of Virginia, by 1607 a ritual swoon when taking possession of the virgin land, and he was particularly impressed by the river on which the colony— following instructions—planted its fort, "one of the famousest rivers that ever was found by any Christian" (133, 141). This pastoral, imperial stream, the James, flowed through park-like "grounds bespread with many sweet and delicate flowers of divers colors and kinds," a squire's garment so rich in promise that it would surely prove "as great a profit to the Realm of England as the Indies to the King of Spain" (143). The earliest known map of the river was drawn by Robert Tindall, Gunner to Prince Henry, and Tindall's chart of Percy's sacred river resembles nothing so much as a womb, a type of fertility and promise, and the new-found river was certainly the means by which Virginia—in Raleigh's phrase—lost her maidenhead.

This womb was haunted, however, by a savage presence, and Percy's ravishment was very nearly literal, for on the first night ashore, "when we were going aboard, there came the savages creeping upon all fours from the hills, like bears" (133-34). These were the "naturals" the colonists were not to offend, but before the English could demonstrate their inoffensiveness they were fired upon with bows and arrows, and being Englishmen, they returned the favor twofold, with muskets. So it was that at the very entrance to the new land an initial skirmish repeated the pattern of violent encounter already established in narratives of exploration and settlement, thereby casting a shadow over the pastoral landscape. Still, in the first reports to the London Company a mood of optimism prevails, and the most important of these was the account by Gabriel Archer of the experiences met with by the party of discovery which, as per "Instructions," set off up "our River" in search of, among other things, a passage to the Pacific Ocean (80).

This group was under the command of Captain Christopher Newport, a sometime pirate with a name right out of Jacobean comedy, and his expectations were similarly ridiculous. Making "a perfect resolution not to return, but either to find the head of this river, the lake mentioned by others heretofore, the sea again, the Mountains Apalatsi, or some issue," what Captain Newport found was what all previous explorers had found in America—Indians. Like Columbus and Cartier before him, Newport was given a friendly, hospitable reception, perhaps inspired by the trinkets which the Captain handed out with the generosity of an oriental potentate. The inhabitants were highly informative also, describing the course of the river to the head of navigation and the "Mountains Quirank" out of which it ran. Beyond the Mountains Quirank, as was so often the case, was that "which we expected" (83). Presumably this was the inland sea which they were to hear of again, but Archer leaves only a lacuna of implication, the kind of grail designed to lure questers yet to come.

The English were entertained on their travels by an Indian king called Arahatec, and in the middle of the banquet even greater natural nobility arrived, "the great king Powhatah . . . at whose presence they all rose . . . and with a long shout saluted him" (84). This was not the truly great Powhatan, but his son, Parahunt, known as "Little" Powhatan by his people. But he was a good enough Powhatan for Newport's purposes, and, to ensure his cooperation and loyalty to King James, the Captain was even more generous with gifts, nor was Little Powhatan behindhand in extending the English a welcoming (and open) hand. At his invitation, Newport and his men traveled on up the river to Little Powhatan's town, called Powhatan, where the king lived in Powhatan's Tower on a hill by the river—which was also called Powhatan by the Indians. Despite these *loci siglii* of prior ownership, Archer observed subjunctively that "were any art used to the natural state of this place, it would be a goodly habitation" (85). The present inhabitant was at home, the English were given another banquet, and before the day was over Little Powhatan and Newport had formed a league of friendship, no mean feat considering the barrier of language—and intention.

Except for a minor incident of theft by Little Powhatan's men, the red and white races enjoyed a harmonious meeting of complete (if martial) accord, declaring mutual war on the Indians at the head and foot of the river. On parting, Captain Newport invited Little Powhatan to dine aboard Sunday next, but that second communal meal was marked by a decided decline in Indian accommodation. Perhaps because Little Powhatan was too full of English cooking, he found indigestible an English "Discourse of the River," during which Newport asked "how far it might be to the head thereof, where they got their copper and their iron" and requested that Little Powhatan provide guides, "for our Captain determined to have traveled two or three days' journey afoot up the river" (87). Little Powhatan ignored Newport's "demands," and returned to his village, saying only that he would meet the English later at the great falls which marked the head of navigation.

There, standing like a symbolic guardian at the threshold to the unknown, Little Powhatan described the difficulty of traveling overland, the scarcity of food along the way, the hostility of his enemies, the up-river Indians, seeking "by all means to dissuade our Captain from going any further" (88). Newport, though disappointed, let discretion take precedence over valor, and put off the inland voyage until a later time, contenting himself (after Little Powhatan's departure) with setting up a cross, inscribed *"Jacobus Rex,"* with the date and his own name below. One of the Indians became uneasy at this, but Newport allayed his suspicions by explaining that "the two arms of the cross signified King Powhatah and himself, the fastening of it in the middle was their united league, and the shout was the reverence he did to Powhatah." This clever bit of imperial equivocation was matched by a similar trick of transformational transference, Newport renaming Powhatan River the "King's River," a nice ambiguity which honored both the king who lived by it and the one who lived by another river far to the east, in whose name the cross had been planted. In time the river was openly called the James, as the colony was called Jamestown, and as for the village called Powhatan, that became the future site of an English settlement called Nonsuch, putting the final seal on the colonists' indifference to aboriginal domain, thereby affirming the primacy of *Jacobus Rex.*

Traveling back down the King's River, Newport stopped off on the way to pay his respects to the once if not future monarch, and presented Little Powhatan with an English hatchet. Pleased at the gesture, Powhatan silenced some of his people who had begun to grumble over the English presence by saying (according to Percy) "very wisely for a savage, 'Why should you be offended with them, as long as they hurt you not, nor take anything away by force. They take but a little waste ground, which doth you nor any of us any good' " (141). If these were indeed the words spoken, Little Powhatan's brief speech must be accounted great in prophetic irony, being among the first of many such mistaken gestures made by Indians who hoped to profit from the white man's presence while keeping possession of their power and prerogatives. They were words, at any rate, which increased the English mood of confidence, so much so that they could laugh behind their hands at the sight of Opechancanough, King of the Pamunkey region (and Little Powhatan's uncle), when he tried to be "stately" after his Indian fashion (92).

Opechancanough was of particular interest to the colonists, for they had been told by an Indian that the Pamunkey River watered a land rich in copper and pearls, and that it arose in the Mountains Quirank, where veins of "very flexible" copper (i.e. gold) were to be found. They were careful, therefore, to leave Opechancanough "in kindness and friendship," the basis of which is revealed by Archer's remark that the Indian king wore "a chain of pearl about his neck thrice double, the third part of them as big as peas, which I should not value less worth than 3 or 400 pounds had the pearl been taken from the mussel as it ought to be" (93). While willing to take the pearl from the mussel, the English were not foolish enough to be caught by the hand in so doing, and though they were encouraged by Opechancanough's hospitality, Captain Newport declined an invitation to spend the night alone in the Indian's village.

The confidence game is a comedy of gullibility mixed with suspicion, greed of gain mingled with guile, and the promising New World garden explored by Christopher Newport and his men is a perilous as well as a pastoral territory, much like the terrain through which Spenser's

Knight makes his way. Shortly after landing on the site of Jamestown, George Percy and some others went walking in the Maytime woods, following "a pathway like to an Irish pace," which led them through a region "flowing over with fair flowers of sundry colors and kinds, as though it had been in any garden or orchard in England" (139). Keeping their way through "this paradise," Percy and his party came to a "savage town," the most of whose male inhabitants, they were told, were out hunting. They "stayed there a while, and had of them strawberries and other things," but when one of the Indians "ran out of his house with a bow and arrows" and disappeared into the woods, Percy "began to mistrust some villainy," and departed (140). On the way back to the fort "one of the savages brought us to the woodside, where there was a garden of tobacco and other fruits and herbs. He gathered tobacco, and distributed it to every one of us; so we departed."

As Captain Newport's voyage up the King's River provides a diagram of imperial supplantation, so Percy's penetration of that Indian bower is a prophetic configuration also, the "Irish pace," a long, winding way which will end with a Spenserian solution to the problem of the "naturals." The Indian's gift of tobacco is likewise symbolic, becoming in time the mainstay of Virginian America. Most immediate of meanings, however, was Percy's pastoral reading of the New World landscape, for it was not long after Captain Newport departed, his swelling sails matching his optimism, that the settlers began to experience the dark side of their chosen paradise. "Destroyed with cruel diseases," as Percy reported, they suffered also from attacks by Indians, but the greatest enemy of all was famine. In the midst of a land of plenty, teeming with fish, flesh, and fowl, the soldier-adventurers, skilled in fortifications and defense, had no knowledge of the angler's or hunter's mysteries and were forced to buy their supplies from Indians whose gifts began to have increasingly higher prices. So it was that Hakluyt's "Instructions" crumpled like so much paper before the press of event, the glorious prospects of Drayton's poem darkening into Percy's dismal lament that "there were never Englishmen left in a foreign country in such misery as we were in this new discovered Virginia" (144).

viii. Amphibious, Ill-born Mob

Out of that terrible ordeal there emerged a greatly reduced garrison, not otherwise transformed by the wilderness experience, led by men whose suffering had not reduced their lust for profit and power. Bickering even as they died, unwilling even at the final extremity to carry out the part of their instructions concerning the literal planting of the land, the colonists would most certainly have suffered Roanoke's fate had it not been for Captain John Smith. Having arrived in America under a shadow of suspicion, Smith is not mentioned in the report which Newport carried back to England, but in the interval of Newport's absence it was the soldier, not the sailor, to whom fell the duty of supervising the next stage of settlement. Smith's attempts to carry out Hakluyt's "Instructions" resulted in a year of heroism mixed with folly, his achievements and misadventures being recorded in a unique document of New World encounter, the report which Smith himself filed in June 1608. His *True Relation of Occurrences and Accidents of Noate in Virginia* has been called the first work of American literature, having been composed in the New World, and certainly it is American in theme and material. But the shape of Smith's account is also an expansion of the essential fable, a pattern which gives form likewise to the relations of Cartier, Lane, Waymouth, and Christopher Newport.

There are two versions, early and late, of Captain John Smith's adventures at the head of New World rivers, and both were written by Smith himself, providing an unsolvable contradiction. Because we have only his word as to the facts, we will never know the truth, and both of his stories shaped events to suit changing circumstances. But that is the wonderful thing about Captain Smith, his uncanny ability to shroud himself in mystery while declaring himself in unequivocal terms, a mixture which is the root and branch of what we are pleased to call the American character. Smith's two stories provide alternative possibilities, a duality and a disjunctiveness endemic to the New World experience, and an acting out of the implications of Ralph Lane's two-hearted River—with the help of his twin-headed Indian.

The romantic version of Smith's journey is the one which has endured, for his rescue by Pocahontas is an icon of popular myth: in that version the material of chivalric legend is interwined with the matter of America, the red princess invested with the role of fair (and royal) protectress. But the story, even if true, is founded on a lie, event warped into the fabric of fiction, for Smith's rescue by an Indian maid was not typical of his adventures in America, nor did he give it the stress it has received. Still, it was he who first set the story in motion, thus adding a romantic dimension to the ongoing myth, giving the image of the virgin land as Indian princess a specific identity—Pocahontas in a welcoming guise, a sometime maiden in the posture of a whore. Whoever John Smith was and whatever happened to him in America will always be a putative affair, of mind more than matter, with the result that his story is the kind of history that opens into fiction, the stuff of the truths which transcend fact.

III

CAPTAIN COURAGEOUS

Captain John Smith, Father of Us All.

i. Predestination in the Stride

The bitter experience of the Jamestown Colony dictated revisions in the literature of settlement, and though the pastoral note holds, it is less Arcadian than Georgic, the aesthetics of imperialism taking on a Hesiodic and Horatian bias. Pastoral language and idealistic motives characterize a typical work of propaganda like Robert Johnson's *Nova Britannia* (1609), in which Virginia is described as an "earthly paradise," but there is added a new emphasis on the need to impose order on the rich but chaotic plenty of the New World garden: "If bare nature be so amiable in its naked kind, what may we hope, when Art and Nature both shall join, and strive together to give best content to man and beast?" (12). The need for "Art and Industry" in the garden is a refrain in the Jacobean propaganda for plantations, a motif shaping the notion of civilized man's role in a barbaric America, and the word "strive" soon enough takes on a less ambiguous function. Notably, the labors of Hercules are among Johnson's favorite analogies for the American necessity, suggesting that Nature will not always be a cooperative partner in colonial enterprise.

Robert Johnson's rage for order is a mercantile equivalent to Ben Jonson's neoclassical ideal, testifying to the aesthetic dimension of early English imperialism. In Johnson's case it is abetted by a middle-class abhorrence of waste, shock over the extravagance of Indians who roamed their thick forests like herds of deer, negligent of plenty and living with "no law but nature," which is no law at all. Johnson recommended the reduction of American forests to useful products—timber and soap ash—and urged the Indians be converted to a more utilitarian form also, "brought" through Christianity "to our civility," and trained "by gentle means to manual arts and skills," welcomed "to conjoin their labors with ours, and enjoy equal privileges with us, in whatsoever good success, time or means may bring to pass" (13-14).

59

Johnson's Indians are "an infinite number of lost and scattered sheep" reserved by God "to be won and recovered by our means," a conventional metaphor, but one which illustrates his emphasis on domestication (14). Where Hakluyt saw America as a vast trading post, a port of call on the way to the far greater markets of Asia, Johnson thought of it as a gigantic farm, and his favorite figure for colonial growth is the transplanted, fruit-bearing tree—Virginia figured as fertile soil for the surplus scions of native English stock.

Still, with that plenitude which characterizes Renaissance propaganda for colonization, Johnson mixes heroic with pastoral analogies, alluding to Hannibal, Alexander, Joshua, and David—familiar types in the literature of conquest. In calling for the civilization of the Indians, he cites Caesar's beneficial effect on "poor and naked Britons," and ends with an appeal to the spirit of the Crusades: "If those undaunted English and Scottish captains that so often ventured their lives, and spilt their blood, to reconquer Palestine from the Turks and Saracens, had seen the gap so open in their days, and the way leading to so many goodly purchases, certainly it had not now been left for us to do" (27). These references remind us that the word "frontier" (like "pioneer") was a military term in Jacobean England, and that the heroic line of advance in Virginia is characterized by the equally linear configurations of martial technology. Moreover, they give an iron-edged meaning to Johnson's proposition that "good" be done to the Indians, "and in no way to their hurt, unless as unbridled beasts, they procure it to themselves" (13).

Johnson's heroic analogies at once substantiate the epic intention of the Virginia endeavor and contradict its humble achievement, for no Alexanders emerge from the annals of James Fort. Indeed, given the utilitarian, mercantile motive, something less than classical in the pattern of courageous captains might be anticipated, and that is precisely the case with the American Hercules, who has a distinctly Falstaffian profile, being something of a *Miles Gloriosus*. Whatever the authenticity of Captain John Smith's *True Travels, Adventures, and Observations,* the book has a fabulous quality suggesting that the whole cloth of truth had been patched out with colorful fabrications, and the result is a montebank appearance, a sort of clamorous advertisement for the author himself.

Still, the *intended* effect was to certify Captain Smith as a modern knight errant, to provide a pedigree, as it were, of adventures at martial (and in female) arms which earned him an armorial escutcheon and the cherished title "Gentleman." Though Spenser's epical handbook of courtesy is not listed by Smith among the other moral and military guides he read while practicing as a youth with "lance and ring" in the Lincolnshire woods, he apparently took the pattern of the Red Cross Knight for his own (T&W: 823). It was an anachronistic (even quixotic) role in 1600, but it was certainly warranted by the Captain's common and rural origins, for like England's patron saint he was a *georgos,* being the son of a propertied yeoman farmer. Moreover, we should distinguish between the penniless braggadocio that was Captain Smith in his later years and the young officer, fresh from continental wars, who enlisted in the Virginia Company, for his presence and activities in America did much to cement the intimate connection between mercantile and military affairs in the Jacobean meaning of the word "Adventurer." Given the miserable state of affairs when, from attrition and circumstance, the command at James Fort fell to him, Smith's accomplishment was considerable: as an American *Miles,* he had something to be *gloriosus* about.

ii. England's Anvil

The longest of Smith's several versions of his American adventure is a combination of epic and autobiography called *The Generall Historie of Virginia, New England, and the Summer Isles* (1624). An exercise in self-promotion and self-justification, Smith's book was designed to gain him further employment, a strategy revealed by proportions and pitch. Of its six parts, the first four are devoted to the discovery, exploration, and settlement of Virginia, and of these four, the second and third are concerned with Smith's role in founding the colony at Jamestown. The fourth part continues Virginia's history from the year of Smith's departure, 1609, to the Indian massacre of 1622, a chronicle of some dozen years that occupies 125 pages, compared to the 145 taken up by the two and a half years Smith was in Virginia. And these later pages emphasize the stupidity and sloth of the colony's administration after he left, blundering ineptness resulting in the increased boldness of the Indians and their devastating attack.

The *Generall Historie* is informed throughout by Smith's martial spirit and his pragmatic means to an end, his militant utilitarianism. Benefiting from his past experience and plenty of hindsight, Smith's view of Virginia is anything but paradisiac and is designed to dim hopes for quick riches: "There is," he wrote, "no country to pillage as the Romans found: all you expect from thence must be by labor" (619). As for gentle handling of the Indians, Smith takes his text from a prophetic parson, Jonas Stockham, who wrote in 1621 that "fair means" to the end of conversion are rewarded with scorn, that English boys sent among the savages to learn their language (and thus speed the missionary work) "return worse than they went," and that if "Mars and Minerva go hand in hand, they will affect more good in an hour, than those verbal Mercurians in their lives" (564). Instead of inviting the Indians to join the English in cooperative labor, Smith by 1624 was for forcing "the treacherous and rebellious infidels to do all manner of drudgery work and slavery for them," using the once abhorrent Spanish example as his "anvil," beating out "an armor of proof hereafter to defend us . . . and make us more circumspect" (579).

"Smith's forge mends all," wrote Samuel Purchas in a poem affixed to the *Generall Historie*, "makes chains for savage nation," and his was only one of several poetic tributes playing on the conceit latent in the author's name—including some spare lines by the old gold-beater himself, John Donne (282 ff.). But it was Purchas who hit upon the happiest metaphor, comparing the *Generall Historie* to Achilles' shield, "armor 'gainst Time . . . with best arts charged," the book characterized as an instrument with a double-edged intention, a shield against calumny and a weapon of policy. In all his poetic roles, Smith is a Herculean bringer of order through strenuous means, and since his reputation has indeed survived because of his *Generall Historie,* it is ironic that the popular image of the militant author pictures him in the protecting embrace of Pocahontas.

For not only does the pretty story occupy but a single page in Smith's voluminous book, but it is anomalous, the merciful princess related only by blood to Smith's chief antagonist, Powhatan, who is portrayed

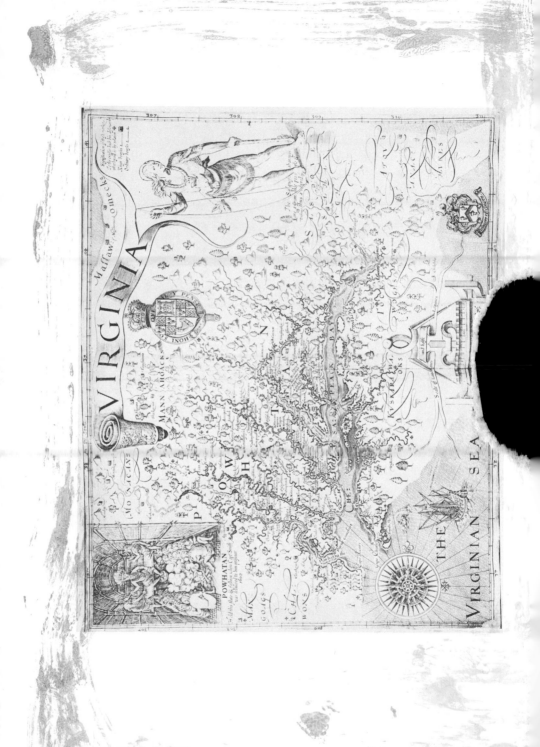

as a wily, cruel, and unrelenting enemy. Even in the series of illustrations ornamenting the map in his *Generall Historie* the picture of his rescue by Pocahontas is outnumbered by scenes of menace and violence, showing Smith being taken prisoner or wrestling with giant Indian kings, pistol or cutlass in hand. More important, if the story of Pocahontas is not much to the point of Smith's *Generall Historie,* neither does it conform to the actual English experience in the American wilderness, which provided the materials from which Smith's adventure and his book were fashioned—as the map which accompanies it shows the symbolic confluence of the Roanoke and Chowan, not the rivers of Chesapeake Bay.

Ralph Lane's adventures on the Roanoke indicated that Art and Nature would seldom work in tandem in America, especially when Nature was represented by a red personification of savage wilderness, and that the ordering of the New World would be a martial, not a missionary effort chiefly. This was also Smith's message, and for both captains symbol of settlement was a fort, Lane regarding it as a means of attaining and exploiting a gold-bearing interior, Smith (by 1630) seeing a "castle or citadel," a stronghold which would serve as the "center or a permanent state to follow (*T&W:* 960-61). This difference was created by changing geopolitical notions concerning the possibilities of land in America, but it did not alter a common military strategy as a means to whatever end: "The wars in Europe, Asia, and Africa," wrote Smith, "taught me how to subdue the wild savages" (925). Though this sentence appears in one of his last tracts—*Advertisements for the Unexperienced Planters of New England*—we may be reasonably sure that he never did entertain any Golden Age illusions about Indians, that he regarded the red man from the start as just another Turk, a potential enemy, not a possible friend. In sum, before the Hesiodic plan could be affected, a certain amount of heroic action was necessary.

Certainly by the end of Captain Smith's first year in Virginia he had sufficient proof of the wisdom of conducting himself always as if in hostile territory. The *True Relation* which he sent to England from James Fort provides an image of the author and his enemies—white as well as red—which differs little from the one contained in his more ambitious and better-known *Generall Historie.* Founded on facts but shaped to a personal motive, Smith's narrative line is beaten out with

Illustration of Captain John Smith's Adventures in Virginia. From *The Generall Historie of Virginia* (1624). Courtesy Rare Book Division, New York Public Library.

Smith's Adventures. Drawn by Captain Smith's friend Robert Vaughan and first published in somewhat different form in his *Map of Virginia* (1612), these panels provide an important example of a critical stage in the metamorphosis of Anglo-American iconography. The Indian figures and the inset map are adapted from Theodore de Bry's illustrations for his edition of Hariot's *Briefe and True Report* (1590), the both taken from John White's drawings and watercolors. Smith has, in effect, introduced himself into Raleigh's Virginia, a scene dominated by the Chowan and Roanoke rivers, much as he imposed his own place-names on a region he never explored, honoring his friends (including Samuel Purchas) but somewhat distorting historical and geographical record. Notably, however, it is the picture in the lower right-hand corner that has survived the otherwise egregiously heroic imagery, including Smith's coat-of-arms, with the motto "To Conquer Is To Live." See W. P. Cumming *et al., The Discovery of North America* (1972), 204, 209, 281.

an urgency that transforms it into a design, thus contributing to the genesis of the ur-myth of American literature, a myth in which the accommodating savage—as Indian princess—plays a role that is distinctly minor, however prominent. As with other reports coming from James Fort, it has an element of unintended as well as intentional humor, and like earlier captains' narratives it takes its impetus from an inland voyage up a wilderness river.

Smith's *True Relation* belongs to the genre established by Cartier and Lane, and likewise contains the shape of adventure, the heroic line associated with the epic. But because of the humor in John Smith's story, the line takes a picaresque as well as a heroic road, a lowering level that suits the Captain's reduced stature—both literal and figurative. The *True Relation,* then, belongs to the literature of adventure, a mode in which humorous and heroic elements are mingled, suggesting that at the heart of encounter violence explodes with a sound much like laughter. We can call Smith's accomplishment the "Epic of Virginia" if we wish, and it is certainly the best we have, but let us remember also that his (and our) adventure lacks the high seriousness of classical heroics. Like so many agents of British empire, Smith muddles rather than marches along, slog-slog-slogging through the muck of a wild, wet woods, infested not by Saracen knights but by a sullen, slippery people.

And yet the Captain remains one man in a thousand, a gentleman unafraid who traveled best alone, and if he is given to strong delusion, wholly believing a lie, his faith results in pure, unmitigated act, a fight at the end of which lies an ultimate conclusion, an imperial lesson, wrought on England's anvil from cold iron. In Smith's *True Relation* the nascent aesthetics of adventure are transformed into steel-hard flesh, as the advancing line becomes a sword, symbol of martial technology representing the absolute utilitarian contingency. *"Whatsoever thy hand shall find to do, do it with all thy might,"* wrote Robert Johnson, "wisdom of the wisest" with which Captain Smith—and Kipling— most surely agreed (26). They are Hebraic but also American sentiments, a key to our paternity, signifying that the out trail, the Long Trail, the trail that is always new, is a way west along the line cut across a vast white space on Richard Hakluyt's map.

iii. To Go and Find Out

Smith's purpose in writing his *True Relation* was similar to that behind Ralph Lane's "Discourse," a desire to explain his conduct in handling the Indians. Though written as "a letter to a friend," Smith's narrative is for the most part a justification of his actions, which had increasingly run counter to the tenor of Hakluyt's "Instructions." Moreover, when he sat down to write his report he was very much a man in the middle, caught between the threat posed by the Indians and the problems posed by a wrangling, faction-torn colony. Though a member of the governing council, Smith had not yet become President, and the impotent Edward Maria Wingfield had been succeeded in that post by rascally John Ratcliffe, under whose rule the fortunes of Jamestown continued to decline. By the end of its first year the colony had more rivalries than a touring repertory company, for every man had his own little drama to enact, and few of the performances involved planting, supporting, and defending a tiny, fever-ridden, famine-haunted outpost on the edge of a vast wilderness. What unanimity there was involved the search for gold, and what they found turned out to be so much "gilded dirt."

Smith eventually convinced the settlers that hard work and unglamorous commodities would result in slow but sure profit—and survival—but he did not succeed in doing so until the second year of the colony, after he became President. Under Wingfield, Smith was made Cape Marchant, with the responsibility of providing food for the colonists, which meant trading with Indians for corn: "the Spaniard never more greedily desired gold than he victual" (*Map:* 387). Though this meant much traveling along the rivers that empty into Chesapeake Bay, it left Smith little opportunity to look for a passage to India. Still, the Captain carried out the "Instructions" as best he could while journeying through the interior, listing profitable native commodities, getting

67

information from the Indians concerning the great "back sea," marking locations for future settlement, and spotting possible mine sites. Smith found little evidence that he was regarded as a god, and though he was remarkably successful in dealing with the Indians, he found them to be drivers of hard bargains, asking outrageous prices for their grain. This was particularly true of the tribes nearest the fort, who, when they could not obtain what they wanted through barter, regarded it as a gift outright and simply took it, walking off with the colonists' precious iron tools. By the end of the first year the Indians Smith was warned not to offend had become very offensive to him, and he felt that only by dealing severely with them could he guarantee the colony's safety and survival—hence the purpose and bias of his report.

The most troublesome of the Indians was the leader of the Paspahegh, who lived near James Fort, but the most problematic was Powhatan, who lived many miles away. Since many of the tribes in the region were under Powhatan's control, gaining his fealty to King James was an important object of the English, but the Indian chief kept away from the fort on the river, preferring to be represented by agents. Powhatan's distance and his power, along with his wilderness seat on the Pamunkey, one of the great rivers of the region, gives him a symbolic stature, and he emerges from Smith's account as a dark force, being enigmatic to the point of mystery. Though hardly an Incan or Aztec prince, Powhatan has a certain grandeur (as Smith has his undoubted courage), and he emerges from the *True Relation* as rather a noble savage, a stern wilderness presence, secretive, moody, even treacherous, yet possessing an undeniable grace. As all rivers led into and out of Powhatan's realm, so the voyage central to Smith's *True Relation* took the Captain into the heart (if not the confidence) of that world, a route which has the ritual and romance of a symbolic quest.

For the sake of literature, it would have been better if Smith's voyage had gained a certain elevation by following the lordly King's River, but exigency dictated a humbler route, in keeping with the picaresque dimension of his adventure. It was up one of the tributaries of the James—the lowly Chickahominy—that the brave Captain sailed, not, like Newport, looking for gold and pearls but, as the name of the river suggests, for supplies of corn. The Chickahominy Indians, unlike many of the tribes in the region, were willing to trade at a reasonable rate, and encouraged by their hospitality, Smith decided to explore the headwaters of their river. Having gone as far as he could in his barge, he left it near an Indian town with seven of his men aboard as guard, then, taking two armed companions and two Indian guides, he set off upstream in a canoe, putting himself "upon the adventure: the country only a vast and wild wilderness" (179). In this, the second stage of his journey, Smith stepped off into a great green mystery, disappearing into the interior for a month. Since the two white men with him were killed, we have only his word as to subsequent events. What really happened is of no consequence here, but the story Smith told most certainly is, being an important myth in the process of creation.

iv. Never-never Country

Like Cartier on the St. Lawrence and Lane on the Roanoke, Smith went up the Chickahominy in search of a passage to India, and it is typical of his version of the great adventure that his journey ended in a swamp. Hoping to find Hakluyt's lake and Verrazzano's Sea beyond, Smith took an Indian guide with him and went on alone, straight into an ambush, and since his conduct in this affair raised some questions as to his wisdom, he rendered the particulars of ensuing events in minute detail. As usual in Smith's writings, specificity swells with the implications of fiction, and as in a novel by Cooper, Smith's Indians seem to have been extremely obliging to the needs of narrative. Though their marksmanship on the Captain's English companions appears to have been excellent, the "20 or 30" arrows they let fly at the Captain either fell short or inflicted minor wounds. Smith's personal Indian, his "consort," was similarly obliging, allowing himself to be held fast by the Captain as a shield in the line of fire, which permitted Smith to load and fire his pistol "3 or 4 times." His consort then volunteered to serve as translator between him and the hostile savages surrounding them with drawn bows, a delicate conversation during which Smith somehow backed into a quagmire, pulling his *ad hoc* Chingachgook with him. Having become literally bogged down, he surrendered to the inevitable—and to the Indians—but instead of being killed or tortured, Captain Smith was treated by his captors as an officer and gentleman.

This is not to say that Smith's story was a fabrication in the absolute sense, only that it resembles fiction mightily. What happened to Smith at the headwaters of the Chickahominy (and afterward) bears a remarkable similarity not only to earlier accounts of European adventures in America, but to certain romantic nineteenth-century novels, and his narrative acts therefore as a sort of bridge, composed of those coincidences which form a conduit of New World marvels. Thomas Hariot had described the savages' awe of the white man's "instruments," his lodestone and compasses, telling how he took advantage of their superstitious curiosity to explain the mysteries of Christianity, and Rosier likewise brought the Indians "to love and fear us" by tricks with a knife, needle, and lodestone (H: 375-76; R: 371-72). So Smith with his chief captor, Opechancanough, who "so amazedly admired" his compass that the Captain was able to discourse on "the roundness of the earth, the course of the sun, moon, stars, and planets," leaping high over the barrier of language (181). For his part, the obliging Opechancanough rivaled Ralph Lane's accommodating Menatonon in describing the country about, including a "great turning of salt water" near the source of the King's River (182).

Smith's encounter with the Indians of the interior may have begun with some traditional touches, but it soon enough took a turn that adds a completely new dimension. The difference between the relationship of Smith and Opechancanough, Lane and Menatonon, is indicative, for this time it is the white man who is captive, a condition of enforced passivity which determined Smith's conduct thenceforth, the Captain resorting to his wits in lieu of his missing weapons. In the accounts of Cartier, Rosier, and Lane, the river adventure is a sortie, a tentative probing of mystery, but in Captain Smith's it becomes a captivity narrative, hence a complete immersion, akin to a baptism, the high point of which in one version of events may have been, according to some authorities, an Indian ritual of initiation, but the outcome of which was most certainly a kind of rebirth.

Yet it was an imperfect baptism, for Smith's head stayed above water, and the English Captain in the wilderness became a herald of civilization. The effect of savagery on him was minimal, even nugatory, boding ill for the hoped-for accommodation between red men and white. Like the needle on his magical compass, Captain Smith held steady on his enforced wanderings through the seemingly endless maze of trails, rivers, and villages of Indian America, his gaze always fixed on a farther north. In all his dealings with the Indians—as reported by himself—Smith proved as wily and cunning as his adversaries, pressing always for advantage and information, his eye ever on the main chance. The result is an overflow of the comic spirit, despite the very real hazard involved, for having lost the arms of Mars, Smith develops the head of Minerva: thoroughly middle-class in its set, yet extremely flexible in action, Smith's mind was adaptable to a high degree, a signal virtue for imperial man.

v. Half-devil and Half-child

Smith's inland journey culminates in his encounter with Powhatan, a meeting which, like his interview with Opechancanough, compounds what had happened earlier in America with what was yet to be, a mingling of the marvelous and mischievous in a splendidly comic interview, conducted on the banks of yet another imperial stream, not the Powhatan/James but the Pamunkey—soon to be Englished "York." There Captain Smith was led into the presence of the very image of noble savagery, Powhatan "proudly lying upon a bedstead a foot high, upon ten or twelve mats, richly hung with many chains of great pearls about his neck . . . with such a grave and majestical countenance, as drove me into admiration to see such state in a naked savage" (185). This perfect figure of a savage king treated Smith with magnanimity, and like his brother, Opechancanough, expressed an interest in the greater world, particularly in the affairs of the English.

What, for example, were they doing in his country?

To this forthright, ingenuous, but perhaps Socratic question, Smith responded with a bare-faced lie, claiming that the English had been attacked by the "Spaniards our enemy, we being overpowered, near put to retreat, and threatened by extreme weather put to this shore," etc., etc., a likely fiction whose acceptance by Powhatan depended upon

71

the less likely chance that he had no knowledge of the interview some six months earlier between Newport and his own son. Pressing some such advantage, perhaps, Powhatan persisted in this line of questioning, asking why the English were interested in exploring the interior. Smith touched upon the subject of the "back sea," and then, in a lie gauged to earn Powhatan's allegiance, told him that Captain Newport had had a man slain by the Monacans, Powhatan's enemies, "whose death we intended to revenge" (186). This properly savage motive seems to have turned Powhatan's attention in the desired direction, for "after good deliberation" he described "the countries beyond the falls," an Indian tale which enjoyed universal circulation in North America.

The source of the King's River, according to the Indian king, was in a region so close to a sea that in storms the salt water made "the head of the river to be brackish": "He described also upon the same sea a mighty nation . . . that did eat men and warred with the . . . nations upon the top of the head of the Chesapeake Bay. . . . He signified their crowns were shaven, long hair in the neck, tied on a knot, swords like pole-axes. Beyond them, he described people with short coats, and sleeves to the elbows, that passed that way in ships like ours. Many kingdoms he described to me, to the head of the bay, which seemed to be a mighty river issuing from mighty mountains betwixt the two seas. . . . He described a country called Anone, where they have abundance of brass, and houses walled as ours are" (186). As with the stories told to Cartier and Lane, Powhatan's description was improved by translation, becoming the desired fiction. Shaven crowns, scalp locks, and war clubs—typical of the Iroquois—suggest also pigtails and poleaxes, and northern lakes become an inland ocean, while the Gulf of Mexico is shoved far north, permitting Spanish sailors to put ashore in Mandarin dress. Like Menatonon's "wassador," moreover, Powhatan's brass leaves golden traces on the touchstone of hope.

Smith in his turn drew the longbow himself, describing "the territories of Europe, which were subject to our great king whose subject I was, the innumerable multitude of his ships . . . the noise of trumpets, and terrible manner of fighting" (187). Powhatan was properly impressed, and invited the English to come live on the Pamunkey, where he would give them land and food and protect them. They, in return, would provide him with hatchets and copper, a proposed exchange which suggests Powhatan's motive for treating Smith so kindly, the Indian's outstretched hand more often than not having an open palm. But whatever his ultimate design, Powhatan is nothing if not an accommodating savage by Smith's account, and he ended their pleasant interview by letting the Englishman return to his people, Smith having promised that they would accept his invitation—yet another glib if understandable lie.

Powhatan's hospitality contrasts strongly with the reception given Smith on his return to James Fort, for his enemies used the death of the two men on the Chickahominy as warrant for his execution. The Captain was saved from the gallows by the timely arrival of Captain Newport, but the generous old pirate soon became a troublesome addition to enterprise, at once a gall and a hindrance. Powhatan, while remaining on the Pamunkey, sent down a flood of presents, importuning the return of his friend and desiring to meet Captain Newport, whose bravery Smith had described at length. Always one for visits of state, Newport lacked his soldier-counterpart's business sense, and when he accompanied Smith on his second encounter with Powhatan, he was every inch a sailor ashore. Powhatan, on the other hand, emerges from the second meeting as less a noble than a politic savage: though assuming at first "such a majesty as I cannot express, nor yet have often seen, either in Pagan or Christian," he quickly descends to the petty tricks of a mercantile swindler, a low cunning which emphasizes Newport's gullibility and Smith's cleverness (191). With "a kind countenance" bidding Smith welcome, Powhatan inquired after the guns which the Captain had pledged as his ransom but had neglected to furnish—or to mention before in his *True Relation*. Smith reminded Powhatan that the Indians who had escorted him back to James Fort had been offered two cannon, "in that he desired a great gun, but they refused to take them. Whereat with a loud laughter, he desired me to give him some of less burden" (192).

It is in this cony-catching vein that the second interview unfolds, a sinister if laughing game, for Powhatan soon asked that Smith's soldiers put away their arms, but the Captain refused—pleading the custom of his country. Next Powhatan demanded that the English display all their trade goods before the bargaining for corn began, and when Smith scorned this "ancient trick," Powhatan, pretending "to despise the nature of a merchant," proposed that they not trade, but rather "we freely should give to him, and he liberally would requite us" (194). This was Newport's favorite pastime in America, and to Smith's great disgust he began to distribute copper at a ruinous rate. Captain Newport was also eager to accept Powhatan's offer of guides into the interior, a "fair tale" which "almost made Captain Newport undertake by this means to discover the South Sea," but which Smith suspected would "not be without treachery, if we ground our intent upon Powhatan's constancy" (197). The South Sea was one thing, depending on Powhatan's help to attain it another: "Experience had well taught me to believe his friendship till convenient opportunity suffered him to betray us" (194).

Captain Smith gives no particulars to substantiate his suspicion, and it may, like much of his *True Relation,* have been illuminated by hindsight, for in the months which followed that second journey he was given sufficient grounds to doubt Powhatan's intentions: As Percy earlier observed, when Indian gifts of venison arrived, "sauce" (insolence) was sure to follow close after (140). In the end, the uncovering of a plot to seize Captain Newport provided a dramatic conclusion to a series of offensive if relatively harmless gestures. The change in Powhatan's portrait, from the accommodating Menatonon-like king of the first voyage to the scheming Pemisapan of the last pages of Smith's narrative, is a sequence which serves the double purpose of preparing the reader for a final revelation while giving Smith the advantage of perceptions more acute than those of his nautical counterpart—and rival—Newport.

That Smith had his suspicions is (again) more than likely, but it is in his staging of events that a craftsmanlike hand is revealed. More important, though Smith's *True Relation* was intended as an instrument of policy, as a work of literature it transcends its occasion. Smith's frontier, his point of contact with the red man's world, is a symbolic field of opposing forces, Powhatan's royal residence on the Pamunkey the center of power opposing the imperial outpost on the James. The one man is wilderness incarnate, a personification of deceptive prospects, the other represents the martial, heroic impulse in the New World. Both provide a pattern of encounter, engaged in an antagonistic duet of cross-purposes, linked by outstretched hands of mutual trust and greed as they maneuver to gain the advantage over one another, protestations of friendship mingling with veiled threats of harm.

vi. A Neater, Sweeter Maiden

There is little room in the several encounters between Powhatan and Captain Smith in the *True Relation* for "the king's dearest daughter" as princess protectress, and Pocahontas is notably missing from the first and second meetings on the Pamunkey. When *La Belle Sauvage* finally appears it is late in the story, and she is sent by her father as hostage for several Indians who had been imprisoned at James Fort for pestering the English. Powhatan's daughter is described by Smith as "a child of ten years old, which not only for feature, countenance, and proportion, much exceedeth any of the rest of his people: but for wit and spirit, is the only nonpariel of his country" (206). Still, like the "maiden child" given Cartier by the Lord of Canada, Pocahontas is another Indian gift, and her companion-escort is the very type and symbol of ignoble savagery, Powhatan's "most trusty messenger, called Rawhunt." In contrast to her beauty and her father's majesty, Rawhunt is "much exceeding in deformity of person," a warped body containing a Machiavellian intelligence, "a subtle wit and crafty understanding."

Smith's description of Powhatan's agent gives a certain warp to Rawhunt's presentation to the English Captain of his fair hostage, "a long circumstance" in which "he told me how well Powhatan loved and respected me, and in that I should not doubt any way of his kindness." And this earlier, even younger Pocahontas is very much her father's child, for "his little daughter he had taught this lesson also, not taking notice at all of the Indians that had been prisoners till that morning that she saw their fathers and friends come quietly, and only then in good terms to entreat their liberty" (206-7). Pocahontas's subsequent friendship with Smith and her loyalty to the English settlers is borne out by witnesses, but in the *True Relation* she is as yet an unregenerate savage, lovely but animated by cunning and guile.

When the material of Smith's first report from America was adapted to his *Generall Historie* it was considerably shortened, with the result that Powhatan's savagery is simplified, at once Romanized and abbreviated, reduced to a generalized portrait which lacks the psychological complexity of the earlier presentation. By 1624 he had become just another Indian, while the addition of Pocahontas as a Savior Princess provided a dramatic element with great human interest. Small wonder, then, that the story took hold of the popular imagination in later years. But there is a mythic dimension to her subsequent emergence, one stemming from her marriage to John Rolfe, the first Virginian to raise tobacco as a money crop and one of the few to take an Indian for his wife. That union, with the bride's conversion to Christianity, held out hope for a permanent, peaceful relationship between red men and white, a hope which, with Pocahontas, suffered a premature death. Christened Rebecca, Pocahontas in death became the mother of the terrible twins of supplantation, English Jacob and Indian Esau, yet another illustration of the mystery of iniquity.

Pocahontas's association with tobacco endured, and like those legions of wooden Indians cut in her image, she became an opulent symbol of New World wealth, the very type of pastoral accommodation. The color of copper (Venus' metal), Pocahontas became the erotic incarnation of a fertile land, a friendly female presence, offering with open arms America's bountiful promise. The endurance of this symbol is not surprising, considering the long-lived hopes of Richard Hakluyt, but Pocahontas, as accommodating Indian princess, represents a myth that has little to do with the history of the English in America or with the subsequent fiction derived from that history. Taken from context, the story expresses the other kind of myth, a Golden Age fable like that purveyed by Arthur Barlowe, Thomas Hariot—and William Shakespeare. It is a tale of a virginal New World greeting a brave Old World clad only in robes of morning, yet it is not gold or pearls she holds out in welcome, nor does she point the way west. Her gift is tobacco, like the land itself, the Indian's inadvertent contribution to English empire.

Pocahontas was first called Matoaka, meaning "Playful," but Powhatan later gave her the name by which she is known—"Wantonness." And it was Pocahontas's "pocahontas" which aroused Rolfe's passion for "our country's good, the benefit of this plantation, and the converting of one unregenerate to regeneration" (236-37). But it is a quality notably missing from her portrait in Smith's *True Relation,* and

76

even in subsequent accounts the relationship between the Captain and the Indian Princess is strictly avuncular. Though resembling Falstaff in his defensive boastfulness and his large way with facts, Captain John in America lacks Sir John's sensual aspect, his chastity symbolizing the sea change suffered by chivalry when it moved from the Old to the New World. Smith's martial asceticism is more than knightly restraint, but is deeply anchored in Anglo-Saxon attitudes toward savage people, an aversion to relationships other than commercial and military. Powhatan sensed this English reticence and objected to it, hence the hopes attending the Rolfes' marriage. But that fated union was exceptional, and Captain Smith's restraint established the frontier pattern, in literature if not in life: a militant asceticism which necessarily emphasized the male bond, an uneasy alliance between red and white dictated by martial and mercantile considerations that produced misunderstandings often erupting in violence.

Though Captain John Smith was responsible for the pleasant story of Pocahontas and himself, the occasion for its telling having been her visit to England in 1618 and his own consequent hope of gaining recognition and reward for his achievements in Virginia, he cannot be blamed for the uses to which it was later put. We should credit him rather with providing a less charming but perhaps more accurate picture of colonial relationships, a landscape with figures engaged in questionable acts. Thus his *True Relation* ends with a minor but indicative anecdote, a story about an Indian who tried to lure Captain Smith up the river and into the woods by showing him a glittering rock, but who, when his account of its discovery became tangled with contradictions, was seized by the exasperated Captain and flogged. This incident took place one year to the month from the landing of the London Company fleet at the site of James Fort, by which time Smith had accumulated sufficient evidence as to the inutility of Hakluyt's "Instructions" concerning the handling of the natives. It marks a wry anniversary, a Jonsonian finale to a year of reciprocal greed and deceit, a satiric complement to the tragic explosion of violence which signaled the end of Ralph Lane's first year in America.

If Smith's beating of the deceitful Indian was on the anvil of his past experience, still, the near success of the Indian's scheme reveals a continued willingness on his part to believe stories of gold and a northwest passage. Captain Smith's great Powhatan is a more complex portrait of savagery than Captain Newport's Little Powhatan, yet as symbols as well as kin they are related, for in a double sense both Captains found Indians who reflected back their own desires, in specific terms and general, savages who not only told them obliging stories but who mirrored their duplicitous intent. This is the covert burden of Captain Smith's adventure, another version of the imperial experience, lending his story a paradoxical dimension. For Powhatan did nothing to Captain Smith that was not a reversal of what Smith intended for him, the Indian King, like his River, merely reflecting back the Captain's own countenance. Traveling up the devious course of the Chickahominy toward the commodious breadth of the Pamunkey, moving from his island stronghold into "the heart of the country," Captain John Smith found a darkness cast before him on the water, that obscurest of self-images, his shadow. It is, once again, a Conradian fable, one in which the tender-hearted Indian maiden plays no part.

vii. Clear the Land of Evil

Toward the end of Smith's *True Relation* there is a description of Virginia's Nansemond River which can serve to express his expedient, utilitarian, and martial view of the New World and its people:

This river is a musket-shot broad, each side being shoaled bays, with a narrow channel, but three fathom deep. His course for eighteen miles is almost directly south and by west, where beginneth the first inhabitants; for a mile it turneth directly east, towards the west, where is a great bay, and a white chalky island convenient for a fort. His next course is south, where within a quarter of a mile, the river divideth in two, the neck a plain high corn field, the western bend a high plain likewise, the northeast answerable in all respects. In these plains are planted abundance of houses and people; they may contain 1000 acres of most excellent fertile ground: so sweet, so pleasant, so beautiful, and

so strong a prospect, for an invincible strong city, with so many com-
modities, that I know as yet I have not seen (200).

The direction of the river's course is described in terms of an upstream voyage, the imperial necessity in America, a male, progenitive, and heroic line which transforms the Nansemond into a masculine presence, providing a setting for that "invincible strong city" which is Smith's favorite figure of orderliness. It is a symbolic landscape much like the Pamunkey region as described by Smith in his account of his departure from captivity, "a fat, fertile, sandy ground," through which the Pamunkey runs "his course northwest, and westerly" (187).

Captain Smith was a man of many parts, but no more a believer in Arcadia than a lover of Indian maidens, reserving his faith and his passion for other matters. A virgin land for him was no Eden, but a waste of plenty itching for a plow; no sacred vestal, but a fat and fertile presence to be possessed by means of rivers like the male Pamunkey, which "keepeth his course without tarrying some twenty miles" into an interior big with the promise of empire. Smith measured both the Pamunkey, and the Nansemond in terms of a musket shot, a martial unit of measure which did not promise well for the "abundance of people" who already occupied the abundant land, "warlike and tall" and with a concept of territory as fierce as it was primitive. For Captain Smith did not seem to entertain much hope of making pliable Christian sheep out of heathen wolves, and though we hear much concerning the conversion of the land in his *True Relation*, of the conversion of the Indians we hear very little. There is absolutely nothing in his account of the people of the New World which would warrant the cheery assurance of "I.H." 's prefatory comments concerning "the erecting of true religion among infidels . . . and the winning of many thousands of wandering sheep unto Christ's fold who now, and till now, have strayed in the unknown paths of paganism, idolatry, and superstition" (168). Smith's account is heavy on the "till now" element, and he devotes several pages to the "unknown paths"—describing the Indian's repellent rites—but as for the erection of true religion among the heathen, Captain Smith preferred erections of a more military nature.

If aboriginal possession has priority over subsequent supplantation, then Captain John Smith is the villain of his own story, for his was clearly an imperial errand, however inflated with a darkly comic spirit. Though his advice concerning the handling of the Indians was ignored during the early years of Jamestown, and though his *Generall Historie* and other late writings failed to earn him the employment or reward he most certainly deserved, that single-minded soldier cast a prophetic shadow on the land. What followed in America during the next two centuries bore out, through repetition, Captain Smith's experience, the hard and pointed facts from which his narrative was forged into coarse-hammered steel. There was no compromise, no truce possible between the English and the Indians, and though popular waves of sentimental idealism would succeed waves of frontier hostility, few frontiersmen were able to share that popular mood.

The native American hero who emerged from the wilderness context was to share a number of Captain Smith's traits: his courage, his cunning, his ingenuity, his faith in the future, his utilitarianism, and his generous way with the truth. The American hero's progress would also be inland by waterways, along rivers which were but greater versions of tidewater streams, a course shaped by a mixture of quixotic idealism and expedient means, greed licensed by a sense of destiny. From first to last it would be a picaresque adventure, a mock chivalric romance, yet it is also a tale of arms and the man, linking the American experience to neoclassic precedent, the strategic dimension of imperial design. Shedding clouds of chivalric glory, Captain Smith is a Red Cross Knight with a star-spangled manner, his river voyages putting a seal on the land, yielding both a popular myth and a darker version, too. We can see in his epic a sum of all previous encounters and a determination of the pattern for centuries to come, for as American Aeneas, Captain Smith is father of us all, Captain and Captive, clue to the meaning of our savage heart, primal author of our gigantic tale.

viii. Work on Water

Captain John Smith's heroic reach is further demonstrated by his continued explorations in Virginia, journeys by barge which ended only when injuries from a gunpowder explosion forced him to return to England, late in 1609. A circumnavigation of sorts, Smith's voyages in search of a river route to the "great salt water, which by all likelihood is either some part of Canada, some great lake, or some inlet of some sea that falleth into the South Sea" took him around the Virginian Mediterranean, Chesapeake Bay (361). Despite the reduction in scope, Smith's adventures on the Bay do amount to an American *Aeneid*, and they occupy a central position in the *Generall Historie*. First recounted in an epical twelve chapters appended to Smith's *A Map of Virginia with a Description of the Country* (1612), they are given a neoclassical tone by having the Captain's praises sung by other voices than his own. Moreover, the map itself is as much a diagram of empire as a record of exploration, a design dominated by the great Bay and its many tributary rivers, the largest of which Captain Smith explored to their falls. Terminus to his penetration of each river is marked on his map by that chivalric device, a Maltese Cross, thereby defining the limits of settlement for a century to come, establishing the boundaries of a world centered at Jamestown, an equivalent though humble enough Rome. But then "even Rome herself, during the reign of Romulus, exceeded not the number of a thousand houses" (*T&W:* 488).

At the top of Smith's map of Virginia, above the head of a giant "Susquehanna" warrior that decorates it, there is a descending loop, the generalized coastline of the rumored "back sea." The gigantic warrior is actually a copy of Theodore de Bry's engraving from a watercolor sketch by John White of a Roanoke werowance, a noble if plagiarized image which, like Smith's account of the inland ocean, will have a long iconographic life through the power of maps to convince.

Corrected page 82

John Smith's Map of Virginia. From *The Generall Historie of Virginia* (1624). Courtesy Rare Book Division, New York Public Library.

Smith's Virginia. First published in Smith's *Map of Virginia* (1612), William Hole's engraving, like Vaughan's, is indebted to de Bry and John White for iconographic details. But this is very much Captain Smith's theater of operations, dominated by Chesapeake Bay and the many navigable rivers that reach inland toward the rumors of an even greater "sea" beyond, on whose banks live the powerful "Massawomacks" (Iroquois). See Cumming *et al., Discovery of North America,* 259.

Even as Smith was looking for his great grail, Samuel de Champlain was pressing an identical search in Canada, and within three years of the publication of Smith's map, his French counterpart encountered the reality. Yet the certainty that there was a river flowing west from the Appalachians of the Pacific remained a potent Virginian myth for more than a century, a lure lying beyond the barrier of the Blue Ridge Mountains. By his explorations, Champlain continued the baseline of French empire, an extended zone of power which would a century later threaten the English from beyond the mountains, as in Smith's day the "great nation and very populous" which lived on the "back sea" periodically raided the Indians at the head of Chesapeake Bay. In 1608, Smith encountered a war party of that "nation" as they descended the Potomac, and in that same prophetic year Champlain made hostile contact with Iroquois as he explored the lake that bears his name, twin events that were tentative probes of imperial pincers, initial thrusts of epic ambitions.

Smith, through barter, obtained war shields from the "Wassawomacks" which later protected him and his men from the arrows of other Indians, and which earned their respect when paraded as trophies of war by the sly Captain, who shared with Ulysses a measure of Mercury in his martial alloy. Prototypical frontiersman that he was, Smith evinced the transformational touch of wilderness technology by adopting a savage means to a civilized end, making a wily way through the woods. Like Sir William Johnson, whose league with the Iroquois resulted in the English victory over the French on the lakes first explored by Champlain, Smith trained his men "to march, fight, and skirmish in the woods," so as to meet Powhatan's warriors on their own terms, a tactic also favored by a Virginian colonel of militia who was born a century after John Smith died (202). The Captain's intended campaign came to nothing, and yet, like Champlain's initial skirmish with the Iroquois, it was a forboding catspaw over waters obscure as prophecy.

"Chesapeake" is derived from an Indian phrase meaning "big-river-at," and so as an inland sea the Bay was also an elongated, expanded Potomac, a waterway which is thought to take its name from an Algonquin word connoting "something brought." However accurate the tradition, it contains in mythic terms a very large truth, much as Captain Smith's epic journey took him at its farthest end past the swamp that would become the District of Columbia. Like the Admiral for whom that swamp was named, the Captain brought with him something more than trinkets, much as the warpath and trading route which the Potomac provided for the Iroquois would in time permit passage for the English through the mountains to the rivers beyond, a second surge of empire led by the man for whom the place called Washington was named.

ix. The Glory of the Garden

Smith's description of Virginia that accompanies his map marks several strategic changes in his version of America, for the account of his Chesapeake epic is accompanied by a distinctly georgic paean, vibrating with the resonances of Robert Johnson: "Heaven and earth never agreed better to frame a place for man's habitation . . . were it fully manured and inhabited by industrious people. Here are mountains, hills, plains, valleys, rivers and brooks, all running most pleasantly into a fair bay compassed but for the mouth with fruitful and delightsome land" (337). This fertile prospect, along with a Hesiodic catalogue of Virginia's commodities, were dictated by Smith's hope of selling his services while peddling America's commercial potential. As Aeneas, that is to say, the Captain was also something of a Virgil, alternating his heroic with his pastoral pen, putting both instruments in the service of empire—and self. Still, Smith's stress on the need for industry and manure bears out his favorite utilitarian theme, that beauty bare is apt to be barren.

Ironically, it was in 1612 also that John Rolfe manured the first crop of tobacco on his James River plantation. The King for whom the river was named detested the odious stuff, nor did Smith care for that Indian plant any more than for the Indian himself, failing to list it in 1612 as either a "planted fruit" or a "commodity" that "may be had by industry" in Virginia. In his *Generall Historie* Smith conjoined tobacco with the Indian as a nuisance, a crop which made "some grow rich but many poor," inducing false hopes of profit and encouraging

85

Indian habits of sloth (599). By 1629 in his *True Travels and Observations,* Smith saw tobacco as a curse, a figurative as well as a literal soporific: "For discoveries they have made none; nor to any other commodity than tobacco do they apply themselves unto, though never any was planted at first" (886). Where the original colonists hoped to find gold, Virginians now planted tobacco, with similar expectations of easy riches, and as Smith earlier scored his companions for neglecting slower but surer sources of profit, twenty years later he pointed out to his countrymen the dangers of a single-crop economy, not only in terms of stability, but in its effects on patterns of settlement: the Virginian planters were so thinly scattered, "so disjointed, and every one commander of himself, to plant what he will," that the centralized control which Smith valued so highly was impossible to maintain (888).

Smith, again in the minority, was again right, though he was not alone in decrying the effects of the commodious land he had earlier explored and praised. The Virginia Company and, later, the Royal Commissioners deplored the economic result of raising tobacco, and clergymen lamented the effect of thinly spread settlement on church-going, but the expansion of plantations along the extensive, convenient network of tidewater rivers was inexorable. The authoritarian, fortress-dominated colony which was Captain Smith's ideal became a "disjointed" system of independent planters, each man "commander of himself" and subject to none. Hardly a pastoral idealist, Smith was unable to appreciate the mood of agrarian independence fostered by the topography of Virginia, a geopolitics with a republican shape. He recommended instead the formation of productive cooperatives, factories producing simple commodities needed in England, "soap-ashes, iron, rape-oil, madder, pitch and tar, flax and hemp" (888). But those Virginians who had been lured to America by Hakluyt's promise of oriental riches were not willing to manufacture such labor-consuming products. When they discovered that tobacco would make them rich, they grew tobacco and tobacco only, and all the King's taxes and all the King's men could not make them stop.

Thus the georgic ideal reverted to a more easy if not Arcadian pastoralism in which neither industry nor manure played an important part, a mood of opportunism fed by beautiful rivers which resulted in an unstable economy and an independent, centerless, restless population. By the end of the century Virginians had converted the Indian weed and Indian rivers to an economy of waste, one requiring a system that depended upon the labor of slaves. It was during the subsequent period of illusory agrarian peace and prosperity that the symbol of Virginia in America became the Indian Princess bearing her dubious gift. We should perhaps recall the cancerous career of tobacco in America when we contemplate that copper-colored maiden with her proffered leaves, and we might think also of that subtle savage her father, and the river which once bore his name, famous among Indians, lord of the wilderness, Powhatan.

x. Soldier an' Sailor Too!

Captain John Smith's effect on the course of Virginia's subsequent economic development is comparable to his reward for securing the colony's safety—a cluster of "barren rocks" off her coast, inadequate recompense (as he himself observed), but fit symbol for the neglect he suffered, both in terms of fame and fortune (*T&W*: 947). Bearing his name, those rocks are a monument, one of those hard facts to which he was so fond of referring, testifying to the New World's resistance to the imposition of hope. So also Hudson's River and Bay, carrying the name of the man who explored them in a continuing quest for northwest passage, the one giving way to shallow soundings, the other to silence, coldness, death. But Henry Hudson shares more than a mocking memorial with John Smith, for when he sailed up the lordly "North" River in 1609 he was pursuing a figment made real on a rough sketch-map that Smith sent from Virginia the year before, a wishful draft based on the earliest accounts the English received from the Indians concerning the great "back sea" beyond the mountains. Smith's maps, both early and late, like Michael Lok's were mythic diagrams, and by their means he left his mark on the landscape, the Hudson along with the Potomac providing imperial corridors stretching northward to challenge French domain.

Nor were they the only broad strokes with which Captain Smith gave shape to English empire in America, for in 1614 he put on his nautical dress and cruised the coast of Northern Virginia in search of whales and gold. The most considerable result of his new employment was yet another book, a propagandistic *Description* of the region he named "New England," rendering one more amazing prophecy concerning the territory he had explored. Drawing upon his own experience, as always, but this time citing the Dutch instead of the Spanish example, Smith insisted that the "main staple" to be "extracted" from New England was fish, "which however it may seem a mean and a base commodity, yet who will but truly take the pains and consider the sequel, I think will allow it well worth the labor" (194). Fisheries were the "mines" of the Dutch, "the sea the source of those silvered streams of all their virtue, which hath made them now the very miracle of industry, the pattern of perfection for these affairs: and the benefit of fishing is that *primum mobile* that turns all their spheres to this height of plenty, strength, honor and admiration."

Smith's earlier hard-nosed realism is here irradiated almost to invisibility by rhapsodic hyperbole, recalling the Elizabethan vision of America and explained by the fact that his pamphlet was written in the service of Sir Ferdinando Gorges, whose earlier interest in Northern Virginia had been reawakened by Smith's discoveries. Sharing for the time Sir Ferdinando's self-hypnotic ability, Smith converted the honorable but laborious trade of fishing into an easy pleasure: "What sport doth yield a more pleasing content, and less hurt or charge than angling with a hook, and crossing the sweet air from isle to isle, over the silent stream of a calm sea?" (213). Not only men may play at this game, but women and children, whose families gaily sailing forth from "their own doors, in their own boats upon the sea. . . . And is it not pretty sport, to pull up two pence, six pence, and twelve pence, as fast as you can?" (213). At times, Smith's version of New England seems neighbor to the Virginian Cockayne, being a paradise so crowded with fish and fowl that "worthy is that person to starve that here cannot live" (208).

Despite his prescience concerning fisheries, Captain Smith's New England is still Northern Virginia, another virgin zone, "her treasures having yet never been opened, nor her originals wasted, consumed, nor abused," a prize to be taken by an imperial stream, the Charles, noble kin to the James, which "doth pierce many days' journey the entrails of that country" (197, 205). The Charles is but the chief of several rivers stretching "far up into the country," coursing through "large dominions" toward the northern equivalent of the great back sea, "divers great lakes, where the Indians kill and take most of their beavers and otters" (192). These were the same lakes which Champlain in 1616 was exploring, a parallel venture which, like Smith's, did not so much dispel an earlier myth as set another, complementary force in motion. The contemporary fashion for Flemish hats endowed the lowly beaver with golden fleece, and though certainty of passage to India by means of the Great Lakes would endure for another century or more, the sure profits from pelts proved an even stronger lure. Drawing enterprise north and west, it contributed to a geophantasy that haunted New England and New York as well as New France, a mercantile epic scheme that would result in a martial epic action.

xi. A Pentecostal Crew

Captain Smith was never so taken with his New England "Paradise" as not to acknowledge once again the sweaty necessity of Adam's children. "Savage gardens," he pointed out, were not the same as cultivated land, and the region remained mostly "as God made it when he created the world," less an Eden than a wild, unordered tract of nature needing to be "cultured, planted, and manured by men of industry, judgment, and experience" (T&W: 197). Such men were in the offing, the self-exiled English Separatists of the Leyden congregation already thinking of emigrating again, this time to America, so as to escape the poverty and spiritual pollution of their life in Holland. It is ironic that the very people who first heeded the Dutch example in New England came themselves from the Dutch homeland, albeit as aliens. Ironic also is John Smith's subsequent claim that the Pilgrims used his printed advice concerning the way to wealth in the New World while refusing to hire his services, thinking (foolishly) to save money thereby.

The Pilgrims may have given Smith cause to grumble, but it is doubtful if they carried his map and description of New England with them when they sailed for America, planning as they did to settle on the Hudson River. Moreover, being just the "worthy, honest, industrious spirits" that Smith prescribed for the enterprise, it is not surprising that they founded a fortified, cooperative enterprise similar to that which the Captain recommended. As the Pilgrims' landing at Plymouth was a matter of circumstance, not intention, so their method of planting was perhaps due less to Smith's influence than to attitudes they held in common with him. Like the Virginians, who acted so differently, they did what they did because they were what they were, sharing with Smith his experience perhaps, but most certainly his common-sense, utilitarian view of the New World, a pragmatic attitude deeply rooted in the rural origins they also held in common with Captain Smith, even to region and district.

In other respects, however, the people from Scrooby were different from their Yorkshire-Lincolnshire neighbor, indeed, from most of mankind, a difference which made their New World enterprise unique. Seeking religious asylum, not a chivalric arena, a Gethsemane, not a paradise, the Pilgrims added a distinctly otherworldly element to American enterprise, a transcendental tangent to the heroic line. Still, because of their middling origins they were willing to render unto Caesar as well as to Christ, and undoubtedly agreed with (while shaking their heads over) Smith's opinion that only the prospect of wealth would ever "draw company from their ease and humors at home" (212). If the Pilgrims were able to found a Puritan utopia, it was only by promising a profit to the Westons of this wicked world. From the start, the business of America was business, which, as the Parable of the Talents suggests, is not inimical to the Gospel message.

There were, therefore, two wheels to the Puritan cart, and that its *primum mobile* was a spiritual, not a material motive gave the Pilgrims a decided advantage, a synchronization which became an effective engine of enterprise in the unharvested garden of the New World. New England, reported Edward Winslow in 1624, was a place where "religion and profit jump together (which is rare) in honorable action," and if profit eventually out-jumped religion, we cannot deny the initial efficacy of that coordinated motive (*CPF:* 372). The Separatist experiment failed during the lifetime of William Bradford, providing through his chronicle of the colony a sad memorial, a cornerstone to a tradition of uncompleted utopian structures in America. Like John Smith's futile search for gold and northwest passage, the Pilgrims' otherworldly venture resulted in a powerful parable, adding to the vocabulary of images through which the developing idea of America would find expression, an epic in which the Hesiodic, not the Virgilian dimension dominates.

Rivers had their importance to Plymouth Plantation, as harbors and a source of food and fertilizer, and, in search of the furs that made their utopia possible, they set up trading posts on the Kennebeck and the Connecticut. But the Pilgrims made no effort to realize the Virginian dream of finding a route to an inland sea, and though they set out for the great Hudson, they were satisfied to set down by the humble waters of Town Brook. The name and fact of that stream is a paradigm of the Pilgrim experience in America, itself an epitome of the Puritan experience altogether, for the ideal community for the people of Scrooby was a village, and between the immensities of wilderness and ocean they established that parochial unit. Though they voyaged up and down the coast of New England, like the beavers that were their chief source of profit the Pilgrims always came back home. There is something comical about their provincialism, and something touching as well, and despite the suffering which marked their first days in America and the failure in which their experiment ended, the Pilgrims were a bright spot on a dark coast, just such a candlestick as they favored for the chief image of their errand.

xii. English Earth

The asylum and harbor which the Pilgrims found within the greater bay of Cape Cod is a symbolic configuration, complement to the imperial womb at the entrance to the James. "The bay," reported the Pilgrims of Plymouth harbor, "is a most hopeful place, with innumerable store of fowl, and excellent good, and cannot but be of fish in their seasons. . . . It is in fashion like a sickle or a fish-hook" (*CPF:* 164). As the encircling spit of land would protect them, so the humble

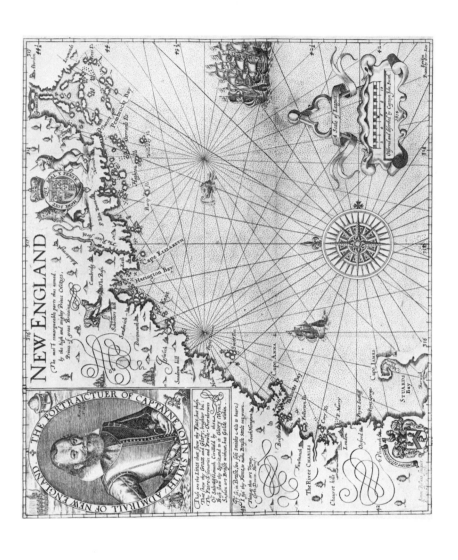

John Smith's Portrait and Map of New England. From *The Generall Historie of Virginia* (1624). Courtesy Beinecke Rare Book Division, New York Public Library.

Smith's New England. First published in Smith's *Description of New England* (1616), this chart, like Smith's map of Virginia, provides an accurate survey of the area explored. Had the Pilgrims brought it with them to America, it is doubtful they would have spent time looking for a navigable river on Cape Cod, since the Charles occupies such a prominent (and near-by) place. Still, "Plimouth" became Plymouth before the first year was out, and a number of Smith's other place-names gave a tentative but familiar reality to English settlement and were later adopted by the Massachusetts Bay Colony, even though the names were supplied by a Prince who became the King the English Puritans beheaded. Smith's reward for his labors was likewise ironic, for though he "fixed" his "fame" by having his likeness engraved on the region he explored—making certain his "brass" would endure—the gold he hoped to earn thereby never materialized.

sickle and fishhook it resembled would sustain them, supplying the necessities of life as beaver skins provided the profit demanded by their backers. Moreover, as fertilizer and seed, fish and corn jumped well together also, and among the dominant images in New England iconography is Squanto showing the Pilgrims how to plant Indian maize, three dead fish in each quick hill, a trinitarian token of the industry and manure which was John Smith's religion. A pastoral figure, Squanto is the male counterpart of Pocahontas, his Indian corn an alternative gift to her tobacco, being a nourishing, golden plant which only flourishes in communities of its kind, sustained by a communal presence.

William Bradford, that genius of broad crossings, regarded Squanto as an instrument of Providence, and certainly his helpful presence at Plymouth was a kind of miracle. When Captain Smith put ashore in the same place nearly ten years earlier, he was attacked by the Patuxet Indians, and after Smith departed, Captain Thomas Hunt, the master of his sister ship, revenged himself by taking a number of that tribe, including Squanto, to sell as slaves. Saved thereby from the epidemic that killed off the rest of the Patuxets, Squanto also learned enough of the English language to be helpful to the white men who occupied the land that was manured by his ancestors. Squanto's history is one of those shadowy affairs characteristic of the first stages of England in America, his return to his homeland as paradoxically fortuitous as his departure, another of those mysteries of iniquity which, as in prophecy's dark glass, illustrate the drama of supplantation. Captain Smith was not directly responsible for Squanto's strange fate, for Hunt's act was against his express orders, but the Indian's assistance may be attributed as much to John Smith as to God, one more passing of the Captain's face over the waters of a new heaven and a new earth.

And once again Smith's reward was a cluster of bare rocks bearing his name, this time off the New England coast, nor could he even claim legal title to that ironic muniment. Despite his hard-headed, practical advice to Virginia and his prophetic schemes and providential help for New England, Smith had little monetary return from his investment of self and suffering, yet his was most certainly immanent domain, certified in the north as in the south by the map he drew of the region. Where in Virginia Smith emphasized the great imperial system of interior rivers emptying into Chesapeake Bay, in New England he charted the coastline only, a diagram terminated by the beckoning, sheltering arm of Cape Cod, an accident of time and space that would develop into another symbolic configuration which we may credit to the universal author of England in America. Never modest in that regard, Captain John Smith by 1622 thought of himself as the father of both New England and Virginia, who were a sort of Romulus and Remus "as indifferent to my heart as my left hand to my right" (*T&W*: 265). But the right hand is the sword hand, and New England would prove at last to be his truest child. Of Virginia, Smith wrote in 1612, that "here is a place, a nurse for soldiers, a practice for mariners, a trade for merchants, a reward for the good, and that which is most of all, a business (most acceptable to God) to bring such poor infidels to the true knowledge of God and his holy Gospel," a perfectly encapsulated description of the Puritans' intended New World errand and its ultimate results, the "business" of promulgating the Gospel becoming a mercantile, military, and maritime mission (353-54).

Though they put spiritual matters before all others, the Pilgrims were as aware of the military as of the commercial necessity. They refused Captain Smith's services, but they hired a Miles to their liking—like Smith, a tough-minded veteran of Continental wars. In a number of ways, Captain Standish was a replica in miniature of the peppery Virginian soldier-adventurer, beginning with his short stature and equally short temper. And during the first month of the Puritan presence in New England, Standish led a search which imitates to the point of parody Captain Smith's quixotic adventures in Virginia, a mock-heroic journey across Cape Cod in quest of a river on which to plant a colony. What Captain Standish found at the end of his search was a mere creek, insufficient for the Pilgrims' purposes, but his overland march led him to a most remarkable discovery, similar in implication to what Cartier, Lane, Newport, and Captain Smith found at the end of their river voyages, a prophetic figuration beyond the capacity of the discoverer to comprehend. For that reason, perhaps, Miles Standish's first military mission on the American strand has no important place in the Puritans' version of their New World experience. And yet a century of subsequent events in New England may be seen as a sequence unfolding from the seed uncovered on Cape Cod, additional signs that America, as epic action, is but the further adventures of Captain John Smith, whose "accidents," according to John Donne, were great "precedents," being metaphysical maps to mind (*T&W*: 285).

IV

A MODEL
OF MOSES

The Pilgrims Lend a
Prophetic Presence
to the Land.

i. History and Mystery

Hakluyt's successor in England was his coadjutor and John Smith's friend, Samuel Purchas, whose *Hakluytus Posthumus,* or *Purchas His Pilgrimes* (1625) was not so much an *Odyssey* continuing Hakluyt's *Iliad* as an English *Aeneid,* less an epic of discovery than of establishing empire, a story necessarily left unfinished but one which closes on a hopeful note. Toward that end, Purchas incorporated large sections of Smith's *Generall Historie,* in effect by his chronological sequence providing the American Aeneas a monumental pedestal of historical precursors, including such fabled pagan "pilgrims" as Hercules, Ulysses, and Aeneas himself. But as his controlling epithet suggests, Purchas's anthology of travels has a Judao-Christian emphasis, and among his peregrinators are Christ, His Apostles (especially Paul), and patriarchal wanderers, chief of whom is Moses. Purchas thereby lends the mechanics of imperialism, whether figured in mercantile or missionary terms, both an epical and a millennial thrust, his catalogue of pilgrim adventurers supplying not only historic precedent and heroic elevation, but a mystical sense of progress toward a glorious future.

Purchas's introductory chapters, intended as a symbolic keystone to his collection of travels, are dominated by a typological interpretation of the voyage of King Solomon's navy to bring back precious materials for his temple from Ophir (identified as "not Peru," but India). Reading the story on several levels in sequence—"allegorical, anagogical, tropological"—Purchas sees it as, among other things, an allegory of the building of New Jerusalem and as an illustration of "the lawfulness of discoveries and negotiation by sea" (I: 9). This latter, or "moral use," of the biblical story, is the most important to Purchas's purposes, being "a kind of preface or preamble to the many histories ensuing," for "negotiation" (trade) is presented as an important part of God's plan for mankind. According to Purchas, "mutual Necessity" is the "Mother

99

of mutual Commerce," for "the superfluity of one country supplies the
necessities of another, in exchange for such things which are here also
necessary, and there abound, that thus the whole world might be as
one body of mankind, the nations as so many members, the superabundance in each concocted, distributed, retained or expelled by
merchandizing" (10-11).

It is for this purpose that God hath "encompassed the earth with the
sea, adding so many inlets, bays, havens and other natural inducements
and opportunities to invite men to this mutual commerce . . . by
everlasting canons decreeing community of trade the world through"
(11-12). If Solomon's navy is Purchas's chief imperial type, then the
ocean is his dominant mercantile metaphor, being the "great purveyor
of the world's commodities to our use, conveyor of the excess of rivers,
uniter by traffic of all nations," providing "portage to the merchant,
passage to the traveler, customs to the prince, springs, lakes, rivers, to
the earth" (46-47). Hence the mystical importance of the two great
pillars supporting Solomon's temple, "printing and navigation, both in
manner given at once to the world by divine goodness" so as to facilitate commerce and speed the Gospel light, "that in the sunset and
evening of the world, the Sun of Righteousness might arise out of our
West to illuminate the East, and fill both hemispheres with His bright-
ness' (171-73). While disclaiming the role of prophet, refusing to take
upon himself "the revelation of the Revelation in that prophecy of the
holy Jerusalem descending out of Heaven from God"—to say nothing
of applying it "to the reformation of the Church in the last times"—
Purchas manages to polish his dark conceit until it becomes a glass in
which a dim but shining future may be detected (173). It is such a time
when "mystical Babylon" (Roman Catholicism) shall disappear, when
"true Catholicism recovering her venerable and primary antiquity, may
without distracted faction, in free and unanimous consent, extend her
demesnes of universality as far as the earth hath men, and the light of
her truth may shine together with the sunbeams, round about the hab-
itable world" (177-78).

As prophetic glass, however, Purchas's vision is but an intensified
reflection of his times, a glory not unlike that which irradiated the sails
of Winthrop's Fleet as it sailed for New England five years later.
Purchas's reliance on scriptural and classical precedent was by 1625 a

propagandist's convention (as the elements of his argument may be found in Robert Johnson's *Nova Britannia*), but his concentration in the manner of an anatomy on the idea of pilgrimage provides—despite his own Anglican persuasion—a literary transition from Hakluyt's mercantilism and Captain Smith's militarism to the transcendent millennialism of the Puritan errand, providing a model for subsequent writers on the American strand. From *Purchas his Pilgrimes* to *Of Plimoth Plantation* is not merely an alliterative bridge, for even as the Vicar of Eastwood gathered his magnum opus, "out of a chaos of confused intelligences framing this historical world," the people who would be best known as *the* Pilgrims were busy framing a mercantile and missionary community on the chaotic verge of a vast western woods (xxxvii).

Always alive to a good story, Purchas included in the last pages of his final volume the first good news sent out of New England, providing a symbolic link to what was yet to come—the voluminous literature turned out by the Puritans in America. In that regard, his most prescient moment occurs in the second chapter of his first volume, where the Mosaic exodus is discussed as a Christian allegory, "the life of Faith, passing through the wilderness of this world" (180). Thus Canaan, "the type of their hopes," is the place of rest which cannot be taken "possession of but by loss of life itself, passing that Jordan which floweth the way of all flesh into the Dead Sea." Purchas in another place cites the supplantation of the Canaanites as an historical precedent (hence warrant) for invading a populous country, being but the first of many "national . . . colonies and new alterations of the face of the world in each part thereof" (185). But the biblical text cited is Deuteronomy 2, which keeps things "this side Jordan," a geopolitical and metaphorical consistency that anticipates a dominent theme in the literature engendered by the Puritan experiment in Massachusetts. Yet it is the Pilgrims of New Plymouth who provide a dramatized prologue, their American adventure acting out even as Purchas wrote his mystery-filled history of profitable peregrinations. Their encounter with the unknown, like *Hakluytus Posthumus,* extends the past into the future by linking the Old World with the New, much as it would provide Puritan chroniclers with an opening chapter in a unique testament of works, the epic of Israel in New England, where Jordan forever rolls between.

ii. Stiff-necked People

Sir George Peckham had as early as 1583 established the parallel between Exodus and emigration to America, and in 1609 Robert Johnson had cited Moses as a type of ideal colonist: "Ten of such will chase a hundred: no adversity can make them despair" (21). Virginia, however, continued to attract and to disenchant less single-minded folk, and it was left to the Puritans of New England to exemplify the rule, both in terms of literature and life. Boston theocrats were chiefly responsible for promulgating the Mosaic metaphor, sermonic hard lines which drew parallels between wilderness conditions in Massachusetts and the region about Mount Sinai, but it was the Pilgrims of New Plymouth who most closely resembled the Jews in transit to the Promised Land. A tribal community tightly knit at the core through long association and mutual adversity, they were led by a patriarchal Elder Brewster through dangers to a land of refuge, a separate place. Like Moses' people, also, the Pilgrims owed their cohesiveness in large part to a respect for law, their covenantal religion binding matters of spirit with language borrowed from contractual terms.

The chief symbol of this legalistic faith, the Pilgrims' Deuteronomy as it were, was the Mayflower Compact, a civil equivalent of their congregational contract with God, a symbol of social order both among themselves and with those Strangers who shared their ark if not their covenant. At Jamestown order was finally imposed by declaring martial law, thus putting a seal on the military character of the enterprise, but at the heart of the Pilgrims' adventure was the idea of the family, a social unit fenced round with laws, just as their church was protected by a hedge of heavenly grace. These communal and otherworldly emphases contributed in large part to the success of Plymouth Plantation, a cohesive enterprise whose spirit was expressed by the Pilgrims' Leyden pastor, John Robinson, who urged them in their New World venture to keep their "common affections truly bent upon the general good" (*CPF:* 94). Because of their strong sense of spiritual community, Robinson's Crusoes were a group well qualified to succeed where the Sagadahoc adventurers had not, taking hold on the wintry margin of a "vast and empty chaos" (245).

The Pilgrims were given further strength by an abiding sense of destiny, of being in the care of a benevolent Providence, yet another Old Testament parallel. Certainty of God's approval is a questionable quality in a complex and crowded society, but it is well suited to the ends of wilderness settlement. To the Puritan turn of mind, adversity as well as advantage had its blessings, and so strong were they in their sense of communal divinity that all things appeared to conspire with them and their desire to settle in the New World. Rather than interpret the many delays in departure from England as God's displeasure with their purpose, rather than regard the navigational error that took them to Cape Cod instead of to the Hudson as a similar sign, they praised Him as One from whom only blessings flowed, attributing to His good favor their safe passage and thanking Him for bringing them to land—any land.

Adversity was sweet in the Puritan mouth, giving savor to the salvational encounter with the New World. Thus William Bradford could see a special providence in the fall of a sailor—a "profane young man" who had tormented the ailing Puritans—while their illness was read by him as a blessing, being the fulcrum and lever of the sailor's death: "And so was himself the first that was thrown overboard" (*HPP* I; 149). This capacity for casting a providential bias on event was common to many intended settlers of the period, of whatever faith, and even the Roman Catholic Rosier sounds like a canting Barebones: "Because we had set out of England upon a Sunday, made the islands upon a Sunday, and as we doubt not (by God's appointment) happily fell into our harbor upon a Sunday; so now (beseeching Him still with like prosperity to bless our return into England our country, and from thence with His good will and pleasure to hasten our next arrival there) we weighed anchor and quit the land upon a Sunday" (389-90). But in this we may compare the Pilgrims to the first Roanoke colonists, who decided that the hurricane of 1586 was a sign of God's disfavor and took ship with Sir Francis Drake for home. For so sure were the Pilgrims of divine favor that they were able to withstand a series of

103

reversals—disappointments, deaths, and disasters—which would have discouraged settlers of less firm conviction.

Putting ashore at Cape Cod was a transitional experience, a respite from the crowded, filthy conditions aboard ship and a foretaste of adversity to come, the Bay being so shallow that the intended colonists were forced to wade ashore, "which caused many to get colds and coughs, for it was nigh times freezing cold weather" (120). But from the first the Pilgrims were determined to make the best of what increasingly seemed to be a bad bargain, and set to work with a busy if not cheery optimism, exploring the region, testing the topsoil for depth and sweetness, and assembling a boat to make further discoveries along the coast. Because of the lateness of the year and the impatience of the *Mayflower*'s Master—yet another New World Christopher, named Jones—to disembark his passengers, they resemble a castaway party, surveying the Cape with hope bred of desperation. Even so, there was a certain stubbornness to their proceedings, signified by their reluctance to be pushed by the importunings of the Captain whose name they spelled "Jonas." Their activities and discussions demonstrate their desire to make a rational decision, to consider alternatives, and in the end they did settle elsewhere. This stiff-necked character is as English as it is Hebraic, but it also is a prime requisite to survival in a wilderness, whether the errand be exodus or emigration.

Thus the Pilgrims' first days in America, like Captain Newport's voyage up the James, are paradigmatic of much that was to follow, and as the Pilgrims themselves were dissimilar to the mixed bag of self-serving purposes that spilled upon Virginia's shore, so the record of their encounter is much different, in style and content, from Archer's report of that other Christopher's trip. Along with so much of the earliest literature to come from or be inspired by the prospects of America, the Pilgrims' report has a propagandistic motive, but they had no desire to attract the kind of settlers who, in Edward Winslow's words, "seeing their foolish imagination made void, are at their wits' end, and would give ten times so much for their return, if they could procure it" (*CPF:* 373). Winslow, writing in 1624, was careful to emphasize that New England was no Cockayne, where fountains "stream forth wine or beer or the woods and rivers be like butchers' shops, or fishmongers' stalls, where they might have things taken to their hand," yet he also gave a favorable account of New England's potential, proposing profits to be made from trading with the Indians for furs, growing tobacco, or harvesting fish—"a better and richer commodity, and more necessary" (374; 371).

That word "necessary" is the definitive adjective, and contains the Puritan aesthetic in a nutshell, dictating the shape, the bias, and even the language of their first printed report, published in 1622 and known as *Mourt's Relation,* surely one of the most remarkable works of literature to be inspired by events in America. It is a little volume that perfectly expresses the simple, even modest nature of the Pilgrim enterprise, contrasting sharply, on the one hand, with the pastoral exuberance of earlier prose inspired by contact with the New World, and, on the other, with the elaborate and self-conscious accounts of their American experience written by Puritan historians during subsequent decades. Given the onus of their Separatism, it is easy to understand why the Pilgrims' sanctity is not the main burden of *Mourt's Relation,* nor was it, in any event, to the purpose of the pamphlet. Writing to inform, not inflame, to convince, not convert, the authors of *Mourt's Relation* stressed matters of fact, not faith, and the events they described do not always put the Pilgrims in the best light. When William Bradford reshaped those early events into a providential drama, his history of "Plimoth Plantation," he dropped a number of scenes and altered the lighting, but in *Mourt's Relation* we have New England and the Pilgrims plain—an honesty of reporting unusual in New World annals.

"What could they see," wrote Bradford in his later version of the Pilgrims' first sight of Cape Cod, "but a hideous and desolate wilderness, full of wild beasts and wild men? and what multitudes there might be of them they knew not. Neither could they, as it were, go up to the top of Pisgah, to view from this wilderness a more goodly country to feed their hopes; for which way soever they turned their eyes (save upward to the heavens) they could have little solace or content in respect of any outward objects. For summer being done, all things stand upon them with a weatherbeaten face; and the whole country, full of woods and thickets, represented a wild and savage hue" (*HPP:* I: 156). But *Mourt's Relation* declares that Cape Cod's "appearance much comforted us, especially seeing so goodly a land, and wooded to the brink of the sea" (117). Though not a Pisgah prospect, the Cape was a sight for salt-sore eyes, opening to a "good harbor and pleasant bay" filled with "the greatest store of fowl we ever saw" (119). Given the propaganda motive, perhaps the truth falls between the two descriptions, but in a larger sense it encompasses both, for whatever their initial reaction, the Pilgrims' subsequent experience bore out the pastoral view and the biblical figure also. Along with Captain Smith's *True Relation,* their report of encounter provides a prophetic text in which we can read what we were to become, the Pilgrims, like the naked quaternity on their seal, being men invested with a glory they could not put out.

iii. An Ornament to His Profession

Authorship in much early American writing is uncertain, and Captain Smith is unique in his strident sense of self, his love of the first person singular—even to the point of avoiding it by commissioning witnesses. The decorum of propaganda—advertising—is a corporate anonymity, the use of imperial "we" rather than the heroic "I," and this self-effacement in the name of enterprise is no more obvious than in *Mourt's Relation,* in which the identities of the several authors are either anonymous or revealed by initials only—and in one instance, at least, garbled by the printer. The Pilgrim's report from America, moreover, not only gives formal shape to the joint-stock nature of colonial ventures, but also suits the communal nature of their own experiment, in which "every man represses in himself and the whole body in each person, as so many rebels against the common good, all private respects of men's selves, not sorting with the general conveniency" (*CPF:* 94). It thereby forms a mystical link between the literature of primitive capitalism and the record of fundamental, even atavistic, Christianity, with the apostolic seal of Plymouth Colony putting the stamp of corporate man on American colonial affairs.

However, despite this significant difference, the Pilgrims shared with Captain Smith a desire to render a realistic but an encouraging report of conditions in the New World, and, as in Smith's *True Relation,* the literary strategy of *Mourt's Relation* is dictated by that American necessity, the shape of a questing journey. The Pilgrims' story has a decidedly unheroic cast, despite the dangers and hardships met along the way, for their combination of pragmatism and naïveté—other-worldliness, if you will—is not a mixture conducive to high romance. Then too, the democratic consensus which decided all important questions acted against the emergence of a single "identity" as the leader or hero of their fortunes—unlike the divisive bickering in Virginia which produced a Captain Smith. This communal emphasis even extends to proportion and pitch, for where Smith's narrative is strung on a tension produced by Indian threat and English disunion, the action of *Mourt's Relation* moves rapidly through the Pilgrims' first month on Cape Cod to the landing at Plymouth, the orderly setting up of their fort, their various dealings with Indians, planting crops, and other communal concerns. Despite adversity, the Pilgrims, like Robinson Crusoe, move right along, gaining three feet for every one lost, and theirs, like his, is a positive accomplishment, a victory over considerable odds. It is not heroism in the romantic sense of that word, yet it amounts to an epic action, being like Hercules' story labor for salvation's sake.

Mourt's Relation consists of a number of related narratives, the longest and most important of which is the first, the "Relation or Journal" which gave the book its name, being an account of "the beginning and proceedings of the English Plantation settled at Plymouth in New England by certain English Adventurers both Merchants and others." Half of this narrative is taken up by the events of the first month on Cape Cod, the remainder with "their joyful building of, and comfortable planting themselves in the now well defended Town of New Plymouth," and it is the latter part which contains the familiar material of Bradford's later history, recounting those tribulations and triumphs that have been combined into a national parable, images so well-worn as to have gained the blurred features of legend. Dominated by the celebration of the first Thanksgiving, it is a pageant in which Samoset-Hobbomok-Squanto become one unctuous Indian showing the Pilgrims how to plant corn and then helping them enjoy the fruits of their harvest, a tableau in which sweet harmony between the white and red races is stressed. But the opening part of the original "Relation or Journal" was severely reduced when Bradford adapted it to his *Of Plimoth Plantation,* with the result that the events of the first month, like John Smith's account of Powhatan sans Pocahontas, is less well known, and for similar reasons. It is not because the first month of the Pilgrim adventure cannot be bent to the myth of pacific relations with Indians, but rather because what happened on Cape Cod does not fit the *other* myth, of the Pilgrims as the peaceful planters of New Plymouth, a story with a static, communal stress.

In effect, by diminishing the action of the Pilgrims' first weeks in America Bradford strategically reduced the most adventuresome part of their initial experience, removing from it the narrative movement characteristic of earlier relations. Since Captain Miles Standish was in charge of the several expeditions sent out to explore Cape Cod, Bradford's revisions somewhat clipped the soldier's laurels also. We may compare the Pilgrim chronicles in this regard to *Purchas His Pilgrimes,* which includes the Cape Cod expedition at the cost of the more pacific (and dull) parts of *Mourt's Relation.* Purchas also found space for a condensed version of Edward Winslow's *Good Newes,* which stresses Standish's adventures among the Massachusetts Indians, his fiery temper and undeniable courage carrying him to the closeted moment of fury when he turned Pecksuot's own knife against him and decapitated the bragging Wituamet.

In Purchas's epic version of the English in America, therefore, Standish is Captain Smith's companion in arms, but Bradford did not include his bloodier exploits in *Of Plimoth Plantation,* excusing himself on the ground that they had "already been published in print more at large" (*HPP:* I: 296). Whatever the reason, the end result was to sacrifice Standish's military fame to the dominant myth, and in Bradford's big book the soldier serves chiefly as Plymouth's policeman, a Sheriff of Nottingmuch, blustering combination of Dogberry and Fluellen: "Captain Shrimp" he was called by Thomas Morton, whose outlaw retreat the little Miles Standish stormed, and the title sticks. So far as New England literature is concerned, the Captain's derring-do had to wait for Longfellow's poem, and even there Standish plays a supporting role, his campaign against the Indians taking second place to the domestic themes of courtship and marriage, equivalents to the establishment of community that preoccupies Bradford as historian.

Covenant and communion were ever the great Puritan concerns in America, and though the authors of *Mourt's Relation* provide compass for Miles Standish's march along Cape Cod, they do little to advance his fame, for because of their consensus viewpoint he is mentioned only occasionally by name. Moreover, the Captain's quest was hardly the grand, geopolitical errand assigned to John Smith, being merely a search for a river big enough to serve as a dependable source of fresh water and to provide a harbor better than that in which the *Mayflower* first anchored. It does resemble Smith's, however, in being a quixotic mission, based on an impossible geographical premise equivalent to Hakluyt's Great Divide, for narrow capes do not great rivers yield. Smith found several noble streams, but no northwest passage, and Standish discovered a creek, the reduction in purpose and results increasing the comic dimension of the Pilgrim encounter, the persistence of expectation in the face of a decidedly spare reality. The absurdity of Captain Standish's effort is intensified by the serious mood and purpose of the Pilgrims' undertaking, an enterprise whose tenor is perfectly rendered by the earnest, plain style of *Mourt's Relation*.

As an adventure, then, Miles Standish's abbreviated hike is a comedy derived from the exercise of just those stubborn qualities which guaranteed the eventual success of the Pilgrims in America. That initial journey of exploration is yet another variation on the theme of first encounter with the interior and the inhabitants of the New World, and their account of that experience, as with earlier reports, serves to epitomize the intentions and character of the participants. As the Virginians' greed was displayed by their journey up the Powhatan in quest of mythical mines and seas, so the Pilgrims' talent for making virtue out of necessity is dramatized by their search for a harboring river. The Indian once again contributes to the action, again inadvertently, as a shy and shadowy but ubiquitous presence, providing tension and subsequent release through sudden violence, a terminal episode which has its prophetic aspect also.

Abandoning Cape Cod after the first, fruitless month, the Pilgrims settled on the harbor which would dominate their enterprise thenceforth, a closed prospect antithetical to the imperial outlook provided by the James, and a view perfectly suited to their commercial and religious plans. Their subsequent, hard-earned success made the experience of the first month seem irrelevant, and it was virtually expunged from the record, resulting in the familiar pageant of the official fable. Yet the Pilgrims' search for a river that was not there loomed over their future, much as Captain Smith's experience gave a cast to later events in Virginia, and by following Purchas in restoring it to the action we considerably alter the myth, giving it a new point and urgency. The Pilgrims' wanderings over the dunes of Cape Cod not only emphasize the castaway aspect of their adventure—the most romantic element—but link it as well to the Mosaic analogy, further substantiating the essential Puritan metaphor and providing the basis for more ambitious literature to come.

iv. Wilderness Walk

By the time the Pilgrims anchored off Cape Cod nearly fifty years of English experience in America had pretty much dispelled notions of noble savagery. Though faced by the necessity of surveying the area, and hoping also to purchase seed corn from the Indians, the Pilgrim leaders allowed Miles Standish and his men to go ashore only after much discussion of the dangers which they might encounter, and the expedition was "rather permitted than approved," with many "cautions, directions, and instructions" (*CPF:* 125). Standish was accompanied by William Bradford and two other civilian authorities, "for counsel and advice," a traveling bureaucracy further hampering his militant exercise. Indeed, it is to Standish's credit that he made his presence felt at all, muffled as he was under such a mattress of civilian caution, but he did, and there are signs that he had a hand in composing the "Relation" itself, particularly the brisk, military language that flashes out here and there: "They ordered themselves in the order of a single file and marched about the space of a mile" (127). Whoever the pen, the line has the distinct thrust of martial penetration, Standish leading his tiny column of sixteen armed and armored men into the unknown, a miniature version of Cortez, Coronado, Cartier, and Champlain—those great C's of continental conquest—and once again the tentative probe ends with Indian encounter, characteristically comic.

Having marched their first mile, Captain Standish and his men spotted "six people with a dog," whom they mistook for Captain Jones and his sailors, but realized their error when the "people" ran into the woods. Anticipating ambush, the Captain proceeded with caution, but "when the Indians saw our men following them, they ran away with might and main and our men turned out of the wood after them . . . but they could not come near them." This passage also has a military style, undercut by the thought of Standish and his corseletted men puffing over the dunes after six fleet-footed savages (and a dog). Rather than stressing danger, it introduces a broad note of humor, a characteristic which reaches a climax on the third day, when the future Governor Bradford walked unawares into a deer trap, thereby being elevated prematurely, but hardly to sainthood.

As the shy Indians fled before them, Standish and his party had to settle for less mobile evidence of tenancy, including corn fields, burial grounds, houses made of bent saplings, and—what they wanted most from the Indians—corn stored in primitive granaries, baskets buried against winter scarcity and marauding strangers. Ignoring the Indians' necessity (and intention), the Pilgrims reckoned their own: "And sure it was God's good providence that we found this corn, for else we know not how we should have done, for we knew not how we should find or meet with any Indians, except it be to do us a mischief" (141). But, being experienced businessmen who knew that the basis of credit is trust, the Pilgrims eventually took care to pay for the corn they appropriated, a crude form of capitalization that provided the wherewithal for their first year's crop, and to carry it they likewise borrowed an abandoned iron kettle, the first evidence they found of earlier European presence on Cape Cod—but not the last.

For after marching down the beach toward a place where "there seemed to be a river opening itself into the main land," they discovered the remains of "an old fort, or palisade, which as we conceived had been made by some Christians" (125, 134). Near by also they found their "supposed river," a cove or inlet which was divided "into two arms by a high bank." The opening arms were not very large, but, perhaps because of the signs of prior occupation, the Pilgrims hoped that the place might prove "not unlike to be a harbor for ships," and decided to explore it further when their shallop was ready. It is this willingness to hope for the best, along with the providential gift of seed corn, which anticipates the *Robinsonade,* and the forlorn yet hopeful sight of a ruined palisade adds a romantic touch, creating expectations of a wild Ben Gunn lurking somewhere in the woods, the first in a long line of Cape Cod hermits. And such, in fact, was the eventuality, albeit in grimmer form. Hawthorne's lament concerning the lack of ghost-ridden ruins in America was mistaken, and in turning back to his Puritan ancestors he failed to go far enough. At the very beginning there was a ghostly presence that would haunt the Puritan enterprise in ways that Hawthorne would have appreciated.

v. Signs and Wonders

When the Pilgrims returned in their shallop to explore the twin arms of the Pamet River, they put ashore a larger party than before, a combined force of soldiers and sailors under the command of Captain Jones—in recognition of his generous offer of additional men. As in Virginia (and elsewhere), a certain tension resulted from this combination, the antagonism of traditional rivalry not at all smoothed over by a wintry voyage by water and a snowy march overland. "Cold Harbor," they named the little cove, and it provided cold comfort, being too shallow for ships. But undiscouraged as always, the Pilgrims agreed it "might be a good harbor for boats," and decided to search out the headwaters of the two streams, in the hope of finding fresh water beyond the tidal flow (139). But after four or five miles of trudging along the biggest of the two branches (now called "creeks"), tramping "up and down the steep hills and deep valleys which lay half a foot thick with snow," some of the explorers tired of the mission. Chief of these was the commander of the party, sailor Jones, who declared himself "wearied with marching, and desirous we should take up our lodging, though some of us would have marched further." That this second part of the party included soldier Standish is likely, and the divided opinion became fact the following day.

The "soldiers' stomachs" (again the martial note) with which they ate their supper turned sour in some the next morning, and "because many liked not the hilliness of the soil, and badness of the harbor," the search for "the head of this river" was given up (140). The party instead trudged over to the smaller stream, ferrying themselves across in an Indian canoe, and headed for the place where they had dug up the Indian's grain—now Englished as "Cornhill." The ground having frozen in the interval, they used their swords and cutlasses to dig up the buried baskets, hard work that apparently sharpened Captain Jones's weather eye, for he announced that "foul weather" was "towards," and declared himself "earnest to go aboard" his shallop. At this the incipient cleavage was realized, Jones heading back to his boat with the lame, the halt, and the corn, while those who "desired to make further discovery and to find out the Indians' habitations" headed off in a contrary direction (141). These "eighteen"—presumably, Captain Standish, his soldiers, and his civilian board of review—spent the night near the source of the littlest river, and next morning set off along "certain beaten paths and tracks of the Indians." The largest trail led them into the woods, and they kept the wicks of their muskets lit in anticipation of trouble, but once again expectation came to nothing, for the "broad beaten path" (as so often in Puritan literature) was a snare and delusion, being merely a *cul-de-sac* used to "drive deer in, when the Indians hunt" (142).

Discouraged, the explorers returned toward the creek by a different route, and in so doing made a remarkable discovery, coming across "a place like a grave," only "much bigger and longer than any we had yet seen." During their first journey, Standish and his men had opened one Indian grave out of curiosity, then left off, thinking "it would be odious unto them to ransack their sepulchres." But this unusual mound piqued their conjecture as to "what it should be, and we resolved to dig it up." Beneath protective boards and woven mats they found something akin to a miracle, counterpart to the corn they had earlier unearthed, and equally important in symbolic terms to the future of England in America:

We found first a mat, and under that a fair bow, and then another mat, and under that a board about three quarters of a yard long, finely carved and painted, with three tines, or broaches, on the top, like a crown. Also between the mats we found bowls, trays, dishes, and such like trinkets. At length we came to a fair new mat, and under that two bundles, the one bigger, the other less. We opened the greater and found in it a great quantity of fine and perfect red powder, and in it the bones and skull of a man. The skull had fine yellow hair still on it, and some of the flesh unconsumed. There was bound up with it a knife, a pack-needle, and two or three old iron things. It was bound up in a sailor's canvas cassock, and a pair of cloth breeches. The red powder was a kind of embalmment, and yielded a strong, but no offensive smell; it was fine as any flour. We opened the less bundle likewise, and found of the same powder in it, and the bones and head of a little child. About the legs and other parts of it was bound strings and bracelets of fine white beads; there was also by it a little bow, about three quarters of a yard long, and some other odd knacks. We brought sundry of the prettiest things away with us, and covered the corpse up again. After this, we digged in sundry like places, but found no more corn, nor any thing else but graves.

What strikes the modern reader is the explorers' equanimity concerning this strange discovery, for though the Pilgrims discussed the identity of the man, pondering whether he was an Indian "lord or king," a "Christian of some note," or one killed by Indians and buried thus in triumph, their account lacks the sense of wonder which we experience even now in confronting the event. Enormous odds are involved, not only in the burial of a white man with Indian honors, but in the chance uncovering of his grave by a small band of Englishmen in their haphazard route through an immense wilderness. It is one of those coincidences which glorify the American experience, lending it the quality of an extended fiction. Here, moreover, we are not dealing with the quixotic imposition of images imported from the Old World, but with the inadequacy of that iconography when confronted by an indigenous symbol: always alert for marvels of providential favor, the Pilgrims were blind to the light emerging from that singular, even miraculous grave.

The skeleton of a blond sailor buried with (his?) Indian child for companion, the white man painted with red ochre, the red (half-white?) infant wrapped in white beads, this incredible couple is a transcendent extension of the meaning of the little, two-armed river. In the austere, snow-covered landscape of New England, near the lesser branch of an Indian stream, lay a figure of prophecy as meaningful as the beckoning, sheltering Cape itself. For whatever brought the castaway sailor to America; whatever bound him to the red man, planted him with an Indian child in the earth of the New World, left him like a Corn God to flower as a nation; whatever brought the Pilgrims to his grave—whatever caused all those patterned accidents is a mystery intimate with the destiny of the Old World in the New. Like Praxiteles' Hermes carrying the infant Dionysus, that sailor is a male madonna with child.

Putting a period to the Pilgrims' search for a river on Cape Cod, the sailor's grave was also the occasion for yet another demonstration of their matter-of-factness, as the search itself was proof of their ability to persist in the face of adversity, to endure hardship, to survive. These are the qualities of castaway heroes, but they are also the strengths which enabled the Jews to prevail in the wilderness, and New England, like the Sinai Peninsula and Cape Cod, would become a metaphorical island, like Crusoe's a reformatory crucible, working a marvelous transformation. It is a genesis foretold in the opening pages of *Mourt's Relation*, where the spirit of wildness flees before the advance of purposeful strangers, but is forced at the last to give up its seed and its secrets to the inquisitive, acquisitive hands of invaders from another world. For in planting their Indian corn those aliens took a first step toward realizing the prophecy in the miraculous grave, and though the great Hudson remained beyond their reach, the Pilgrim adventurers grasped river enough. It is a wilderness stream haunted by the red face of man, a mystery holding in its arms the future of the new people of New England who, even in their portraits, put forth something of a savage look, much as "English" became "Yankee" by way of Indian mouths.

vi. A Line of Scarlet Thread

An initial gloss on the meaning of the buried sailor is provided by the name given by the Pilgrims to a place farther on down the Cape, where Captain Standish at last had his anticipated clash with the local Indians. Called "First Encounter," it commemorates a brief, nearly bloodless battle which ended with an English victory: "It pleased God to vanquish our enemies and give us deliverance" (158). Deliverance from wilderness vicissitudes provides a motif echoing through the narratives of far more important incidents in New England's history, and the episode is significantly preludial. Like Standish's later knife-work with the Massachusetts Indians, it is not typical of the Pilgrims' relations with the aboriginal inhabitants, which were relatively pacific, but like the head of Wituwamat which Standish set on a pole as a warning to enforce that peace, it looks to the future.

Counterpoint to that first collision was the meeting between the Pilgrims and Massasoit, leader of the neighboring Wampanoags, an uneasy but finally a productive negotiation which resulted in the kind of alliance the Virginians had tried in vain to make with Powhatan. Had the Pilgrims been successful in landing on the banks of the Hudson, their relations with red men might have been somewhat different, for the Mohawks did not suffer strangers gladly. But the Wampanoags were reduced in numbers by the plague that had killed off the Patuxets, and were therefore glad to join forces with the English against mutual enemies, fear and hate even more than love being color-blind. Whatever the impulse, the union was long-lasting, a peace propitious for the Pilgrims, whose relationship with the Indians, from the Cape Cod corn quest on, tended to their advantage. Consider Samoset, marching boldly into the unfinished settlement at New Plymouth and greeting the Pilgrims in their own language, like helpful Menatonon, willing to tell them what they wished to know concerning "the whole country, and every province, and their sagamores, and their number of men, and strength" (183). But it was the Wampanoag named Hobbomok and the Patuxet Squanto who provided the most signal services for the settlers, acting as go-betweens in their dealings both with Massasoit and with the powerful Narragansetts.

Hobbomok-Squanto played Ariel-Caliban in the Pilgrims' castaway drama, but it was their Man Squanto, the Last of the Patuxets and the First Uncle Uncas, who emerges supreme, a prototype of the Good Indian who used his privileged position to bully and blackmail the Wampanoags. And like an obliging character in a bad play, Squanto died at the end of the second act, joining the rest of the Patuxets in Mother Earth. On that common grave the Pilgrims built their palisaded Utopia, planting Indian corn in fields once tilled by Indian hands, commencing the fulfillment of the prophecy contained in the Cape Cod grave, a symbolic supplantation and genesis resembling that which Gibbon saw "amidst the ruins of the Capitol, while the barefooted friars were singing vespers in the temple of Jupiter." For the Pilgrims proposed the salvation of the Indians, but in terms of physical survival the relationship was reversed, and their Pauline mission soon enough became a mercantile errand. Buying corn from the Indians, they also bought land, and when profits from the sale of corn and cattle to their neighbors on the Bay exceeded profits from the sale of furs sent to England, they bought more land, by means of legal documents duly signed and sealed. But their contracts were made with red men who had only a vague notion of property, yet a fierce sense of proprietorship, a territorial imperative that did not diminish with the extent of their domain.

That Plymouth Plantation managed to coexist in peace with Indians for many years, this during a period when Virginia was suffering a number of bloody massacres, was exceptional, if not providential. But the pacific period lasted only so long as white settlement did not crowd the native inhabitants, and it ended at about the same time that the Utopian purpose of the Pilgrims died, and for the same reasons. As New Plymouth became Plymouth the New Englander began to share with the Virginian an aversion to the Indian who had been his salvation, until at mid-century the image of the red man in Puritan literature had become a close facsimile of John Smith's Powhatan—cunning, treacherous, and cruel—a mask of Satan and a symbol of iniquity. This metamorphosis came to a grim conclusion in 1675, a year in which those otherwise dissimilar arms of English empire in America took up the sword together, evincing an imperial unanimity which bears witness to the heritage north and south of the American Aeneas.

Massasoit as a symbol of noble savagery and accommodation is Powhatan's antithesis, but his son, Metacomet, is the northern counterpart of Opechancanough, Powhatan's brother, who plotted the massacre of 1622. For Metacomet is better known as King Philip and best known by the war to which he gave his name—and his life. The treaty that Massasoit signed with the English was equivalent to the Mayflower Compact in being a contractual basis for peace, establishing a neutral zone between the red and white worlds. But when that zone became an area of friction, the same treaty served as Metacomet's death warrant, for his war against the English was regarded by them as sedition. The enduring sign of Massasoit's friendship was his appearance at the first Thanksgiving, a token of the Indians' intention to remain "very faithful in their covenant of peace with us, very loving and ready to pleasure us" (*CPF:* 82). But there was another communal feast, fifty-five years later, at which Metacomet made an appearance in the truncated manner of Wituwamet, his "Leviathan" head arriving in Plymouth on a "day of public Thanksgiving" celebrating the "wonderful success against the enemy which the Lord had blessed them with, *ever since they renewed their covenant with Him*" (196).

The words (and the italics) are those of Boston's Increase Mather in his history of King Philip's War, but the sword that cut off Metacomet's scheming head belonged to Captain Benjamin Church, a frontier soldier of Miles Standish's stamp and a son of Plymouth Plantation. Less a Pilgrim than a homespun Perseus bearing home in triumph a Gorgonian head, Captain Church is likewise a Yankee Joshua, the result of letting convenantal notions loose in a wilderness. A half-century elapsed before the emergent New England champion picked up the bloody burden of John Smith's *Historie*, but as Miles Standish lends the first months of Puritan residence in America a martial dimension, so his search for a good-enough Hudson sketches out the territory and action for a subsequent epic, taking on an additional luster thereby. Winding through the Puritans' metaphoric landscape as through the wilderness terrain of Exodus is a fiery trace, brilliant against somber hues. At first a minor but at last a determining figure in the larger pattern, it maintains the continuity then asserts the dominance of imperial design, the trajectory of a people who took care to "plant their ordnance" before setting out their corn (*CPF:* 168).

vii. A Delicate Plain

Providential or not, a certain design seems to emerge from the affairs of the Pilgrims in America, which in their early days takes shape from their failure to find a large river. Not only did they miss the Hudson, but they also stopped short of the Charles, which lay just a short distance up the coast from the harbor where they finally settled, in an area described by Captain John Smith as "the paradise of all those parts" (*T&W:* 204). Had the Pilgrims in fact brought Smith's map and *Description* with them, it seems doubtful they would have spent so much much time looking for a river on the Cape—where none appears—and would instead have headed toward the short but broad waterway which Smith shows opening into the mainland somewhat to the north. Indeed, it seems to have been the Charles which Robert Coppin had in mind when he attempted to take the Pilgrims to "a great navigable river and good harbor in the other headland of this bay, almost right over against Cape Cod . . . in which he had been once" (*CPF:* 148).

Second Mate of the *Mayflower,* Coppin was a second-rate pilot, with good intentions but a bad memory. What he took for the mouth of the Charles was Plymouth harbor, "a place where not any of us had been before," but where all (save Coppin) were to remain, the bay within the Bay supplying the plentiful fresh water and deep soundings which they had failed to find on the Cape (160). Exigencies of occasion determined that the Pilgrims would settle for (and on) Plymouth harbor, a combination of inclemencies which they were pleased to interpret as the benevolent will of God. Certainly they would have preferred the advantages of the Charles or the Hudson, but as the Jamestown settlers pursued more ambitious schemes and discovered greater streams, so the Pilgrims were drawn as if by an artistic hand into a protected

119

harbor, a landscape well suited to their errand. Needing no great river, the first Puritans in America succeeded in not finding one, a diverted quest essential to the geopolitical symbolism of New England, their harbor signifying the asylum that was the chief end of their American exodus.

Samuel Purchas saw trade as a divine instrument of harmony, promoting peace and good will among men, but for the Pilgrims and the Puritans who followed them to the New World trade was an expedient merely, and though mercantilism underwrote their millennial plan it was not integral to it. But like the matter of the Indian the meaning of the harbor in New England underwent a significant transformation over the years, and if design drew the Pilgrims to their snug refuge, then it was as part of a larger scheme, for the confines of New Plymouth became a prime factor in an expansionist necessity. As the Pilgrims' harbor involved them more than their leaders liked in the tangled web of trade, so their asylum proved to be less than a pastoral sufficiency. Its relative barrenness resulted in the removal of a second generation, the first in a series of territorial extensions that eventually resulted in King Philip's War. And as Captain Standish of New Plymouth gives way to Captain Church of Duxbury, so we can find in the documents of the Pilgrims' earliest days in America the rootling from which grew the gadding grapevine, a mixture of religion and rapacity that took quickly and held fast to New England soil, providing precedence for (though absorbed into) the mantling Vine of Massachusetts Bay.

Like starlings, smallpox, and other sundry pests, the seedlings of expansionism in New England took up very little space upon arrival, occupying a small, last chapter in *Mourt's Relation,* a lay-sermon by Robert Cushman intended in part to explain the religious basis of the Pilgrim colony. Carefully avoiding a discussion of their Separatist motives, Cushman stressed instead their intention to bring the heathen "to embrace the Prince of Peace," but the sinister implication of this apostolic love feast (not unlike the emblematic union of serpent and dove) was revealed soon enough (244). Saint Paul provided the text for Cushman's missionary exhortations, but he found warrant for "the lawfulness of removing out of England into the parts of America" round about Plymouth by resorting to the other end of his Bible: "As the ancient patriarchs removed from straiter places into more roomy, where the land lay idle and waste, and none used it, though there dwelt inhabitants by them . . . so is it lawful now to take a land which none useth, and make use of it" (243-44).

Cushman's stress on "use" links his sermon with Robert Johnson's *Nova Britannia,* and he likewise cites as "sufficient reason" for supplanting (while converting) the Indians their lack of industriousness: "they have neither art, science, skill or faculty to use either the land or the commodities of it, but all spoils, rots, and is marred for want of manuring, gathering, ordering, etc." (243). This argument, further stiffened with patriarchal precedent, became the cutting edge of Puritan dominion, the doctrine of "Lord's Waste," an important instrument of supplantation. Having obeyed Christ's injunction that they not hide their candles, the thrifty Pilgrims were unwilling to let their upended baskets remain empty, a mingling of piety and proprietorship that resulted in their initial success and ultimate failure, the peaceful message of the Gospels giving way increasingly to the militant burden of the Pentateuch. So it was that Samuel Purchas, by including the adventures of Captain Miles Standish near the end of *Hakluytus Posthumus,* created an unintentional hermeneutic circle of sorts, an alchemical serpent linking the Pilgrim venture to the anagogic imperialism of the Old Testament.

The unity provided by Purchas's continuity between patriarchal pilgrims and those of New Plymouth has yet another dimension, for despite the obvious parallels between Cushman's sermon and the tract by Robert Johnson, there remains a strategic difference in the use of biblical terrain north and south, typological distinctions which place the Anglican vicar aboard the *Mayflower* in spirit if not in body, much as Hakluyt's instructions accompanied the Virginian colonists to America. Hakluyt it was who, in urging heroic precedents on Sir Walter Raleigh, called on him to be "of a valiant courage and faint not, as the Lord said unto Joshua, exhorting him to proceed on forward in the conquest of the land of promise" (376). So also Robert Johnson, who, regarding the need to secure (and succor) Jamestown, observed that "it had been extreme madness in the Jews (when having sent to spy the land that flowed with milk and honey, and ten for two returned back with tidings of impossibility to enter and prevail), if then they had retired and lost the land of promise" (15). But Puritan writers for doctrinal reasons tended to shape the literary map of New England along the lines of Samuel Purchas's typological chart, on which the Jordan provided a boundary not to be crossed. Though willing, on occasion, to emulate Cushman by citing Abraham and Jacob as patriarchal precedents for expansion, Puritan writers preferred Moses to Joshua as a heroic exemplar, picturing the Saints as a chosen people enjoined by Jehovah to a long wilderness walk. "Moses brings not unto Canaan, nor can the Law justify," wrote Purchas, thereby providing terminus for Puritan domain (180).

But here too the Pilgrims anticipate, Robert Cushman paraphrasing St. Paul concerning promised lands, declaring that there was no longer "any land or possession now, like unto the possession which the Jews had in Canaan, being legally holy, and appropriated unto a holy people, the seed of Abraham, in which they dwelt securely and had their days prolonged . . . a land of rest after their weary travels" (240-41). For Cushman as for Purchas the post-Exodus Canaan is "a type of eternal rest in heaven," there being on earth "no land of that sanctimony, no land so appropriated, none typical, much less any that can be said to be given of God to any nation as was Canaan, which they and their seed must dwell in, till God sendeth upon them sword or captivity." The human condition is like that of Moses and his people in the wilderness, for "we are all, in all places, strangers and pilgrims, travelers and sojourners, most properly, having no dwelling but in this earthen tabernacle; our dwelling is but a wandering, and our abiding but as a fleeing, and in a word our home is nowhere but in the heavens, in that house not made with hands, whose maker and builder is God, and to which all ascend that love the coming of our Lord Jesus" (241).

Later, more liberal (and more literate) Puritans might differ from Cushman concerning New England as a promised land, but they never expressed better the common conviction that it was a place of hard work, not ease, one where milk had to be taken from cows and honey from hives. Robert Johnson had called Virginia an "earthly paradise," describing it in the words of Joshua's account of Canaan as "a very good land, and if the Lord love us, he will bring our people to it, and will give it us for a possession," while Cushman called New England merely "another country," a place "to which they might go to do good and have use towards others of that knowledge, wisdom, humanity, reason, strength, skill, faculty, etc., which God hath given them for the service of others and His own glory" (J: 8, 10; C: 242). Yet here, too, in

sounding the great Puritan theme of "doing good," Cushman necessarily opened a wide western gate, pointing to a "way through the sea"
to "a spacious land" beyond. Calling upon "outcasts, nobodies, eye-
sores" to "lift up their eyes and see whether there be not some other
place and country to which they may go," Cushman inadvertently encouraged material ambitious, showing the way to a better place here
on this earth. Whether or not it was a promised land, New England
was property there for the taking, an opportunity too good for a land-
poor people to pass up.

In the end the New World wilderness was transformed not into a
Separatist asylum, but into separate tracts of land, a metamorphosis
which began to take place not long after the first Pilgrims landed.
Ironically, Cushman's sermon in *Mourt's Relation,* like many Puritan
exhortations that were to come, seems to have taken its bias from the
strategy of admonition, and his otherworldly emphasis is perhaps less
a statement of Puritan principles to prospective settlers than a repri-
mand to those Saints already planted in America. Such, certainly, is
the burden of an earlier sermon by Cushman, read to the Pilgrims at
Plymouth on the first anniversary of their landing, another incunabu-
lum in which, as in a palimpsest, a dim, secondary script may be read
beneath the intended message. Like *Mourt's Relation,* Cushman's anniversary sermon contains sections of prophetic writing, unintended
ironies which add still another dimension to the Pilgrims' ultimately
futile quest, illuminating further the symbol of the furtive waterway
which became Plymouth Harbor. Despite the restrictions of theocratic
metaphor, the continuity of Miles Standish and Captain Benjamin
Church testifies that, in New England as in Exodus, Joshua is the
shadow of Moses, the prophet becoming the soldier of God as the
wilderness becomes the threshold to Canaan. Yet Jordan, as we shall
see, continues to roll between.

viii. A Grievous Crab-tree Cudgel

It must be said at this juncture that if the Pilgrims to whom Cushman addressed himself were mixed in their motives, their admonitor was not a purely disinterested commentator, for his personal oar was deep in the mercantile waters bearing up the New Plymouth enterprise. Cushman, a wool-carder who entangled the Separatists in a costly contract with Thomas Weston, was a determining if distant factor in their venture, typical of the uneasy marriage between spirit and substance which characterized the Puritans' New World errand. William Bradford spent his declining years in America trying to trace the pattern in a fabric woven with the warp of trade and the weft of religious idealism, and the saintly weaver regarded Robert Cushman as a tangled thread in God's design, doing the Pilgrims some service and not a little harm, securing a contract that was entirely in Weston's favor but which may have been the best that was possible.

Cushman seems to have been an impulsive, idealistic person, torn between absolute Puritan principles and his commitment to the disadvantageous deal made with Weston, an unresolved combination of the antagonisms contained in the double promise of America, which, as in his sermon in *Mourt's Relation,* held out opportunities for two kinds of salvation. Like Captain Smith, Cushman was a man in the middle, caught between plans framed in England and the reality of the New World, and his equivocal position at the start of the Pilgrim venture is a Puritanic equivalent to the Captain's chivalric stance. Like Smith's, Cushman's uncomfortable attendance was acerbated by his persistence in reminding the settlers of their intended errand, a symbolic role given dramatic force by the fact that he was one of the few who stayed behind in England when the ill-named *Speedwell* transferred its passengers to the *Mayflower.* As a result, he did not arrive in America until late in 1621, on the *Fortune* (another misnomer), a reminder in a number of ways of earlier agreements and resolves, not the least of which was the contract with Weston which Cushman carried in his baggage.

When Cushman stayed behind in 1620, it was apparently an expression of his resentment over the Pilgrims' refusal to sign that contract, and when he came to New England he stayed only as long as it took to get the necessary signatures, returning on the ship that had brought him. He continued to serve as the Pilgrims' representative in England until 1625, when he died—along with the Weston connection—and from first to last his role in the Pilgrim drama was determined by that commercial consideration. As middleman, therefore, Cushman was in a position which made him acutely aware of the ingratitude and greed of supposedly otherworldly Christians. "Friend," he wrote to Edward Southworth in 1620, "if ever we make a plantation, God works a miracle; especially considering how scant we shall be of victuals, and most of all ununited amongst ourselves, and devoid of good tutors and regiment. Violence will break all. Where is the meek and humble spirit of Moses? and of Nehemiah who reedified the walls of Jerusalem, and the state of Israel?" (*HPP:* I: 145). It is to Bradford's credit that he included this letter in his magnum opus, that *omnium gatherum* which is as much an archive as a history proper, and it is to our good fortune. For in Cushman's complaint about the impurity of the Pilgrims' motives we have the germ of his sermon of 1622, which was in turn a seed from which a tree would grow, yielding a full measure of those crab apples of early New England literature, the jeremiads with which Puritan preachers tried to temper the sweet taste of Yankee Jonathan's success. As such, it provides a third part to the Puritan New World view, in which the contingency of wilderness and river, of mercantilism and Christian mission, is given additional meaning by transforming the New England settlers into backsliding Israel, expressing yet another tension between prophecy and the profit motive.

ix. Here Little, and Hereafter Bliss

Given the eventual drift of New England enterprise and its secularization of theocratic sanctions, it is fitting that the first published sermon delivered in Puritan America was entitled *The Sin and Danger of Self-Love*. A complement in many ways to John Robinson's farewell to the Pilgrims in Leyden, Cushman's sermon also urged cooperation and community, but in an admonishing, not a hortatory vein. Adopting the persona of Paul, Cushman taxed the Pilgrims for the "disease of self-love so dangerous in us," and while commending them for traveling "into a wide wilderness . . . to carry the gospel and humanity among the brutish heathen," Cushman feared that "there may be many goodly shows and glosses, and yet a pad in the straw," that the "bird of self-love which was hatched at home . . . will eat out the life of all grace and goodness" (24-25). Illustrating scripture with homely, rural figures, Cushman's sermon is in the best Puritan tradition, his emphasis on the danger of hypocrites to the community laying in place the foundation stone for a whole edifice of jeremiad literature.

Though a layman, Cushman anticipated not only the theme, but the biblical types employed by later preachers, for in urging his fellow Pilgrims to "purge out this self-love," to work for the welfare of the whole, he made reference to "the days of the Jews, returning from captivity. . . . It is now no time to pamper the flesh, live at ease, snatch, scrape, and pill, and hoard up, but rather to open the doors, the chests, and vessels, and say, brother, neighbor, friend, what want ye?" (29). Evoking the Jews during the Restoration of Jerusalem, Cushman linked his analogy to the American necessity, irradiating it with a millennial light, "the dawning of this new world," though as yet a "raw country," where "land is untilled, the cities not builded, the cattle not settled," a host of "present necessities" crying out for attention. In citing their trespasses, Cushman did not forgive the Pilgrims their debts, and at the center of his sermon there is a pertinent reminder that "We also have been very chargeable to many of our loving friends, which helped us hither, and now again supplied us, so that before we think of gathering riches, we must even in conscience think of requiting their charge, love and labor, and cursed be that profit and gain which aimeth not at this." Here again Cushman spoke as Weston's agent, and his saintly stress on selfless, shared endeavor should remind us that the Pilgrims' communism was a capitalist arrangement. No willing bond which held all property in common, it was a joint-stock venture, and they soon broke that part of their contract with Weston, dividing up the land into separate lots.

It was in vain, therefore, that Cushman scolded those who would, like the Prodigal Son, "come forth and say, give me the portion of lands and goods that appertaineth to me, and let me shift for myself" (32). And yet, as in the hopeless admonitions of Captain John Smith, we can see in Cushman's remonstrations the shape of the future, for his sermon outlines a major tension and dominant metaphor in early New England writing, not only a contrast between the ideal pattern of community provided by the Jews and the always imperfect Puritan facsimile, but also between "this wandering wilderness" and "that joyful and heavenly Canaan" which lay beyond mortal peregrination (35). If Robert Cushman, the Pilgrim from Canterbury, was something of a Pardoner, having mixed motives behind his sermons, he resembled Chaucer's pilgrim also in having an angelic tongue. Seldom has the idealism of the Puritans been more lyrically stated than in his rhythmic apostrophes to otherworldliness written in the service of Thomas Weston, crying out to his fellow voyagers to heed the Scriptures: "the voice and word that must call us, press us, and direct us in every action" (*CPF:* 240).

We may amuse ourselves with conjecture as to how the Pilgrims of New Plymouth, at the end of a year of unremitting toil, received the communal cup which Cushman held out in passing through, filled as it was with the taste of iron ("our abiding is but a fleeting," etc.). And we may imagine likewise their reaction to being lectured at in the voice of St. Paul, the master finger-shaker of the New Testament, especially since their mission was conceived in the Pauline spirit. But Cushman was right, despite his self-righteousness, for among his auditors were sufficient hypocrites to pervert the Pilgrims' errant to imperial ends. While converting the wilderness to a garden and attempting to pay off the burdensome debt which Cushman's contract placed on them, the Pilgrims in any event found precious little time for converting the Indian to loving and useful ways. And when the land was first divided up, "as near the town as might be," it was not only to harness the energies of self-love, but "for more safety and defence," which called to William Bradford's mind not the example of the Jews, but "what I had read in Pliny of the Romans' first beginnings" (*HPP:* I: 372-73).

x. Water Out of Rock

The Jordan for the Jews of Moses marks the eastern terminus of their wilderness terrain, but by means of their circumambient passage, it becomes a western stream and the eastern border of the Promised Land. The Hudson River occupies a similarly paradoxical place on the Puritan map, a half-century of progress in New England being in effect a retrograde movement toward the river which was the Pilgrims' original destination, a lengthy demonstration of the Puritan willingness to make up through enterprise what God had neglected to provide by a gift outright. As a geopolitical force, the lure of the Hudson Valley was equivalent to a Land of Canaan, but as they moved toward it the sons of the Puritan Fathers exchanged a transcendental for a terrestrial faith. Still, as Cushman's sermons suggest, the metamorphosis was a matter of degree, not kind, and among the ironies of his contradictory career is the verbal map of New England which he included as a dedicatory epistle to his sermon against self-love. Published in England to encourage further emigration to New Plymouth, Cushman's sermon, like his contribution to *Mourt's Relation,* is a most perverse document, being one more arrangement of internal contradictions, a prophetic configuration which would later characterize the Puritan Commonwealth as a whole.

New England takes its name, explained Cushman, from its resemblance to the mother country, being "full of dales, and meadow ground, full of rivers and sweet springs" (3). In contrast to the emphasis of the sermon which follows, this landscape is no desert wilderness, but a promising prospect much like that of Captain Smith's *Description,* a pastoral vein which quickens with an imperial pulse as Cushman considers the Hudson. In his description, as on Michael Lok's map, the river is "a great arm of the sea, which entereth in forty degrees, and runneth up north west and by west, and goeth out either into the South Sea, or else into the bay of Canada." That great arm provides another reason for New England's name, giving her an insular identity, being "cut out from the mainland in America, as England is from the main of Europe." Cushman was as wrong in his geography as he was ineffective in his sermons, but as prophetic also, for though New England was no literal island, she became a figurative one, and the Hudson turned out to be a strong arm of western empire.

It is a river the "secrets of which we have not yet so found as that as eye-witnesses we can make narration thereof, but if God give time and means, we shall, ere long, discover both the extent of that river, together with the secrets thereof; and so try what territories, habitation, or commodities, may be found, either in it, or about it." Here again Cushman was factually wrong, prophetically right, for if the Pilgrims showed little interest in exploring the Hudson—his allusion being perhaps a lingering echo of their original plan—it would remain thenceforth a powerful geopolitical factor in New England, not so much as a possible northwest passage as a constant symbol of "habitation and commodities" superior to those close at hand. For where Virginia was haunted by an epical prospect, New England's genius was pastoral, yet in time the prophecy in her name would be realized, the Puritan asylum of covenantal and communal uniformity transformed into a center of intercontinental trade, just such a mixture of mercantilism and millennialism that was Samuel Purchas's imperial ideal.

Having by the end of his last volume "brought all the world to England," Purchas concluded by tracing all the lines of his travels "to this center, and this center to the basis and ground thereof, that is to his country" (132, 130). As for Virginia and New England, Purchas prayed that God would make them "as Rachel and Leah, which two did build the house of Israel, that they may multiply into thousands, and there enlarge the Israel of God, and the Church's Catholic confines, doing worthily in America, and being famous in Great Britain" (134). Some one hundred years later, observing the centennial of the founding of the Bay Colony, the Reverend Thomas Prince delivered an election sermon in Boston, a full-dress occasion for the rehearsal of the original and continuing errand which concludes with David's benediction: "Now therefore in the sight of all Israel the congregation of the Lord, and in the audience of our God, keep and seek for all the commandments of the Lord your God: that ye may continue to possess this good land, which the Lord hath given you, and may leave it for an inheritance to your children after you forever" (220). Israel in America was indeed doing worthily, but was perhaps no longer so famous in Great Britain, being beyond the Church's catholic confines and well on the way to becoming a center of its own. Like the England of Samuel Purchas, the American Israel had by 1730 "combined a trinity of kingdoms into a unity . . . made the ocean the wall to her inheritance, and rooted out the wonted barbarism of borderers" (131). An island that was not an island, a wilderness that would become a garden, New England was an asylum that opened to empire, by 1730 located to the west of Jordan's stream.

V
GLORIOUS ENTERPRISE

Governor John Winthrop's Wonderful Wall.

i. A Plat of Rising Ground

Something of the mood that attended the great Puritan migration of 1630 is suggested by an inscription in a book which Edward Howes sent from the Inner Temple to John Winthrop, Junior, "at the Massachusetts in New England" shortly after his arrival there. The book was Sir Dudley Digges's *Of the Circumference of the Earth,* the most recent proof that a passage to India could be found, and on the verso of its title page Howes wrote that he would be "happy, thrice happy . . . if this little treatise should add anything to your knowledge, invention, or industry, to the achieving of that Herculean work of the Straits of New England, which I am as verily persuaded of, that there is either a strait, as our narrow seas, or a Mediterranean Sea, west from you" (*WP:* III: 95n). Howes's epic geography has a Hakluytish look, but his inscription ends on a mystical, millennial note reminiscent of Samuel Purchas's mercantile vision:

"Doubtless," Howes wrote, "there is a man (or shall be) set apart for the discovery thereof, thereby to communicate more freely, more knowingly, and with less charge, the riches of the east with the pleasures of the west, and that the east and west, meeting with mutual embracements, they shall so love each other, that they shall be willing to be dissolved into each other; and so God being manifested in Christ through all the world, and light shining in thickest darkness, and that palpable darkness being expelled, how great and glorious shall that light appear." Sent from England late in November 1632, the book bearing its hopeful inscription would have arrived in Boston sometime during "the extremity of the snow and frost" of the month following, when the Winthrops, father and son, were having difficulty enough launching a bark to put down pirates plaguing their coast, never mind searching for a northwest passage (*WJ:* I: 95).

The contrast between Howes's millennial, even Miltonic language and the dreary reality of the "Herculean work" then going on in New England is typical of the expectations and realities that characterize colonial enterprise in the New World, but so far as the Puritan errand was concerned, it is doubtful if the work for which the Winthrops saw themselves chosen ever involved such grandiose geopolitical schemes. Theirs was most certainly a spiritual goal, for the "principal end of this plantation" according to their Charter was to "win and incite the natives of the country to the knowledge and obedience of the only true God and Savior of mankind" (*RM:* I: 17). But their immediate purpose was to forge the bonds and establish the boundaries of a community "so religiously, peaceably, and civilly governed, that their good life and orderly conversation" would bring the heathen flocking to the fold (in the words of John White of Dorchester) "as doves to the windows" (17). As the name "Winthrop" suggests, both father and son were founders of towns, winning strongholds of purified Christianity on the edges of America, a mission in which mutual embracements was most definitely a social, not a metaphysical idea. The Governor's chosen image was a City on a Hill, a single beacon in the wilderness rather than Howes's western blaze of glory, and the "Mystic" on whose banks John Winthrop planted his personal acreage was no transcendental conduit of wonder, but a stubby, utilitarian stream taking its name from the Algonquin word meaning "tidal river."

The terms of Winthrop's Charter extended the borders of his Patent "throughout the main lands from sea to sea," but his chief concern was in securing the sanctity and safety of his people within the immediate bounds of his colony, which were defined by the courses of the Merrimack and Charles rivers (*RM:* I: 3-5). His first months in America were so busy that he seldom found time to record the day's events in his journal, which as a result provides a rather breathless chronicle of that period of great trials and small triumphs. The Governor was so preoccupied with the details of administration that it was early in 1632 before he found the time or felt the need to survey his Patent by traveling up the Charles, a journey that was little more than a day's outing. His delay in this regard is indicative of Winthrop's sense of priorities, and the very shortness of his brief passage, like Miles Standish's truncated epic on Cape Cod, has meaning also, a prophetic cast which begins with the names that his party gave to prominent landmarks along the way.

Name-giving is the primal mark of empire, and while Christopher Newport was bestowing gifts on the Indians he met on Powhatan's River, he did not neglect that other imperial game, which he played with like abandon. The names recorded by Gabriel Archer suggest a mood of wild pastoral, mingling Indian words and English, signifying the hoped-for union but facetious withal: "Arahatec's Joy," "Mulberry Shade," "Kind Woman's Care," "Queen Appomattox' Bower," "Careless Point." Thereby was founded a carefree tradition which held for two centuries in the South before moving westward, and in this as in other matters the New England custom was different. Expressing a quiet humor, the names given by Winthrop's little group are dull indeed when compared to Newport's exotic creations, as the sober playfulness of the Puritans contrasts with the egregiously sportive mood of Newport's party. Wrote Winthrop in his journal:

They named the first brook Beaver Brook, because the beavers had shorn down divers great trees there, and made divers dams across the brook. Thence they went to a great rock, upon which stood a high stone, cleft in sunder, that four men might go through, which they called Adam's Chair, because the youngest of their company was Adam Winthrop. Thence they came to another brook, greater than the former, which they called Master's Brook, because the eldest of their company was one John Masters. Thence they came to another high pointed rock, having a fair ascent on the west side, which they called Mount Feake, from one Robert Feake, who had married the Governor's daughter-in-law (WJ: I: 73).

Like the Cape called Cod and the place there called "Cornhill" by the Pilgrims, Beaver Brook has a promising if homely enough significance, for the beaver was both an emblem and a mainstay of New England enterprise during Winthrop's first years in America. More meaningful, perhaps, is that Adamic chair, identified with the rising generation whose future was so closely paired in the Puritan mind with the New World errand. And the reverential (if joking) compliment paid to the eldest "of their company" has similarly communal connotations, as does the familial name given to the little mountain

135

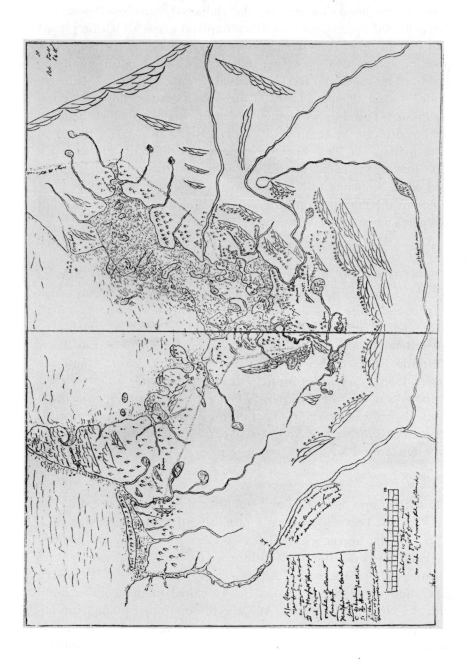

John Winthrop's Map of Massachusetts Bay (c. 1633). From Justin Winsor, *Narrative and Critical History of America* (1884-89). Courtesy New York Public Library.

Winthrop's Massachusetts. Governor Winthrop's Patent is cradled by the long arm of the Merrimack ("it runnes 100 miles up into the Country, and falles out of a ponde 10 miles broad"), which extends even farther by means of the Musketaquid (Concord) River. "The waye to Plimouth" crosses the Weymouth as it winds south by west from Dorchester, and the beginnings of Boston are visible, as is "Newtowne" — from which the road to Connecticut will soon be run.

which marked the end of the Governor's inland voyage, putting the stamp of kith and kin on that terminal point. From its modest height, moreover, Governor Winthrop obtained a view which contrasts sharply with the sight from Cartier's Mount Royal or the prospect obtained at the barrier falls of the James. What Winthrop saw was Wachusett Mountain to the west and Monadnock to the north, montane counterparts to the rivers bordering his Patent, being geographical symbols of the Puritans' enclosed world.

Governor Winthrop's topographical ideal is best expressed by a rough sketch map he made of his Patent shortly after taking the trip up the Charles. Dominated by the Bay, it is a system of many confluencies encircled by the Merrimack and Musketaquid rivers, and like certain aerial photographs, panoramas made possible by a distorting lens, the Governor's map expresses a concentric perspective, all the more symbolic for its inaccuracy. It provides counterpoint in that regard to the expansionist maps drawn by Captain John Smith, on which rivers reach toward inland seas or open to the great white space of an unknown hence promising interior. For the Governor's was a microcosmic demesne, a circumscribed and centripedal world, as inward-looking as the introspective Puritan mind itself. Though a larger and more complex sphere than the one centered by Plymouth, the Bay Colony was likewise shaped to a harboring, not an expansionist ideal, a concentric geopolitics. It was only a larger version of that village utopia, and, indeed, it would soon contain Plymouth within its greater sphere, for like the Pilgrim commonwealth, Winthrop's city was at the center of a circle that would not hold.

ii. A Mind Not To Be Changed

The Humble Request signed in 1630 by Governor Winthrop and five of *The Company late gone for New England* disavowed Separatism, declaring they were not of that party "that dreams of perfection in this world" (*CFP:* 295-96). They were certainly a more sophisticated, worldly group than the migrant farmers of New Plymouth, but despite their disclaimer, the Bay Puritans soon became fast friends with their New World neighbors—perhaps too fast, so far as the Pilgrims were concerned. While claiming a tie with the Church of England, Winthrop's people severed all possible ties with the Crown, and with their brethren at New Plymouth they intended to find a haven and found a religious state filled with the spirit of God. Their sacred mission was likewise mercantile, a dual errand which they hoped to achieve by adopting Plymouth's form of governance, a marriage of corporate and covenantal principles, communal in structure and function, theocratic in spirit if not in fact, and insular in purpose and extent.

John Winthrop was university-educated and a lawyer by profession (though a preacher by inclination), a member of the gentry and the perfect model of manor-house aristocracy. A citified country gentleman, he was something of a sixteenth-century Puritan Jefferson, with an elitist appreciation of the beauties of ordained order and social forms, yet with sufficient experience in politics to understand the expedient basis of power, to realize that the exercise of authority is facilitated by appeals to the self-interest of the governed. He was quick, therefore, to appreciate the functional simplicity of the Plymouth plan, which was democratic in tendency, in that it extended the franchise to all partners—Freemen—in the enterprise, but authoritarian in practice, delegating considerable power to the ruling executives—the Governor and his Assistants (or fellow Magistrates, as they were sometimes called). Because of a traditional English acknowledgment of the prerogatives of superior place and education, the most prominent men of Plymouth Plantation were usually reelected for years on end, in effect granting them nearly lifetime tenure. Governor Winthrop undoubtedly saw the system as a convenient mechanism, a means to expedite the exercise of magisterial authority rather than as a device by which the Freemen could have a deciding voice in their government.

In his treatise on religiously motivated rule, "A Modell of Christian Charity," which he read to his people on the voyage over, Winthrop echoed John Robinson and Robert Cushman by stressing the communal necessity of being "knit together in this work as one man . . . as members of the same body" (*WP:* II: 294). But his corporate idealism did not confuse Christian Love with Levelling: "God Almighty, in his most holy and wise providence, hath so disposed of the condition of mankind, as in all times some must be rich, some poor, some high and eminent in power and dignity; others mean and in subjection" (282). Winthrop, obviously, was of the first part, that "one man" through whom the communal "one man" would express itself, his Christian commonwealth, like Massachusetts, radiating out from one central source of power. Selling his home in England, Winthrop apparently expected to be lord of an expanded manor in America, but as with other such expectations carried over from the Old World to the New, his were doomed to disappointment. What worked reasonably well in little Plymouth, where the Governor had the distinct advantage of being at the center of a small group of old friends and associates, worked to opposite ends on the Bay, where New World occasions transformed Winthrop's wonderful machine of government into an infernal device, an engine whose power came increasingly from below, not above.

On the recto of the sixth leaf of the Governor's American journal is a design (one of three) for a fort, a system of interfaced squares, at the center of which is a sketch of a crenelated castle or keep, its banner bravely flying, the whole perched on what must be a hill but looks like a cloud (*WP:* II: 276). The drawing is most likely a plan for the fort which eventually dominated Boston harbor—largely at the cost of the Governor—but it will stand as well for Winthrop's projected City on a Hill, which turned out to be a veritable castle in Spain. Designed with a view to danger from without—like the palisade at Plymouth a defense against "common enemies," including Dutch, French, and Indians—the Governor's fort did not anticipate division from within, against which no number of squares can hold. At the very start, his plan to settle all his people within the protective walls of one city was changed by circumstances, rumors of Indian attack causing his "community of peril" to form several strategic villages. The dispersal was an effective (though unnecessary) tactic, but like the diaspora of the Jews, it promised ill for Winthrop's Holy City.

Subsequent attempts were made to consolidate authority in the colony by bringing the magistrates together in one town, Boston, which only created an effect counter to the one intended. The continued influx of immigrants destroyed forever Winthrop's ideal of a single, centralized community, but the tiny settlements established during the Governor's first year, spread out along the Mystic, Charles, and Saugus rivers, were waymarks of defeat. The concentricity of the

Massachusetts Bay rivers, like the system of government which Winthrop set in motion, facilitated a centrifugal movement, not a centripetal one, radiating out from, not in toward Boston at the center. Even as the Governor surveyed his Patent from Mount Feake, his marvelous machine was working against the end for which it was designed, being a mechanism much like Samuel Purchas's planetary system, which in "breeding New Britains in the spacious American regions" created new centers and new circumferences, a galactic explosion that was not at all what Purchas meant (XX: 132).

iii. Long the Way and Hard

Robert Cushman, in his epistolary complaint of 1620, established by way of antithesis twin ideals for New World leadership, Moses and Nehemiah. Cotton Mather, drawing on several score years of intimate association between Puritan experience and Old Testament precedent, could do no better, and in his *Magnalia* he defines the essential similarity and distinguishing difference between Governors Bradford and Winthrop by comparing the yeoman-weaver of Plymouth to Moses and the lawyer-gentleman of Boston to Moses *and* Nehemiah. A Moses in his capacity of wise leader and just lawgiver, Winthrop, like the great restorer of Jerusalem, was a Wall-Builder, an ideal Governor on the Judaic-Puritan plan. In his treatise on Christian Commonwealth Winthrop himself singled out Nehemiah as a perfect type of leader, and as things fell out in America, he had manifold opportunity both to "exhort" and to "dispose liberally of his own." His people come close to Dryden's Jews, being "a headstrong, moody, murmuring race / As ever tried the extent and stretch of grace"—but so were the Jews of Moses. The exodus from Egypt was hardly a country dance of sweet accord, and the derelictions, demurrers, and defections of his people inspired from Moses a whole literature of tongue-lashings, a vocabulary which stood the Puritans in good stead.

The Moses of Plymouth Plantation had his troubles, too, with sundry Strangers and Sojourners whose motives proved beams in the Pilgrim eye. Still, these were few in number, and most of them were simply driven out of town. But Winthrop had a number of towns in his care, and a fleet, not several boatloads of settlers. To this large and disparate company was added the remnant population of Old Planters, a conglomeration of opportunists and solitaries, mavericks for the most part and seldom amenable to the Puritan persuasion. After the *Anne* and *Little James* dropped their unwelcome passengers at Plymouth in 1623, the Pilgrims were pretty much left alone to work out their problems, but wave followed wave of immigrants to Massachusetts during the first ten years of Winthrop's rule, establishing an ever-widening periphery of settlement, moving farther and farther from the center at Boston.

The Massachusetts Moses had a magic wand denied his Plymouth counterpart, his Charter—which invested the Governor with great local authority—whereas Bradford's autonomy was mostly a matter of indifference (and perhaps some relief) in England. Yet political instruments without effective support are empty scabbards, and while Bradford was very much a consensus administrator, a man in the midst, Winthrop was another man in the middle, the central figure in a *Laocoön*-like struggle. Bradford's influence gradually waned, his *History* a demonstration of the erosion of principle in the name of immediate interest, but Winthrop's *Journal* provides a much different story. From first to last, the Governor's was a losing battle to maintain centralized power and institutional purity, to implement an autocracy which never reached the desired perfection. He perpetually tinkered with governmental machinery to further his end, but only weakened the efficacy of the Magistracy as prime mover, transferring power to popular forces which accelerated the expanding rim of the great wheel. The Governor's journal is also a record of continual strife, in which the Puritans' passionate adherence to principle and deep faith in their own sanctity threatened the precarious stability of the colony and dissipated the strength of brotherly feelings on which the commonwealth depended for singleness of purpose and rule.

Nor were all of Winthrop's problems internal. As he had anticipated in his shipboard sermon, "common enemies" did indeed threaten his "community of peril," Winthrop having good cause to share Bradford's fears of Dutch and French attack. Even if he was not interested in competing for the discovery of the Northwest Passage, the Governor was jealous over the sanctity of his boundaries, and like Bradford (at times in competition with him), concerned with securing advantages in the beaver trade. As always there was the problem of the Indian, whose conversion to Christianity was an important part of Winthrop's errand, an item in his Charter symbolized by the lone savage on Massachusetts' Great Seal. But the Macedonian cry for help took on increasing irony as time went on, for the souls of the heathen remained closed to the light of the Gospels and their minds became increasingly set against incursions by Christians who were more interested in helping themselves to land than in helping the Indian to heaven. Then there was the constant threat posed by Sir Ferdinando Gorges in England, whose baronial ambitions and prior claims to New England were a constant danger, especially since he was associated with the Puritans' "greatest enemy," Archbishop Laud. During a critical period Winthrop was in danger of having his precious Charter recalled, and was periodically pestered by the operations of Captain John Mason from Gorges's own patent to the northeast.

But Gorges and his agents, like licentious Strangers and rebellious Saints, were at least visible, identifiable antagonists, and the Dutch, French, and Indians likewise could be dealt with by means of treaty and threat. The Governor's single greatest antagonist was a much more Protean quantity, the multiplicity of motives that animated the settlers of Massachusetts, only a minority of whom were Puritans, and among that minority undoubted but unprovable hypocrites. Moses also had under his charge a "mixed multitude" picked up in his wilderness wanderings, and that became a favored phrase in Puritan annals, for what provides a minor note of dissention in Exodus is a powerful discord in New England literature. "Satan," Winthrop wrote in his first letter to his wife after arriving in New England, "bends his forces against us, and stirs up his instruments to all kinds of mischief, so that I think here are some persons who never showed so much wickedness in England as they have done here" (*WP:* II: 303).

Like Satan's legions, the mixed multitude was numerous, invisible, powerful, and associated with the material temptations of this world, being ambitious to obtain as much temporal advantage as opportunity would provide. For some this meant charging exorbitant wages for necessary services, for others it meant beaver pelts, but for most it meant land, the possession of which meant moving out from the center which the Governor tried to hold at Boston. Winthrop needed the immigrants, who were the colony's single greatest source of income, keeping the price of cows and corn high, and skilled workers were also in demand, so much so that few questions could be asked (at first) about purity of sect or motives. But these compromises not only acted against Winthrop's long-range plan, they resulted in an inflated, lopsided economy, creating a materialistic mood which made even some Saints turn piggish.

Still, the center might have prevailed longer had it not been divided against itself. The group of Puritan leaders who signed the Agreement in Cambridge, England, in August 1629 soon enough found out that the anticipated "difficulties and discouragements which in all probability must be forecast upon the prosecution of this business" acted to dissipate rather than strengthen "the joint confidence we have in each other's fidelity and resolution" (*WP:* II: 151-52). Almost from the start, Winthrop's rule was a matter of unspoken tensions and hotly debated antagonisms, not only with the "popularie" but also the "principalitie." The former, the newly created Freemen of Massachusetts, responded with something less than gratitude at being allowed the rights and privileges of the corporation, their new status in the New World apparently having suspended the old "law of nature, order, and antiquity," so that the law of "conformity and submission" was no longer "inviolable" (cf. *WP:* I: 284). The "principalitie," Winthrop's fellow Magistrates, likewise fell out over the matter of "perpetual precedence and dominion," which some were reluctant to surrender to the Governor.

So Winthrop's City on a Hill became "Trimountain" Boston, hardly a model of Christian Charity. Separated from the rest of the colony by topography, Winthrop's insular, fortified city was a symbolic center whose three hills signified the trinitarian antagonists—religious, social, and commercial—of which the spreading population at large consisted. Seldom in accord with each other or with themselves, these factions were aggravated rather than accommodated by the system of government Winthrop created, nor was the friction eased by the oil of magisterial generosity. With the moderation of true conservatism, Winthrop deemed "that in the infancy of plantations, justice should be administered with more lenity than in a settled state" (*WJ:* I: 171), but his

144

leniency only acerbated the situation, further offending reactionary (and jealous) magistrates like Thomas Dudley while sounding hollow to Freemen who, having experienced a degree of independence, wanted more. What the Governor thought of as flexibility was interpreted as the arbitrariness of a despot, and the very forces he set in motion to facilitate his rule evolved into counterweights which hampered the exercise of centralized, magisterial authority ever after.

One important difference between the Mosaic exodus and the Puritan errand was that the Jews were merely passing through while the English had come to stay. Where Moses could count on the instability of migration acting to increase dependency on his power, Winthrop could only watch as his authority drained away along the rivers on which his people settled. With Bradford, he was eager to gather evidence of providential approval, but here too he was denied the dramatic demonstrations of the Old Testament. Like Nehemiah Winthrop might give of his own to the needy, but unlike Moses he could not always count on supplies from heaven. The list of providential gifts which he compiled in his journal are small potatoes compared to the manna Moses stuffed into complaining mouths. Winthrop raised his hands to heaven when he discovered that a mouse had devoured the *Book of Common Prayer* in preference to *Saint's Rest,* but that was dusty diet for a malcontent people who might, upon occasion, have eaten the mouse.

In his "Modell of Christian Charity" Winthrop clinched the Mosaic analogy by referring to the Atlantic as a Red Sea and by twice speaking of the "good land" to which they all were going. Yet something of his controlling strategy is revealed by his closing words, a benediction to his people in which Winthrop assumed the persona of Moses, "that faithful servant of the Lord, in his last farewell to Israel," a patriarchal blessing that couched a warning: "If our hearts shall turn away so that we will not obey the Lord our God, but shall be seduced and worship other Gods, our pleasures, and profits, and serve them; it is propounded unto us this day, we shall surely perish out of the good land whither we pass over this vast sea to possess it" (*WP:* II: 295). There is a certain sly legalism operating in this use of Scripture, for Winthrop has not only interpolated the alliterative (and Puritan) proscription against "pleasures and profits," but he has substituted a "vast sea" for Moses' River Jordan, in effect commencing the Puritan errand at the

145

beginning of the wilderness passage. The result is a kind of *quietus in-terruptus,* by means of which the Puritans are brought to the very brink of the Jordan only to have it turn once again into the bitter waters of the Red Sea.

The development and improvements upon Winthrop's reversible wilderness was the work of several generations of theocratic rhetoricians, but the basic strategy remained consistent. As the Charles and the Merrimack were the physical, civil boundaries to Winthrop's Patent, so the Jordan was that invisible line bordering the Puritans' spiritual realm beyond which they could not go. This compound, theo-, geo-political metaphor provided a counterpart to Winthrop's Nehemian Wall, likewise identified with the peculiar New England emphasis on limitations—whether in architectonic or cartographic terms—enclosing frames intended to curb the expansionist spirit. But like Winthrop's governmental devices, the distant Pisgah view tended to work against his intention, serving as temporal, not salvational bait, Saints as well as Strangers salivating at the prospect of property without end. The Mosaic metaphor was never more than the imposition of theocratic ideology on the common will, the work of a decided minority, however powerful, and it was largely ineffective in stemming the movement of the multitude toward prospects of Canaan, however illusory.

In his old age Roger Williams fulminated against "God Land," who was "as great a God with us English as God Gold was with the Spaniards" (VI: 319). "God" and "good" share a common etymology, and in Winthrop's "Good Land" we have the root of his chief evil, "God Land," for if the theocrats thought to impose limitations on expansion and material profits by setting bounds which identified geopolitical barriers with paradisiac rivers, they achieved the opposite end. But the cumulative effect of their writings was an image of New England which gave an epic form to Puritan affairs, lending not only the sanctity but also the shape of Scripture to their experience, forging parallels with the events of the Old Testament which were warranted by Puritan experience in America to an amazing degree. In figurative language as in forms of government, Governor Winthrop provided a determining if inadvertent shape to emerging patterns of literature and life in New England, a Mosaic counterpart to the Aenean adventure initiated by Captain John Smith in Virginia.

iv. The Region, the Soil, the Clime

Winthrop's evasion by means of revised Scripture is backed by his refusal to identify the "good land" specifically with a promised land, an omission which makes his figure consistent with Cushman's theogeographical doctrine. But that Puritan thinking on this matter was not consistent—at least not in the early years—is suggested by the sermon which John Cotton read to Winthrop's departing Fleet at dockside, *Gods Promise to His Plantations,* a discourse which provides a distinct antithesis to Cushman's stern message to the Pilgrims, being a theological brief proving that New England was truly God's gift to the Puritans. Indeed, as Winthrop later found it necessary to correct Cotton's thinking regarding the Antinomian controversy, so his shipboard lecture may have been designed as a counter to the other man's sermon. Though Cotton had been careful to allude only to the land promised to Abraham and Jacob, subsequent events suggest that his auditors had heard what they wanted to hear.

Aside from this unintentional emphasis, John Cotton's greatest contribution to the subsequent literature of Puritan New England is his figure of the transplanted Vine, the spiritual scion from which an American arbor will grow. It is to the divine protection of this plant that the title of Cotton's sermon refers, giving "consolation to them that are planted by God in any place, that find rooting and establishing from God . . . that what He hath planted He will maintain," and Cotton's Vine would become an essential trope expressing the New England Way, the matter of their emerging epic (15). Vines would not figure greatly in the horticulture of Massachusetts—save the kind bearing pumpkins and such—but the theocratic variety became a sermonic commonplace, a pastoral figure central to the Puritan motif of the well-tended garden. Unlike the "found" paradise of Virginia, the Puritan garden is an arena carved out of the formless chaos of raw na-

147

ture, georgic acreage surrounded by a Hedge of divine protection which is the pastoral equivalent to Winthrop's urban Wall. A figure springing from biblical literature, the garden metaphor took a distinctive dimension from the Puritan experience in New England, the emphasis on redemptive hard work an equivalent to perilous passage through the desert wilderness.

But this metaphor, like the Exodus idea, took years to perfect and was an exhortatory device, being rhetoric designed to correct the tendency of Puritans to go and do otherwise, to check the energies released by the prospect of boundless domain. It is, notably, a one-sided literature for the most part, the other side of which is recorded in deeds, documentary and dramatic, which make up the bulk of New England's archive and actions. Moreover, as with Cushman's, Cotton's, and Winthrop's sermons, the earliest literature engendered by the Puritan experiment tended to work against itself, a disjunctive dimension revealed as early as the spring of 1631. Writing to the Countess of Lincoln, a season of suffering behind him, Thomas Dudley grumbled about certain "letters sent us from hence into England, wherein honest men, out of a desire to draw over others to them, wrote somewhat hyperbolically of many things here"—winter discontents similar to complaints from Virginia (*CFP*: 324). And yet the "letters" to which Dudley refers seem to have been the manuscript of the Reverend Francis Higginson's pamphlet, *New-England's Plantation,* sent from Salem in 1629 and published several times during the following year, a document which differs greatly from the paradisiac propaganda describing Virginia.

Taking his tone from *Mourt's Relation* and Winslow's *Good Newes,* Higginson presents, or at least attempts to convey, a balanced account of New England, his form and language designed to appeal to ambitious but industrious settlers, the hard workers whom all authorities by 1630 agreed were the best hope of intended plantations. Rather than painting a land of milk and honey, Higginson labors to convey the impression of a middle ground, a georgic ideal that was "neither too flat in the plainness, nor too high in the hills, but partakes of both in a mediocrity, fit for pasture or for plough or meadow ground, as men please to employ it" (244). Yet that last phrase suggests a certain license, and there creeps into Higginson's Hesiodic catalogues of commodities a vision of plenty, if not paradisiac surplus, as he fills an imaginary larder with "fish, fowl, deer . . . muskmelons, watermelons, Indian pumpkins, Indian peas, beans," plain fare given added flavor by "the healthfulness of the country, which far exceedeth all parts that ever I have been in" (265-66).

Complement to Higginson's pamphlet is provided by *The Planters Plea,* by John White of Dorchester, also published in 1630. Where Higginson avoids the Puritan's spiritual errand, the Reverend White stresses it, and with Samuel Purchas he identifies the route to the New World with the progress of Religion, which "hath always held a constant way from East to West," and with the invention of the compass, which led to "that almost miraculous opening of the passage unto, and discovery of these formerly unknown nations" (7-8). While, with Higginson, calling for men who are "willing, constant, industrious, obedient, frugal, lovers of the common good, or at least those such as may be easily wrought to this temper," White adds to Higginson's georgic prospect a utopian dimension (20). For not only does White assert that the "larger scope of ground" available in a new country makes "the life of man every way more comfortable," but he declares that "the husbanding of unmanured grounds, and shifting into empty lands, enforceth men to frugality and quickeneth invention: and the settling of new states requireth justice and affection to the common good: and the taking in of large countries presents a natural remedy against covetousness, fraud, and violence, when every man may enjoy enough without wrong or injury to his neighbor" (2-3).

Even the thinness of New England's soil makes it a more virtuous terrain, encouraging piety, not profits and profligacy: "If men desire that piety and godliness should prosper, accompanied with sobriety, justice, and love, let them choose a country such as this . . . which may yield sufficiency with hard labor and industry" (18). This is hardly the Cockayne-Canaan of Virginian projectors, yet the landscape is irradiated with a certain visionary gleam, a millennial atavism evoking a Hesiodic "golden times, wherein men, being newly entered into their possessions, and entertained into a naked soil, were enforced thereby to labor, frugality, simplicity, and justice," a peaceful scene of useful endeavor, where men have "neither leisure, nor occasion, to decline to idleness, riot, wantonness, fraud, and violence, the fruits of well-peopled countries" (3).

There is latent here the ideology of a later, primitivistic agrarianism, a suggestion that space itself is a virtuous and regenerative element. White is careful to refute Hakluyt's old notion that a virgin land can cure the diseases of the body social, "that colonies ought to be emunctories or sinks of states, to drain away their filth," but his America is still a transformational terrain, his landscape, like Higginson's weather, bound to improve the best of men (19). While illusory, perhaps, White's idealism and Higginson's materialism provide the nucleus of a powerful myth, a green glow of pastoral felicity in the West that encouraged the subversive expectations which were Governor Winthrop's nemesis. Nor can we discount the effect of rumor, news of New England passed by word of mouth, a grapevine far different from the one which John Cotton proposed planting there. The Puritans might deny the possibility of paradisiac Canaans here on earth, but the implication of a contemporary broadside poem mocking the spiritual *Summons to Newe England* suggests that hope as well as satire feeds on exaggeration:

> *There milk from springs, like rivers, flows,*
> *And honey upon hawthorn grows;*
> *Hemp, wool, and flax, there grows on trees,*
> *The mold is fat, and cuts like cheese;*
> *All fruits and herbs grow in the fields,*
> *Tobacco it good plenty yields;*
> > *And there shall be a Church most pure,*
> > *Where you may find salvation sure (27).*

Such doggerel indicates that while Puritan propaganda might have been dry of Jordans, the New England mind was not, that there existed a vast, subterranean current of popular feeling which associated the western world with fertile valleys. In the silence between the sermons you can hear the river's whispered challenge, the still, quiet voice of the wilderness.

v. Fresh Woods and Pastures New

The closest thing we have to overt expression of that voice is *New Englands Prospect* (1634). Written by a man appropriately named William Wood, it was the most considerable report of accomplishment and promise to be generated by the Puritan enterprise during its early years. Though Wood was a layman and plain citizen, not a preacher, his *Prospect* seems to have been commissioned or at least authorized by the Magistrates of the Bay Colony, who voted a "William Wood" a letter of thanks in 1634 in recognition of his services to Massachusetts. By 1633, the year in which Wood returned to England and readied his book for the press, expansionist forces were already beginning to push against the restraints of Governor Winthrop's Wall, and *New Englands Prospect* does promote a view resembling the one obtainable from Mount Feake, much as the map printed with the book resembles and was probably copied from Governor Winthrop's early sketch of his Patent. Both convey a topography dominated by an encircling network of waterways, a Hesiodic plan, and Wood's prose likewise seems gauged to direct the further movement of settlers along lines which the Governor would have approved, in both geopolitical and moral terms. Conveying a restrained but undeniable excitement over the opportunities present in the New World for settlers willing to work hard to realize them, Wood is careful to contain the promise of New England within the limits of Winthrop's river-bound demesne.

What is missing from Wood's *Prospect,* as from Higginson's *Plantation,* is the spiritual aspect of the Puritan errand, and though this may be a strategy dictated by the increasing threat to Winthrop's colony posed by Archbishop Laud, it does promote a terrestrial, secular thrust. Moreover, while framing a pattern of expansion acceptable to the Governor, Wood employs images and references which, like the pastoral life proposed by White and Higginson, amount to a kind of

151

code, expressing in literature those attitudes already providing counterforce to Winthrop's geopolitical restraints. This undoubtedly inadvertent, unintended stress reflects the inherent disjunctiveness of the theocratic scheme, and if the sermons of Cotton at dockside and Winthrop under way state the religious, hence idealistic, purpose of the Puritan plan, Wood's little book reflects the everyday aspect of Bay Colony life, which (as one hard-working colonist reminded Cotton himself) involved some sweaty alternatives to fishing for and planting souls.

This representativeness extends to William Wood, about whom we know little more than is reflected in his book. One of the many whose identity merged with the larger purpose of settlement, providing the underpinnings of the Puritan commonwealth, Wood was a relatively invisible citizen and is thereby all the more representative. Whoever he was, he was a master of a simple style who could also turn out a passable poem, and he had a wry sense of humor, a flash of color peeping out from under his sober, Puritanic cape, which must have been as welcome on the New England frontier as it is in his description of it. Theocratic writers were fond of punning on the names of their four chief Apostles—Cotton, Mather, Stone, and Hooker—who provided cloth, dye, building material, and food (fish) for the spiritual commonwealth, but we may add to that figurative list the name of Wood, whose kind provided the timber without which the Cambridge Platform could never have been built.

Wood begins by continuing the convention that New England is "an Island" or "Peninsula," and likewise maintains a circumambient pose, promising not to "wander far from our Patent" (2). His *Prospect* in effect takes in a greater Plymouth harbor (and Plymouth, too), the two major capes of Massachusetts reaching out to "embrace" newcomers in their "arms, which thrust themselves out into the sea." This hospitable, harbor shape extends also to New England's rivers, which Wood, unlike John Smith, does not see as piercing the entrails of the land, but as "venting themselves into the ocean, with many openings, where is good harboring for ships of any burden." Providing "seats" for "many towns," rivers supply the inhabitants with fish for food and fertilizer, Wood stressing throughout the importance of "alewife rivers" to settlement. Along those same streams trees grow "straight and tall," fit for "good masts" and "mill posts," proximity allowing the timber to be "conveyed to any desired port" where it can be converted into "good board, rosin and turpentine" (16-18). And the many lesser streams contribute to this benevolent system: now providing water for cattle, they can also turn "water mills, as the plantation increases" (16).

"As the plantation increases"—this is the key phrase, with many variants throughout. "Water mills" are not an important feature of Wood's landscape, which is predominantly agrarian, its prosperity linked to the settlement and cultivation of land, to corn and cattle. But the promise of mills, along with the certainty of "increase," imbues his *Prospect* with a note of futurity, a progressive perspective. Employing Higginson's strategy of listing difficulties and dangers as well as facilities and benefits—and making sure, likewise, that the latter outweigh the former—Wood also animates his *Prospect* with a secular version of John White's millennialism, teasing his reader with expansionist phrases, pointing out "the very sweet places for situation" which "stand very commodiously, being fit to entertain more planters than are yet seated" (42). In describing New England, Wood moves from southwest to northeast, and waxes more enthusiastic as he approaches the unsettled region along the Merrimack, "a river 20 leagues navigable," teeming with "sturgeon, salmon, and bass, and divers other kinds of fish" (46). The less settled the region, the more attractive its resources, and "the country hath not that which this place cannot yield."

Wood's strategy was certainly in accord with the policy of Boston Magistrates—to encourage the planting of towns along the Merrimack— but like other devices set in motion by the Governor, Wood's book contains a covert antithesis couched in its expansionist rhetoric, for what the Merrimack contained in abundance, other, more distant regions had in superfluity. *New Englands Prospect* is a skillfully articulated instrument of propaganda, managing to convey an impression of harbor-bound industry while evoking an image of limitless opportunity associated with the outermost perimeters of settlement, but the result is a system of counter-motions, the effect of which may not have been predictable, but was soon enough ascertainable. Consider his image of the Indian, an important feature in his accommodating landscape, Wood having devoted an entire half of his book to "their persons, clothings, diet, natures, customs, laws," etc. Dividing the several tribes of New England "as it were into shires," Wood's distribution emphasizes the peacefulness of "our" Indians (the Massachusetts), whom Wood calls Aberginians (aborigines?), and the ferocity of "those" Indians, which, whether the western Mohawks or the eastern Tarrantines, "be more desperate in wars" than the Indians near by (59-61). If the inner circle of settlement contains peaceful Indians, and the outermost perimeter of New England is populated by ferocious savages, given to rape and cannibalism, the middle (contact) ground is occupied by correspondingly middle-range Indians, the "stately, warlike" Pequots, who are "just and equal in their dealings," and the Narragansetts, "the store-house of all such kind of wild merchandise as is amongst them" (64-65).

Wood's account of the Indians promotes his optimistic, utilitarian view, and though making no mention of White's hope concerning the use of native populations as a work force (though he does recommend harnessing the moose), Wood's scheme adapts them to mercantile ends and enforces his closed view of New England. Yet it contains a paradox, for though Indians form a savage wilderness wall against further expansion, they also by their cruel bloodiness provide warrant for their own extermination, dooming all save those who evince "civility and good natures," and encouraging an outward-moving, unstable rim of settlement. This is a dramatic irony, beyond Wood's intention and control, but just as the lure of land which he promotes was already drawing settlement toward a direction different from and farther than that desired by the Boston Magistrates, so his diagrammatic difference between "good" and "bad" Indians would soon be converted from an anti-expansionist device into an instrument of supplantation.

Wood's outer ring of cruel savagery realizes, as did the Indian, Winthrop's shipboard anticipation of "common enemies" and a "community of peril." Moreover, though the *Prospect* surveys what is generally a peaceable inner kingdom, a georgic terrain, the poems which Wood includes, rather charming catalogues in heroic couplets of the flora and fauna to be found in New England, add at times a threatening note to the Hesiodic aura. Thus peaceable beasts are "immured" in the "castle" of an old hollow tree, "Least red-eyed ferrets or wily foxes should / Them undermine, if rampired but with mold," and his timber-laden forests conceal "The grim fac't ounce, and ravenous howling wolf, /

Whose meager paunch sucks like a swallowing gulf" (20). Wood's fruitful rivers and streams are likewise inhabited by an ominous crew, "The bellowing bittern, with the long-legg'd crane, / Presaging winters hard, and dearth of grain," as well as "fearful" birds who "in whole millions flee" the hunter's "murdering piece" (28-29). Wood's natural world is suited to man's purposes, supplying food, drink, and even medicines: "Snake murdering hazel, with sweet sassafrage, / Whose spurns in beer allays hot fever's rage, / The dyer's sumac, with more trees there be, / That are both good to use, and rare to see" (17). But New England's woods are an "Indian orchard," neither a cultivated garden nor entirely a benevolent place. A version of wild pastoral, his landscape is a terrain needing man's art and industry to render it tame and useful.

It is, moreover, a landscape centered by the village, the river, and the harbor, the basic unit in Wood's Horatian scheme, promoting a peaceful, self-contained emphasis. His image of New England is illustrated perfectly by his map, a crude woodcut that delineates a watery domain, framed by ocean, bay, and rivers, an enclosed region filled with the meandering courses of waterways so generously drawn as to resemble estuaries—canal-like in their regular and systematic permeation of the countryside. Most of the important rivers, moreover, including the Charles and the Merrimack, do not end in the sharp points which characterize the expansionist maps of Michael Lok and Captain Smith, but in rounded, lake-like sources, culs-de-sac emphasizing a circular, georgic pattern. Hesiodic rather than heroic, the shape of Wood's rivers implements his mercantile, agrarian design.

Wood's New England is a pacific, communal Island-on-the-Bay which resembles that other pastoral island across the sea, differing from it only in the matter of available land. As in England, rivers in Winthrop's Patent are working streams, peaceful waterways feeding agrarian activities or providing power for mills. Latent in Wood's diagram is the idea of New England as a grand machine, for despite their meandering courses, her rivers connote a systematic articulation of waterways and sources of power, the means by which the land's potential will be realized. Though the pattern is circular, the rivers are in their function but contributory spokes to a larger configuration whose form belies its own linear function. A vast, watery wheel, the fixity of New

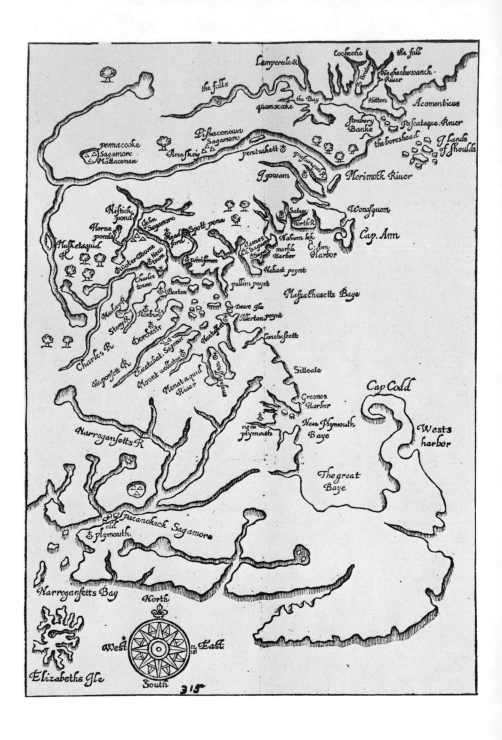

William Wood's Map of New England. From *New Englands Prospect* (1634). Courtesy Rare Book Division, New York Public Library.

Wood's New England. Drawn to accompany his *New Englands Prospect,* Wood's map resembles Winthrop's as his book reflects the Governor's policy concerning expansion. In terms of imagery, the map not only demonstrates the rapid growth of the Bay Colony, but emphasizes the importance of rivers as mechanisms of settlement. Wood's New England is a world enclosed in circles, a contrast to John Smith's heroic Virginia, with its linear geo-iconography. Smith's version of New England likewise has an adventuresome face, opening to the wide Atlantic, while Wood's is dominated by bays and harbors.

England is illusory, for as it takes its being from rivers, so rivers draw to it the raw energies of the wilderness, a system of confluencies which like its counterpart on Chesapeake Bay proved to be a powerful instrument of metamorphosis, a centripedal shape that, when set in motion, generated a centrifugal force.

VI
WOMB OF NATURE

Thomas Morton and the Call of the Wild.

i. Odors from the Spicy Shore

Shortly after his journey up the Charles, Governor John Winthrop took another short, wintry voyage, this time "over Mystic River at Medford" to survey his own property there. Traveling "among the rocks" for several miles, "they came to a very great pond," also filled with "divers small rocks, standing up here and there in it, which they therefore called Spot Pond" (*WJ:* I: 73). Having amused themselves with that great New England sport, walking "all about it upon the ice," Winthrop and his group hiked on until "they came to the top of a very high rock," from which he obtained a view of "a goodly plain, part open land, and part woody, from whence there is a fair prospect, but it being then close and rainy, they could see but a small distance. This place they called Cheese Rock, because, when they went to eat somewhat, they had only cheese (the Governor's man forgetting, for haste, to put up some bread)" (74). As in the Pilgrim adventure on Cape Cod, there is a silent satire taking place here, the rocks, the ice, the "close and rainy" prospect, and the thin meal of cheese somehow allegorical in a small way of the realities of Winthrop's great errand.

Only a Puritan could obtain "a fair prospect" from a Rock named "Cheese," and in New England generally the Mosaic contingency of water and stones somehow congeals into ice, which was what enterprising Yankees mined out of the Walden Pond they called "bottomless." Again, it was a matter of finding in the New World what one came for, the lesson of that intentional allegory by Nathaniel Hawthorne, "The Great Carbuncle," based on a native New England legend transplanted from Connecticut to the banks of the "Amonoosuck" in New Hampshire, among the "Crystal Mountains." There is, in that regard, another relevant entry in the Governor's journal, one written ten years later, concerning the exploit of "one Darby Field, an Irishman," from that pest-hole up the coast, the Piscataqua River. Climbing to the

161

top of the White Mountains, Field "saw to the north a great water which he judged to be about 100 miles broad, but could see no land beyond it" and to the west he spied "some great waters . . . which he judged to be the great lake which Canada river comes out of" (II: 62-63). Field's was a most Cartier-like prospect, and like the French Captain the Irish explorer brought back "some stones which they supposed had been diamonds, but they were most crystal," as his great lakes were entirely fog, being carbuncles of a truly mystic order.

There is a certain smug satisfaction in Winthrop's subsequent entry concerning some of Sir Ferdinando's agents who followed up Field's discovery, "the report he brought of shining stones, etc., causing divers others to travel thither, but they found nothing worth their pains" (85). By 1642 Sir Ferdinando was no longer a potent adversary, but the Governor had a long memory, and Gorges's patent and the Piscataqua region are a frequent source of the troubles recorded in his journal. Yet we may derive another meaning from Darby's diamonds and his mystical lakes, for such a long-range view was essential to Sir Ferdinando's quixotic presence in the New World, a purpose antithetical to that of Governor Winthrop, on geopolitical as well as religious grounds. Where Winthrop was content with the view from Cheese Rock and satisfied with Spot Pond, Sir Ferdinando sought a much more glorious prospect, and the very name of his American venture—"Laconia"—indicates that the distant lakes were an important feature of his plan.

As in Darby Field's description, one of those many lakes looms especially large in Sir Ferdinando's New England, Lake Champlain in reality, but in mythic terms a gigantic and watery equivalent to the fabulous Carbuncle, an elusive, ever-distant jewel of emerald green, translucent with light and mystery. Lying beyond the boundary hills of Massachusetts and associated with the headwaters of the Connecticut and the Hudson, the lake was a powerful zone of influence, uniting the riches to be made from beaver furs with persistent rumors of a northwest passage. It could hardly be seen from Mount Feake, yet its presence was felt in Boston, for the great lake intensified and concentrated westward the lure which pulled people outward from Winthrop's walled world. That lake, and the rivers reaching toward it and (reportedly) flowing out of it, provide a reverse image of the Bay, an inland mirror mirage exerting wilderness magic, a wildwood alternative to the Puritan pastoral purpose in New England, a cynosure putting forth a green and golden glow.

One version of the mysterious lake had haunted Jamestown, and Captain Smith had searched for it as for some vast grail, but Smith's quest was never Winthrop's errand. Yet from the beginning the Governor was aware of the lake, and one of the earliest entries in his American journal, made before the *Arbella* left England, concerns Sir Ferdinando's plans "for discovery of the great lake in New England, so to have intercepted the trade of beaver" from the Dutch and French (I: 29). And in 1633 a proposal made by Bradford & Winslow that Winthrop & Company join them in trading with the Indians along the Connecticut River turned the Governor's mind toward the lake also. While declining the Pilgrim offer because of the "warlike Indians" and difficulty of navigation on the Connecticut, Winthrop had some privy thoughts concerning the contingency of that river and the Merrimack, the nature of which defines his Bay-bound view of New World enterprise. The Connecticut, Winthrop noted,

runs so far northward, that it comes within a day's journey of a part of the Merrimack . . . and so runs thence N.W. so near the Great Lake as to allow the Indians to pass their canoes into it over land. From this lake, and the hideous swamps about it, come most of the beaver which is traded between Virginia and Canada, which runs forth of this lake; and Potomac River in Virginia comes likewise out of it, or very near, so as from this lake there comes yearly to the Dutch about ten thousand skins, which might easily be diverted by Merrimack, if a course of trade were settled above in that river (I: 110).

Though Winthrop exaggerates the proximity of the Connecticut to the "Great Lake," he locates that body of water more accurately than does a Dutch map of the day, which places it north of Boston. Moreover, Winthrop's linking of the lake with the Potomac and the St. Lawrence suggests a more considerable body of water than Champlain, but so does the Dutch name for the lake—"Iroquois"—which was later given to Lake Ontario, for the "Great Lake" was often confused with *the* Great Lakes. Moreover, Winthrop's geography is precision itself, his plan for diverting the beaver trade down the Merrimack a modest proposal when compared with the schematic scope of Sir Ferdinando's vision of that same region in the West, where lay "so many excellent lakes, of so mighty extent, from whence issue so many rivers" (91). Gorges is Winthrop's antithesis in New England enterprise, as William Bradford was his complement, for Sir Ferdinando had a classically expansionist sensibility, sharing with his cousin Sir Walter a generous conception of American possibilities. His *Brief Narration,* though written late in life, resonates with excitement in the presence of wilderness great enough for a kingdom, conveying a lust for empire undimmed by age, a design made possible by "the means and opportunity of those great and goodly lakes and rivers" of New England, "which invite all that are of brave spirits to seek the extent of them" (92).

Sir Ferdinando was also like Sir Walter in that he never had set foot on the territory to which he lay claim, but with the Don of La Mancha, the Governor of Plymouth Harbor in England was fond of fantastic voyages, his chivalric enthusiasm undampened by repeated failure. Gorges had a Hakluytish head, a mystic alembic transforming rumor and report into golden certainties:

It is already known that some of these lakes contain fifty or sixty leagues in length, some one hundred, some two hundred, others four or five hundred . . . the land on both sides, especially to the southward, fertile and pleasant, being between the degrees of forty-four and forty-five of latitude; and to the west of these lakes that are now known, they pass by a main river to another sea or lake, which is conceived to disembogue into the South Seas; where the savages report that they have a trade with a nation, that comes once a year unto them with great ships . . . the people being clothed with long robes, their heads bald or shaven, so as it is conceived they must be . . . Chinese (92-93).

Here once again is the latitudinarian view, carried along a line that expands the vista as it goes, lakes magnified from fifty to sixty to one hundred, two hundred, four and five hundred leagues long, then opening into the Pacific Ocean, a vertitable diagram of the expansionist spirit. It is a familiar route, but one with the quality of a religious pilgrimage for certain kinds of Englishmen—though lacking perhaps the millennial glow which Edward Howes detected in western skies. Like many anachronisms revived by American space, Sir Ferdinando's was a prophetic vision, his symbolic passage to India a poetic idea that would remain very much alive for another century and a half.

Again, it was not a dream shared by Governor Winthrop, who had the disadvantage of actual residence on one bit of the vastness over which the imaginations of Gorges and Howes moved with ease on wings of mind. But physical contact, as the poems of John Donne suggest, does not necessarily diminish a metaphysical breadth of vision nor always reduce desire. Consider the example of the most notorious agent who worked for Sir Ferdinando in New England, whose adventures were so filled with wonder that they proved an irresistible lure for such diverse talents as Hawthorne, John Lothrop Motley, Charles Francis Adams, and, more recently, William Carlos Williams— Thomas Morton of Merry Mount, wildwood master of rough-hewn revels. If the Lake of Iroquois was the mystic diadem of seventeenth-century New England, then no man more reflected in himself its green and golden light than Morton, symbol of all the forces with which the Puritan authorities were forced to contend, those Protean powers with which Governor Winthrop wrestled from the moment he set foot on the American shore. Giant serpent in the Massachusetts *Laocoön*, snake in the Puritan garden, Thomas Morton is associated in New England's annals with lawlessness and expansion, with the fluidity of boundaries and the ubiquitous Indian threat. A man of lakes and rivers, Morton was what was not wanted in the Puritan utopia, yet for all that, indeed, perhaps because of it, he is very much in the American grain, albeit cut from English oak.

ii. Solemn Troops
and Sweet Societies

It is easy for us to love Thomas Morton, to regard him as a spirit of wilderness freedom, his Maypole a halfway mark between pagan monuments to priapic power and the liberty pole of later times, but it is not hard to understand why the Puritans hated him. Morton was a Green Man, an outlaw who personified the lawless plenty of Nature, a threat to any well-ordered community. He held out the promise of America as an earthly paradise, a pagan, not protestant prospect, a zone of pleasure, not salvation through suffering. Morton transplanted in his own person the exiled Dukes and Robin Hoods of Elizabethan romance to the American woods, his lawlessness providing a blank warrant upon which the Puritans' worst fears could be written. He threatened their morality by consorting with Indian "maids" and posed a mortal danger by bartering guns for furs with Indian braves (thereby gaining an advantage in the beaver trade), and his pagan maypole, his anarchic revels with manservants, and his fondness for venery (as well as veniality) only worsened the situation, Morton tramping through orderly fields in search of fun and game. A prototypic Borderer, Morton settled, cuckoo-like, in the abandoned nest of Captain Wollaston atop a hill between Plymouth and the Bay, thereby offending the eyes of both colonies. Symbol of the anarchic wilderness and the "beast-like" men who were its personification, Morton was a doomed alternative to the rule of order through grace, serving as scapegoat for the collective anxiety of his neighbors.

By profession Thomas Morton, like Winthrop, was a lawyer, and law (after patriotism) was always his first resort, but he was a scoundrel by inclination, and survives as a symbol of outlawry, master of the masterless, governor of the ungoverned. "Lord of Misrule," Bradford called him, "thinking himself lawless," and the Pilgrims set about correcting his thought, siccing Captain Standish on Morton and his riotous company like a dog on "so many fairies, or furies, rather," and furious the merry host became (*HPP:* II: 48-51). Protesting his rights, Morton was packed off to England, and in his absence John Endecott landed at Salem. The foul bird was gone but the dirty nest remained, offending maypole still erect, and the generous terms of the Bay Colony charter put it all in Endecott's care. Arriving with sword in hand, he chopped down the pole and in similar terms admonished the remnant of Morton's crew "to look there should be better walking" (50).

No sooner had the pole fallen than Morton popped up again, returning in the company of Isaac Allerton, the Pilgrim factor and (like his predecessor, Cushman) a bad connection. Having been remanded to Sir Ferdinando, who, as Royal Governor of Plymouth in England, was the proper authority in the case, Morton had used his quicksilver tongue to good effect, returning to America as Gorges's man. But John Endecott was not to be swayed so easily, and soon enough had Proteus clapped in bands of steel, part of the program to restore law and order that Governor Winthrop had launched on his arrival. The full weight of the Puritan errand fell on Thomas Morton, who was hauled up before the Massachusetts Magistrates as a bad example: his property seized, his improper person put in the stocks, in short time "mine host" was hoisted aboard the *Handmaid* by block and tackle- a sort of *deus in machina*. With that grim completeness so dear to the providential mentality, a Puritan version of poetic justice, the *Handmaid* was instructed to sail past Mount Wollaston (*vice* "Merry") so that Morton could enjoy the full measure of his sentence, the sight of his house burning to the ground (*RM:* I: 75). The Puritans thought that by banishing Morton and burning his temple of ungodly delights they could purify New England, making sacred the soil within Winthrop's wall. But that signal cloud rising from Mount Wollaston would prove to be something more than sacrificial smoke, for it would fill the former host with a new afflatus, lifting him to transcendent heights of desire for revenge. From out of the pillared cloud would come green fire, an intense beacon lighting the way to a Canaan beyond.

Having earlier recommended himself to Sir Ferdinando's attention, Morton upon his return to England hastened to enlist in the knight's campaign against Winthrop's colony. His chief contribution to the cause was "an infamous and scurrilous book," his *New English Canaan*, in which Morton graced his American revels with orthodox Anglican and anti-Separatist sentiments, making himself out to be an innocent victim of persecution, indeed, a martyr to the English cause. A harum-scarum exercise in libelous tomfoolery, the book was an embarrassment to Sir Ferdinando—who had always remained on polite terms with Governor Winthrop—and in 1637 Gorges observed the occasion of its publication by disburdening himself of the author's services. But when Morton was writing his book, anticipating the effect it would have on his Puritan adversaries, his fortunes never seemed higher, and in a letter to a friend in Massachusetts he crowed that he soon expected to "see my desire upon my enemies" performed visibly, "and in such sort as may be subject to the senses in a very lively image," including "the cropping of Mr. Winthrop's ears" (*WJ:* II: 195-96). Morton's desire for visible vengeance may be attributed to the image burned into his brain of his flaming house, but his book (and the letter) were his undoing, not only with Sir Ferdinando but with John Winthrop as well.

For the New England Puritans seemed to be the only readers who took Morton's *New English Canaan* seriously—very seriously—and they likewise were not pleased by his letter when it came into their hands. So when Morton, for reasons known only to himself, chose to return to Massachusetts in 1643, John Endecott took him in charge once more, with what must have been a certain pleasurable set of his jaws. Hailed before what amounted to a vigilante tribunal, "that the country might be satisfied of the justice of our proceeding against him," Morton was charged with several unsubstantiated and ridiculous crimes, among which was that he had "set forth a book against us"—thin proof of indictable offense, but mighty witness to the Puritan awe of the written word (*WJ:* II: 194). Jailed for a year, "in expectation of further evidence out of England," Morton was thereby given what amounted to a death sentence, for a winter in close confinement broke his health. When he was brought once again before Winthrop, "we thought not fit to inflict corporal punishment upon him, being old and crazy, but thought better to fine him and give him his liberty . . . to go out of the jurisdiction, as he did soon after, and he went to Agamenticus, and living there poor and despised, he died within two years" (196).

Morton's harsh treatment and miserable death come down to us as a symbol of Puritan bigotry at its worst, persecution masquerading as justice, yet he was hardly an innocent victim, his fate a tangled knot of mixed motives. Morton is an American version of Falstaff, not the *Miles Gloriosus,* but the impromptu Host, his Merry Mount a wildwood version of the Boar's Head Tavern, being something of a piggery in the Aeaean vein. What England was to Falstaff in the last act of *Henry IV, Part II,* New England was to Morton at the writing of his book, a prize to be pillaged, and the climax of his expectations was similar also. Morton's futile return to America, his baseless claims and flaunted documents of outdated authority, his trial by his old enemy the Lord Chief Justice of Massachusetts, his long, debilitating stay in prison, his eventual banishment and lonely death beyond the Piscataqua, all evoke nothing so much as Falstaff's last days. Like that sad tale, it takes place off-stage, and is told to us by unsympathetic third persons, recited by the indignant, dry-eyed chorus of Puritan worthies.

Yet we must, as with the death of Falstaff, acknowledge the fitness of Morton's demise, for as Lord of Misrule he claimed more license than society can allow, his renegade revels symbolic of the dark side of New World freedom.* Dangerous in life, Morton, like Falstaff, is immortal as literature, and his book is a triumphant memorial, a unique mingling of expansionist propaganda and anti-Puritan impudence, the most effective antidote available to the tocsins sounded by Winthrop and Bradford over their achievements in the New World. Claiming Ben Jonson as a friend, Morton provided a Jacobean antimasque to the Puritans' cherished allegory of spiritual progress in the wilderness, and though his enemies wrote the last act to that drama, Morton had his revenge, conveying in a lively image a well-cropped Winthrop. The Puritans got rid of Morton, but Morton had his say, for what he was in person his *New English Canaan* is to early American literature—a baroque, sensual, and outlaw seed. Long before Puritan historians fashioned their wilderness condition into a sober epic of orderliness, Morton created its antithesis, a picaresque vehicle, a bacchanalian car filled with joyous, pagan plenty, a classic anthology of underground prose and poetry. At its heart is a vision of a virginal interior—fertile, green, inviting—and a dream of naiad voices laughing in the American wilds.

---

* Whatever the subsequent mythic interpretation, the contemporary record states that Morton was prosecuted in Massachusetts in 1630 not for offenses against the English, but for "many wrongs he hath done the Indians from time to time" (*RM:* I: 75).

iii. A Wilderness of Sweets

Thomas Morton was a salty rub in the Puritans' collective eye and *New English Canaan* was no salve, but an intended insult, like the poem he affixed to his maypole for Miles Standish to find. As the title suggests, it is framed as a reverse image of the Puritan plan for New England, a mocking mirror for the Massachusetts Magistrates. Each of its three parts attacks, directly or indirectly, an aspect of the Puritan errand, presenting an image of the wilderness as a pastoral playground, a picture of the Saints as "cruel Schismatics," and a portrait of the Indian as immeasurably superior in character to the canting hypocrites who would convert him into a facsimile of their own image. His book amounts to geopolitical pornography, being an inversion of the Puritan restraint concerning the uses of the Lord's Waste, and as if to make his intention beyond question, Morton makes abusive misuse of William Wood's *Prospect* throughout, setting it up as a tilting post with which to refute the Puritan purpose in the New World.

Morton refers to Wood's book as a "wooden prospect," thereby distinguishing the other's overview from his own much more lively perspective. Certainly one would be hard put to find two works with more antithetical qualities. Where Wood's presentation is factual and restrained, his world an enclosed, snug harbor, Morton's is vague, vast, and verbose, his geopolitical expansiveness expressed by sensual images and organic metaphors. One thinks of Longfellow versus Whitman, genteel versus wild romanticism, paleface versus redskin—though in Morton's case perhaps "wineskin" is the better term, as he had some assistance from the grape. It is a classic American dichotomy, but an archetypal antagonism, Morton playing Dionysus to Wood's Apollo, Sir Toby Belch to his Malvolio, setting himself up as a spokesman for all those lovers of cakes and ale for whom Puritan moral rigor was self-seeking hypocrisy. Wood was hardly a reforming Barebones, but as his book is a slim shadow of Morton's bulky volume, so his account of the New World is thin stuff when compared to the glories of the *New English Canaan,* his prescription of hard work countered by Morton's recipe for skimming the cream from the land of milk and honey. Wood invests his landscape with an element of progressive optimism, but this too is meager matter next to Morton's wizard transformations, in his book as at his revels converting the wilderness into a pastoral paradise of joyous ease, his Indians not industrious co-workers, but coinhabitants—and, sometimes, cohabitors.

A mystic, Hesperian portal, Morton's New England is, like Robert Johnson's Virginia, "a country whose endowments are by learned men allowed to stand in a parallel with the Israelites' Canaan," a land that is not merely a facsimile of Old England, but "far more excellent . . . in her proper nature" (180-81). Where Wood mapped out a middling, georgic zone, a landscape of mild adversity, Morton gives the Via Media a mystic power, identifying his Promised Land with a "Golden Mean," a *"Zona Temperata"* distinguished by "a very beautiful land, not mountainy nor inclining to mountainy" (121-22). There are no mountains, only valleys in Morton's country, "set forth in this abstract as in a landscape," depicted by a rhapsodic style that swells with sensual, even Ovidian imagery, ringing changes on the paradisiac theme:

And when I had more seriously considered the beauty of the place, with all her fair endowments, I did not think that in all the known world it could be paralleled, for so many goodly groves of trees, dainty fine round rising hillocks, delicate fair large plains, sweet crystal fountains, and clear running streams that twine in fine meanders through the meads, making so sweet a murmuring noise to hear as would even lull the senses with delight asleep, so pleasantly do they glide upon the pebble stones, jetting most jocundly where they do meet and hand in hand run down to Neptune's Court, to pay the yearly tribute which they owe to him as sovereign Lord of all the springs. Contained within the volume of the land, are fowls in abundance, fish in multitude; and I discovered, besides, millions of turtledoves on the green boughs, which sat pecking of the full ripe pleasant grapes that were supported by the lusty trees, whose fruitful load did cause their arms to bend: among which here and there dispersed, you might see lilies and the

Daphnean tree: which made the land to me seem paradise: for in mine
eye t'was Nature's masterpiece; her chiefest magazine of all where
lives her store: if this land be not rich, then is the whole world poor
(179-180).

The gist of Morton's images reminds us of the difference between the
golden lyricism of Elizabeth's courtiers (and Raleigh's couriers) and
the grosser stuff of the Cavaliers. This is not Hakluyt's evocation of a
royal virgin-in-waiting, but a saucier figure, a wanton metaphor hiding
in the pastoral imagery like a willing savage consort, revealing through
purposeful half-concealment those "dainty fine round rising hillocks"
attesting that Merry Mount was a hill sacred to Venus.

That Morton's New England is a Woods of Eros is made clear by the
poem which serves as Prologue to his book, a series of sensuous couplets
proposing that his Canaan be properly "possest," compared in this regard to "a fair virgin, longing to be sped / And meet her lover in a
nuptial bed":

> *Deck'd in rich ornaments t'advance her state*
> *And excellence, being most fortunate*
> *When most enjoy'd: so would our Canaan be*
> *If well employ'd by art and industry;*
> *Whose offspring now, shows that her fruitful womb,*
> *Not being enjoy'd, is like a glorious tomb (114).*

Here Hakluyt's fair Virginia is tricked out in Cavalier trumpery, yet
the result is a remarkable analogy, Morton having combined several of
the dominant (indeed, rampant) motifs of early propaganda concerning the New World: the idea of the virgin land, the emphasis on art
and industry improving bare Nature, and the sanction against letting
land lie waste. The result is a metaphysical conceit recalling John
Donne's erotic geography, but where Donne uses "my America, my
new-found land" to compliment his mistress's charms, Morton employs
the erotic burden to complement his concept of America, an available
virgin whose womb, though fertile, is like a prison, in which "admired

things" languish, "fast bound in dark obscurity," a fate much like Morton's own in Boston.

That Massachusetts Theopolis was the heart of Puritan America, but the womb of the womb of Morton's country is Lake Erocoise ("Iroquois"), surrounded by land so fruitful that it is compared to "Delta, the most fertile part in all Egypt, that aboundeth with rivers and rivulets derived from Nilus' fruitful channel, like veins from the liver" (240). This "famous lake" is "far more excellent than the Lake of Genneseret . . . both in respect of the greatness and properties thereof, and likewise of the manifold commodities it yieldeth" (234). Teeming with fish and fowl, it is the breeding ground for more beaver, deer, and turkey than can be found elsewhere in New England, and Morton proposes that a "metropolis" be built there which will "have intercourse" with other "brave towns and cities" by means of the rivers to which Erocoise gives rise, one of which promises to be the long-sought "passage to the East Indies" (235, 239). Like John Winthrop (and others), Morton has confused Lake Champlain with more westerly and larger bodies of water, a perspective which permits his conception of Erocoise as the source of the Potomac, the Hudson, the St. Lawrence, and yet another undiscovered river which will trend toward Cathay.

"Erocoise" evokes not only "Iroquois" and "Erie," but it coincidentally contains "Eros," an unintended key to Morton's erotic apprehension of the "Great Lake" and distinguishing it from Winthrop's otherwise similar topography. "New Canaans Genius," the poem which serves as epilogue to the central third of his three-part book—the section containing his erotic geography—further expands this sensual dimension, describing not only the fish, and "beaver fleeces" to be found in the "admired Lake of Erocoise" and along her "fertile borders," but also "what pleasures else" are to be obtained there:

> There chaste Leda, free from fire,
> Does enjoy her heart's desire;
> 'Mongst the flowery banks at ease
> Live the sporting Naiades,
> Big limb'd Druids, whose brows
> Beautified with green boughs.
> See the Nymphs, how they do make

Fine meanders from the lake,
Twining in and out, as they
Through the pleasant groves make way,
Weaving by the shady trees
Curious anastomoses. . . . (241-42).

In the opening pages of his *New English Canaan*, Morton identifies the "middle" or "temperate" zone with the "choice of Love," and his imagery is certainly consistent with the position of Lake Erocoise on his erotic map, images of plenty giving way to suggestions of pastoral pleasures like those decorating certain walls in Pompeii.

Morton's imaginary geopornographics bear no relation to the real landscape of North America, but is an imposition of erotic classical images on the wilderness scene. In John Smith's description of Virginia, his militant, expansionist view of the New World occasionally falls into unconsciously sexual metaphors of penetration and possession, but Morton (like Hakluyt) knows what he is doing, his prurient personifications calculated to offend the Puritans' prudery, his book but an extended impudence, a defiant, literary Maypole. And yet because of his allusions, however remote, to the actual topography of New England, Morton's description of Lake Erocoise accomplishes something more than what he intended. Giving vent to a sexual manifestation of the expansionist impulse, Morton has provided another possibility for America, his obliging landscape a penultimate expression of the pastoral spirit that gave definitive shape to the New World, a form here at last given the color of copper and wearing only a smile.

iv. The Paradise of Fools, to Few Unknown

Thomas Morton joins earlier propagandists in calling for art and industry to help him bed his virgin, but the Venusian terms of his portrait suggest he will not need much assistance. Moreover, the pastoral plenty he catalogues is less a Hesiodic harvest than the heroic heap of fur and feathers which follows a day of hunting, whether in Merry England or around Merry Mount. Figured as an Arcadia, Morton's America is but a farther Greenwood, himself the Earl of Huntingdom, but it is a forest so filled with available game as to be a paradise of the fool's variety, a Land of Cockayne. To William Wood, the beaver is a totem of Puritan enterprise, a creature of "Art and Industry," but Morton associates the beaver not with the improvement of the country but with "the advancement of Priapus," his tail no trowel but a source of aphrodisia, much as his fur provides "beaver coats" for Indian "lasses" (W: 27; M: 205, 280). All things conspire to produce a life of pleasure and ease in Morton's ardent forest, Indian men as well as maids joining in the dance around the maypole, an image of savagery accommodated to his landscape of fun.

Ignoring Wood's evidence of Indian cruelty, Morton scoffs at that "article of the new creed of Canaan . . . that the savages are a dangerous people, subtle, secret, and mischievous," claiming instead that the Puritans circulate such reports so that the beaver trade will remain "under their lee" (256). Having traded "southward of Plymouth," Morton can report the "Indian more full of humanity than the Christians" —indeed, he prefers the heathen to such godly folk as he encountered in New England, "as all the indifferent minded planters can testify" (257). Morton does not bother to mention the fact that he traded guns for furs with those same amenable savages, then took potshots at them and stole their canoes—thereby doubly endangering his fellow planters of whatever degree of disinterestedness. This is the genial host's other side, the dark half, the outlaw aspect of his Falstaffian picture of the New World wilderness which the Puritans associated with the numerous perils surrounding their fragile communities.

The Puritans' attempts to deal with Morton provide the comedy of his book's third and final part, in which the author ridicules the martial pretensions of "Captain Shrimp" (Standish) and "Captain Littleworth" (Endecott), his mock epic providing a prototype for Hudibrastic humor. John Winthrop enters the action late, but Morton is accurate as ever, pinning the Governor as "Joshua Temperwell"—a reference to his steel, not his justice. The Puritans are characterized by Morton as a pack of Malvolios, as in the prefatory poem by Sir Christopher Gardiner, "men full of spite, / Goodness abusing, turning Virtue out / Of doors, to whipping, stocking, and full bent / To plotting mischief gainst the innocent" (112). Like Captain Smith's history of Virginia, Morton's *New English Canaan* was written largely on the author's own behalf, and Gardiner (like Purchas) promised that it was a "glass" that "Shall sing thy praises till the day of doom."

As magic mirror, however, Morton's book is clouded quicksilver, his attack on the Puritans garbled by mendacity or inarticulate rage or both, and though published in England within a year of *Lycidas,* the *New English Canaan* did not enjoy the fortunes of that far more discreet version of pastoral. Brought forth on the very eve of the Puritan Revolution, Morton's glorious prospect of New England suffered a fate much like that of its author. Though Englishmen of the 1630's were interested in reading about the opportunities of planting in America, they apparently felt little concern for the trials of one Morton there, obscurely if hilariously rendered. Surfeited by an age of euphoric pamphlets, moreover, they had not much use for Morton's paradisiac tract. Still, as murky glass the *New English Canaan* does contain prophecy, images whose relevance is much more clear from our own retrospective view. Morton's book may have seemed to its own age the guttering of a false beacon, a smoky, foul-smelling lamp illuminating the anachronistic schemes of that "noble-minded gentleman, Sir Ferdinando Gorges, Knight," but to us it seems more like the first flickerings of a slow-rising glory, a celebration of absolute personal freedom associated with the lambent greenness of a distant interior.

As literature, Morton's book is (in Gardiner's phrase) an "Interlude," a comic entertainment sandwiched between dramas of greater pitch and moment. It is, moreover, the kind of act dominated by the antics of the Reverend Vice, for though Morton celebrates plenty and pleasure enjoyed free of all restraint, he also in effect widens the bounds of license until it resembles outlaw country. A little man with a tall story, Morton was an exploiter and a knave, seeking his own profit at the expense of others, and if his artwork seems to redeem him, that is one of the mysteries of iniquity which the drama of supplantation illustrates at length, being a mixed mode in which heroes have shadowy corners, while villains possess a spark of grace. Morton was essentially a nobody magnified into a symbolic presence by the very emptiness of the stage onto which he blundered, a wastrel and opportunist transformed into a figure of romantic outlawry by those other transmogrified nobodies who were his persecutors. He is the first in a long line of Strangers in American literature whose presence is haloed by a certain glory, suggesting an advent perhaps more demonic than divine, pointing from a hilltop to a paradise of gain. Shifty creatures whose hinder parts are obscured in myths of obliquity, they are incarnations of borders and boundaries, those neutral grounds where facts take on monstrous proportions, gargantuan children of violence and loud laughter.

Morton's Mount of Pleasure and his Lady Lake signify the absolute opportunity signaled by the wilderness, his West a New World womb that is the source of four great rivers not unlike the Edenic quaternity, a green zone toward which all rivers reached and from which flowed a spirit animating the settlers of New England even as they established their churches and distributed plots of land according to rank and wealth. In their ritual exorcising of Thomas Morton, the Puritan Magistrates purged their community of the outlawry which the wilderness engendered, but they could not curb the less anarchic but powerful forces which were a more orderly expression of that same restless spirit, a pastoral urgency which transformed Governor Winthrop's autocratic rule into an embryonic democracy. Whatever the facts in Morton's case, it is best perhaps, as with Captain Smith, to take him at his word, leaving him looking westward from Merry Mount toward his paradisiac Lake, back to back with Governor Winthrop, who stands munching his meal of cheese, peering eastward over his wilderness of rock.

v. Levell'd Rule of Streaming Light

Morton's mystic Lake provides equipoise to Winthrop's harboring Mystic River, being an Alpheus of plastic, pastoral power, a vision of transcendental beauty. But it was an impossible extreme, counter to Winthrop's utopian plan, and his vision was not shared even by the multitude who followed the Governor's beacon to America for reasons of their own. They may have caught a glimpse of a furtive carbuncle, but they, with Hawthorne's honeymooners, hoped for a hearthside contentment: for Saints and Sojourners alike the New England ideal was communal, familial, and agrarian—nothing like Morton's bachelor hall of delights, his domain of pleasure. The New England prospect was a "goodly plain" filled with godly, hard-working folk, not Morton's green and golden grove, and the Indians who served for nymphs and satyrs on Merry Mount would soon be identified by them with the imps of Satan. Theirs was a georgic ground located between Winthrop's urban ideal and Morton's wildwood alternative, half way between the Governor's strict rule of law and the host's licentious liberty, a dream of pastoral contentment contained within the bounds of understanding, the middle but not an erotic zone.

As epic, the New England experience of the early years was distinctly Hesiodic, a contained, agrarian scheme that lacked the longer view, whether of Captain Smith or Cavalier Morton, a parochial outlook no better defined than in a little poem which prefaces William Wood's *Prospect*. By playing on the conceit in the book's title, the poet converts it to a "Mount" of "thine experience," from whence an over-all view of New England may be easily obtained: "And if the man that shall the short cut find / Unto the Indies, shall for that be shrin'd; / Sure thou deservest then no small praise, who, / So short cut to New England here dost show." Along with the inept verse, the reduction of the great quest for passage to India to the "small room" provided by New England's boundaries provides a note of unintended humor, that Lilliputian provincialism which often characterizes Massachusetts matters, counterpoint to Morton's Brobdingnagian brag.

Yet the fact remains that while Morton's saga remained unread, Wood's modest prospect was several times published during the 1630's, and it was his and therefore Winthrop's view which obtained in New England. In later years, moreover, Wood's image of the bustling river valley of farms and mills would continue to appeal, the village and not the town, the meandering river, not the paradisiac stream dominating the scene—an image familiar to Englishmen, yet somewhat transformed by being transplanted to American soil. Because of the theopolitical laws framed by Winthrop and his fellow Magistrates, settlement in New England took the orderly shape of church-centered units, and though the Governor lost his dream of a metropolitan commonwealth, he gained in its stead a multitude of Puritan communities, a hundred Plymouths, a diaspora that was, in all senses, Congregational. It was a genesis very different from the pattern of settlement in Virginia, a communal movement dictated by the form of an expanding circle, unlike the linear, inland thrust of individual plantations along the multitudinous system of waterways contributing to the Chesapeake Bay. Though the Governor's vision was another imposition of a quixotic design on the blank American map, his plan doomed from the start by the many rivers which soon filled out the New England terrain—mirrored and matched by the multiplicity of settlers who came and did likewise—because Winthrop persisted, in the end he prevailed.

The transformation of the Puritan errand is symbolized by the only two biblical place-names taken by Massachusetts towns during Winthrop's lifetime, "Salem," the first settled, meaning "peace," and "Rehoboth," founded in 1645, meaning "enlargement." But the names of other townships, echoing the places left behind and carrying over the insular conceit, are symbolic also, testifying to the essentially conservative pattern of settlement, resembling the manorial model familiar to the Governor and the governed, resulting in a sense of community lacking in the South, a thoroughly middle-class as well as a middling ground. Though the tensions of expansion resulted in a rapid and radical shift in governmental power, equivalent to the mood of independence felt by Southern planters, it was a process distinguished by consensus and compromise, marking the emergence of a new man, not only the mass man of Massachusetts, the increasingly independent freeholder who drew strength from his land, but a different kind of ruler, willing to adapt while holding to principle, accommodating the increasing power of the populace but never surrendering to it, accepting the enlargement of his domain but doing what he could to keep the center firm at Boston. Authoritarian by heredity and training, Winthrop could also be amazingly flexible, and his experience in the New World transformed him, from hereditary autocrat to adept politician. He is the incarnation of Boston itself, toward which the contributory rivers of his colony flowed, and though the movement of his people was outward along those same rivers, what they created in their pursuit of independence and wealth bore the impress of the Governor's measured rule.

Again, however, we cannot deny the powerful thrall exerted by the pastoral promise set in motion by the view from such prospects as Wood's, as in time the bordering streams of Winthrop's Patent yielded to rivers nearer Morton's range, defining zones that exerted a new kind of force, not diagonal, but lateral, inspiring an outward, transfluvial movement which would characterize expansion in America in subsequent centuries. For the word "Prospect" connotes not only the roundabout view, but also a forward, futuristic one, being an opening as well as an enclosed vista, and Wood's book is both a survey of present conditions and a list of the kinds of opportunities which promoted the burgeoning mood of freedom. It is significant in this regard that Wood's *Prospect* was reprinted once again in 1764, this time in America, contributing to the literature feeding the imperial fires nourished by the French and Indian Wars, converting them to revolutionary and proto-nationalistic ends. Published with a militant preface aimed at British restrictions of colonial trade, Wood's book served as a stage from which to protest suppression of American enterprise—the earliest manifestation of which it so ably represented—becoming thereby a Grey Champion among books.

vi. By Slow Meander's Margent Green

In 1638, at the midpoint of his American career, Governor Winthrop enjoyed a rare moment of relative though misleading stability and prosperity in his commonwealth, and took the opportunity to make peace with his frequent antagonist but now his relative through marriage, Thomas Dudley. The result of this mutual pledge of amity was a river voyage much like that first trip up the Charles, only now it was down the Musketaquid, newly named "Concord" for the frontier town planted on its bank, a name redolent of civil and social harmony, as were the events of that journey:

The Governor and Deputy went to Concord to view some land for farms, and, going down the river about four miles, they made choice of a place for one thousand acres for each of them. They offered each other the first choice, but because the Deputy's was first granted, and himself had store of land already, the Governor yielded him the choice. So, at the place where the Deputy's land was to begin, there were two great stones, which they called the Two Brothers, in remembrance that they were brothers by their children's marriage, and did so brotherly agree, and for that a little creek near those stones was to part their lands (WJ: I: 269-70).

There is a touch of ponderous comedy here, not only the sober Puritan fun which also characterized the excursion on the Charles, but the elephantine minuet of power, prerogatives, and property which is the essence of Puritan manners, the perfect unity of familial love cemented by establishing definite bounds to adjoining plots of land. It is the sort of tangency which gives the word "neighbor" in New England a cer-

181

Adriaen Block's Map of North America from Chesapeake Bay to Penobscot Bay (1614). Courtesy Algemeen Rijksarchief, the Hague.

Adriaen Block's Map. Attesting to Dutch primacy in northeastern exploration (the Hudson, Long Island, and the Connecticut and "Pequot" rivers are clearly shown), Block's map also contributed to the mistaken, mythic geography of the region. His *"Meer Vand Irocoisen"* (Lake Champlain) is Thomas Morton's "Erocoise," and is located in the vicinity of Walden Pond. Even Champlain's great *Map of New France* (1632) perpetuates the error. See Cumming *et al., Discovery of North America*, 214, 287.

tain poetic ambiguity, symbolized by the stone walls that divide the region into a crazy quilt with orderly if irregular borders, miniature versions of Winthrop's Wall.

Many of those walls are now tumbled down, but the twin stones still stand, a fit monument to John Winthrop in America. A memorial split in twain near the bordering stream, they form a kind of gnomen, megalithic plinths casting Druidical shadows. Settled along the main tributary to the Merrimack, Concord was the first inland town in the Governor's Patent, a prophetic thrust toward an interior which would result in a turning away from the harbor prospect. Though within the borders of the Bay Colony, Concord was symbolic of the forces which would render those boundaries obsolete, a spirit of expansion which neither streams nor stones could restrain or withstand. Expressing a mood of unity, the name "Concord" is anomalous in Puritan annals, having neither a British or a Biblical precedent, nor did concord often characterize Puritan affairs. In later times, moreover, Concord would be a monument in itself to the fiery sense of community independence fostered by Winthrop's commonwealth of love, given a new identity by a new "common enemy," memorialized at last as not a place of peace, but as a battleground.

And still later the Concord River would mirror the tranquil faces of poets and philosophers, true sons of the Puritans who nursed millennial fires on hereditary hearths, hatching utopian schemes. Concord was the stream in which a certain hermit went fishing, a maverick sojourner who planted his cabin on Walden Pond, sealing himself off from the world so as to perfect his own institutions, a tidy community of one. But one (as Winthrop discovered and as the hermit's teacher knew) soon splits in two, like a bean giving birth to a sprout becoming a trine, the sum of growth and being, and though his soul was nourished by solitude, Thoreau enjoyed his meals at Emerson's home. Yet in his loneness, the hermit expressed something intensely intrinsic to the New England experience, that yearning toward spiritual perfection which he felt as he floated in the clear azure of earth's eye, drifting in blue purity reflected from heaven above.

For what is Walden Pond but a spiritualized Erocoise, close to the eaves of Emerson's house, only a short walk through the woods away. And on an early Dutch map, a mystic diagram in pastoral greens and gold, the lake called Iroquois occupies a region to the north and west of Massachusetts' shore, separated by a range of hills which feed a triad of rivers tributary to the Bay. Though sketched within a rigid reticulation of navigational lines, the map is anything but exact, and even shows a narrow strait separating Cape Cod from the main, as well as a large river directly across from the harbor where the Pilgrims first landed—one of the three reaching toward that lake beyond the hills. As a picture, therefore, the map is an icon, being more truthful than factual, and so is the meaning of that mystical Lake Iroquois which fed the streams along which Winthrop's people settled, infusing them with a spirit intolerant of walls. The lake is a force gathering all lines to itself, vectors converging at the vanishing point where heaven touches earth, a spot of glorious splendor, the momentary blaze of the western, setting sun an absolute equivalent to Mosaic fire.

"Here then is an eye of God that opens a door there, and sets him loose here, inclines his heart that way and outlooks all difficulties." So John Cotton in *Gods Promise to His Plantations,* and so the meaning of Erocoise to New England, a womb of spirit set loose along her rivers, those westering blue veins reaching toward the green fire at the radiant center of God's golden eye.

VII

BY WAY
OF NEWTOWN

How Thomas Hooker
Crossed his Rubicon
and Started the Pequot War:
A Hudibrastic Interlude.

i. A Gift Horse

In the spring of 1631 Governor Winthrop was paid a visit by "Wahginnacut, a sagamore upon the River Connecticut, which lies west of Narragansett," who expressed an earnest desire "to have some Englishmen to come plant in his country," describing his valley as "very fruitful," and promising a yearly tribute of eighty beaver skins (*WJ:* I: 61). The Governor treated Wahginnacut to dinner, but that was all the Indian emissary of good will got out of the English at Boston, for Winthrop found out "that the said sagamore is a treacherous man," who hoped to engage the Puritans in his "war with the Pequots," a "far greater" nation than his own. It was for similar reasons that Governor Winthrop declined the Plymouth proposal to trade with Indians on the Connecticut, hoping instead to circumvent the danger posed by the quarrelsome Pequots by drawing the beaver business down the Merrimack. But within three years of Wahginnacut's visit the Connecticut began to rival and then exceed the Merrimack as an instrument of New World opportunity, the central focus of a series of events which are paradigmatic of the Governor's problems in America. A drama of imperial supplantation, the unfolding action demonstrates the futility of Winthrop's dream of a self-contained theopolis in a vacuum of wilderness.

The drama began long before the Puritans came to New England, making the issue of guilt and innocence as obscure as the original cause of succeeding affairs. At about the time Sir Humphrey Gilbert's trumpet was winding an imperial summons, a tribe of Mohegan Indians was obeying a similar impulse by shouldering its way eastward into the Connecticut Valley, pushing aside weaker tribes and even crowding the Narragansett nation, acts of aggression which earned it the name "Pequot"—"Destroyer." Hence the efforts of Wahginnacut to enlist the support of Winthrop's forces, an appeal which found more sympathetic ears in Plymouth, the Pilgrims having heard good things about the great western river from the Dutch. It was this arrangement that brought Bradford and Winslow to Boston, and when Winthrop again refused to involve himself with Connecticut matters, they proceeded on their own.

These several developments in the play for power along the western river receive a covert dimension through another entry in Winthrop's journal, one suggesting that his interest in Connecticut possibilities remained quietly active. Late in the summer of 1633, several months after Bradford and Winslow visited Boston, "John Oldham, and three with him, went over land to Connecticut to trade," and were received hospitably by the Indians, returning with beaver skins, hemp, and lead ore (108). Winthrop admired the sample of hemp, regarding it as "much better than the English," and he seems to have been impressed by the kind treatment extended to Oldham. But the lesson of Wahginnacut should have warned him about Indian gifts, for that bit of hemp would provide the initial strand for a fatal cord, a sequence of events set in motion by John Oldham, himself a symbol of forces working in opposition to Winthrop's rule.

Typical of the self-seeking and far-ranging individuals whose propositions often went against Puritan disposition, Oldham first arrived in New England in 1623, one of those troublesome Strangers in whose midst Thomas Morton looms supreme. John Oldham became involved in John Lyford's Anglican conspiracy against the Separatist utopia, and with Lyford was banished to Cape Ann. Setting up as a trader, Oldham sailed as far south as Virginia, where he fell ill and claimed an experience of grace, which last brought him back within the Pilgrim pale. In 1628 he served as Thomas Morton's escort to England, and he seems to have been for a time thereafter in the service of Sir Ferdinando himself. But bonds of affinity weaken with distance, especially when possibilities are replaced by real advantage, and after Oldham returned to America he cut his Gorges connection, thenceforth identifying himself with Winthrop's colony. Settling in Watertown, he signed the Freeman's Oath in 1631, and three years later was awarded a large tract of land on the Charles River in the shadow of Mount Feake.

Despite these signs of acceptance, Oldham was an expedient anomaly in Winthrop's world, useful for his courageous willingness to open up trade with the western Indians, but hardly typical of enterprise on the Bay. Equally important, Oldham was elected a Deputy by his fellow Watertown Freemen when that office was created in 1634, and though the Deputies were supposed to make the governing process less unwieldy, they soon became a political force acting in opposition to the strong, centralized power preferred by Governor Winthrop. Indeed, one of the first consequences of the change was Winthrop's loss of his own office, a result of popular discontent over his authoritarian rule and a turnabout in power and position assisted by expansionist engines set in motion by Oldham's Connecticut adventure. In the end the restless trader proved to be a pioneer in both the old and what would become the new sense of that word, his westward rambles acting to undermine Winthrop's Wall, in effect hoisting the Governor with his own petard.

ii. The Saints Engage in Fierce Contests

The Dutch, who were seldom idle, did not stand by while the Pilgrims made preparations to set up a trading house on the Connecticut. By virtue of Adriaen Block's exploration of that river in 1614, they lay claim to the region it watered, and having heard of the Pilgrims' plans, they set up a fort below the property bought from the Indians by Edward Winslow, so as to abort his embryonic enterprise. This defensive action in turn involved Governor Winthrop in Connecticut affairs where the friendly overtures of Indians and Pilgrims had failed, for if he had little enthusiasm for doing business beyond the Charles, he had even less for dealing with the aggressive Dutch, whose presence on the near-by Connecticut would be a perpetual menace. So the *Blessing of the Bay* was sent to Manhattan bearing the Puritans' covenant and charter from the King, by which he had "granted the river and country of Connecticut to his own subjects" (*WJ:* I: 109). Governor Wouter van Twiller was not behindhand in this display of prerogative, and responded by referring to *his* commission, wherein "the Lords the States" had given the Connecticut to the Dutch.

While this tactful exchange was taking place, the Plymouth traders, feeling that their cause was both just and, as with all their endeavors, sanctioned by an authority higher than civil, opted for direct rather than diplomatic action. In one of those maneuvers which made a comic opera out of the relationships between English and Dutch forces in America, the Pilgrims sailed defiantly past the blustering commander of the Connecticut fort, carrying a prefabricated trading post concealed below decks. They set up shop on Winslow's land, thinking that was the end of the Dutch and the beginning of the beaver business. The Dutch never did prove much of a threat to the English on the Connecticut and the beaver trade thrived, but the Pilgrims soon found themselves once again in uncomfortable proximity to an old enemy—John Oldham. Taking advantage of the English presence on the Connecticut, he set up there for himself, planting south of the Dutch fort in company with a few of his fellow Watertown Freemen whose interests he so well represented.

Oldham's maneuver was as silent as it was sly, and seems to have escaped the watchful eye of Governor Winthrop, whose attention was held by the noisier activities of wards within his Wall at Newtown. Laid out between Watertown and Charlestown in 1631, Newtown was intended to serve as both a fortified community and the seat of government, a symbolic keystone in the defensive perimeter along the Charles. But Boston was shortly afterward selected as the capital of the colony, being better watered and more easily defended, and the abandonment of Newtown as the cynosure of the Puritan commonwealth created both a psychological and a geopolitical problem. After Winthrop removed his own house to Boston, Thomas Dudley, who had settled in Newtown, planning to grow up there with Massachusetts, stubbornly remained behind, nursing a grudge as his poetic daughter swallowed her distaste for the raw wilderness to which her sensibilities had been forcibly transplanted. Thomas Hooker, the minister of Newtown, seems likewise to have resented the prominence enjoyed by John Cotton in Boston, nor were the less prominent residents of Newtown any happier with their lot collective or their lots individual, the both considered mean and getting meaner as the population increased.

Well-placed in a military sense only, Newtown was short on grazing land, and her people therefore were unable to share in the profits from selling cattle to newcomers.

Intended as a main supporting member, Newtown from the start was a flaw in Winthrop's Wall. It was Watertown's resentment over being taxed to pay for the palisade around her neighbor that led to the Freemen's demand for more say in colony legislation, and this, in turn, resulted in the creation of the Deputies and Winthrop's fall from office if not power, his rival Thomas Dudley succeeding him as Governor. It was, moreover, at this same General Council of April 1634 that Newtown "complained of straitness for want of land, especially meadow, and desired leave of the court to look out either for enlargement or removal, which was granted; whereupon they sent men to see Agawam and Merrimack, and gave out they would remove, etc." (*WJ*: I: 124) It was at this time also that John Oldham got his five hundred acres, and William Wood received his somewhat less substantial reward for his benefactions to the colony when the General Council met the following September. But the people of Newtown were less impressed than Wood by the advantages of the Merrimack, and asked in September "that they might leave to remove to Connecticut" (132). Once again pleading the lack of grazing land, the Newtown proponents for removal pointed out "the fruitfulness and commodiousness of Connecticut, and the danger of having it possessed by others, Dutch or English." They likewise stressed the "strong bent of their spirits to remove thither," thus investing their restlessness with a providential aura for what Saints proposed was in general assumed to be divine disposition.

In general, but not necessarily in particular. John Cotton, in his dockside sermon, had encouraged the Puritan planters' determination to go to America by assuring them that their "inclination" was evidence of God's will, that Providence is "an eye of God that opens a door there," that "inclines" hearts toward New England "and outlooks all difficulties." But in Boston Cotton preached a different line. Siding against those who thought to follow God's eye to Connecticut, he gave his blessing to the opinion that, "in point of conscience, they ought not to depart from us, being knit to us in one body, and bound by oath to seek the welfare of this commonwealth" (132). Though no longer Governor, John Winthrop remained a Magistrate,

193

and his notion of commonwealth still carried considerable force. During the summer, moreover, the General Council had celebrated its new liberal character by cracking down on women's fashions and speeding up fortifications in Boston and around the Bay. Though Thomas Hooker's objection to the "fundamental error that towns were set so near each other" may have been received with applause by the Deputies, the Magistrates still thought otherwise.

It was, they claimed, "in point of state and civil policy" their duty to deny the people of Newtown their wish to depart the Bay, since their removal would not only expose them "to evident peril" from the Dutch and Indians, but would weaken the Massachusetts Wall even further by encouraging other communities to remove. Some salve for Hooker's burnt ego was included, for his departure (the Magistrates said) would "not only draw many from us, but also divert other friends that would come to us," and their opinion ended on a religious note: "The removing of a candlestick is a great judgment, which is to be avoided" (133). The decision drew a hard line between "the strong bent of spirits" and Winthrop's "state and civil policy," in effect giving primacy to the Wall over the Motions of Grace, and the debate and vote which followed cut the line even deeper. For the issue fell between the party of the Wall and the party of Motion, between autocratic and popular, consolidative and expansionist forces, and it is notable that Governor Dudley was the only Magistrate who sided with the Deputies for Newtown's removal. But because of the power of their veto—the "negative voice"—the Magistrates and the Wall held, and John Cotton once again emptied his bottle of balm upon the scene. "The congregation of Newtown came and accepted of such enlargement as had formerly been offered them by Boston and Watertown," noted Winthrop in his journal, "and so the fear of their removal to Connecticut was removed" (134).

Winthrop would have his triumphant little pun, but while the battle was being fought he was losing the war. During all this high-minded (and high-handed) play of power, principle, and piety, John Oldham had been following his own inclination, and without benefit of clergy. The Watertown defectors were soon followed to the Connecticut by some equally silent incliners from Dorcester, a precedent which acted just as Winthrop feared the Newtown removal would, one collapsing block in his Wall causing others to tumble also. So it was that in May

1636, only two years after Newtown had complained of being crowded, Thomas Hooker led his congregation and their cattle overland to the Connecticut Valley, there to increase and multiply—and, of course, divide. It was a momentous event, surely, but one noted in marvelous brief compass in Winthrop's journal: "Mr. Hooker, pastor of the church of Newtown, and the most of his congregation, went to Connecticut. His wife was carried in a horse litter; and they drove one hundred and sixty cattle, and fed of their milk by the way" (180-81).

The record is also thin-lipped concerning the genesis by which the several settlements along the Connecticut River became a separate colony, but the method was similar to the amoebic growth of Massachusetts towns—an extended foot containing a bit of nuclear church—and so in a larger sense Governor Winthrop's ideal prevailed once again. Yet if it was as John White of Dorcester, England, had said, if the progress of religion indeed followed the sun, then it also followed Dorcester, Massachusetts, along with Watertown and Newtown to the Connecticut Valley—thereby diminishing the Boston Beacon. But by 1636 that light had a very real counterpart "set on the sentry hill to give notice to the country of any danger," and it was likewise cannon, powder, and shot that first followed the westward course of Puritan empire, whatever the millennial glory that may have trailed after. For in June 1635 the General Court voted to grant "three pieces to the plantations that shall remove to Connecticut, to fortify themselves withall" (*RM:* I: 148).

And when, in March of the following year, a commission was granted "to several persons to govern the people at Connecticut" until such time as they elected their own, it was in recognition "that where there are a people to sit down and cohabit, there will follow, upon occasion, some cause of difference, as also divers misdemeanors, which will require a speedy redress" (170). In more than one way did Newtown represent five years of experience in establishing a community of love in Massachusetts, whose peacefulness and harmony was supposed to bring Indians flocking like doves to the window. As for that palisaded and problematic plot on the Charles, its name was changed soon after to Cambridge, thus dignifying the place where Harvard College was to rise, a walled Garden within the larger Wall whose purpose was similarly strategic, being a shield of truth against the incursion of doctrinal error—nor were Indians particularly encouraged to flock within.

iii. Dialect and Discourse

There is no contemporary account of Thomas Hooker's migration to Connecticut written by a participant or a sympathetic observer, only the documents of record and the accounts by later Massachusetts historians who relied on Governor Winthrop's journal for an account of the affair. Nor was Hooker's the kind of enterprise which occasioned (or even permitted) an exchange of letters and the engendering of propaganda, and if he exhorted his congregation before departure concerning their prospects in Connecticut, no record of the sermon seems to have survived. Indeed, the best proof of the Puritan sanction against finding post-Exodus Canaans in the New World is the silence concerning the obvious Old Testament parallel to Hooker's western hegira, for the Newtown emigrants literally acted out the Mosaic pageant, marching through the wilderness terrain and crossing their river to plant on the western side.

Though we do not know the thoughts of Hooker and his people on the subject, succeeding events may well have dimmed any hope of finding a land of peaceable promise beyond the Bay, for their first year was marked by a severe winter and great hardship. Hooker had missed the purgatorial prelude which had introduced Winthrop and his Fleet to "the paradise of these parts," but he soon had his full measure of suffering and starvation. Whatever it was he sought in the western valley, he found wilderness enough, and that there may indeed have been some reversal of expectations is suggested by the account of Newtown's removal written by the Puritan historian, William Hubbard, some forty years later. Hubbard had been a boy in his teens when Hooker had made his western journey, but he was most definitely of the founding generation of ministerial planters, credentials given further warrant by his graduation in the first Harvard class of 1642. He was doubtless aware of the conditions and conflicts which resulted in

196

Newtown's removal, and it is his account of the matter which alone mentions the rivalry between Hooker and Cotton, a flash of the honesty that distinguishes Hubbard's *General History of New England* from all others. His is likewise the only account which allows the Canaan allusion in describing Hooker's wilderness passage, but the terms of the metaphor are ironic, for Hubbard's description of Newtown's defection epitomizes conservative reaction in Massachusetts:

It was generally accounted no wisdom to be straitened in a wilderness, where there was land enough, and therefore these people, with Isaac, preferred a Rehoboth before a Sitnah; and it were to be wished, that men's desires being obtained as to room, there may never be contention about their bounds. But whatever were the cause, or gave the occasion, of setting up these western plantations, the design being resolved upon in the year 1634, some were deputed from amongst the towns in the Bay to view the country, who returning from this Eschol with a large commendation of the commodiousness of the place, and fruitfulness of the soil, they took up a resolution forthwith to begin several plantations there; accordingly, in the year 1635, several families, with the approbation of the authority of Massachusetts, undertook the removal of themselves to that Canaan of Connecticut; and in the way thereunto, whether they so well expected it and prepared for it or no, they met with many difficulties and trials of a wilderness, before they were comfortably settled there. For those their hasty resolves, that had so early budded, were sorely nipped, and almost quite blasted, by the sharpness of the winter season that year, and other sad occurrences, which they were called to encounter with, in the following year, by the barbarous outrage of the Pequot Indians, who, like Amalek of old, that set upon the rear of Israel in the wilderness, did sorely annoy those plantations upon Connecticut River, at their first settling there (306-7).

Much in the manner of Winthrop's adaptation of Moses' apostrophe to his people on the threshold of the Promised Land, Hubbard's account of Hooker's passage to "that Canaan of Connecticut" stops the emigrants short of the Jordan, the prospect of plenty transformed into yet another wilderness. The Connecticut experience is thereby warped to the terms of the dominant theocratic metaphor, providing a pattern of westering expectation and consequent disillusionment that acts to reinforce the sanctity of Winthrop's Wall. Thomas Hooker of Newtown had taken issue with the Governor's geopolitics, but Hooker of Hartford soon saw the world as according to Winthrop: The Chosen of God, he wrote in *Application of Redemption,* "must come into, and go through a vast and roaring Wilderness, where they must be bruised with many pressures, humbled under many overbearing difficulties . . . before they could possess that good land which abounded with all prosperity, flowed with milk and honey" (IX: 5). As Winthrop had noted, the Newtown emigrants were plentifully supplied with milk during their passage, but it all came from cows.

The Pequot War served Hubbard as a convenient pivot on which to swing Connecticut back into the Mosaic wilderness, for Amalek by 1680 was a conventional type for the Indian who is figured on the Great Seal of Massachusetts as a Macedonian and missionary subject. The outbreak of war the year after Hooker's people removed was a signal event in the process of transforming the Indian from an object of charity to one of hatred and fear, catalytic to the conversion of the Puritan errand from Pauline to patriarchal purpose. And it certainly illustrated Winthrop's fears concerning the reaction of the quarrelsome Pequots to the movement by large numbers of Englishmen into their territory. However, the cause of the war was not Newtown's removal westward, it was a combination of mishaps and blunders the most of which originated in Boston, the result of that peculiar myopia afflicting Massachusetts, a perspective glass which diminished instead of enlarging events taking place beyond Winthrop's Wall. There is, most certainly, a kind of poetry in the Pequot War, the event providing a finale to the epic of supplantation in Connecticut, but like the complex circumstances which brought about that move, the war itself was a product of Boston manufacture, a marvel of misdesign. If Connecticut proved indeed a howling wilderness, it was Massachusetts that caused the howl.

iv. As You Sow

The Pequot War as well as the Newtown removal were general effects which may be traced to single causes, in both instances to that individual whose presence in America was usually a matter of "perticulers," John Oldham. Once again it was the result of his trading ventures, but this time the exchange was decidedly to Oldham's disadvantage, the good luck (or providential assistance) he enjoyed while dealing with Indians finally having ended, along with his life. In July 1636 Oldham's pinnace was sighted off Block Island, "the deck full of Indians," a circumstance which aroused the suspicions of John Gallop, a fellow trader putting out from Connecticut (*WJ:* I: 183). After overhauling the fleeing pinnace, Gallop engaged in a brisk exchange, his "two pieces and two pistols, and nothing but duck shot" against Indians "armed with guns, pikes, and swords," and finally won the day. Oldham was found "under an old seine, stark naked, his head cleft to the brains, and his hand and legs cut as if they had been cutting them off, and yet warm" (184).

Oldham's body was consigned to his proper element, the sea, and his property to the proper authorities in Boston, who took steps to determine the cause of his death, a geopolitical, not medical autopsy which perfectly illustrates the tangled affairs of Indians and Englishmen, the shifting allegiances and little lies that kept the situation not only fluid but sometimes volatile. For Oldham had been the object of a plot set in motion by the Narragansetts, who like most Indians had a primitive but powerful conception of business conduct, a somewhat Sicilian sense of the proprieties of commerce. Oldham had violated that stiff decorum by trading with their enemies, the Pequots, so Narragansett sachems ordered a subordinate tribe on Block Island to kill him. The Boston authorities learned of this from an Indian taken prisoner by Gallop, and it placed them in a delicate situation, since the Narragansetts were, as William Wood described them, "the most numerous people in these parts," living hard on the exposed southern frontier of Massachusetts. So the Magistrates preferred to believe the version of the plot according to the powerful Narragansett sachem Canonicus, the Boston delegation that visited him finding "marvelous wisdom in his answers and the carriage of the whole treaty, clearing himself and his neighbors of the murder, and offering assistance for revenge of it, yet upon very safe and wary conditions" (186).

Some kind of swift and prompt retaliation was in order, and since Canonicus had no objection, the Block Islanders were singled out for the honor. A small army of ninety men was dispatched thither, "to put to death the men but to spare the women and children" for the gentler fate of servitude, a punitive expedition put under the command of John Endecott—perhaps to enlist his sword in more useful work than redesigning the British ensign. And Endecott was ordered, almost as an afterthought, it seems, "to go to the Pequots to demand the murderers of Capt. Stone and other English, and one thousand fathom of wampum for damages, etc., and some of their children as hostages, which if they should refuse, they were to obtain it by force." The said Captain Stone was a Virginian trader who had been driven out of Massachusetts in 1633 for dissolute, drunken, and adulterous behavior "and ordered upon pain of death to come here no more" (108). He subsequently offended the Pequots by his rude manner of doing business, and in their direct way they put the second part of his sentence into effect. The Boston Magistrates had no great regret over Stone's demise, but an Englishman was an Englishman, even if he was from Virginia, and they looked into the matter of his death. The Pequots proved very obliging, and told their story "with such confidence and gravity, as, having no means to contradict it, we inclined to believe it" (139). The Pequots having gravely offered to deliver up the two men who had killed Stone, four hundred fathom of wampum, and a number of pelts, throwing in "all their right at Connecticut, and to further us what they could, if we would settle a plantation there," the Boston authorities agreed to "be at peace with them, and as friends to trade with them, but not to defend them, etc" (140).

It was under this arrangement that John Oldham had commenced commerce with the Pequots, but the Indians were very slow in making good the matter of Stone's murderers, the wampum, etc., hence the second part of Endecott's commission, the first part of which he undertook with great dispatch but to little effect, for the Block Islanders fled when they saw the English coming. Endecott, his officers, and his men were reduced to staving in canoes and burning wigwams, mats, and corn, and they must have departed the island in a prickly mood, which could not have been improved by the four days they sat windbound in the mouth of the Connecticut River. They sought shelter in a fort being built there by Lion Gardiner, an engineer newly arrived from England, on land owned by the Puritan Lords Saye and Sele and Brooke, who intended to found a settlement for persons of tender conscience and high degree. Put off by the leveling tendencies of government in New England, the Lords never made the move, and Saybrook shortly thereafter became absorbed by Hooker's colony—but not before it bore the brunt of the Pequot War.

Designed by John Winthrop Junior as a defense against the Dutch, the Saybrook fort soon provided signal service against the Indians, a consequence of Endecott's expedition which Lion Gardiner foresaw: "I said" he recalled twenty years later, "you come hither to raise these wasps about my ears and then you will take wing and flee away . . . but go they did as they came without acquainting any of us in the river with it" (9). Endecott's spine of steel extended far into his head, and like a javelin hurled he could not in motion be stayed until brought to earth. So he set sail for the Pequot River, where he repeated his Block Island tactic with Block Island results, wreaking great havoc among empty wigwams. Only one Pequot was killed, by a Narragansett who had come along as an interpreter, but that was enough. As Gardiner prophesied, the single swat from Endecott's sword brought the Indians swarming out of their riverside nest.

Having unleashed the Pequots against the Connecticut settlers, the Boston Magistrates turned to matters closer to home—including their treaty with the Narragansetts. Winthrop took care to note in his journal the several outrages perpetrated against the English by the Pequots, and he duly recorded the letters of protest sent from Connecticut and Plymouth concerning the effects of Endecott's expedition, but he seems to have been more concerned during this period with Anne Hutchinson's dangerous notions of grace. Not only was her insistence on individual intuition of election—as opposed to the evidence of "works"—contrary to church doctrine, but it was also subversive of duly constituted authority, a two-headed threat within Winthrop's world which diminished the importance of a few Indian ambuscades in the west. Boston was never more Lilliputian than during the course of the Antinomian controversy that was sparked by Hutchinson's opinions and popularity, and Winthrop was at the very center of the microcosm, having used the antagonisms aroused by the turmoil to unseat the liberal Governor, Sir Henry Vane. So busy was he prosecuting the great big-endian debate and defending his prerogatives of office ("The new Governor [J.W.] was fain to use his own servants to carry two halberds before him, whereas the former Governor [Sir H.V.] had never less than four") that by the time he got around to the troubles in Connecticut they were about over (*WJ:* I: 216). Nor was Plymouth's conduct and contribution any larger, the Pilgrims using the occasion of the war as a platform from which to air old grievances concerning Massachusetts' trespasses and unpaid debts, claiming, besides, that the affair was none of theirs, etc.

One of Governor Vane's last acts in office was to send Captain John Underhill, a veteran of the Block Island and Pequot River campaign, back to Saybrook fort with twenty men, to assist in its defense. Underhill was soon called upon to join forces with the small army raised by Captain John Mason (the "good" John Mason, of Connecticut, not Gorges's man in Maine), who carried in his van a renegade band of Mohegan-Pequots led by a sachem named Uncas, an ambivalent quantity soon to play an equivocal role in the drama of supplantation. Setting sail from Saybrook, Mason had the good sense not to repeat Endecott's mistake, and though his orders instructed him to land on the Pequot River, he went instead to Narragansett Bay. There his army was augmented further by Miantonomo's men, who were curious to see how the English would do against the fierce Pequots, and, marching westward, Mason laid the Narragansetts' skepticism to rest, falling suddenly on the Indian fort commanding the Mystic River (the "other" Mystic, of Connecticut, not Massachusetts). Nearly all of the Pequots were killed, the English using a combination of swords, muskets, and fire in a holocaust that horrified even the Narragansetts but reduced the war to a cleaning-up operation. Additional forces from Massachusetts arrived in time to help wipe out the remaining pockets of resistance, but the triumph was really Connecticut's. Some measure of Winthrop's perspective at this time may be taken from his observation that "the general defeat of the Pequots at Mystic happened the day after our general fast," thus keeping things in general within Boston's precincts (221).

To similar effect was the arrival there shortly afterward of Thomas Hooker, whose liberalism had been somewhat tempered by his wilderness experience. Not only did he join in the prosecution of the Antinomians, but Hooker met with Winthrop to discuss a confederation between Connecticut, Massachusetts, and Plymouth, a union that was a direct consequence of the Pequot War. It would be several years before that federation would be a fact—it was put off by fears on the part of her sister colonies concerning the tendency of things to drift within Massachusetts' borders—but the plan would be symbolic of Winthrop's enlarged geopolitical scheme, the center still holding at Boston—the mountain to which the Hartford Mahomet came. Still, if the war served to promote further unity, the Antinomian controversy produced further division, and though the party of works won out over the party of grace abounding, the excommunication and exile of Mrs. Hutchinson and her supporters increased considerably that misbehavioral sink, Rhode Island. It also added to the population along the Piscataqua, an eastern counterpart to the Connecticut River and a particularly troublesome feature on Winthrop's map—his diagram of widening but not necessarily welcome domain.

The region that became New Hampshire in later years is associated with every crime in Winthrop's book, from piracy to sodomy, and since it bordered the territory commanded by the agents of Sir Ferdinando Gorges, it was identified with that zone of threat also. Rhode Island was both anarchy and anathema, but it was given a certain high tone by Roger Williams, whereas the Piscataqua was a backwoods anti-utopia, a perpetual garboil on the backside of the Bay. In Winthrop's eyes it was a receptacle of human garbage, being a gallery of refugees and rogues seldom graced with the excuse but merely giving the pretext of religious dissent. If the Connecticut River provided a geopolitical margin equivalent to the advancing frontier of later epochs, the Piscataqua was border country, like Merry Mount a neutral ground harboring cutthroats, buggers, and Captain John Underhill. For the erstwhile hero of the Pequot War had enlisted himself on the wrong side in the Antinomian controversy, and a subsequent charge of adultery did nothing to redeem him to Boston's good graces. Underhill was exiled to the

Piscataqua, where his activities on the river east of the Bay gave further point to the Governor's distaste for both the region and the man, which alone should recommend him to our attention.

v. A Lawless, Linsey-woolsey Brother

Throughout his rule, Governor Winthrop managed to maintain civil relationships with those of his enemies who kept his respect because of their station and power, like Sir Ferdinando, or because of their superior intelligence, like Roger Williams, and one gets the impression that had the Governor met Satan face to face he would have given the Devil his due—much as he granted the Canadian Governor, La Tour, the courtesy of Boston. Winthrop was also capable of generosity toward former antagonists, and when (in 1644) the Reverend John Wheelwright renounced his stand in the Antinomian controversy—having been brought to his senses by a term of residence on the coast of Maine—Winthrop was glad to regain that luminary for God and Massachusetts. Anne Hutchinson, who never recanted, Winthrop never forgave, and he seems likewise to have reserved a special place in the darker corners of his heart for Captain Underhill. A capable commander of Boston fort, in politics Underhill comported himself so as to become an incarnation of folly and divisiveness, an identification firmly cemented during the Captain's two years of inconstant exile on the Piscataqua. After founding the town of Dover, Underhill found himself involved also in civic wrangles with his fellow settlers and in border disputes with Massachusetts, and though he returned to Boston from banishment in 1640, his tearful, public confession and statement of contrition seem to have struck Winthrop as somewhat contrived.

Tired of the cares of absolute liberty, the Piscataqua region, like Captain Underhill, finally submitted to Boston rule—in fact, Underhill was instrumental in the move—but through Winthrop accepted unholy Dover into the sacred precincts of Massachusetts, he never found room for the town's founder. As a consequence, Captain Underhill fell under a long shadow, and despite his pardon by proclamation, had difficulty finding work. In the end he went west to fight Indians again, this time in the service of the Dutch, who appreciated his talents in such a generous manner that the Captain became a prominent resident of Long Island, which did nothing to raise him in Winthrop's eyes. Not only was Long Island colored Presbyterian true blue in the Governor's book, but it was associated with increasing westward migration, desertions and defections from Winthrop's domain during the 1640's which were a result of the economic depression that followed the falling-off of immigration during the Civil War in England. When, in 1643, news reached Winthrop that Anne Hutchinson had been killed by Indians along with others from Rhode Island who had moved west and "dwelt under the Dutch," he made a grim observation in his journal concerning those who "had cast off ordinances and churches, and now at last their own people, and for larger accommodation . . . dwelt scatteringly near a mile asunder" (II: 138). Underhill fell under this same general category, associated with Dutch dominion, western lands, and Indians, and in 1644 was accused by Winthrop of complicity in a Dutch plot "to engage the English in a quarrel" with the Mohawks (161).

Even the matter of Underhill's election was under a cloud, the Spirit having delivered "an absolute promise of free grace . . . as he was taking a pipe of tobacco" (I: 275). And yet, despite their unbridgeable differences in character and conviction, the Captain and the Governor were one in their emphasis on the necessity of community in the New World, Underhill following the accepted pattern—if not the paternity —of Massachusetts by founding a town in New Hampshire. Despite his faults, which were soldierly vices, Captain Underhill was a family man whose instincts (even when adulterous) were gregarious. Of good heart but impulsive, too spirited to accept the rigid morality and centralized authority of Boston, Underhill was (understandably) susceptible to the Gospel according to Saint Anne. In terms of the Puritan drama, moreover, he was in the vanguard of the next stage of settlement after the initial westward thrust symbolized by Hooker's hegira and Major Mason's march against the Pequots. Underhill's association with the Hudson was especially prophetic, for the English frontier would follow him there, the tide of empire pushing toward that great river, his departure for fairer fields, like his earlier role fighting Connecticut's battles and his exile on the Piscataqua, being symptomatic of changing times and realigned forces.

Where Thomas Morton posed an impossible alternative to Winthrop's improbable plan, Captain Underhill entertained a median and meliorating vision, and though his was distinctly a minority view in 1638—so far as power politics in Massachusetts were concerned—it would gain strength as the westward movement of New England's population continued. Like Morton, Underhill left his own memorial, a pamphlet giving his account of the Pequot War, important not only as a first-hand narrative of that epochal event, but as an expression of Underhill's generous (if occasionally confused) soul, conveying his version of New England vistas—both geo- and psycho-political. Connecticut's John Mason also left a narrative of the war, which likewise expresses a point of view at variance with the idea of America obtaining in Boston, suggesting that there may have been as much truth as ruth in William Hubbard's mocking use of the Canaan allusion.

vi. Holy Text . . .

Captain John Underhill's *Newes from America* (1638) is the last pamphlet associated with the planting of Massachusetts printed during the first decade of great growth, and it provides an aesthetic third to the georgic prospects of Puritan propagandists and the gorgeous views promulgated by Thomas Morton, a view in which not the Plow nor the Pole but the Pike defines the landscape. Some sense of Underhill's purpose is indicated by his lengthy subtitle, which advertises a "true relation" of the Puritans' "war-like proceedings these two years past," along with "a discovery of those places that as yet have very few or no inhabitants which would yield special accommodation." It is very much in the tradition of Captain Smith's relation of thirty years earlier, with, if anything, an increase in the martial dimension. Instead of a map, moreover, Underhill includes "a figure of the Indian fort, or palisado," which shows the English forces busily exterminating the Pequots, a flaming circle with implications antithetical to those of William Wood's accommodating diagram.

Where Wood provides the fertile arena for a Hesiodic epic, Underhill transplants the Puritans into a more troubled terrain, his own experience resolving through violence the tensions provided by Wood's outer ring of savagery. Published the year before the first printing press was set up in Winthrop's domain, from whence issued a literature enforcing the theocratic scheme for Massachusetts, Underhill's pamphlet like its author is distinctly in the minority. He was hardly the last refugee from Winthrop's rule who used London presses to oppose hard usage received in Boston, but his argument lacks the theological burden of writings by Roger Williams and Samuel Gorton. His was a war of weapons, not words, and though the "places of accommodation" he describes lay outside the bounds of Winthrop's Patent, his pamphlet evinces a spirit of accord with Massachusetts. Yet, when read carefully, it can be seen as proposing a radical departure from the kind of community espoused by John Winthrop, an expression of the democratic ethos that new-world conditions and Anne Hutchinson's teaching inspired.

Underhill's narrative begins *in medias res,* proposing no long view of the conflict but rather "interweaving" his relation "of our warlike proceedings" with descriptions of "the special places fit for new plantations" (13). The effect and form is antithetical to Wood's Hesiodic scheme, being a martial version of expansion, and instead of enforcing Boston's concentric containment, Underhill's narrative expresses a linear thrust, moving out from Winthrop's Patent in a generally western direction. Like Captain Smith's Virginia, Captain Underhill's New England is dominated by rivers, not only the battle zones of the Pequot and Mystic, but also the pastoral Connecticut ("pity it is so famous a place should be so little regarded"), the Quinnipiac ("which rather exceeds the former in goodness"), the Piscataqua ("pity it is it hath been so long neglected"), but most particularly the Hudson: "if you would know the garden of New England, then must you glance your eye upon Hudson's river, a place exceeding all yet named" (13-14). By placing these pastoral prospects within his heroic action, Underhill in effect supplies a third strand, the green impulse that is the reality behind the heroic action against "that insolent and barbarous nation, called the Pequots" (3).

There is in this regard a note unique in captains' narratives engendered by the American experience, first sounded in Underhill's account of the Block Island campaign, during which he was saved from an Indian arrow by his helmet, worn only at the insistence of his wife. There follows an amusing digression on the issue of women's rights in New England, for Underhill's willingness to take his wife's advice was a refutation of the rumor "that New England men usurp over their wives, and keep them in servile subjection" (5). Given his adulterous history, these reflections on marital piety in the midst of a martial narration are doubly anomalous, but they do serve to emphasize the essentially domestic bias of the narrator, echoing as well his loyalty to Anne Hutchinson. It also introduces a distaff emphasis which soon takes another and more significant form, Underhill putting particular stress on the "two maids captives" whom the Pequots seized during their raid on Wethersfield, utilizing the event in an ingenious fashion, in effect providing his narrative a contrapuntal stress, the fate of the female captives acting as counterpoint to his masculine tale of arms.

Having described the insolent passage of the Pequot canoes past Saybrook Fort after the Wethersfield attack, Underhill leaves the reader in suspense as to the fate of the two girls, embarking instead on what is in effect a commercial for the "accommodations" of Connecticut real estate, including his encomiums on the beauties of the Piscataqua and the Hudson as well. Then, further neglecting the two maidens, he recounts the sad end of John Tilley, tortured to death by the Pequots because he did not "suspect the bloody-mindedness of those persons" (15). This incident provides further motive for the march (and fiery vengeance) on the Indian stronghold ("would not this have moved the hearts of men to hazard blood, and life . . . ?") but it also increases the reader's apprehension as to the treatment of the Wethersfield maids in such "wicked, insolent" hands. Further delay is provided by Underhill's account of the marshaling of Connecticut forces under Captain John Mason and the desire of Uncas and his Mohegan renegades to join the English expedition, all doubts as to their fidelity laid to rest by prayers and the hard evidence of "five Pequots' heads" produced during a Sabbath layover (16). Only then does the Captain return to the maidens, who were rescued from the Indians by Dutch traders, a circumstance which lends particular meaning to the incident. Since the Dutch were forbidden by the English from trading with the Pequots, their presence in Connecticut was illegal, but having broken the law, they were able to rescue the girls. So ill will drew out good deeds, God having been "pleased, out of His love, to carry things in such a sweet, moderate way, as all turned to His glory, and His people's good" (17).

This theme of apparent ill turned to real good gives purpose to the rest of Underhill's narrative, a providential pattern of reconciliation which has at its center the figure of the "two maids captives." During her examination by the soldiers at Saybrook Fort, the oldest of the girls, "about sixteen years of age," assured her interrogators that the Indians "did solicit her to uncleanness," but that she had resisted temptation. Assuming her captivity was "God's just displeasure," the girl was careful not to commit further "evil and sin against her God," but instead drew a kind of strength from her suffering (18). As captives, the girls are figured by Underhill as Israel in bondage, for "hope was their chiefest food, and tears their constant drink. Behind the rocks, and under the trees, the eldest spent her breath in supplication to her God" (19). The allusion to the punitive sojourn in Babylon is definitive, for theirs is a penitential bondage: "Poor captivated children," the maidens are the "prisoners of hope," whose chief consolation is the "sweet comfort" of adversity, God's punishing hand sure evidence of His presence in the wilderness. They were, notes Underhill, "more affected with the sense of God's fatherly love, than with the grief of their captivity," for it is better to be in the lion's den with Christ "than in a downy bed with wife and children" without Him—a notion of sweet bedfellowship which may have inspired wry Boston smiles (20).

But Underhill's main point must have lifted Boston eyebrows, for having delivered the Puritan platitude that "the sweet relish of God's comforting presence" increases appetite for adversity, he moves on to conclude that "the greater the captivities be of His servants, the contentions amongst His churches, the clearer God's presence is amongst His, to pick and cull them out of the fire" (20). This is the crux of Underhill's little sermon, binding the ordeal of captivity to sectarian controversy, the both being purifying processes: "You cannot have Christ in His ordinances, but you must have His cross" (21). Whatever John

Winthrop may have wanted from Christ, His cross was not on the list, nor was he ever party to the notion that "contentions" were signs of "immanent grace in the souls of His servants." Underhill was correct in warning "You that intend to go to New England, fear not a little trouble," but this was hardly the kind of news that Winthrop wished to broadcast in 1638 (22).

Governor Winthrop wasted little space in his journal on the "two maids, who had been well used by the Pequots, and no violence offered them," and he would likewise have given short shrift to Underhill's notion that "truth" is a matter of "contentions" (*WJ:* I: 219). Instead, his emphasis was always on the need for communal love and self-sacrifice, a monolithic Congregationalism demanding the submission of individual wills to the consensus invested in authority. Asking of oneself what one can do for the common good is a recipe of benevolent tyranny, against which dissent is predictable, as in the case of Anne Hutchinson and her many followers. And if we translate Underhill's doctrine of "contentions" into political terms, we find a notion abhorrent to Winthrop's idea of commonwealth but intrinsic to the form and manner of emerging government in Massachusetts, the play of forces which resulted in a bicameral split between executive and legislative powers in the Bay Colony, a direct result of the mock-epical wrangle over the ownership of Mrs. Sherman's sow—"a great business upon a very small occasion" (*WJ:* II: 64) Governor Winthrop would have regarded Underhill as an advocate of anarchy, much as he saw Anne Hutchinson as a bomb tossed in the lap of authority, but from our perspective the Captain's ingenious application of adversity has a mighty forward thrust, his thesis that contention leads to the sorting of truth being very much in the spirit of that most democratic of institutions, the New England town meeting.

The rest of John Underhill's narrative, his account of the attack on the Pequot fort, has a much more conventionally Puritan sound, the battle being a Bunyanesque business with "the providence of God in it" (23). Sharpening the edge of the Puritan errand, Underhill removes it from the Pauline to the Patriarchal arena: in anticipation of the question, "Should not Christians have more mercy and compassion?" Underhill responds by switching Testaments, invoking the precedent of "David's war" (25). Moreover, if the English soldiers acted "without compassion," it must have been because their ferocity was God-given, their errand being one of divine vengeance: "When a people is grown to such a height of blood, and sin against God and man, and all confederates in the action, there He hath no respect for persons, but harrows them, and saws them, and puts them to the sword, and the most terriblest death that may be."

This is the reverse of Underhill's Davidic coin, a militant Judaic counterpart to the passive Hebraic image of the maiden comforted by adversity, the both proof against onslaughts of self-doubt—and Indians. Combined, both sides constitute a considerable addition to the metaphoric language of New England, the meaning of which is further amplified by the march overland of Captain Mason's little army. "The bush may be in the fire," observes Captain Underhill, "but so long as God appears to Moses out of the bush, there is no great danger" (22). Quite clearly, the face of God appeared to John Underhill from out of the Mystic holocaust: "We had sufficient light from the word of God for our proceedings" (25). By such a light may the consequent history of New England be read, as the landscape is transformed from a pastoral to a punitive terrain, the Hesiodic scheme becoming an Israelite chronicle of holy wars.

vii. Of Pike and Gun

Despite his many differences with Winthrop's geopolitics, Underhill does manage to keep the Connecticut campaign this side the Jordan, but if we turn to John Mason's account of the Pequot War—in effect, the official Connecticut version—we find a definitive difference in metaphorical terrain. In considering the implications of that transformation, it is necessary to keep in mind the fact that Mason's narrative was written nearly a quarter of a century after the event, by which time he owned a considerable portion of Connecticut real estate. Having been made "Major General" of Connecticut as a reward for his great victory at Mystic, Mason was thenceforth a considerable citizen of his colony, and he was in 1660 elevated to the office of Deputy Governor.

Where Underhill wrote from under a cloud, suffering adversity, Major Mason wrote from a height of prosperity, which is not quite the same thing as transcendence, as we shall see.

Mason as architect of his own adventures seldom attains the ideal of objective (and epic) detachment which he claims in the opening pages of his "history" of the war to which he owed his fame and fortune. Humbly maintaining that his "principal aim is that God may have His due praise," and begging that the General Court at Hartford (who had requested his account of the war) be sparing in the use of his name, Mason declares that his intention is to purvey an overview of the whole affair rather than a narrative of his personal contribution (126-27). Having assumed that modest posture, Mason proceeds to reverse it, writing an account of the Pequot War in which his own name appears with monotonous regularity—second only in that regard to the Lord's—and though the Major assiduously avoids the first person singular, the effect (as with Adams's Henriad) is of less modesty rather than more. The general impression conveyed is that God and John Mason won the great war, the author emerging as a veritable cliché, the canting Cromwellian Soldier of God, a Hudibrastic self-satire of monstrous proportions: "It was the Lord's doings, and it is marvellous in our eyes! It is He that hath made His work wonderful, and therefore ought to be remembered" (144-45). And likewise the handiwork of His humble servant, Major General John Mason. *Selah!*

As record, Mason's history of the Pequot War is a dramatic monologue of inadvertently revealed Puritan character, but as literature it is slight. And yet there is a consistency of scriptural allusions which lends his narrative a certain pattern of implication, a transcendent tactic matching his brilliant Narragansett maneuver, one which counters Underhill's stress on wilderness suffering-as-redemption. "In a word," according to the Major, "the Lord was as it were pleased to say unto us, The Land of Canaan will I give unto thee though but few and strangers in it . . . and the Lord was pleased to smite our enemies in the hinder parts, and to give us their land for an inheritance . . . by His special Providence to lead us along in the way we should go" (130, 151, 152). These allusions provide a symbolic strand in his narrative, equivalent to Underhill's praise for distant river valleys, but unlike the Captain from Massachusetts the Major General of Connecticut transforms them into equivalents of the Jordan.

The crux of Mason's account of the war is neither Christ's cross nor the suffering of the "two young women taken captives," who are barely mentioned, but rather the Major's decision to disobey orders, to which he devotes considerable space, an interlude demonstrating the legalistic, contractual, and covenantal thinking of the Puritans. Dropping from the third into the first person, "making bold to present this as my present thoughts on the case," Mason justifies his action not only by logic, but by its successful which is to say providential outcome: "What shall I say? God led his people through many difficulties and turnings; yet by more than an ordinary hand of Providence He brought them to Canaan at last" (135). Aligning his own disobedience of temporal authority with divine dispensation, Major Mason goes on to put his feet in the fiery sandals of Joshua, and in breaking out of the "too narrow compass" of his commission, he breaks free from the limitation of the theocratic metaphor. In similar fashion, we may presume, did Major Mason break out of Winthrop's Wall in 1635, being one of that select party from Dorchester which followed John Oldham and the motions of grace to the western valley.

Again, we must remember that hindsight is a powerful shaper of prior motives, yet Mason's history of the Pequot War does indicate that a somewhat different view of the New England landscape held in Connecticut, suggesting that William Hubbard was essentially correct in his ironic allusion to the Connecticut Canaan. In any event, by the time the Major sat down to write his history of the Pequot War he had affected the crossing of an invisible Jordan in his own mind. When he sent his narrative to the General Court in Hartford, he gave a quietus to his imperial sum by dating it from "Norwich, in New England, in America," a trine of concentric circles radiating out from the head of navigation on the river once called "Pequot" but by 1660 styled "Thames," like the Connecticut a paradigm of the drama of supplantation beyond the Bay, and in that respect, at least, as good a Canaan as one could desire.

viii. Thick and Thin

Governor Winthrop may have looked down his long nose at the democratic tendencies of Hooker's colony—"The best part is always the least, and of that best part the wiser part is always the lesser"—but he welcomed Connecticut's overtures concerning a New England Confederation, which amounted to a strategic widening of his Wall (*WJ:* I: 290). A certain urgency was given to the matter by territorial rivalries between the Mohegans and Narragansetts consequent upon the defeat of the Pequots, but, ironically, the chief impediment to the desired Puritan union was disagreement over the common boundaries of the three colonies, in effect but a more sophisticated version of the quarrels between Uncas and Miantonomo, the affairs of the English once again mirroring (and mingling) with Indian imperatives until motives become indistinguishable. Boston, again, was the aggressor, for the border disputes resulted from the terms of Winthrop's Charter—which gave the Bay Colony all land lying between the north "part" of the Merrimack and the south "part" of the Charles—wording which the Governor interpreted generously on his own behalf. Drawing latitudinal lines from the northernmost point of the one river and the southernmost tributary of the other, he drew into his domain not only that dubious addition, the Piscataqua region, but also Agawam, a trading post on the Connecticut, and Scituate, a town planted by Pilgrims.

Winthrop's legalistic geopolitics were characteristic of the Governor's rule throughout, a constant maneuvering for advantage while promoting the general good. When, therefore, a group of settlers left Massachusetts in 1638 to plant a fourth colony in Connecticut, at New Haven on the Quinnipiac, Governor Winthrop accepted this "great weakening" of his own domain as "a good providence of God," being both the possession of "those parts which lay open for an enemy, and the strengthening of our friends at Connecticut" (I: 265). That his reasoning echoes Newtown's petition to remove suggests Winthrop's willingness to forget if not always to forgive, a changing position in respect to western regions which was helped along by the presence there of his son and namesake. For on the tenth anniversary of Hooker's removal Winthrop noted that John Junior's plantation was "begun at Pequot River," and though he was bothered somewhat "whether it would fall within our jurisdiction or not, because they of Connecticut challenged it by virtue of a patent from the King which was never showed us," still, it "mattered not much to which jurisdiction it did belong, seeing the confederation made all as one" (II: 275).

As things fell out, Connecticut did get the Pequot River region, but the Governor's remarks reveal his expanded perspective: "All" is "One," *Pluribus* is *Unum,* Connecticut as well as Massachusetts stamped with Winthrop's quarry-mark, his family seal. The year before he died, the Governor noted in his journal that "a new way was found out to Connecticut, by Nashua, which avoided much of the hilly way," whereby the path that God's eye opened for Hooker through the wilderness was abandoned for a road articulating Winthrop's revised plan for New England (343). But the name "Nashua" expresses a certain ambiguity, being an Algonquin word meaning "between," suggesting both unity and separation, like the bordering stone "Brothers" by the Concord River. And the road leading from Boston west by way of Newtown soon stretched to the Hudson and beyond, reaching ever toward more fertile fields, mapping an impulse that cannot abide the restraint of walls.

The Winthrop family crest displays a running hare on a green hill surmounting a helmet and an escutcheon on which is a rampant lion, an emblem glossed by the motto, *"Spes Vincit Thronum."* But New World conditions lent a certain ambiguity to the phrase, permitting an alternative glossing, for Hope Wins (*Vincere*) but it also in America Confines (*Vincire*) the Throne, and in the end Winthrop was himself held prisoner by the very forces with which he thought to secure his citadel of salvation. "Turn you to the strong hold, ye prisoners of hope," advised the Lord, through the mouth of Zechariah, wisdom with which both John Underhill and John Winthrop agreed, but the Prophet of Hope foresaw a Holy City without walls, and a mountain giving way to a valley of eternal peace. So the course of New England's history during the years of the Governor's reign suggests that hope turns ever outward in search of greener hills than Boston's, *"spes"* becoming a sublime pun associated with the vastness that perpetually diminished domination by extending domain. And so that Adamic chair on the upper reaches of the Charles became at the last an equivocal symbol, affirming that in America the drama of fathers and sons will assert an Aenean impiety, a version of Exodus: as John Winthrop Senior sold his Adamic patrimony to gain a new world, so in 1657 the heir apparent to the Massachusetts throne, John Winthrop Junior, became the Governor of Connecticut, identifying the family fortunes thenceforth with Hooker's western hope.

VIII
ECCLESIASTIC DRUMS

Puritan Theocrats,
Despairing of the Present Generation,
Reform the Past.

i. Something Like Prophetic Strain

"Through a wise and salutary neglect," observed Edmund Burke of the Thirteen Colonies in 1775, "a generous nature has been suffered to take her own way to perfection," and though New Englanders might have chosen different adjectives, what was true of the colonies in general during the eighteenth century was especially true of the New England Confederacy through the middle years of the seventeenth. From 1642 until 1660, when Charles II turned an unmerry eye in her direction, the Puritans in America were allowed to perfect their Way if not their generosity, for no one neglected them more than their own Oliver Cromwell. The Civil War removed the threat posed by Archbishop Laud and Sir Ferdinando Gorges, but it also cut off the flow of immigrants on which New England's prosperity was dependent, causing an economic depression that was followed by a psychological one. For as Cromwell's victories challenged the sanctity of Winthrop's errand, so his policy of toleration had the sharp, rebuking sting of a whip on a bare Quaker back, and his indifference to the brilliance of Boston's beacon is revealed by his suggestion that it be removed to the West Indies. And yet if Cromwell neglected Winthrop's wick, he in effect trimmed it, causing it to burn with a harder flame, the better to be seen from afar, still another demonstration of the increasing New England talent for turning adversity to advantage.

1642 was an especially bad year for the Puritans in America, the troubled economy, internal quarrels, and threats of Indian uprisings combining with Cromwell's success to inspire painful and even angry questions. The various border disputes between the New England colonies were forgotten in the face of similar wrangles between Uncas and Miantonomo, but where danger strengthened the Confederacy, economic depression seemed to increase the mood of materialism and internal disarray. Boston was torn asunder over the ownership of a

219

single pig, and Plymouth was aghast over a monumental case of buggery involving "a mare, a cow, two goats, five sheep, two calves, a turkey," and one (appropriately named) Thomas Granger. This epidemic of wickedness caused Governor Bradford to marvel how such crimes could occur "in a land where the same was so much witnessed against, and so narrowly looked into, and severely punished when it was known," and he devoted much of the year's entry in his chronicle to pondering the reasons thereof (*HPP:* II: 308). Governor Winthrop, likewise, was exercised over the love of cattle, the fall in the price of which put "many into an unsettled frame of spirit, so as they concluded there would be no subsisting here, and accordingly they began to hasten away" (*WJ:* II: 82).

This was not the removal of whole communities, which, if it dimmed the luster of Massachusetts, at least strengthened her boundaries. Instead, it was the seeking of "outward advantages" by single families or small, defecting groups, who did not depart his Wall by "an open door" of providential inspiration, but "crept out" through cracks of opportunity, desertions and defections in time of trouble which weakened the defenses of those left behind in a "wilderness, where are nothing but wild beasts and beast-like men" (83-84). "Ask again," Winthrop thundered from an angry cloud of ink, "what liberty thou hast towards others, which thou likest not to allow others towards thyself; for if one may go, another may, and so the greater part, and so church and commonwealth may be left destitute in the wilderness, exposed to misery and reproach, and all for thy ease and pleasure" (84). The net effect of Winthrop's exhortation is to present a picture of community antithetical to his ideal City, divided against itself and threatened by a hostile world outside ruined walls, a dubious sanctuary set in a fearsome territory inhabited by bestial men whose spiritual welfare is no longer a relevant concern.

Yet it was only a year later that *New Englands First Fruits* was published in London, an anonymous little book with a large public purpose, to "let the world know," as the author put it, "that God led not so many thousands of his people into the wilderness, to see a reed shaken with the wind, but amongst many other special ends, this was none of the least, to spread the light of His blessed Gospel, to such as never heard the sound of it" (430). In marked contrast to Winthrop's imagery, red-skinned Macedonians glow like well-scrubbed apples amid the general harvest gathered in *First Fruits,* including not only "flesh, fish, and fowl," but the first graduating class of Harvard College. Unlike the endangered commonweal described by Winthrop in his journal, the New England of *First Fruits* has such a "form and face" as the Governor prescribed in 1630, being a "good land" purged of "vile persons and loose livers," and planted with God's *"precious ordinances"* (440-46).

New England's blessedness is a sign of Divine Investment, "an earnest-penny of more to come," *First Fruits* throughout being a tale of *"beginnings whereof and progress hitherto,"* of things "which in part already are, and will in time further be improved" (437; 442). All these evidences of progress—backed by "remarkable passages of His providence to our plantation"—is presented as proof that "God means to carry His Gospel westward, in these latter times of the world; and . . . as the sun in the afternoon of the day, still declines more and more to the West, and then sets: so the Gospel (that great light of the world) though it rose in the East, and in former ages hath lightened it with His beams; yet in the latter ages of the world will bend Westward, and before its setting, brighten these parts, with His glorious lustre also" (430-31). That was New England's destiny according to John White of Dorcester as well, and the shift in pronoun suggests Whom the Gospel prefigures, implying that He is already packing His bags for departure to America.

But if Christ's arrival in Boston was imminent, John Winthrop's angry outcry suggests that many New Englanders were not biding His advent, but were lighting out for a farther west themselves. *First Fruits* is patently propaganda, a stretching of facts so thin and tight that they squeak, and if the pulpit is an ecclesiastical drum, in New England it sometimes has a hollow as well as an ominous sound. Published in London the year after the outbreak of the Civil War, *First Fruits* was as much a product of the Puritan Revolution as *Areopagitica,* published a year later, and like Milton's great pamphlet it was written in protest, albeit in an indirect vein. Sent down from the Hill of Matthew (and Winthrop), not Mars, it is a book whose purpose and point is revealed by the quotations on the title page, from Zechariah—"Who hath despised the day of small things?"—and Job—"Though thy beginnings be small, thy latter end shall greatly increase." Packed like many another Yankee basket with the biggest apples on top, *First Fruits* is a marvelous example of special pleading, containing the seeds of a whole literature to come, Puritan authors in America being from first to last responsive to events in England.

The first writing engendered by the Puritan presence in the New World was different in emphasis only from the propaganda for settlement associated with Virginia, but with the outbreak of the Civil War it took a distinctive turn. The Cavalier defeat produced a silent echo in Virginia, but Cromwell's victory raised a competitive clamor in Massachusetts, for any way one wishes to view it, Puritan literature in America is a child of calamity. The Puritans on both sides of the Atlantic were great explainers, but in New England they felt they had to raise their voices to be heard, and the Cambridge Platform was erected that they might be even more audible, a sort of dais set up in Harvard Yard the New England Way to show. Something of that urgent necessity prevailed in the American experience, the felt need to justify one's existence through testament and testimony, an unwillingness to let the naked deed stand unseen but to immortalize it in that most fragile of monuments, the printed page.

This American impulse is not wholly Puritan in its origins—witness the writings of Captain John Smith—but the uniqueness of the New England contribution is evidenced by that indisputably native product, Ben Franklin's *Autobiography,* which was, like so many of his inventions, less an original creation than an improvement. Franklin's great book is, among other things, a secularization of a favorite Puritan genre, spiritual autobiography, a literary manifestation of the habitual sifting of the stuff of one's days and deeds for signs of election, writing not *apologias* but *apocalypses,* uncoverings of the evidence of divine purpose. The writing of Puritan history in America is a variation on this same impulse, perhaps more *epochalypsis* than *apocalypsis,* being a matter of covering up as well as selecting events the better to display the indisputable evidence of God's presence in New England.

As a version of prophecy, Puritan history is untrustworthy as fact, yet as it is more fiction, so it approximates myth, providing a communal equivalent to the perilous adventures of Captain John Smith. It is, as Cotton Mather suggested, a song of arms and the men ("Virosque")—a significant variation of the Virgilian tag. As the Virginian map resulted from a dream of Cathay, so the New England

"Christianography" (again, Mather) was derived from the millennial hope, a gleaming sequence which became the golden thread of true epic. Milton's grand design was certainly touched by his experiences during Oliver Cromwell's reign, and Bunyan's *Holy War* took its metaphor directly from the campaigns of the man with peace in his name but a sword in his hand, yet both were anticipated by Edward Johnson's *Wonder-Working Providence* (1653), the most considerable response in America to the Civil War at home. A mingling of martial figures with a sense of providential purpose, Johnson's provincial epic put forth an early version of Manifest Destiny, thereby transforming forever the Puritan errand and giving a primacy to the narratives of the Pequot War over the pacific emphasis of *First Fruits*.

In terms of numbers, the chief artifacts of Puritan literature are sermons, which contributed much in terms of metaphor and allusion to the gathering tradition. But the sermon lacks the narrative line essential to an epic plan, and while exhorting to deeds, it seldom contains (save in a restrictive sense) action. Moreover, though responsive to political as well as pious issues, it hardly responds to the landscape, sharing with the secular literature of seventeenth-century England an aesthetic limitation which accentuates the Puritan tendency to see the New World as through their Bibles—darkly. Filtering the American scene through an ecclesiastical sieve of typological images, the Puritans' sermons paint holy landscapes which may have reinforced their sense of being a special people, but which resemble ancient Israel more than contemporary New England. Puritan histories often are guilty of similar aesthetic liabilities, and are dominated by biblical analogies, but because of the historical necessity to pay heed to the press and heave of real event, theocratic chroniclers could not ignore the determining lie of the land. The difference between the account of the Pilgrims' first impression of the New World in *Mourt's Relation* and Bradford's revisionist apostrophe is the difference between Cape Cod seen plain and seen through a typological porthole, yet the landscape remains recognizably New England and cannot be confused with the Sinai Peninsula. Compare William Hubbard's allusion to Exodus in his account of Hooker's migration to Hooker's own use of the same in his exhorting sermon and you have the difference between metaphor and mere analogy.

In Puritan histories, as in their sermons and on the title page of their Geneva Bible, it is the Red Sea crossing which dignifies their testaments of faith, a picture in which Canaan is marked by only the dimmest of distant clouds. But since the wilderness in fact gave geopolitical shape to events by means of western rivers as well as an eastern ocean, those rivers play a definitive part in the unfolding action, influential in determining the imperial design, lending symbolic meaning as keys to tragedies and triumphs on the boundaries of the Puritan world. As in matters of undeniable record, New England rivers in New England histories become thresholds of advance, and thereby contribute to the pattern of progress, being waymarks of providential passages quite different from—even antagonistic to—the kinds of evidence garnered by John Winthrop in his journal-catalogue of events especially selected to prove New England's singular blessedness.

That journal is the primary stuff of subsequent histories, being a record of the rhythms of expansion and contraction in New England, the painful throes of reluctant imperial birth. It is, however, a chronicle dominated by the Governor's bias, providing a definitive warp for the several works which were dependent on it for matters of fact, a slant which tended to be accentuated by the nostalgic impress of later writers. And yet in those histories, as in the Governor's journal, we get occasional flashes of light through imperfect seams, a disjunctive dimension equivalent to those inadvertent emphases in the earliest propaganda for settlement. A joint in the Puritans' shining armor, the disjunctiveness reveals the strain between fact and official fiction, the kind of tiny opening through which those American Sir Johns—Oldham, Mason, and Underhill—could slip like Proteus himself, and bending to that hole in Winthrop's great Wall, with the linsey-woolsey brotherhood we detect the green and golden gleam of a distant river valley.

ii. Assert Eternal Providence

Governor Bradford's *Of Plimoth Plantation* is at once the most provincial and the most cosmopolitan of Puritan histories, for if the Pilgrim adventure at times resembles *Robinson Crusoe*, Bradford's heroes, like Defoe's, take a long time getting to their island. To borrow their own favorite figure, the Pilgrims wander about Egypt through nearly half of Bradford's book, the two volumes forming something like the Old and New Testaments in that respect. As if to reinforce the difference, the first of his two books is divided by chapters, the second by years, suggesting that time began for the Pilgrims with 1620, the *Anno* in which they came into their American domain. And there is meaning also, though unintended, in the fact that Bradford's history was not so much left unfinished as abandoned, his increasing doubts concerning Plymouth's future trailing off into a disconsolate *"Anno 1647. And Anno 1647,"* even the *"Domini"* of earlier entries dropping off, a signature of doubt resolved by silence.

The failure of the Pilgrim utopia is signaled by the Puritans' eventual loss of mastery, their drift into disarray, and the manner as well as the matter of Bradford's history gives expression to decline, being latterly a rumination on the ruins of hope. John Winthrop may accord room to defeats as well as victories in his journal, but Bradford accommodates them, even exaggerates them, running a magnifying glass over the grosser warts on the face of event. This is what lends his book its distinctive quality of drama, a tendency to promote, consciously or otherwise, the Pilgrims' conflicts and confrontations. Where Winthrop maintains a dry and matter-of-fact (if occasionally acerb) manner, Bradford further enlivens his narrative with a highly charged, personal account of things, and though he reflects the communal nature of the Pilgrims' enterprise by avoiding the first for the third person, the overall effect is of a considerable investment of self. A maker of fustian when a weaver in Holland, as a writer Bradford produces much homelier cloth, the Puritan "plain style" by which "simple truth" is best rendered, but the pattern still reveals the driving force of a masterful shuttle.

As a narrative, Bradford's history has a highly episodic appearance, separate parts which upon close inspection reveal a subjective unity based on association. It is by such means that rivers take on symbolic meaning as zones of conflict triggered by trade, the Connecticut a scene of successive quarrels with the Dutch and Bay Colony Puritans, Bradford's several entries providing an epitome of the comedy of supplantation there. The highest point of unintended humor occurs toward the end, when the quarrel with the Dorcester interlopers on Winslow's property became a matter of prior providential claims, the Pilgrims maintaining "that if it was the Lord's waste, it was themselves that found it so, and not they" (II: 221). But rather than push their priorities, the Pilgrims finally "thought it better to let them have it upon as good terms as they could get," "forcible resistance being far from their thoughts (they had enough of that about Kennebeck)" (223).

The Connecticut comedy is matched by the tragedy on the Kennebeck, which likewise arose from the presence of a Plymouth trading post there, succeeding events providing a diagram of those conflicting necessities, mingled with circumstances, that define the Pilgrim experience as rendered by William Bradford in his great ledger of profit and loss. His version of the Kennebeck affair, like so much of his history, is padded with letters received and accounts still receivable, a considerable amount of both relating to Isaac Allerton, the dubious factor responsible for establishing the venture on the northern river, in 1628. Commencing with a discussion of Allerton's role, Bradford goes on to discuss the consequent introduction by the Dutch of wampum as a medium of exchange in New England, its acquisition and manufacture by the Narragansetts making them rich, powerful, and arrogant. The Indians' new-found wealth, moreover, gave them the means to buy guns and powder from unscrupulous traders, rendering them more dangerous than ever to the colony. From this gloomy topic, Bradford moves on to Thomas Morton's career in America, his arrest and punishment for teaching Indians the use of guns occurring in the same fatal year as the founding of the Kennebeck trading post.

Ranging back and forth in time, and up and down the coast, Bradford employs a method that is cumulative and associative, the Kennebeck episode turning on the issue of Indians and firearms and framed by the dealings of Allerton, both early and late, on the river and elsewhere. An epitome of the ills of trade, the Kennebeck venture limped on for years, providing no end of troubles between Plymouth and Massachusetts, a version of sibling rivalry that like the Connecticut affair spelled the doom of the first born but weakest of the two. The rivalry on the Kennebeck erupted finally in bloody violence, darkening into melodrama, "one of the saddest things that befell them since they came," tragedy triggered (as so often was the case) by a person from Piscataqua, "one Hocking" who "went with a bark and commodities to trade in that river, and would needs press into their limits, and not only so, but would needs go up the river above their house (toward the falls of the river), and intercept the trade that should come to them" (II: 174-76). When it was over, Hocking was dead and so was a Pilgrim named Moses Talbott, but that was just the beginning of the trouble, not the end.

The incident was also recorded by John Winthrop, who "feared it would give occasion to the king to send a general governor over, and besides it had brought us all and the gospel under a common reproach of cutting one another's throats for beaver" (I: 124). That there be more forebearance than beaver the matter was taken before the General Court of Massachusetts, and John Alden was bound over as a witness, clapped in jail until such time as he could speak for himself and the other Pilgrims involved. The bloody events of 1634 ended with mutual expressions of "love and thankfulness," but, as with most such embraces by Massachusetts, Plymouth went away feeling her pocket had been picked. The final symbol of that feast of love is Bradford's account of the wrangling with the Bay Colony over their boundary line, which turned on a tributary to the Charles: "A small river, or brook rather, that a great way within land trended southward" (II: 278-79). Bradford's progressive reduction of the "small river" to a "brook," and (later on) to a "runlet or small brook," is a study in geopolitical rhetoric dominated by the ridiculousness inherent in the petty terms of the quarrel. But it was also prophetic, for Plymouth would herself become a diminished tributary to the Bay, as meager a current as her own Town Brook.

There is some meaning, therefore, in the coincidence that blends the guttering out of the Plymouth candle with Edward Johnson's lighting the Boston beacon, Bradford abandoning his chronicle about the time that the Massachusetts man was publishing his, but other than this chancy connection there is little in common between the two books. For while Bradford's history commences with affairs in Europe, it becomes increasingly reduced in scope and scene, at the last an example of monumentalized minutiae, local history as epic, its intended audience merely "the children of these fathers," who would be made to say, following the words of Deuteronomy, *"Our fathers were English men which came over this great ocean, and were ready to perish in this wilderness, but they cried unto the Lord, and he heard their voice, and looked on their adversity, etc."* (I: 156-8). But Johnson intended his voice to be heard beyond the Bay, and though the burden of his *Wonder-Working Providence* is on events in America, its weight is thrown in quite another direction. Without openly attempting to snatch the victory from Cromwell's triumphant army, Johnson hints heavily that the decisive battle has been fought in western wilds, that the true Church is building in New England, where Christ's "golden candlesticks" provide a harbinger of millennial glory.

Where Bradford's chronicle fades into silence, Johnson's fairly trumpets with brassy assurance, a hallelujah chorus as scored by Bunyan. In *First Fruits*, providences were presented as evidence of Christ's impending arrival, but for Johnson Christ is already come, Winthrop's model commonwealth no longer a peaceable kingdom of love but an epic territory. For Johnson's is a Cromwellian Christ, a New World Achilles, "our first simile of a soldier," leading the Puritans in a series of victories over all manner of iniquity (121). The militant and manifestly predestinarian quality of Puritan New England is epitomized by Johnson's strenuously heroic line, the author himself a symbolic blend of carpenter-and-militia-captain, well qualified to create an armor-clad Christ. The effect is to shape the details of the Puritan experience in America—the "Wilderness Work"—into a coherent and sometimes poetic narrative, a legitimate epic dominated by a pervading millennialism and given shape by a martial conceit. Johnson's opening and closing chapters are keyed to the apocalyptic language of Revelation, but his narrative throughout is colored by military language, his version of New England's progress being an alliterative quick-march toward Armageddon: "Behold the worthies of Christ, as they are boldly loading forth his troops into these western fields, mark them well man by man as they march, terrible as an army with banners" (49). In Johnson's terms, New England is less an asylum than a proving ground for Christ's "ordinances," a word which has for the Captain a sulphurous smell of powder and shot.

Johnson evokes the Exodus analogy for the Puritans' wilderness errand, and John the Baptist too, but his favorite biblical type is the archetypal supplanter of Esau, Jacob, whose "mighty God" is the "God of Armies" (85). Johnson styles the Puritans "Jacobites," perhaps not the most happy choice in the long view, but one which preserves theocratic sanctions against finding post-Exodus Canaans in New England, and toward that end also he figures Jordan on his metaphoric map as a "boisterous, billow-boiling ocean," typological equivalent of the Red Sea (238). Still, Johnson's dominant figures are explicitly expansionistic, and though Massachusetts is presented as a staging area for apocalypse, the realities of wilderness encounter impinges on the biblical landscape. The outbreak of the Pequot War made it necessary for the Puritans to "face to the front," which was in the back parts of New England, to the west, and it is in Johnson's history that "frontier" begins to take on American connotations, not as a permanent, national border, but as a quasi-military, geopolitical line—an advancing edge of civilization and Christ (147, 90).

Because of his dominant metaphor, Johnson figures the process of settlement as a relentless attack on the wilderness, colonists "tearing up the roots and bushes with their hoes . . . coming through the strength of Christ to . . . readily rush through all difficulties" (85). It is a heroic work, "the toil of a new plantation being like the labors of Hercules, never at an end" (114). As the Crossing dominates his imagery, so the river becomes more a barrier than a blessing, progress in Johnson's book being symbolized by the importance of bridges to the advancing process: "The constant penetrating farther into this wilderness, hath caused the wild and uncouth woods to be filled with frequented ways, and the large rivers to be overlaid with bridges passable, both for horse and foot" (234). This linear, technological thrust is epitomized by affairs in Concord, where the river is blocked by falls which keep salmon downstream and cause flooding of the meadows. In Herculean fashion, the people of Concord have tried to divert the water by cutting through the falls, "but cannot, yet it may be turned another way with an hundred pound charge, as it appeared" (110). It is at this critical juncture that the advancing edge of civilization takes on a heroic shape, suggesting that topographical barriers are not to be confused with providential design. Where the eye of God does not open a way, gunpowder will.

Thinking to facilitate navigation from Concord to the Bay, Johnson had no use for passages to India, alluding to explorers who "believed they had found out another sea" so as to ridicule the "phantastical revelations" of sectarian "opinionists" (243). Johnson's world is Winthrop's, "towns close compact in desert land," and at the center is fortress Boston, its three hills "like over-topping towers keeping a constant watch to foresee the approach of foreign dangers, being furnished with a beacon and loud babbling guns, to give notice by their redoubled echo to all their sister-towns" (258; 71). "The wonder of this modern age," epitome of mercantile and military progress, Boston serves as symbol of a "nation born in a day," nascent nationalism which is a strategic revision of the "chief end of the plantation," as stated in the Charter (61). Captain Johnson's account of New England's accomplishment pays little attention to the Pauline part of Winthrop's original errand, identifying the Indians as antagonists chiefly: "not only men, but devils" (165). As for the labors of John Eliot and his associates, "the particulars . . . being already published, no further need be spoken" (264).

Because of his militant emphasis, Captain Johnson, like Captain John Smith, gives English America a martial identity, no longer as a spearhead of empire but as the imperial thing itself. Setting forth the rudiments of a technological consciousness, a progressive, pragmatic attitude which champions the straight line as an heroic version of utility, Johnson lends his forward thrust an extra measure of velocity by means of his religious zeal, chewing through God's plenty with a triumphant (if whining) resonance—not unlike the singing of a saw. Bridging rivers and blowing obstructions clear, the Massachusetts' mechanism of progress stretched out roadways where rivers did not go, lines of communication that spelled the end of the Puritans' original errand even as they put forth the lineaments of an independent nation. Celebrating the Cambridge Platform, Johnson's *Wonder-Working Providence* lends it the glory of imperial fire, and when the smoke and flames have cleared away, it proves to have been the scaffolding of Manifest Destiny.

iii. Apostolic Blows and Knocks

Johnson's Holy War anticipated by more than twenty years the Bunyanesque mode, but his tale of Christian soldiery in Massachusetts seems to have found few readers in Cromwell's England, nor was it particularly well received in Connecticut and points west. By Johnson's account, the Pequot War was won by Bay Colony forces, a slight which seems to have inspired the General Court at Hartford to commission Major Mason's account of the affair and which most certainly moved Lion Gardiner to record his thoughts on the subject. "Our New England 12-penny chronicle" he growled, is "stuffed with a catalogue of the names of some as if they had deserved immortal fame, but the right New England military worthies are left out for want of room, as Major Mason, Captain Underhill, and Lieutenant Sielley &c, who undertook the desperate way and design to Mystic Fort and killed 300, burnt the fort, and took many prisoners, though they are not once named" (30-31). Nor is Gardiner, and his grudge against Massachusetts for neglecting to mention Lion's share of the war is matched by his resentment over Connecticut's failure to reimburse him for expenses incurred while he was commander of Saybrook Fort.

Some such slight caused Gardiner in 1638 to leave Saybrook for an island on Long Island Sound, and by 1656 he had moved to Long Island itself, from whence, like Winthrop, he viewed the Puritan's glorious victory as through a telescope, backwards. Apologizing for his lack of skill with the "smoothing plane," Gardiner characterized his narrative as "a piece of timber scored and forehewed, unfit to join to any handsome piece of work," and suggested that someone should be found "to smooth it lest the splinters should prick some men's fingers, for the truth must not be spoken at all times" (3). Gardiner's pose resembles that stock Elizabethan character, the Malcontent, and the "piece of work" described sounds mightily like the club of Juvenalian satire, Gardiner having hewn the events of the war into a cudgel. While acknowledging Mason's great victory, he regards the war itself as no providential drama, but a series of blunders with a lucky conclusion, an action in which near tragedy emerged from a trifle. Underhill and Mason see themselves as soldiers of God, but Gardiner casts himself as Mordecai, the Jew at the Gate, challenging all who would enter the Connecticut Israel by means of the river road. But unlike Mordecai, he is also a victim of neglect, a watchman unheard, a wilderness voice finding a deaf ear in Connecticut.

Gardiner's controlling figure and fact is the fort, and by sticking to things as he saw them, he necessarily sees them from Saybrook, a point of view which gives his *Relation* a certain unity, but one which presents an eccentric perspective, the "victory to the glory of God and the honor of our nation" at Mystic being accorded something less than a sentence (20). By contrast, the fate of the Boston trader, John Tilley, is given a page and a half, his capture having taken place within sight of the fort as a result of Tilley's rude refusal to heed Gardiner's warning about the dangers of Indian attack. Where Underhill depicts Tilley as an innocent victim of Pequot treachery, Gardiner flays him as an example of stubborn greed, part and parcel of his main stress on preparedness, his lament concerning "the pride and security which hath been the ruin of many nations, as woeful experience hath proved" (22). For Gardiner's lecture on the stupidities which resulted in the Pequot War (his account of Endecott's campaign is a delight) is chiefly intended to forewarn New England lest history repeat itself, emphasizing past blunders so as to illustrate present dangers.

A builder of fortifications in the Old World and the New, Gardiner was by profession an advocate of preparedness, and half his narrative is devoted to repeating the rumors of Narragansett plots against the English spread by Uncas after the war, old fears through which Gardiner hoped to renew the mood that inspired the long-neglected Confederation. He complains that he had warned "the Governors of these parts" about the danger of Indian uprising, but

I see they have done as those of Wethersfield did, not regarding their peril till they were impelled to it by blood, and thus we may be sure the fattest of the flock are like to go first if not all together, and then it will be too late to read. Jer. 25. For drink we shall if the Lord be not the more merciful to us, for our extreme pride and base security which cannot but stink before the Lord, and we may expect this yet if there should be wars again between England and Holland, for our friends the Dutch and our Dutch Englishmen would prove as true to us now as they were when the fleet came out of England. But no more of that, a word to the wise is enough. And now I am old, I would fain die a natural death or like a soldier in the field with honor, and not to have a sharp stake set in the ground and thrust into my fundament and to have my skin flayed off by piecemeal and cut in pieces and bits and my flesh roasted and thrust down my throat as these people have done, and I know will be done to the chiefest in the country by hundreds if God should deliver us into their hands as justly He may for our sins (23-24).

Gardiner's view of the wilderness as punitive terrain has a sharpness missing from Underhill's picture, his stake suggesting nothing so much as the splintery Juvenalian implement evoked in his opening pages, planted in historical precedent and pointed toward one overwhelming truth—the Swiftian premise that felicity amidst savagery is possible only by massive doses of self-deception and foolish pride.

Designed to refute Johnson in particulars, Gardiner's *Relation*, by its emphasis on fundamental facts not conformable to firmamental views, amounts to a more general rebuttal. The Puritans usually made short shrift of contradictory opinions, and when Gardiner's manuscript was placed in the hands of John Winthrop Junior—by then the Governor of Connecticut—he in turn placed it in a document box, where it remained for more than two centuries. As a result, unlike Mason's *History*, Gardiner's narrative had no influence on subsequent versions of the Pequot War, yet his rough-hewn work would have a long heritage in New England. Aside from his burden of refutation, Gardiner shared with Johnson a fortress-centered sense of New England, and his defensive view of the landscape is but a counterpart to Johnson's antagonistic advance, giving the wilderness a human and hostile shape.

233

About the time that Gardiner sat down to his chisel and holdfast, William Bradford wrote a quaint version of medieval complaint, a poem entitled "Some Observations of God's Merciful Dealing with us in this Wilderness." Despite its title, Bradford's poem shares the doubtful mood with which his history of Plymouth Plantation closes, evoking an atmosphere of omnipresent threat which serves as Jeremian complement to Gardiner's Juvenalian view of New England's hazardous condition. For Bradford's "camp of Israel" is a garden choked with "noisome weeds" of "pride and oppression," an American Gomorrah: "Whoredom, and drunkenness, with other sin, / Will cause God's judgments soon to break in" (473). As in Gardiner's *Relation,* the chief instrument of divine judgment will be the Indian, hitherto filled by God with "dread" of the English, the Puritan community remaining inviolable: "No woman wronged in her chastity / By any of them, through God's great mercy" (467). But as divine immanence is withdrawn, rape becomes imminent, for the Puritan instrument of power, the musket, is now in the hands of New England's devilish adversaries: "Like madmen we put them in a way / With our own weapons us to kill and slay" (475). Reading these signs, and thinking on the "fair precedent" of Israel after "the elders and Joshua were dead," Bradford fears for "New England's fate" (477).

Like Gardiner's lambasting, Bradford's lament remained in manuscript, but both are signs of the times, being registers of altered moods produced by new occasions. They are also prophetic, looking forward to the general Indian uprising which both men feared, the revolt that was sparked if not lead by King Philip, a conflict far more devastating both to Indians and English than was the Pequot War. Thenceforth the character of the Puritans' errand and their literature would lend a painful meaning to the symbol on Massachusetts' seal: as in Drowne's copper image atop the Province House, the iconographic Indian in Massachusetts had by century's end set his arrow to his bow. It was apparently in reference to the beckoning Macedonian that Philip received his royal sobriquet, a droll bit of Puritan fun, but like Pocahontas-Rebecca, Metacomet-Philip proved an agent of ironic reversal. From Macedonian to Amalek, from spawn of Satan to minister of divine vengeance, from Canaanite to instrument of papist Canada, the metamorphosis of the American Esau is a bloody register of the shifting winds of change.

iv. Devilish Engines

In his dockside sermon, John Cotton quoted Jeremiah 2:21, warning against the danger of letting the noble and holy Vine of Psalm 80 decline in the second generation. But that Psalm is also a lament, like Bradford's poem, expressing anguish during a period of tribulation, the Psalmist looking back to a time of prosperity in Israel when the garden was green and God's protective hedge was strong. John Winthrop aboard the *Arbella* likewise warned his people about the dangers of neglecting contracts with God—a decidedly testy sleeping partner to enterprise—in a negative but (like Cotton's) minority note. By 1670 this Jeremian strain had begun to swell in New England, as the theocracy strove to maintain its hold over the minds and hearts of a second and (by all pulpit accounts) heedless generation. As a consequence there was a significant revision of the magic-lantern show with which Puritan preachers gave biblical shape to the Massachusetts landscape, and the panorama was no longer Moses and his wandering Camp of Israel, but the threatened, accursed Garden of Jeremiah.

When Samuel Danforth took his election-day auditors out into a metaphorical wilderness to consider New England's errand in 1670, he did not show them a reed shaking in the wind (though he may have left them trembling somewhat when he was done). But neither did he speak of spreading "the light of the blessed Gospel" among the heathen, which was the purpose of the Bay Colony according to Winthrop's Charter and *First Fruits*. Though he shared his Roxbury parish with John Eliot, Danforth spoke only of "enjoying the pure worship of God in the wilderness," an "errand" which in his opinion "we have in a great measure forgotten" (61, 65). In the language of the Prophets and Paul, Danforth scolded his listeners and reminded them of the signs of God's displeasure, not only "blasting and mildew now seven years together, superadding sometimes severe drought, sometimes great tempests, floods, and sweeping rains that leave no food behind them," but "blazing stars, earthquakes, dreadful thunders and lightnings, fearful burnings" (74). It would not be long before Boston's Samuel would be proven a prophet, for New England was engulfed by a very red sea as a passing meteor set fire to heaven and hearth.

In 1654, Edward Johnson did not neglect to list negative providences, but they are mere "jogs of the elbow" by a paternalistic deity, broad hints written "as in great capital letters" to remind the Puritans "of the end of their coming over" (253-54). But full score and three years later the elbow unbent into a punishing arm, writing letters that burned across the sky, spelling an end that was not an errand but a day of doom, nor was Increase Mather slow to take the hint. Sermons, like poems, often serve occasion, and Mather wrote a sermonic history of King Philip's War that nearly outran event: published in 1676, the ink of his *Brief History* was wet before the blood shed in the war had dried. In accounting for the outbreak of King Philip's War, Mather called it a "dreadful judgment" on the people of New England for not having "pursued, as ought to have been, the blessed design of their fathers, in following the Lord into this wilderness, whilst it was a land not sown" (47). The narrative history which Mather constructed from this basic premise is antithetical to Johnson's *Wonder-Working Providence*, being a negative epic of cosmic reverses not advance.

The strategy of the jeremiad is a crabbed providentiality, taking painful comfort from punishment as evidence of God's continued if angry presence. Since the advent of Jesus Christ in Massachusetts (and the restoration of the Old Charter) seemed to have been indefinitely postponed, Puritan prophets were perversely pleased to find Satan in their midst. Like children begging for the rod in preference to parental neglect, they came to need Indians as they earlier needed a wilderness, not as objects of charity, but as engines of torment. But in assuming the angry posture of the Jewish Prophets, the theocracy realigned the New England landscape, for one effect of abandoning the Pentateuch for the prophetic books of the Old Testament was to transplant Massachusetts beyond the Jordan, not to a Canaan of milk and honey, but to the wormwood world of Jeremiah and Judges. Thus Increase Mather in his *Brief History* may describe New England as "that part of the English Israel which is seated in these goings down of the sun," as a land that "the Lord God of our fathers hath given to us for a rightful possession," but the burden of his account of King Philip's War suggests that what God hath given to the fathers he may take away from the sons (46). New England is Israel, but it is no blessed asylum, and though by a leap of faith the Puritans have managed to cross the Jordan without having wet their feet, Mather's point is consistent with theocratic logic, his punitive landscape affirming the wilderness idea that covenants with God allow for no permanent prospect of peace.

Mather's emphasis and his further reach are driven home by the sermon appended to his short history of the war, a jeremiad proper, holding out a warning easy to read in its running title, "To Hearken to the Voice of God in His Late and Present Dispensations" or risk "another Judgment, Seven Times Greater than any Thing which yet hath been." Reminding his readers of the imperfect results of Samuel's exhortations to reform, Mather in his *Brief History* suggests that despite the defeat of the Wampanoags and Narragansetts sufficient "Philistines" are left to "prove a sore scourge to the children of Israel," so that the people of New England may not "glory in anything that we have done, but rather be ashamed and confounded for our own ways" (205-6). What consolations Mather gives are indirect, as in his transformation of the terrors of an unreasoning, anthropomorphic wilderness into the strokes of a chastising rod, wielded by a rational, anthropomorphic deity. The year of terrible suffering is figured as a visit by a divine physician, who determined "we were not yet fit for deliverance, nor could health be restored unto us except a great deal more blood be first taken from us" (62). Yet Mather's emphasis is on the necessity for complete reformation, insisting that "*praying* without *reforming* will not do" (96).

Because of his prophetic stance, Mather's version of the war conveys the impression that it was largely fought from the pulpit, the turning of the tide of battle coming close upon "a day of humiliation by fasting and prayer attended in the Town-house at Boston"—a perspective not unlike Winthrop's on the Pequot business (144). King Philip's is Samuel's war, not David's, hence inconclusive, planted firmly in the landscape of Judges, and when Mather celebrates the decisive victory of the English at Turner's Falls on the Connecticut, he neglects to give the name of the river but instead fuses the event to scriptural scenery: " 'The river Kishon swept them away, that ancient river, the river Kishon, O my soul thou hast trodden down strength.' And all this

237

while but one Englishman killed, and two wounded" (147). The return from Judges: 5:21 to providential statistics is sudden enough, but the effect of the quotation is to transform the Connecticut into the waters of the Megiddo, which, though they flow into the Mediterranean, on the Puritan map provide a bloody counterpart to Jacob's Jordan.

In terms of sacred geography, Increase Mather clarifies the setting of Danforth's sermon, lifting New England out of the wilderness of Moses, thereby transforming the meaning of adversity and redefining the end of the Puritan errand. For what lies ahead of Jeremiah and the Judges is not the pastoral prospect of Canaan but the wasted, withered Vine, threatened as in Psalm 80 by the boar from the wood, a view which will increasingly obtain from Boston pulpits. But there is in this regard no stronger refutation of the notion of Puritan consistency than the account of King Philip's War written by William Hubbard, in form and function the antithesis of Mather's. Hubbard's *The Present State of New-England, Being a Narrative of the Troubles with the Indians* (1677) is also the patterning seed of his later, much larger *General History of New England* (c. 1680), and since the first was more popular than Mather's version, the second never published by the General Court of Massachusetts (which commissioned it), Hubbard's view and sympathies seem to have been larger than those obtaining (or desirous to obtain) in Boston. Something of a Demosthenes, Hubbard as historian of the Indian War favored the Philippic to the prophetic vein.

v. Equal Hope and Hazard

William Hubbard's personality comes through his writings and helps to explain their difference, for he was a broad-minded and cosmopolitan preacher, as likely to reach for a Latin quotation as a biblical one, and his favorite Jewish ancient is that shrewd maximizer, Solomon. Hubbard evinces a love of balance and proportion which, along with his well-tempered Calvinism and dry wit, suggests an eighteenth- rather than a seventeenth-century sensibility, and in no way evokes that cant-ridden cliché, a New England Puritan divine. Characteristically, Hubbard was slow to accept his ministerial call, studied medicine while at Harvard, and took a skeptical view of the witchcraft hysteria. He seems to have welcomed the restoration of monarchy in England, but his Toryism stopped at ocean's edge, for he took a strong stand against Andros's presence and policies in Massachusetts. His innate political conservatism is revealed by his great election-day sermon, identifying the Happiness of a People with hierarchical sanctions, and in his account of New England's history he is in sympathy with Winthrop's oligarchical way. Yet even here his opinions have a Burkean ring, putting faith in "such a constitution of government as doth sufficiently secure the liberties of the people from oppression," guarding against "popular confusion" as well as "tyrannical usurpation" (185).

Hubbard's stress in his *General History* (as above) on "the general good of the whole" is central to his political philosophy, at once harmonious with Puritan social theory and of a piece with neoclassical political (and aesthetic) conservatism. It likewise informs his account of King Philip's War, and where Mather's version is shaped to a sermonic necessity, Hubbard's more ambitious project takes shape from a skeptical, neoclassical, and balanced view, assuming a narrative rather than a discursive shape. Hubbard pillaged Mather's account for images and allusions, but he built them into a unique version of epic, the neoclassical overtones of which are accentuated by his reduction of the providential and especially the punitive element. Hubbard preferred to stress the civil and territorial aspects of the struggle, and he likewise seems to have felt that the proper observance of Christ's ordinances was less important to the safety of wilderness settlement than were proper fortifications. His stress is on the necessity for law and order in a new country, but he tempers his admonitions of backsliding Saints with observations concerning the positive implications of Metacomet's defeat.

In sum, where Mather's version is theopolitical, Hubbard hews to a geopolitical line, a difference dramatized by comparing their attitudes toward the fate of Thomas Wakely, a Casco Bay settler who was killed by the Indians. Mather, who describes Wakely as a "godly man," portrays him as troubled of soul, believing that God was angry with him "because although he came into New England for the Gospels' sake, yet he had left another place in this country, where there was a church of Christ, which he once was in communion with, and had lived many years in a plantation where there was no *church nor instituted worship*" (89-90). Hubbard, however, describes "old Wakely" as a restless spirit, who "some years before removed from Gloucester, or Cape Anne, out of some discontent, which afterwards he often bewailed, resolving either to have returned back, or else to have removed to some securer place; but he was arrested by the Sons of Violence before he could affect his purpose" (II: 103). In Hubbard's account, Wakely's fate has less to do with the state of his soul than his sole estate, living "so far from neighbors, or else encompassed with creeks or rivers, that no relief could presently be sent to him" (103-4).

This topographical note further separates Mather and Hubbard as historians of the war. Where Mather muddles his geography by lumping Wakely's death with events west of the Merrimack, Hubbard includes it in the second part of his book, subtitled "From Piscataqua to Pemmiquid," a division (and title) which enforces his geopolitical emphasis. Hubbard maintains a distinction between Massachusetts proper and the improprieties beyond the Merrimack, segregating King Philip's War from the related troubles to the east. The main conflict took place between the Merrimack and the Connecticut, and like most Massachusetts affairs, it had a successful and tidy termination, while the situation east of the Merrimack was murky and messy, the struggle there emerging from a long history of misrule and violence and continuing long after King Philip was dead and his people defeated. This is the region of the "Philistines" held by Mather over the heads of his readers, but by Hubbard's accounting it is an American backwoods, and if his divisions and emphases are integral to his neoclassical bias, they also reveal his abiding consciousness of the landscape as a political symbol.

At the center of his history of King Philip's War, Hubbard places a map of New England, drawn to illustrate his "Register" of the "Wars of the Lord," an iconographic alternative to William Wood's melioristic map of some forty years earlier. Not only does it delineate a much larger territory, but it puts forth a martial not a pacific topography, epic not georgic in implication: Framed by the Connecticut and Merrimack, Hubbard's battle map includes the lesser streams of New England, figured no longer as canals but as sharp, imperial blades. Where Wood marked townships by tiny, cross-bearing orbs, Hubbard uses miniature walled communities, surmounted by peaked-roof towers, and in the East, beyond the Piscataqua, two small savages may be seen, bearing muskets as they emerge from a patch of woods. A gloss on this war map is provided by the stress of a poem by Benjamin Tompson, which prefaces Hubbard's history, for though Tompson enrolls Hubbard among Biblical chroniclers like Nathan, they are outnumbered by imperial geographers—Purchas, Hakluyt, and Captain John Smith.

If Hubbard's muse is "old Columbus' ghost," it is a theocratized Christopher where the aboriginal inhabitants are concerned:

> *Former adventurers did at best beguile,*
> *About these natives' rise (obscure as Nile)*
> *Their grand Apostle writes of their return;*
> *Williams of their language; Hubbard how they burn,*
> *Rob, kill and roast, lead captive, slay, blaspheme;*
> *Of English valor too he makes his theme,*
> *Whose tragical account may christened be,*
> New England's Travels through the Bloody Sea (*I: 24*).

As the snide reference to Roger Williams and John Eliot tips Tompson's theopolitics, so his allusion to the Red Sea crossing places the war in an Exodus landscape. Hubbard likewise decorates his title page with texts celebrating Joshua's victory over Amalek, thus stressing the heroic rather than the purgatorial implications of the Puritans' ordeal, but he does not insist on nor does he limit himself to the Mosaic metaphor. His Connecticut is not the River Kishon, but the Styx, and when he evokes the "fiery pillar of the Scripture" and "the dark cloud of Providence," his context suggests a wry condemnation of Mather's eagerness to find evidence of God's presence in New England (II: 249).

In Benjamin Tompson's poetic bulletins on the conduct and course of the war, *New-Englands Crisis* and *New-Englands Tears* (1676), King Philip is portrayed as a lecherous, "greasy *lout*," who proposes to reverse the normal order of things in Massachusetts: "The richest merchants' houses shall be ours, / We'll lie no more on mats or dwell in bowers / We'll have their silken wives, take they our squaws, / They

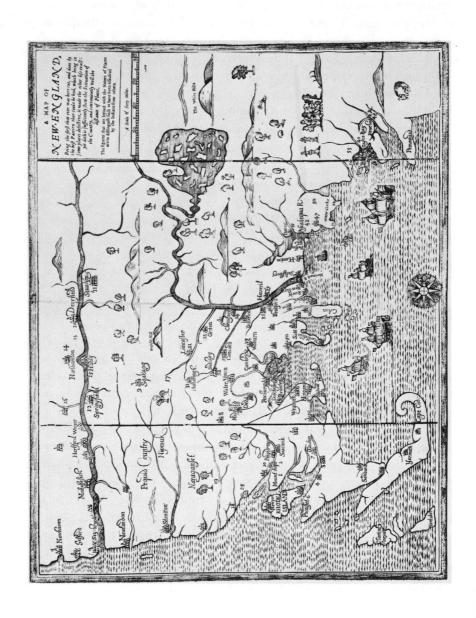

A MAP OF
NEW-ENGLAND,

Being the first that ever was here cut, and done by
the best Pattern that could be had, which being in
some places defective, it made the other less exact:
yet doth it sufficiently shew the Situation of
the Country, and conveniently well the
distance of Places.

The figures that are joyned with the Names of Places
are to distinguish such as have been assaulted
by the Indians from others.

A Scale of forty Miles.

William Hubbard's Map of New England. From The Present State of New-England (1677). Courtesy Rare Book Division, New York Public Library.

Hubbard's New England. Drawn to accompany his account of King Philip's War, Hubbard's militant map should be compared to William Wood's pacific counterpart of some forty years earlier. No longer dominated by the rivers of the Bay, Hubbard's expansionist New England now has the Connecticut as its western border, numerous coastal towns, and the sword-point streams associated with Captain Smith's imperialistic geo-iconography. For an account of the differences between the American and English versions of this map, see Randolph G. Adams, "William Hubbard's Narrative, 1677," Bibliographic Society of America, *Papers*, XXXIII (1939), 25-39.

shall be whipt by virtue of our laws" (54). A figure of misrule, the Indian lurks in "miry swamps better befitting hogs," emerging from his lair in Drydenesque fashion, his "cheeks" providing "banks for grease and mud, a place for leeks," his "locks" resembling ropes or "Medusa's snakes" (64). Tompson's poems add up to a poetic jeremiad, like Mather's sermon, aimed at reforming New England—not her soul, but her manners. As such, they demonstrate the narrow margin between sermonic and satiric whips, and provide a comic counterpart to Hubbard's account of the war, which is a "tragical-historical" action wherein King Philip plays an American version of the Elizabethan hero-villain, chief figure in a drama of purgation—his own and New England's.

Less greasy but still slippery, Hubbard's Philip is portrayed as a veritable Machiavel of evil "designs" and "plots," a ubiquitous figure of iniquity, the evil genius of Revolt. Like Shakespeare's Richard III (and Milton's Satan I), he is cast in the shape of the Devil, "who was a murderer from the beginning," and who has "filled the heart of this savage miscreant with envy and malice against the English" (I: 53). Type and symbol of Rebellion, Philip is a covenant-breaker, a conspirator, a liar, and a traitor, and the issue of the war against him is law and order versus misrule and chaos. If he is characterized as a "Boar out of the Wood," so is Richard III, and Philip is defeated not by an act of God, but by the "staff" and "shields" of the Governors of the Confederated Colonies, to whom Hubbard dedicated his book (9-10). Hubbard's Fence therefore is not a doctrinal Hedge, but "a form and order of government" providing "sufficient fence and security for so great a treasure as is the common good and public safety" (7).

With Tompson, Hubbard depicts Philip and his "crew" as a collective abomination, fit inhabitants of swampy "dens" and "habitations of darkness," bestial symbols of the forces of nature let loose (87; 252). The slayer of this dragon, the hero of Hubbard's play, is "the bold and undaunted champion, Captain Church . . . the terror of the Indians in Plymouth Colony" (82; 262). Benjamin Church stars in the first and last battles with King Philip (like Richmond, he waits in the wings during the intervening acts), yet he is finally disqualified for the role of New England's savior by the circumstances of Philip's death, brought about by a shot from the musket of a deserter from his ranks, "an Indian of his own nation" (266). Still, Hubbard does not see this as a humbling providence, but as a dramatic irony, yet another difference between his use of the war and Mather's. For it is Hubbard's purpose to demonstrate that "although the Almighty hath made use of the Indians to be a scourge to His people, He hath now turned His hand against them, to their utter destruction and extirpation from off the face of the earth, peradventure to make room for others of His people to come in their room, and in their stead" (278-79).

Something further of this difference in strategy between Mather and Hubbard is revealed by comparing their accounts of New England's earlier troubles with the Indians, a *Relation* of which Mather published in the same year as Hubbard's inclusive narrative, in effect providing a backdated supplement to his earlier *Brief History*. Both writers attempted to make up for Edward Johnson's neglect of Connecticut's contribution to the Pequot War by giving credit to Major Mason's decisive victory, each historian depending on the Major's own recollections of his campaign. It is a significant register of their opposing viewpoints that whereas Hubbard cut away Major Mason's references to the Connecticut Canaan and severely reduced the providential matter, Mather retained it all. This discrepancy is enforced by the concluding section to each work, demonstrating the rhetorical means by which Mather and Hubbard employed history to different ends, a disparity which suggests that the word "Puritan," even in Massachusetts, does not always connote a uniform arrangement of blacks and whites.

Thus Mather, instead of ending with another jeremiad, rounded out his 1677 *Relation* with a "Historical Discourse Concerning the Prevalency of Prayer," the body of which is largely made up of proofs "that New England's deliverance from the rage of the heathen is an eminent answer to prayer," a burden which would seem to contradict the argument of his previous *Exhortation* (253-66 *passim*). But in the preface to his melioristic "Discourse," Mather continues to "look for another day of trouble seven times greater" unless "a general reformation takes place in New England" (243-44). Where, in his earlier account, King Philip's War was seen as providential punishment, now it is seen as evidence of divine assistance, a transformation by duration that is further clarified by Mather's use of Mason's conquest of the New England Canaan, the receding past becoming "the TIME when God hath appeared for us" (265). If Mason is allowed his Canaan, it is because New England has become the Israel of the prophets, of whom Mather is the foremost, warning that if the "evils prevailing amongst us . . . be not reformed, the Lord's controversy will not be ended . . . the blessed design of our fathers in coming into this wilderness not being minded and attended as ought to be" (244).

Hubbard, for his part, ends his history of the Indian Wars with a contrary emphasis, an "Epilogue to the Tragical History foregoing," wherein he reassures his reader that God is a wise father who, after whipping His children, throws "the rod into the fire" (II: 261). Having punished them and forgiven them, moreover, He rewards them, "for our enemies to the southward were . . . possessed of many goodly *havens,* many fertile places, as at Mount Hope, and along the Narragansett Country" (261). The Indians having been destroyed by "the special hand of God . . . as were the Pequots before them," the Lord's purpose has obviously been to make way for "a better people," the "troubles" having been a "beautiful work," a cleansing of the land as well as the community (262). In effect, having trimmed the references to the conquest of Canaan from Major Mason's history of the Pequot War, Hubbard reverses Mather's strategy by moving that blessed event forward in time, placing it in the near future. Significantly, he concluded the first half of *Present State*—his account of King Philip's War proper—with Moses' "Tribute of Thankfulness" after Joshua's defeat of Amalek, which took place on the very threshold of the Promised Land (225). While Mather ends with a threatening wave of his Stick, Hubbard gives a tantalizing glimpse of the Carrot, antithetical strategies which have their origins in John Winthrop's ambivalent use of Moses' farewell address to his people.

vi. Where More Is Meant than Meets the Eye

Hubbard's final wilderness stand attests to his loyalty to the forms and language of the literature associated with the Puritan fathers, as he was linked to them through the circumstances of his life, where Increase Mather could only cling to the great chain of his birth, not his being. Mather regards Massachusetts as still troubled ground, but Hubbard makes a clear distinction between the situation on either side of the boundary Merrimack, to the east of which the struggle still goes on. Hubbard places blame for the war in the west squarely on Philip, but the "particulars of the tragedy" in the east indicate considerable guilt on the part of the English, who have angered the Indians by dishonest and callous dealings (II: 93-96). Whereas Massachusetts is a land graced by God and good governance, the recent bloodshed only a blessing in disguise, the eastern region is cursed, being a wasteland of blight and dissention, a *locus sigilli* of divine displeasure: "When a place is *designed to ruin*, everything they take in hand shall tend that way" (173).

Since "place" is the theme, it is also the subject of the opening pages of the second part of his history, "From Piscataqua to Pemmiquid," a region "less frequented, and so more unknown than the other" (70). Where the meaning of events in the "other" place is tied to the breaking of covenants, Hubbard sees the "truth" of the "story" east of the Merrimack as springing from "the places whereon the discourse proceedeth," a territory "being scarce worth half those men's lives that have been lost in these two last years, in hope to save it." Defined by a number of "rivers and havens," which provide "borders," "spots," and "skirts" for settlement, the eastern region has been particularly exposed to "the rage and cruelty of the barbarous and perfidious Indians belonging to that side of the country" (77). But the "tragedy" needs a further "prologue" by way of explanation, "A short Discourse of the first Planting that Side of the Country," for in contrast to the orderly settlement of Massachusetts, the territory beyond the Merrimack was bedeviled by a "multiplicity of grants and patents," conflicting claims acerbated by frequent changes of proprietors and agents (84-86). The result has been a "want of an orderly and settled government" and a lack of "townships and villages," the kind of civil wall which was the protection of the region "this side" the river (89-90).

Set off from Massachusetts by the Merrimack, the eastern territory is divided within itself by rivers and bays, symbolic less of a system of orderly settlement than of faction and misrule. The eastern region is everything that the west is not, a dark and bloody ground whose fate is inextricably bound up in the very fabric of settlement, a tragic territory lacking the redemptive grace of King Philip's War. Where the war in the west is a providential instrument of orderly expansion, the continuing struggle in the east has antithetical implications, suggesting divine disfavor. In the west the dominant frame is provided by the rise and fall of King Philip, while in the east the action is a confusing series of incidents, "treacherous and wicked practices" of white men matched by "bloody and deceitful actions" of the red (82, 94). Hubbard notes in his Epilogue that all of the "irregularities and miscarriages in our transactions and dealings with the Indians" have occurred in the border regions of New England, havens of misrule lacking any *"reprover in the gate,* or Magistrate to put offenders to shame," the inhabitants being free to transform themselves "as well they could into the manners of the Indians they live amongst, and are some of them therefore most deservedly (as to Divine Justice) left to be put under the yoke and power of the Indians themselves" (255-57).

This theocratic gerrymandering carries over into Hubbard's *General History of New England*—like Johnson's, a chronicle chiefly of Massachusetts events—where affairs east of the Merrimack are set aside in two chapters serving for a stage on which Captain Underhill figures prominently (as in a pillory): "As was sometime said of Cain, that he went from the presence of the Lord, and dwelt on the east of Eden, so this gentleman went to the eastward, and made a great bluster among the inhabitants of Exeter and Dover, and ambitiously affected the government amongst them" (353). The irony recalls similar remarks in Winthrop's journal, and since Hubbard relied on that record for the materials of his history, it is not surprising that the symbolic topography of his most ambitious book takes its pattern from the Governor's ideal domain. Moreover, Hubbard shared Winthrop's conservatism, and his version of New England's past tends if anything to be more severely shaped than Winthrop's account of his own times, the historian giving a less random cast to the Governor's chronological record.

Though dutifully recording the providences that Winthrop assiduously gathered, Hubbard is perhaps more loyal to the ideal of the secular Wall, lending a weight of neoclassical unity to asserting the decorum of Place. By his account, God's displeasure tends to fall on Wall-breakers, like the people of New Haven who, having departed Massachusetts for fair western fields, overextended their resources in the vain hope of profit (321 ff.). Wethersfield, similarly, was frequently torn by civil and religious strife which could be traced to Oldham's "indirect means" of settlement, "a kind of surreptitious seizure" (313). In the latter instance, as in his description of troubles beyond the Merrimack, Hubbard colors his providential interpretation with a classical sense of fate, Wethersfield's turbulence attributed to "a kind of fatal necessity," the town "destined to contention." With Underhill's Piscataqua an East of Eden and Hooker's Connecticut a factitious (and faction-torn) Canaan, Hubbard's New England amounts to a fair copy of Winthrop's theopolitical domain—a consolidative, conforming, and concentric world. Careful to point out that it is no "land flowing with milk and honey," Hubbard invokes the standard analogy of Israel in exodus, taking pains to define the essential difference, which was that the Jews had only "to pass through" their wilderness, "and not first plant it," evoking the garden idea and hence a Hesiodic plan (96-97; cf. 52-53).

Though no literal map accompanies his *General History,* Hubbard's metaphoric topography corresponds to William Wood's, being a distinctly middle, which is to say georgic, ground. Preserving the traditional harbor view, in which rivers are "very commodious harbors and havens for ships," Hubbard sketches in a convenient system of waterways that permit passage "into the country with great advantage to the inhabitants on either side" (17, 16). Though he observes regretfully that shipping is blocked by the unfortunate line of falls, he does not involve himself in Johnson's gunpowder plot, nor does Hubbard share the other man's predeliction for militant and millennial metaphors. In contrast to his fiercely vindictive view of King Philip's War, Hubbard's *General History* is a pacific document generally, celebrating not arms, but law and the man in Massachusetts. Progress is measured in terms of due process, and Hubbard is much less interested in the erection of the Cambridge Platform than in the building of the body politic. Hero of the action is Winthrop himself, who had the high purpose, capacity (and estate) to construct a mechanism of government suitable to New World occasions.

It is all the more surprising, then, that the last chapter of Hubbard's *General History* is made up of lengthy exerpts from Daniel Denton's expansionist pamphlet, *A Brief Description of New York* (1670), his consolidationist and conservative emphasis suddenly exploding into encomiums for western regions. It is as if the Governor himself had suddenly thrown off his Puritanic cape and assumed the green mantle of that gay Cavalier, Thomas Morton, kicking a hole in his own wall to display the glories of the Hudson Valley. Hubbard is careful to excise Denton's identification of the Hudson with a "terrestrial Canaan . . . where the land floweth with milk and honey," and yet he preserves the general paradisiac emphasis, including descriptions of "the richness of the soil, the healthfulness of the climate, and the like," adding only a qualifying note concerning "the unhealthfulness of all those places on either side of the Manhattoes, as being flat and low lands, and subject to agues in the summer, which is no small discouragement to them that prize health as they should" (D: 61, 56; H [1878]: 675). But the effect is to enhance the beauty of the other regions described by Denton, like his native Long Island, from which Hubbard trims not a blossom, leaving it "bedecked with roses, and an innumerable multitude of other delightful flowers, not only pleasing to the eye, but smell, that you may behold nature contending with art, and striving to equal if not excel many gardens in England" (H: 671; D: 42-43). Most important, because most paradoxical, Hubbard preserves Denton's expansionist stress: "How many poor people in the world would think themselves happy, had they an acre or two of land, whilst here are hundreds, nay thousands, of acres, that would invite inhabitants" (H: 675; D: 55).

Given Hubbard's ostensible purpose of writing an epical apologia for Winthrop's anti-expansionist policy, it is difficult to understand why he would end his book by including, nearly verbatim, generous helpings from a tract "published as well for the encouragement of many that may have a desire to remove themselves thither, as for the satisfaction of those that would make a trade in those parts" (H: 676; D: 63). Since it counteracts the effectiveness of his own laborious fabric, Hubbard's intrusion of Denton's Doorway in Winthrop's Wall is a massive geopolitical hernia, an extreme example of the disjunctiveness that characterizes Puritan accounts of progress in New England, its strategic location giving it particular weight. Most paradoxical of all is the fact that Daniel was the son of the Reverend Richard Denton, who was involved in the religious contentions of early Wethersfield which were for Hubbard the curse of unwarranted, unlicensed expansion in the early years of New England, spiritual discontent coming in the van of the kind of paradisiac expectations to which the junior Denton gives expression, his a New York version of the Connecticut "Canaan" which Hubbard was earnest to refute.

Counterpoint to this pastoral note is provided by yet another disjunctive element, an anecdote gathered by Hubbard for an intended "further continuation" of his narrative of the Indian Wars that was never published, the material left in manuscript as part of his *General History*. It is the story of Benjamin Wait and Stephen Jennings, who undertook an incredible winter journey into Canada to ransom their wives (taken prisoner in a raid by Indians loyal to France), an adventure which gives expression to a heroic *geist* singular in Hubbard's writings. Traveling from Hatfield on the Connecticut to the Hudson, and from there northward across Lake Champlain (with the help of an Indian guide and a providential canoe), the heroic husbands reached the "Canada River," and then continued on for two hundred more miles to Quebec, from whence they returned in the spring with not only their wives but a band of other redeemed captives. "Their adventure," observes Hubbard, "being attended with so many difficulties and dangers, in the depth of winter, was not to be paralleled with any attempt of that nature since the English came into those parts, wherein they were surely led along by a divine *nutus*, as well as by the innate love to their wives (which would have afforded matter for a large fiction to some of the ancient poets)" (637). Whatever the ancient poets might have done with the story of Wait and Jennings, as Hubbard seems to have sensed it has a deep American resonance, the native epic strain struggling free of biblical analogue, the sacred Puritan family tie given a new dimension by an heroic wilderness journey.

In terms of geopolitics also Hubbard's story is prophetic, the shape of England in America increasingly taking its bias from the north-south axis of the Hudson and Connecticut, reaching forward to empire beyond. In structure and impetus, Hubbard's story prefigures Cooper's *Last of the Mohicans,* a tale of Indian massacre, capture, pursuit, and escape set along the same symbolic corridor, the system of lakes and rivers which was an arena of imperial friction for nearly a century. That long war was just beginning as Hubbard recorded the adventures of Jennings and Wait, and as Cooper's romance is a fictional reprise of historical events of a similar nature, so Hubbard's anecdote is a resonant prelude, anticipating the ur-action of frontier life and literature. With the great Hudson stretching northward out of a paradisiac valley, the concluding pages of Hubbard's *General History* provide a very different diagram from that found in Winthrop's journal, foreshadowing the heroic Kentucky Canaan of Daniel Boone.

During the early stages of King Philip's War it was proposed that a wall be built around the perimeter of Winthrop's Patent, thus giving concrete shape to his mural metaphor while memorializing the failure of his Pauline mission, providing a complex monument to the Puritans' state. But the outcome of the war made such a wall no longer necessary, the Wampanoags and their allies the Narragansetts having been removed, like the Pequots before them, from New England, clearing the ground between the great border rivers, the Merrimack and Connecticut. But as the Indian presence remained on the map by means of Indian names, so as a symbolic device the idea of the Wall endured also, the territorial struggles within the boundary rivers giving way to the border conflicts which followed—acts in a much larger drama. In the process the Puritan engine became a juggernaut, the theocracy trapped within as its wonderful machine moved ponderously into the succeeding century. In the service of consolidation the Wall became a mechanism of expansion, in the dreadful shape of Mather's *Magnalia* heaving toward a fiery conclusion, a Holy War of Yankee design, the Connecticut Canaan giving way to a Carthage in Canada. By century's end the Puritans had finally found their war and their theme, the American Aeneas striding out of the wilderness, and if his features retain a fiercely Old Testament look, so in a certain light they take on a savage hue, redness reflected from a dark and bloody ground.

IX

A FABRIC HUGE

Cotton Mather's Masterpiece:

Or,

The Original Errand Betrayed.

i. Old Experience Do Attain

In his last chapter on Massachusetts proper William Hubbard introduces a new and troublesome note into his *General History of New England,* a list of negative providences, "sad events" which illustrate a historical necessity: "Moses and Aaron must be stoned when the mixed multitude in Israel have not their wills; who, by the perverseness of their minds, become the more obdurate in their errors by the solemn strokes of Providence, which, if rightly improved, might lead them to repentance, which is the use thereof" (641-42). Here is the (by 1680) familiar Jeremian note, but, as Hubbard's qualifiers ("if," "might") suggest, nothing is certain in his world-view, and as if to undercut his own observation, thus piling blackness on darkness, he ends the chapter with a caveat against those who "darc adventure to enter into the secret of the Almighty, and will undertake to give an account of His judgments and actions, assigning the reason of this and that sudden and unexpected stroke of death" (640). This is patently a negative response to the Increase Mather school of history, but it acts also to provide Hubbard's *General History* with a terminal skepticism by weakening his own interpretation of "the solemn strokes of Providence."

Hubbard's was the wisdom of Solomon, but it was not the kind of knowledge wanted in Boston in "MDCLXXX" or afterward, where pulpit and press regularly disseminated Matherish matter, much of which was devoted to a "reading" of events, both past and present, so as to foretell what was to come. In the Mather view, history is a series of dark conceits, the work of *Deus Scriptor,* being writings on the wall of time to match the skywritings of the modern moment. But what the Mathers do share with William Hubbard, and he with other prominent men of the age, is a sense of decline, a pessimism which in Hubbard's history mingles Calvinist gloom with a classical sense of time's decay, for the Ipswich Solomon regarded the early years of New England as a "Golden Age," "when vice was crushed, as well by the civil, as sacred sword" (247-48). Hubbard dates the turn of New England's fortunes from the outbreak of the Pequot War (which Edward Johnson had read as news of an apocalypse soon to come), a reversal completed by the depression of the 1640's, Providence departing with the immigrants "as at the turn of a tide" (238).

Benjamin Tompson imposed a satiric frame on this same cast of mind in *New-Englands Crisis*, looking back when "Pompion" (by which he meant pumpkin, not pomp) "was a Saint, / When men far'd hard yet without complaint," a backward view giving point to his poetic version of King Philip's War:

> *During Plain Dealing's reign, that worthy stud*
> *Of th' ancient planters' race before the flood*
> *The times were good, merchants car'd not a rush*
> *For other fare than Jonakin and mush.*
> *Although men far'd and lodged very hard*
> *Yet innocence was better than a guard. . . .*
> *Freeness in judgment, union in affection,*
> *Dear love, sound truth they were our grand protection (50-51).*

From Langland on, the English satiric tradition assumes this pastoral pose, hearkening back to the "goodly usage of those antique times," when "the sword was servant to the right," in order to display the modern age to disadvantage. But in Tompson's case the perspective has a Puritan bias, a jeremiad-like emphasis on the loss of divinely protective walls. In this, as in other literary matters, the Massachusetts mode was anticipated by William Bradford, whose atavistic poetic complaint about the decline and threatened fall of New England places the bad new times against the good old times. Thus the departure of the "happy and blessed time" is associated with a disappearing older generation, the "grave and godly" clergy and the "prudent" magistrates who are either "gone" or "grow gray." "Men sincere, and upright in heart," they "from justice and right would not depart," but they have been succeeded by men in whom virtue doth decay" and "true godliness doth not shine" (472-73).

The idea of a Golden Age is intrinsic to the Hesiodic scheme, but where Milton reconciles the Fall from Paradise to the idea of benevolent adversity, in America the Calvinist conviction tends increasingly to curb what was once an expectation of Paradise Regained, identifying New England's promise with a receding point in the past. Again, this is a perspective implicit in the jeremiad, Hebrew prophets like Puritan pastors holding up the example of the fathers to the sons, and nostalgia becomes a fine art in the years following King Philip's War. Satire, that is to say, becomes a pastoral care with a Juvenalian vengeance, wielding a club in place of the crook, and whether evidence of moral or theocratic decline, the result in terms of literature is paradoxical. Robert Cushman in 1622 scolded his audience for not observing their own strict canons of Christian community, citing Moses and Nehemiah as ideals for emulation, but Puritan writers held up for a later generation the (by then ideal) example of those same faulty (by then fabulous) fathers whose greed so offended Cushman, comparing them favorably (sixty years thence) to Moses and Nehemiah.

The Puritan exodus was a flight from the Old World in anticipation of a divine judgment, the founding fathers hedging themselves off from corruption by a wide ocean and a wall of purified ordinances, but the wilderness strategy of a subsequent generation was determined by the transformation of the land from "good" to "god," the imposition of material aims tainting New England, bringing it under the threat of the very danger which the fathers had fled. Such was the logic of the jeremiad in New England, but where the biblical prophet looks forward to the restoration of Jerusalem—typological equivalent of the Christian millennium—Puritan prophets tend increasingly to see smoke and fire in the future, the good times receding a sign of bad times ahead. William Hubbard tempered his Calvinism with neoclassical balance, but writers of Increase Mather's persuasion tended to reverse both pitch and proportions, using the classical sense of decay to reinforce their conviction (or at least their message) of universal (and spreading) depravity. Thus Hubbard's contemporary, the Boston merchant and militiaman Joshua Scottow, shed an old man's tears over the decline of New England at century's end. In Scottow's version of time's

257

changes the shores of Massachusetts had once had a "native and natural smell as of a field, which the Lord hath blessed, so that a prome-
nado abroad after rain would have revived a man's spirits" (314). But
because of "land-defiling and desolating sins . . . our sweet scent is
gone, and we smell rank . . . as if we were laid out to be the American Anticyra" (309, 314). This is Bradford's unweeded garden, needing some savior with a hoe, nor was one slow to appear, for even as
Scottow wound his fish-horn bugle, a champion answered his call. In
his election day sermon of 1676, William Hubbard had attempted to
calm a people emerging from the devastation of King Philip's War by
asserting the permanence of God's plan, but the audience assembled
for the election of 1689 was told that "if our youth be permitted to
run wild in our woods, we shall soon be forsaken by that God whom
our fathers followed hither when it was a land not sown; and Christianity, which like the sun hath moved still westward unto these 'goings down of the sun,' will return to the Old World again, leaving
here not a New Jerusalem . . . but a Gog and Magog . . . for the
last of the latter days" (137). Echoing phrases from Increase Mather's
Brief History of King Philip's War, the election day sermon of 1689
is a nostalgic performance throughout, a symbolic rehearsal of well-
worn Puritan tropes given added meaning by the chosen speaker, that
son of the father and heir of those holy ghosts, John Cotton and Richard Mather, that marvelous chattering boy, Cotton Mather—self-elected
savior of New England.

The Puritans may have come seeking a Salem, but as the crazy antics
of the most prominent citizens of that town suggest, their dream of
peace was from the start a troubled one. Thomas Shepard, Hooker's
successor at Newtown (and his son-in-law), thought of New England as
"a land of peace, though a place of trial," tribulations which often
ended before Puritan tribunals, becoming a Levitical process of law
(70). Such was the experience of Thomas Morton, Anne Hutchinson,
and John Underhill, and in later times a number of Salem residents
found themselves in the prisoner's dock also, from whence they followed Thomas Granger to the gallows. As Underhill promised, New
England was a place of frequent contentions, though the truth which
he anticipated was not quite the one that emerged. Conceived as a
community of love, Winthrop's utopia became by century's end a
Melvillean sphere, surrounded and often threatened from within by

images of fear and hatred, a dreadful metamorphosis to which Cotton Mather contributed more than his share, converting the Puritan asylum into a reasonable facsimile of a madhouse. For when Indians grew in short supply, the Puritans looked inward and found witches, satanic fire to which Cotton Mather fluttered as if with a book to a lamp.

ii. Things Unattempted in Prose or Verse

By 1694 the witchcraft hysteria had run its brief course and Cotton Mather had returned to the theme of his election day sermon and to that dependable prime evil from Puritan forests, the Indian. In that year Mather published his *Short History of New England,* a little book with a long trajectory, not a Marlovian but still a mighty big line, for if his book is indeed short history, it is long jeremiad: Mather devotes most of his space to declaiming against the tendency of the Rising Generation to spread laterally, departing the limits of Winthrop's Wall. "Ah! Lord!" he laments, "Is there no way for us to hinder our sons, from *going out* at our *wall,* that they among, I know not what cursed *crews,* offer themselves a *burnt offering* unto the *Devil?*" (48). This language, as in 1689, was a reprise of the imagery engendered by King Philip's War, but where the Indian had before been seen as an instrument of divine punishment chiefly, in Mather's hands he became by 1702 a "rattlesnake" in human form, and "the most scrupulous persons in the world must own, *that it must be the most unexceptionable piece of justice in the world for to extinguish them.*" Such is the logic if not the strategy of Mather's masterpiece, his *Magnalia Christi Americana,* the most ambitious attempt by a Puritan historian to lend epic form to the New England Way, a massive jeremiad and a monument to failure (I: 215).

As memorial, the *Magnalia* is something of a failure itself, being a veritable curate's egg, a sum of parts several of which are quite good, but the whole exceeding appetite for the rest. Where Hubbard's history is dull but dependable, being less art because more fact, Mather's is more art—and more and more. Another and the largest of those Puritan artifacts so carefully shaped as to approximate (though not resemble) fiction, Mather's big book is a mythic counterpart to Captain John Smith's history of Virginia. It is a matching case, also, of authorial heroics, for pedants, like prophets, poets (and Captain Smith), tend to merge Self with Other, becoming the protagonists of their works. In his *Short History* Mather answers his own call for a Boston Ezekiel, filling the gap in the Hedge with his most proper person, and in the *Magnalia* this tendency becomes magnified, the authorial divine increasingly confused with the Divine Author, as from the title page to the final sheet of errata the achievements of Christ in New England are tightly interwoven with the "Endeavors of Cotton Mather." Where Captain Smith achieves the effect of epic detachment by having his deeds sung by others, Mather resorts to devices of unbearably false modesty, an elephantine coyness involving elaborate declarations of anonymity concerning the authorship of the sermons and tracts gathered together, a congregate conglomeration whose putative subject is New England's church history, but which takes its unity from the ghost within the holy machinery.

At times the occasion celebrated seems to be the act of compilation, the ultimate academic exercise, a *Schriftfest*. At the heart of Mather's book is his history of Harvard, an academic norm to which all events refer, and its soul appears to be Mather's desire for the presidency thereof, perhaps the true cause being served by such laborious love. Certainly, if Mather's declared purpose is to memorialize the achievements of the founding fathers, he has set forth their errand in a most inappropriate way, a noisily fulsome, ornate, and self-gratulatory manner which violates the cherished simplicity and modesty of the Plain Style. Mather was aware of this problem, and addressed himself to it in his "General Introduction" by abusing his anticipated critics, a tactic which in itself should arouse suspicion (31). The first generation of American Puritans prized the Plain Style because it was an aesthetic counterpart to their theological program, a simple manner suited to the purification of doctrine. No Puritan historian wrote more plainly than William Bradford, who associated *"a plain style with singular regard unto the simple truth in all things"* (*HPP:* I: 1). Since Bradford's antithesis in this regard is Cotton Mather, we should look carefully (if reluctantly) into the motives behind the manner.

Like Cotton's stammer, his staggering syntax seems to suggest that the weight of his ancestors sat heavily on him. The *Magnalia* asserts an *ubi sunt* motif, a version of Virgilian sadness and an expression of filial piety: "*De Tristibus* may be a proper *title* for the book I am now writing" (II: 537). But unlike pious Aeneas, young Mather appears to be uneasy under the burden of his father, for in fact his mournful numbers often assume a grotesque, antic guise, that strange, even perverse hilarity characteristic of Puritan elegies, which in America tend to take the form of puns and acrostics, witty displays intended, apparently, to puzzle the departed Saint into heaven. Licensed by the Hebraic tradition of anagrammatic psalms, and encouraged by the conceited Renaissance mode, Puritan writers of elegiac verse tended, as in so much else that Puritans did, to carry things too far. Evincing a nervous, oblique risibility, the mannerism of their mortuary mode is a display of extravagance which at times seems to be a substitute of style for spirit, a signature of doubt and a testament of weakening will, the poetic sons falling away from the strong sense of purpose which they celebrate in the prosaic fathers. As in the Stones of Venice, we may read in the entablatures to an older generation that make up the *Magnalia*'s monumental bulk the chronicle of a failed errand, a rococo epic that like the palace at Versailles appalls by its nakedness of desperate decoration, hollowness accentuated, not concealed by craft.

Mather begins by evoking Virgil's muse, and starts off bravely with a conventional account of the Puritan exodus, but this heroic, linear aspect soon loses itself in the intervening architectonic matter, the interior necropolis being a maze much like the catacombs of Rome, a structure which tends to immobilize as well as (in Nicholas Noyes's eulogizing phrase) "embalm the dead," promoting a static and non-epic scheme (I: 20). Mather attempts likewise to elevate his materials by means of classical and biblical analogies, but the effect is merely to bloat and balloon, a mock-epic tendency accentuated by the author's strained jocosity, puns, and paraphrastics, the whole inimical to the high seriousness and objective detachment of the classical epic. As autopsy, Mather's masterpiece is an anatomy, better entitled "*Anatomia Christi Americana*," being of Burtonian, not Miltonic design. Articulated by perilous connections, a loose aggregate forced by authorial desire into Cotton Mather's chief icon of worship—a printed book which spells in flaming letters of gilt his name on covers of golden calf—the *Magnalia* is an alternative Bible, a hugely subversive new testament, bearing massive witness to that inadvertency which often determined Puritan enterprise in America. In mode and manner Mather went so wide of his mark as to promote a gargantuan disjunctiveness, putting old time itself out of joint, for his *Magnalia* is an amalgam of traditional Puritan forms and old-fashioned Renaissance styles that betrays the original Puritan spirit. Its value to us is precisely its faultiness, for it is a good book because it is so bad.

The *Magnalia* is patterned to the inverted cone of nostalgia, permitting a funnel view that glorifies the past by reducing its plenitude to a glorious generality. But if one effect of the nostalgic perspective is to enhance ancestral achievements through simplification, one result is often to lend large relative size to recent events—and the hinder parts of the *Magnalia* that loom especially large are matters in which the author had a prominent hand. John Winthrop may be accorded first place in chronology and a proportionate space among the early Governors of Massachusetts, but his is a modest tomb when seen from our poet's corner. For near by sits the magnificent literary sarcophagus accommodating Sir William Phips, who was the Mathers' chief Magistrate in more ways than one. Likewise, the account of the Pequot and King Philip's wars is shaped to epic ends, but it is succeeded and much exceeded by Mather's "*Decennium Luctuosum,*" a narrative of New England's recent Indian troubles with which the *Magnalia* ends, a massive Appendix providing a catastrophic conclusion to millennial hopes, but a threshold to a fiery imperial way.

iii. Captain or Colonel
or Knight in Arms

In spite of its imperfections, and in part because of them, Cotton Mather's life of Sir William Phips is one of his most important works, the effigy of the late Governor of Massachusetts recumbent on Mather's cenotaph to the memory of "The Shields of the Churches," the dead Magistrates of New England. Of all the *"Ecclesiarum Clypei"* laid to rest in Mather's Second Book of the *Magnalia,* Sir William is the only bona fide knight, but as Mather's preferred usage suggests, it is Phips's military title of Captain Governor which best suits American nobility, much as the title of his biography, *"Pietas in Patriam,"* styles him a Massachusetts patriot rather than a soldier loyal to the King. In implication as well as proportion, Mather's life of Phips is a premier contribution to our national literature, a companion piece to his handbook of ethical Protestantism, *Bonifacius,* or (as it is generally called) *Essays to Do Good* (1710). First published as a separate book in 1697, Mather's life of Phips is another and equally important foundation stone in that mythic erection, the Self-made Man, hero of the Protestant Epic, providing a Dick Whittington for the American Strand.

Consider the implications of the bare outline of Phips's life. Born in 1650 on the Kennebeck River in the Province of Maine, a place deep in the backwoods of New England, Phips was the youngest of twenty-six children, which distinction was guaranteed by the subsequent death of his father. Young William herded his widowed mother's sheep for a while, but being dissatisfied with his pastoral lot, he soon turned to ship carpentry, and then, ambitious to rise in the world, went to Boston. There he first learned to read and write, and next married a well-placed though not a wealthy widow. Then, so as to fully realize the destiny concealed in his name, Phips turned from building ships to sailing them: Hearing sailors' stories of a treasure hulk sunk off the Bahamas, the carpenter become captain went to England to obtain the necessary backing for recovering the gold, and after overcoming numerous obstacles, he finally made his lucky strike. Though the Crown and his backers got the lion's share of the Spanish gold, his sailors likewise being paid off well as part of a bargain forestalling mutiny on the return voyage, Captain Phips received a small fortune—and, by way of consolation, his knighthood from James II.

Sir William was also given the Provost Marshal Generalship of Massachusetts, and sailed back to Boston with banners flying, to be greeted by William Hubbard with a sermon (delivered, coincidentally, on the Fourth of July) which compared Phips to Jason returning with the Golden Fleece. Never was profit so honored in its own country, and Sir William hastened to wrap up his election to Sainthood by joining the Congregational Church, selecting the one presided over by Increase Mather & Son. Phips likewise became involved with the Mathers in the overthrow of Governor Andros, and celebrated the Glorious Revolution which followed (in the Mathers' eyes as a consequence) by sailing off to capture the French stronghold of Port Royal, Nova Scotia. When he returned again in triumph to Boston, the victorious knight found he had been made a Magistrate of the colony in gratitude for his services, a gesture to which he responded in kind by mounting a campaign for the general invasion of Canada. Sailing up the St. Lawrence, Sir William and his army were defeated by a combination of bad luck, foul weather, and superior French forces, a reversal of Phips's personal fortunes which also plunged Massachusetts into an economic depression.

As a result of Increase Mather's bargaining in London for a new Charter, wherein certain rights held unalienable by the people of Massachusetts were surrendered to the King on the condition that Increase could name the first Royal Governor, Sir William was elevated to that position shortly after his ragged return from Canada. But Mather chose a fated commander for the Puritan ark of state, for Phips's defeat at Quebec was a turn downward from which he never recovered. His governorship was more a weight than a balloon, for it shared the hostility which greeted the compromise Charter in Boston, and though the new Governor did rise to the occasion of the witchcraft trials by putting an end to them—after his own wife was indicted—he in other respects proved to be a less than ideal choice for an office requiring tact and statesmanship. A dutiful instrument of the Mathers when it came to levying unpopular taxes to support the Congregational Church, Phips was very much his own man where free trade was the issue, and not only abused his authority by impeding the collection of customs duties, but accelerated the exchange of goods by playing at pirate.

Ironically, the strong-headed qualities which made for Phips's success on the high seas undid him in high place: confusing opposition with mutiny, he crushed his opponents instead of compromising with them, and even resorted to blows in his handling of customs officers who presumed to do their duty. As a result, four years after he had attained the highest office to which the Mathers could lift him, Phips was recalled to England to face charges of misconduct. But before he could be brought to trial, Sir William had a sudden return of the good luck which had eluded him in recent years, and died. Into the grave with him, pinned to his coffin like the funeral ode which Cotton Mather penned for the occasion, went the political ambitions of Increase and his son.

In terms of literature, Phips can be seen as a Marlovian hero, whose rise to power was flawed by a fatal hubris, an overreaching for further laurels (and loot) which tumbled him into defeat and doom. One could, therefore, read his story as the tragic tale of a hero-villain, but Cotton Mather did not, and in "setting up a *statue*" of General Phips, Mather removed most of his blemishes, that being the kind of posthumous undertaking at which Boston's literary embalmer was unbeatable (I: 229). The faults he could not excise Mather advertised as "*spots* in *ermine*," giving a royal touch to his American weasel, and instead of serving as an example of ambition exceeding ability, Phips emerges from Mather's account as the epitome of humble accomplishment in high place (227). An instance of egregious editing, Mather's life of Phips is an example of drastic cosmetic surgery, the General reshaped into a hero for the American shore, a Massachusetts Aeneas. As "PHIPPIUS MAXIMUS," the General is a champion of the Commonwealth, his life exemplifying "the old heathen virtue of PIETAS IN PATRIAM, or love to one's country," and it is this golden strand, this "essential thread," which Mather finds "interwoven into . . . his *history* and his *character*" (219, 175). And yet, by picking at the fabric, we can detect a darker line, not only Phips's personal flaws, but a geopolitical discontinuity intrinsic to his personal failings and to those of the *Magnalia* as well.

To begin with, there is an inherent disjunctiveness in Mather's portraiture, his attempt to employ classical techniques in celebrating the hero of his distinctly middle-class drama. Comparing Phips to Pizarro and Columbus does not elevate so much as bloat, the result resembling Horatio Greenough's George Washington, terribly naked in his white marble and toga. Though driven like Columbus in all his actions by the "most vehement and wonderful *impulse*," the chief evidence of grace in action, General Phips is a most ungraceful hero, his chief virtues being "indefatigable *patience* and a proportionable *diligence*," which are not pagan, but patently Puritan values, for which the sons of New England were praised and her daughters named (43, 171). As elsewhere in the *Magnalia*, moreover, Mather tends to insist too much, a forcing of fact into symbol which cracks the fabric of belief, revealing an essential fallacy. Thus Phips is described as being "of an enterprising genius, and naturally disdained *littleness*: but his disposition for *business* was of the Dutch mold, where, with a little show of *wit*, there is as much *wisdom* demonstrated as can be shown by any nation" (168). But cheeses are also cast in the Dutch mold, and there is a latent Edamic look to Mather's New World hero, who was "of an inclination cutting rather like a *hatchet* than like a *razor*," a useful instrument, but not the heroic sword.

What emerges is less a knight- than a carpenter-errant, whose *"capacity for business* in many considerable actions" puts forth the embryonic lineaments of the businessman (171). Sir William achieved through his efforts not only the wealth that is the sign of providential stewardship, but "the character of an *honest man*," and though he might be styled " '*a knight of the golden fleece*,' " Mather prefers to call him " 'the knight of honesty,' for it was *honesty* with *industry* that raised him," with a little help from God (173-74). Elevated by providence, General Phips becomes a "guardian angel" of Massachusetts, dropped "as it were from the *machine of heaven*" to relieve "the distresses of the land," but one can hear the loud creaking of gears backstage, resulting from the General's rather more than angelic proportions: "For his *exterior*, he was one *tall*, beyond the common set of men, and *thick* as well as *tall*, and *strong* as well as *thick*: he was, in all respects, exceedingly *robust,* and able to conquer such difficulties of *diet* and of *travel,* as would have killed most men alive: nor did the *fat,* whereinto he grew very much in his later years, take away the vigor of his motions" (204, 207, 217). The effect is of bumbling legerdemain which reverses intention, the portrait progressively degenerating into caricature, much like Daumier's metamorphosis of King Louis Philippe into a vegetable.

The king after whom Mather models his statue, however, is David, like Phips an "advanced shepherd," and as David's adventures loom large in the Old Testament, so Sir William's bulk dominates the *Magnalia* (221). The several analogies to the biblical soldier amount to an epic simile and an unlikely similitude, typical of Mather's purpose and his provinciality, for David is not only a type of militant Christ, but was the temporal savior of his country, while General Phips was neither. Because of his great success in fishing up gold for his King, Phips is styled a *"king's-fisher"* by Mather, who declares that New England enjoyed *"halcyon days"* under his administration (202). But a kingfisher is not a fisher king, and in fact New England was very slow to recover from the economic troubles into which she was plunged by the General's botched campaign. Upon his triumphant return to Massachusetts, the newly knighted Phips vowed to venture his "life in doing of good," equated with doing harm to Canada, the "source of New England's miseries," for "as Cato could make no speech in the senate without that conclusion, *Delenda est Carthago,* so it was the general conclusion of all that argued sensibly about the safety of that country, 'Canada must be reduced' " (183-85). Yet "the greatest action that ever the New Englanders attempted" resulted in the reduction not of Canada, but of Massachusetts, a mighty stumbling block in the path of Mather's intended savior-king, and not a small obstacle to authorial intention.

"By an evident hand of Heaven, sending one unavoidable disaster after another, as well-formed an enterprise as perhaps was ever made by the New Englanders, most unhappily miscarried, and General Phips underwent a very mortifying disappointment of a design which his mind was, as much as ever any, set upon" (189). With that Puritan pipe-vise turn of mind, which can get a grip on the roundest defeat and twist it to advantage, Mather's General decides that his debacle was "like Israel engaging against Benjamin," that "it may be we saw yet

but the *beginning* of the matter, and that the way to Canada now being learnt, the foundation of a victory over it might be laid in what
had been already done." But as for the implications of that Heavenly
Hand, the General, "though he had been used unto *diving* in his time,
would say, 'That the things which had befallen him in this expedition,
were too deep to be *dived* into!'" (190). To which Mather adds only
the observation that "the general disaster which hath attended almost
every attempt of the European colonies in America to make any considerable encroachments upon their neighbors is a matter of some
close reflection."

"Of" perhaps, but not "for," and Cotton Mather, usually a very loon
for deep diving, refrains from taking the plunge. Yet that he was aware
of the negative implications of Phips's failed campaign is suggested by
a rabbinical anecdote prefacing his account of the Canadian "business," concerning "a time when the Philistines had made some inroads
and assaults from the northward upon the skirts of Goshen, where the
Israelites had a residence, before their coming out of Egypt" (184).
Presuming themselves "powerful and numerous enough to encounter
the Canaanites, even in their own country," the Israelites "formed a
brisk expedition, but came off unhappy losers in it." For, observes
Mather, "the *time* was not yet come; there was more *haste* than good
speed in the attempt; they were not enough concerned for the counsel
and presence of God in the undertaking; they mainly propounded the
plunder to be got among a people whose trade was that wherewith
beasts enriched them; so the business miscarried."

The parallels between the rabbinical text and Phips's campaign are
absolute, even to the allusion to the Canadian fur trade, and the remark about plunder has a special relevance, for the General had hoped
to cover the cost of the war by sacking Quebec, a foiled expectation
which resulted in the consequent depression. Most important, perhaps,
is the observation concerning "the counsel and presence of God," for
nowhere in Mather's account of Phips's undertaking is there any mention of a religious "impulse," only a patriotic one. Yet as the Psalmist
"going to recite this history says, 'I will utter dark sayings of old,'" so
that mole for dark matters, Cotton Mather, in giving "the true report
of a very memorable matter," keeps his silence on the gloomier aspects
of Phips's defeat. Though the occasion fairly begs for a jeremiad on
profane versus holy warfare, because of political (and politic) reasons,

Cotton Mather holds his tongue—a massive instance of impeded speech.

By celebrating General Phips's exploits and serving as an apologist for his failures, Mather in effect incorporates his hero's tragic flaw into the *Magnalia,* for advocacy of the invasion of Canada is a twofold violation of the original Puritan errand, the "Good Old Way" of which he is self-declared champion, being an assertion of worldly domain involving the wholesale slaughter of heathen. If Phips's great fault was overweening ambition, a wolfish hunger for power and recognition draped by Mather with the sheepskin of *"humility* and *lowliness,"* then the author shares the other half of Satan's portrait, his own sin being the one which the Pauline Puritans most abhorred—hypocrisy (221). Had he been less concerned with apologetics, less involved personally with the fortunes of General Phips, Mather might have delivered a thundering denunciation against the worship of false gods, but in pointing his statue toward the papist stronghold in the north, Cotton paints and plasters over the imperfections in his militant carpenter-saint.

As for the Pauline mission of the fathers, "the principal end of the plantation" as stated in the Old Charter, Mather gives it short shrift. His portrait of the Apostle John Eliot takes up an entire Part of his Third Book—which contains the lives of New England's dead divines— and in terms of proportion forms a pious complement to the patriotic emphasis given Phips, but his stress is on Eliot's personal qualities, his capacity for hard work and self-denial: "The anagram of his name was TOILE" (562). Eliot's labor among the heathen is rendered chiefly by footnotes, and though Mather's brief account of "the miserable people which our Eliot propounded unto himself to teach and save" may have been intended to magnify the missionary's task, it certainly diminishes the Indian as a deserving object of charity (560). Eliot dying provides Mather one more opportunity for a tearful glance to heaven, permitting another sigh over the passing away of the Good Old Days, but over the passing away of the Macedonian the eulogist casts an unmoist eye. Calling rhetorically for a "Timothy" to step forward "in the room of our departed Paul," Cotton Mather—for once—does not obey his own summons (579).

iv. Meteor Streaming to the Wind

The peculiar uses to which Cotton Mather put his nostalgic perspective is dramatically demonstrated by his Sixth and last Chapter to the Seventh and last Book of his *Magnalia*. Entitled *"Arma Virosque Cano,"* it is a Virgilian exercise with a communal Puritan slant, an epitomized history of the Pequot and King Philip's wars derived from the models provided by his father and William Hubbard, but it lacks any Jeremian frame. Much as Increase Mather and Hubbard revised Mason's account of the Pequot War for their own (disparate) purposes, Cotton Mather borrowed their vocabulary of biblical and classical allusions, but by compressing events into one continuous heroic action the younger man achieved a much more intensely epic effect. Excising the Jeremian aspects of King Philip's War, Mather depicts the Puritan army as militant Righteousness, "with a sword in our hands that we might renew and confirm our peace" (II: 562). The backslidings of the English are conveniently forgotten, the greed for land overlooked, and the blame for the war is placed squarely on King Philip and his allies.

As a consequence, Cotton Mather's version of the war more closely resembles William Hubbard's than it does Increase Mather's, a similarity which extends to the son's use of Hubbard's geopolitical dichotomy, distinguishing between "those parts of New England, which had the *glory* of Evangelical churches in them, for a *defense* to be *created* upon," and those regions beyond the Merrimack which did not, where the English "grew too like the Indians, among whom they lived in their *unchristian* way" (II: 577). But the Matherine emphasis on the importance of churches as New England's first line of defense still holds, and Wakely is still "an honest old man" blubbering over God's displeasure with him (578). Unlike Hubbard, moreover, Mather refuses to waste his breath on those "many rude, wild, *ungovernable*" persons in the east, taking refuge in his intention of writing a *"Church*

History," which excuses him from taking "another long walk into the woods after these ravening savages" (577). As a warrant for his refusal to cross Merrimack's waters, Mather imposes a biblical framework on the Puritan epic of arms and the men, their victories analogous to that over "Og, the king of the woody Bashan," by "Joshua, the Lord General of Israel, with all his armies passing into Canaan" (578). The tense is carefully kept transitive, and it is likewise "unto a Shiloh that the planters of New England *have been making* their progress," yet another example of the withheld climax keeping the Saints this side the Jordan (579; italics added).

The same strategy results in the abrupt and surprisingly pessimistic note with which Mather ends his epic of the Indian Wars, suddenly announcing (on the same page) that "we have had one enemy more pernicious to us than all the rest, and that is 'our own backsliding heart,' which has plunged the whole country into so wonderful a *degeneracy*, that I have sometimes been discouraged from writing the church history of the country." From the very brink of the Jordan, within sight of Shiloh, the reader is suddenly yanked into the degenerate present moment, where "the wrath of Heaven has raised up against us a succession of other *adversaries* and *calamities,* which have cast the land into great confusions" (580). "God knows," sighs Mather, in closing his account of the "Wars of the Lord"—the last section of his *Magnalia*—"what will be the END." God knows, but Cotton Mather will provide a good guess, and the "end" of the *Magnalia* opens to his *"Decennium Luctuosum,"* a massive Appendix which amounts to not only a long walk but a veritable incursion into the barbarous regions beyond the Merrimack, the very rocks of which are blazoned with the kind of writing "like that on the wall of Belshazzar," evincing a hand nonetheless Matherine for being "anonymous" (581).*

Having excised the Jeremian aspect of King Philip's War so as to make it conform to his nostalgic epic design, Mather transfers it to his account of the ongoing conflict with the French and Indians. Reinstating Increase Mather's emphasis on reformation, Cotton returns the churchless region beyond the Merrimack to his ecclesiastical map, characterizing it as a troubled ground much like that described by William Hubbard, the scene of a "long war" by means of which God

---

* Once again, the hand is moved by the spirit of John Winthrop, Mather's unEnding being yet another version of the Puritan *quietus interruptus.*

has "chastised a *sinful people* by those [i.e. Indians] who are *not a people*" (589). With Hubbard, Mather concedes that the non-people of the East had ground for their enmity against New Albion, and the French as well as the Indians are regarded as having legitimate grievances (584-86). But this apparent fair-mindedness is misleading, Mather not so much a Francophile as an Androsphobe, the deposed Governor having earlier aroused New France to military action by his high-handed extension of New England's border. Though the issues are different from those associated by Hubbard with the eastern region, they are messy still, a confused, dubious battle played out against a backdrop of many rivers.

The region beyond the Merrimack remains unholy ground and cursed: whether because of theocratic bigotry or schematic intention, Mather refuses to grace it with his usual biblical scenery. As a result, he for once pays attention to the local landscape, and though analogy-prone as ever, he fastens at least one end of his metaphor to the American strand. Where the Connecticut River in his account of King Philip's War is his father's "Kishon," the Saco is the Saco, being the place (again borrowing from Increase) where the *"vein* of New England first opened, that afterwards *bled* for ten years together!" (587). So intimately are the Indians of Maine associated with the fluid element that when a premature peace was signed at Pemaquid, Mather foresees (blessed are the uses of hindsight) that it will be a *"fluctuating* and *unstable* sort of a business," for the treaty was signed "not on the *firm land* but in their canoes upon the *water"* (610). And the *"passions"* of the Indian chief, Bomaseen, are described as having "foam'd and boiled like the very waters at the fall of Niagara," an epic simile taken directly from the American, not the biblical or classical landscape (628).

And yet when eastern violence dips occasionally into Massachusetts, Mather resorts to his usual arsenal of Hebraic allusions. An Indian massacre at Groton recalls to his mind a time when Jewish " 'elders proclaimed a fast in their cities . . . because the wolves had devoured two little children beyond the Jordan.' Truly," Mather reflects, "the elders of New England were not a little concerned at it, when they saw the *wolves* thus devouring their children, even on this side of Merrimack!" (627-28). This lamination of Merrimack and Jordan gives metaphoric consistency to Mather's sense of New England as New Israel, and it is notable that one of the few times he grants the dispensation of Bible imagery to the region beyond the river, the occasion is the death of "our DUMMER, the minister of York," whose murder by the Indians is compared to Abel's death at the hands of Cain (612-13). Dummer is linked by the sacred Harvardine tie to the inner sanctum of Massachusetts, but the land beyond the Merrimack is still very much east of Eden.

Whatever his reasons, Cotton Mather's "little boil'd Indian corn in a tray," as he styles his *"Decennium Luctuosum,"* contains enough native material to place it in the ongoing tradition of American encounter initiated by Captain Smith's voyage up the Chickahominy (581). Counterpart to Smith is the Puritan heroine Hannah Dustin, the female captive from Haverhill who comported herself in the eastern wilderness in a manner quite different from Underhill's tearful prisoners of hope. Hannah's murder of her Indian captors is compared by Mather to "the action of Jael upon Sisera," an allusion which may be an inadvertent twitch of Mather's knee-jerk biblicalism, but which acts to place New Hampshire deep in the landscape of Judges, in effect transforming the Merrimack to the River Kishon (636). This, in turn, gives point to the jeremiad with which Mather concludes his *"Decennium Luctuosum,"* a sermon illustrating a text from Judges—"The children of the east came up against them; and they entered into the land to destroy it; and Israel was greatly impoverished" (658). Mather thereby reveals that despite his narrative emphasis he is not really concerned with reforming the inhabitants of the dubious " 'garden of the east,' " that the region beyond the Merrimack is chiefly useful as an object lesson to Massachusetts (587).

Mrs. Dustin's home was within the holy bounds of the New English Israel, and her close brush with a cruel fate is obviously aimed at the "Daughters of our Zion" that they might consider "what it would be for fierce Indians to break into their houses and brain their husbands and their children before their eyes, and lead them away a long journey into the woods; and, if they began to fail and faint in the journey, then for a tawny savage to come with hell-fire in his eyes, and cut 'em down with his hatchet; or, if they could miraculously *hold out,* then for some filthy and ugly squaws to become their insolent mistresses, and insolently to abuse 'em at their pleasure a thousand inexpressible ways" (666-67). Mather's slithery syntax makes it difficult to determine just who is abusing whom, but it is clear that the Indian has the upper hand, being the chastizing instrument administering "the sharp *strokes* of Heaven" which may yet fall on the matronly flesh of Massachusetts unless she mends her ways (665). By such means the sufferings beyond the Merrimack serve as a version of Inferno, a Hell through which Mather-as-Virgil leads his Boston congregation: "How dolefully am I circumstanced, if I go down from one hell unto another at the last" (666). All that protects Massachusetts from calamity is her great China Wall of Congregational Churches: "The enemy that have come in upon our land 'like a flood' carried all before them as an 'irresistible torrent,' until they came to places that have churches as it were to *garrison* them. There the Almighty Lord hath check'd the 'proud waves,' and said, 'Hitherto, ye shall come, and no further!' " (660).

This is the point of Mather's subsequent sermon, *Frontiers Well-Defended* (1706), which testifies that the defensive wall soon enough becomes an advancing line, and if the arrested flood of red men evokes the drawing back of the Red Sea, so eastern rivers play a role in the continuing drama of supplantation. "It was wholesome counsel given," notes Mather in concluding his "*Decennium Luctuosum*," "and usually taken in the beginning of New England, 'Let Christians nowhere sit down without good ministers, but let them rather tarry where they are, as Ezra tarried by the river Ahava, till he had got some Levites to go with them' " (661). Thus John Robinson, who in his farewell sermon to the Pilgrims at Leyden took his text from Ezra 8:21, "upon which he spent a good part of the day very profitably, and suitable to their present occasion" (*HPP*: I: 121). Bradford does not relate the substance of Robinson's sermon, that pious benediction at the start of "the beginning of New England," but Mather's single sentence at the latter end of the *Magnalia* provides a pocket epitome of the theocratic literature engendered by the first century of Puritan experience in America, past occasions yielding present usage.

First, there is the nostalgic reference to "wholesome beginnings," next, the vital function of the clergy to settlement ("don't venture to form *towns* without the *gospel* in them any more"), and, finally, the unique role of the river, at once border and threshold. The Ahava is a lesser and therefore permissible Jordan, not a permanent but a temporary boundary, and as an allusion it provides a counterpart to the rabbinical anecdote shadowing General Phips's invasion of Canada.

To end an intended epic with a jeremiad would seem a strange and contradictory business, but in Mather's hand his father's rod becomes a scepter, more an implement of power than punishment, his *Magnalia* not so much a caveat against expansion than a recipe for the right way to go about it. Where Increase had hoped to guarantee the survival of Massachusetts, Cotton looks to her prevalence in America, a filial impiety whereby *Johannes in Eremo* becomes Aeneas in Rome.

By picking our way through the maze of the *Magnalia*'s ecclesiastical map we can follow the metamorphosis of the original transcendental errand to the final secular mission, the Exodus of the first book becoming the Armageddon of the last, a fiery crusade during which the landscape of the Old Testament burns away, revealing the recognizable but transformed terrain of New England—no longer a wilderness garden but a fortress New Israel heaving toward regeneration through violent means. Thus the true epic of America emerges at the far end of the process, Mather's terminal Holy War giving heroic point to the mass of his anatomical matter, in effect taking up the Aenean theme from where Captain John Smith left it years before. Intended as a New Jerusalem, the Mathers' Boston became a New Rome, a citadel of proto-nationalist feeling whose watery gates were guarded by Cotton's statue of Sir William Phips, a clumsy, thick-set parody of Michelangelo's David.

His bulk enhanced by the whole armor of God through whose joints there gleams the clear light of day, Sir William strides out of the sea, his sword pointing inland, a shining blunt instrument which, though somewhat short of its intended length, serves its purpose well. For by tracing its direction across Cotton Mather's geopolitical plat, we intersect the Great River of the North at Quebec, an imperial diagram that provides a battle plan for a half-century to come. From a distance, moreover, when irradiated by the dawn's early light (or a rocket's red glare), Mather's statue takes on a rough-hewn likeness, its great stone face resembling the features of another patriot soldier, whose memorial stands near Potomac's imperial tide.

v. Invisible, Except to God Alone

"If a *book* of some consequence be laid open before one that cannot *read*, he may look and gaze upon it; but unto what purpose, as long as he cannot understand it?" (658). With this leading question Mather draws toward the end of the end of his *Magnalia*, the "*Decennium Luctuosum*," preparing for an egregious indirection put forth in a metaphor endemic to his authorial world-view: "This very comparison is by the great Austin well applied unto the *judgments* of God. And I will therefore so far improve the comparison, as to observe, that the judgments of God, under which we have been languishing for ten years together, are a sort of book put into our hands; a book indeed all written in *blood*; a book yet full of *divine lessons* for us." But, asks Mather, can *anyone* read this book? Perpetual master of the rhetorical inquiry, he goes on to render a lengthy demonstration of the visual powers which strangely turned myopic when confronted with General Phips's defeat. Explaining that wall-reading is "a work well becoming a minister of the gospel," Mather plays self-fulfilling prophet once again, turning to an explication of his own preceding text, a "reading" of the events east of the Merrimack he has just recounted.

" 'Whoso is wise will observe these things' " is repeated like a chorus throughout Mather's terminal jeremiad, for as a work of literature the history of the past ten years has been written by God in such a way that "we may read upon it, in a very legible character, those words in Jer. xviii: 1: 'Thus saith the Lord, behold I frame evil against you, I devise a device against you' " (669). As author, moreover, the Lord resembles Cotton Mather, the both having produced "a *work*, a *strange work*," being a "*devising* of ways, very strangely to distress all sorts of people, in all sorts of interests. . . . It hath been as if ways had been deliberately and exquisitely *studied*, and as if with much contrivance plotted for to bring us all within the reach of the general calamity."

Drawing close and peering over Cotton Mather's shoulder, we observe that the face he sees in prophetic waters has Hawthornesque lineaments, the sly, shifting, protean features of the Puritan's chief antagonist in the New World, Satan-as-Scheming-Savage, a paranoiac vision floating up from dark depths indeed.

To isolate the epic strand of the *Magnalia*, to align millennial beginning with apocalyptic ending, is to find a gigantic tale much like the one in *Moby-Dick*, a three-stranded fable in which a heroic quest darkens into insane obsession, a dream of errantry into a nightmare of universal evil, where the difference between God and the Devil becomes hopelessly blurred, even irrelevant. "I hope," protested Cotton Mather, "I am not becoming a *visionary*" (654). "Thou art a monster," cried a Quaker, "all mouth, and no ears—" (649). They were both, in different ways, quite correct. "Sirs," said Mather, in closing his great book, "we have 'wisely observed' the things that have in our afflicted years befallen us, and we have now, to good purpose, heard a sermon of *observations* upon those things, if we will now retire, and ponder seriously with ourselves, 'What is there amiss in my own heart. . . .' " (681). There was nothing amiss in Mather's heart that does not grin through the cracks in his book, the both being of such calamitous character that he who reads should run.

X
PROVIDENTIAL PASSAGES

Wherein a Matron,
a Minister,
a Militiaman,
and a Madam
Display the Cardinal Points
of the Puritan Compass

i. Painful Pre-eminence!

Versions of spiritual autobiography on the tribal scale, Puritan histories are also massive variations of that characteristic New World genre, the captain's narrative. From Columbus's letter to Queen Isabella to the histories of John Smith and John Mason, the captain's account of his adventures in America is informed by a self-explanatory, even exculpatory motive, and Puritan histories likewise are given form by the felt need to explain the New England experience to the world at large, explaining away such theological niceties as the hanging of old ladies, the massacring of Indians, and the flogging of Quakers, etc. Puritan doctrine may have denied justification by works, but Puritan histories are most certainly works of justification, as epics a version of apologiad. They evince, moreover, a gradual metamorphosis of genre, from Johnson's Jacobite to Mather's Jeremian epic, changes testifying to a transition in Puritan purpose. Where Captain Johnson's history, like Captain John Smith's, takes its *élan* from the triumphant narratives of victorious soldiers, Mather's is a more dubious battle, in which a terminal and therefore signal importance is put on suffering.

Dragging the imaginary figure of a distraught and abused female captive before his reader in the last pages of the *Magnalia*, Mather assures us that "such things as these, I tell you, have often happened in this lamentable war," and his "*Decennium Luctuosum*," is spotted throughout with illustrative examples (II: 667). William Hubbard, likewise, concluded his history of King Philip's War with anecdotes of settlers east of the Merrimack who had been put "under the yoke" of Indian captivity, but as in his story of Wait and Jennings, Hubbard tends to emphasize the heroic element, stressing the captives' hardihood and cunning—much in the vein of Captain John Smith's account of his ordeal as the guest of Powhatan (II: 139-41, 194-98, 199-204). Cotton Mather, by contrast, prefers atrocity tales, like the "horrible story" of John Diamond's death by dismemberment, or accounts of women suffering durance vile in the dirty hands of savages (II: 591-93, 597-600, 614-618). It is the "diabolical" behavior of the Indians toward their prisoners which converts the eastern regions to a hell-ground, but equally important is the parallel with the Babylonian bondage of the Jews, and as the Jewish exile is intrinsic to Jeremiah's message, so the Puritan captivity narrative provides a complement to the sermonic jeremiad, establishing one more correspondence between the Chosen People of Israel and those of New England.

The Babylonian exile is a complex and often obscure matter, mingling nostalgic lament with longings for revenge, looking backward to the past victories of Israel and forward to the restoration of Jerusalem and the destruction of her enemies. The New England captivity narrative borrows that complexity, much as it is informed by the vocabulary of the Hebraic songs of triumph and despair which made up the *Bay Psalm Book*. The sufferings of the exemplary captive were just as exciting to the Mathers as were the signs of witchcraft and other signals of divine and demonic presence in New England, holding out hope for the purification of the Puritan state and its eventual triumph, but like the jeremiad itself, the captivity narrative was a double-edged weapon. Used by the Mathers to maintain the consolidative burden of the theocratic plan, the captivity experience illustrated the penalties of breaking through the sheltering Hedge of divine ordinances, yet the vengeful aspect of the Babylonian analogue introduced an alternative motif, calling for the reduction of the northern Babylon / Carthage / Canada / Quebec, whose fall would assure the emergence of either (depending on whether the text was Revelation or Jeremiah) the Millennium or a powerful, united, theocratic Empire.

Captain John Underhill anticipated the genre by comparing the Wethersfield maids to Israel in bondage, and he also paired his "poor captivated children" with the Puritan victory over the Pequots (19-25). But he did not go so far as to imply that the miserable girls were suffering for Connecticut's sins, leaving the association of individual ordeal with collective guilt for a later generation. William Hubbard likewise alludes to the "Tents of Kedar" in describing the wilderness condition of eastern settlers suffering under the yoke of Indian tyranny, but his emphasis was never on divinely ordained punishment (II: 201). That was ever the message of the Mathers, and where Hubbard celebrates the daring adventures of Wait and Jennings, Increase in his *Remarkable Providences* (1684) chose from the same event the story of Quentin Stockwell, an Indian captive whose trek from Hatfield on the Connecticut to Chamblee on the St. Lawrence was along a bloody trail of pain and near starvation.

Hubbard evokes a pagan *"nutus"* to explain the heroism of his Hatfield husbands, but Mather uses Stockwell's narrative to illustrate "the changes of providence which passed over him," in his eagerness to gather evidence of God's grace somehow overlooking the fact that Stockwell himself makes no reference to divine intervention at all (40). It is not, finally, to God, but to plain "Ben Wait" that Quentin attributes his deliverance, and Mather's oversight is yet another of those disjunctive slips that characterize Puritan literature, revealing by betraying theocratic intention. It is a quality of insistence typical of the Matherine muse, the tension between what Stockwell tells us and what Increase wants him to say further demonstrating the distance between the people and the pulpit at the close of the century, a space not unlike the hole in the Hedge which Cotton Mather tried to fill in his self-cast role as Boston's Ezekiel.

A theocratic instrument, the captivity narrative cannot be called a "popular" form of literature, but like the medieval *exemplum* it is both a rhetorical device and a parabolic seed of sensational fiction to come. People in motion (and trouble) are inherently interesting, and underlying the scriptural overlay and theocratic emphasis lies a very good story, an uneasy prisoner beneath an ecclesiastical burden. Moreover, because it is a genre engendered by wilderness encounter, the captivity adventure is alive with a rigorous sense of the landscape. It is supplemented in that regard by a slim miscellany of related early New England narratives, adding up to a unique literature written by otherwise ordinary persons, elevated momentarily from the routine round of colonial life by the singularness of their experiences. Captives, a Captain, and a Madam Knight, like Bunyan's Christian they are in movement against adverse circumstances, providing paradigms of the result when Puritan sensibilities are exposed to the wilderness landscape: seldom a uniform reaction, it consistently accounts for the Puritans' prevalence in and sustenance by their environment. Paradoxically, these narratives also register the changes by which transplanted Englishmen became nascent Americans, metamorphoses associated once again with rivers bearing Indian names. Working Ovidian rather than Christian transformations, immersion in wildwood streams is an equivocal experience, often subversive to theocratic schemes.

ii. 'Tis Chastity, my Brother, Chastity

The first and in many ways the greatest captivity narrative is Mary Rowlandson's *The Sovereignty and Goodness of God* (1682), the publication of which was heralded in the first American edition of *Pilgrim's Progress*, a coincidence of considerable implication. For while Bunyan's great book asserts grace abounding, Rowlandson's little volume dramatizes the conditionality of God's favor in New England, a negative emphasis belied by her title but reinforced by an accompanying jeremiad by her husband, the Reverend Joseph Rowlandson: *The Possibility of God's Forsaking a People, that have been visibly near and dear to Him; together, with the Misery of a People thus forsaken.* "I have seen the extreme vanity of this world," declares Mrs. Rowlandson in concluding her story, "one hour I have been in health, and wealth, wanting nothing: but the next hour in sickness and wounds, and death, having nothing but sorrow and affliction" (166). Hers has been (to borrow one of the Mathers' favorite phrases) a "humbling" experience, but it has also been a blessing, and she concludes, with David, that "It is good for me that I have been afflicted" (167).

By such means does she offer herself as the salutary subject of her husband's jeremiad, displaying the marks of divine chastisement as signs of her blessedness: "When I lived in prosperity . . . I should be sometimes jealous least I should have no affliction in this life, and that scripture would come to my mind: For whom the Lord loveth He chasteneth, and scourgeth every son whom he receiveth" (166-67). No cross, no crown, and in recounting her humbling experiences Mrs. Rowlandson is also asserting the painful pleasures of election. It is, notably, an ordeal that begins with a doomsday note, "the noise of some guns" at sunrise awaking the inhabitants of Lancaster to a scene of pandemonium, "the dolefulest day that ever mine eyes saw" (118). But doomsday soon takes on a regional coloration, for the "dreadful hour" is not one of hell-fire, but a "house on fire over our heads," not devils, but "bloody heathen ready to knock us on the head if we stirred out." This tension between scriptural and eschatological events and the very real episodes of Mrs. Rowlandson's experience holds throughout, her individual sufferings serving to illuminate the purposes of her God, the two-faced Jehovah of the Psalms. There is He who carries His Chosen People through "never so many difficulties," and makes them "see and say they have been gainers thereby," but there is also He who is angry with those who " 'are not grieved for the affliction of Joseph, therefore shall they go captive, with the first that go captive' " (167, 158).

Carried with other prisoners and spoils to a near-by rendezvous, Mrs. Rowlandson is forced to witness a version of Walpurgis Night, a "roaring and singing and dancing, and yelling of those black creatures in the night, which made the place a lively resemblance of hell," not sinners frying, but "horses, cattle, sheep, swine, calves, lambs, roasting pigs, and fowl," a "miserable waste" of good meat which adds grievous weight to her personal "losses and sad bereaved condition" (121). This wanton feast is a prelude to a long ordeal of deprivation, Mrs. Rowlandson separated the next morning from all her children save an injured "babe," and forced to accompany the Indians "into the vast and desolate wilderness, I knew not whither" (122-23). This is the first in a series of "Removes" which take her farther and farther west, a purgatorial journey stripping her naked of all that she holds dear, commencing with her wounded child who soon dies and is buried unceremoniously in the woods. The lonely grave is a cruel reminder of her own "wilderness condition," and Mrs. Rowlandson's grief is increased by the Indians' refusal to let her visit a daughter held near by: "I had one child dead, another in the wilderness, I knew not where, the third they would not let me come near to. . . . And as I was going along, my heart was even overwhelm'd with the thoughts of my condition, and that I should have children, and a nation which I knew not ruled over them" (126). By such allusive means, Mary Rowlandson becomes not only a captive, but *the* Captive—Israel wandering in bondage.

Yet her emphasis on the loss of children has a distinctly New England coloration, a familial element epitomized by the circumstances of

Goodwife Joslin's death, she being "very big with child . . . and another child in her arms" (128). Unable to keep up with the rest, Mrs. Joslin begged to be allowed to go home, and "vexed with her importunity," the Indians "stripped her naked, and set her in the midst of them; and when they had sung and danced about her (in their hellish manner) as long as they pleased, they knocked her on the head, and the child in her arms with her" (129). The English children, who were forced to witness this as a warning, testified that "she did not shed one tear, but prayed all the while." There is in this dreadful anecdote no hint of sexual threat, the story illustrating, rather, the central theme of domestic rapine. As the family was the unit central to the Puritan concept of community, so the captivity narrative gains its power through depicting its destruction, the image of the tormented, naked, pregnant, praying woman (and child) like Mary and *her* "babe," a Puritan madonna of sorrows.

This domestic theme serves also as comic relief, admittedly unintentional, for Rowlandson's chief tormentors are not the men of the tribe —she even has a good word for her "Master"—but the women for whom she is forced to work as a slave, and Mary as Martha maintains a dim view of Indian huswifery. Edward Johnson wrung a bit of wry humor from the Pequots' expectations that the Wethersfield girls would be able to teach them how to make gunpowder, and of like risible kind is the work to which Mary Rowlandson was put—knitting. The necessity of toting along needles and yarn during each Remove results in a ludicrous episode, typical of her sufferings at the hands of callous squaws: "In this travel, because of my wound, I was somewhat favored in my load; I carried only my knitting work and two quarts of parched meal: Being very faint, I asked my mistress to give me one spoonful of the meal, but she would not give me a taste" (130). We cannot doubt her discomfort, but it is something less than Goodwife Joslin's, and it takes effort, sometimes, to feel sorry for Mary Rowlandson, especially if one is aware that the Indians were short of food because of the scorched-earth policy dictated by Puritan authorities, a strategy of constant pursuit and pillage, colonial equivalent to search and destroy.

On the banks of the Baquaug River the English army nearly caught up with the Indians, a burdensome straw on Mrs. Rowlandson's suffering hump. To begin with, the crossing itself was in a manner ludicrous, being on makeshift rafts: "By the advantage of some brush which they had laid on the raft to sit upon, I did not wet my foot (while many of themselves at the other end were mid-leg deep) which cannot but be acknowledged as a favor of God to my weakened body, it being a very cold time. I was not before acquainted with such kinds of doings or dangers" (130). A wet foot in wintertime is no joke, but there is bitter comedy in Rowlandson's perilous crossing, her providential position on the high and dry end of the raft a burlesque illustration of Puritan election, inspiring a suitable quote from Isaiah: " 'When thou passeth through the waters, I will be with thee, and through the rivers, they shall not overflow thee.' "

God may have been with Mrs. Rowlandson as she crossed over the Baquaug, but He seems to have left the English army behind, and the same river that serves to demonstrate the Lord's high regard for Mary soon turns into a punitive instrument against her: "On that very day came the English army after them to this river, and saw the smoke of their wigwams, and yet this river put a stop to them" (131). The soldiers seem to have been as unwilling as she to wet their feet, but Mrs. Rowlandson reads the event as a "strange providence of God in preserving the heathen." For where many hundreds of Indians, including "old and young, some sick, and some lame," managed to get over the river, the English army could not: "God did not give them courage or activity to go over after us; we were not ready for so great a mercy as victory and deliverance; if we had been, God would have found out a way for the English to have passed this river." Rowlandson brings up this incident later on, in summing up "a few remarkable passages of providence," and, by praising the all-seeing and mysterious workings of the Lord, she manages also to castigate the bumbling English army, "the slowness and dullness" of which was derided by the Indians (158-59). This pious insult is a complex insinuation, the minister's wife "admiring to see the wonderful providence of God in preserving the heathen for farther affliction to our poor country," sentiments revealing what everyday conversation may have been like in a Puritan village, thin innuendoes issuing from the patient smiles of the uncommon good, pious superiority masked by a Socratic manner.

A similar revelation is provided by an episode that occurs at the farther end of Rowlandson's Removes, on the western bank of the Connecticut. Ferried across in a canoe, the rumpled, ragged, dirty, and distraught matron finds herself in the midst of "Philip's crew," like

Captain Smith at the head of the Pamunkey thrust into the very heart of darkness: "I could not but be amazed at the numerous crew of pagans that were on the bank on the other side. When I came ashore, they gathered all about me, I sitting alone in their midst: I observed they asked one another questions, and laughed, and rejoiced over their gains and victories. Then my heart began to fail and I fell a-weeping, which was the first time to my remembrance that I wept before them" (134). Surrounded by savages, overwhelmed by a sense of absolute estrangement from civilization, the Puritan heroine nevertheless takes a kind of comfort from her tears, those bitter streams that carry her likewise into the heart of the Hebrew experience: "Now may I say . . . 'By the waters of Babylon, there we sat down: yea we wept when we remembered Zion.' "

But from metaphorical Babylon the New English Israelite is hurried into the presence of King Philip himself, her river-side epiphany giving way to a comic interlude of temptation refused: "He bade me come in and sit down, and asked me whether I would smoke (a usual compliment nowadays among saints and sinners) but this no way suited me. For though I had formerly used tobacco, yet I had left it ever since I was first taken. It seems to be a bait the Devil lays to make men lose their precious time . . . such a bewitching thing it is: but I thank God, He has now given me power over it; surely there are many who may be better employed than to lie sucking a stinking tobacco-pipe" (134). This is high comedy, the bedraggled minister's wife refusing the Indian's traditional gesture of hospitality, interpreted by her as a satanic "bait." It is a caricature of virtue preserved, her reason for rejecting the pipe less a caveat against the pleasures of the flesh than a lecture on the evils of wasting time, with a clearly Yankee intonation. But the scene gains a further comic dimension if we compare it to that prototypical iconograph of woman tempted, not Eve and the Serpent, but Comus and the Lady Alice. The correspondences are coincidental, yet the suitability of the captivity narrative to the Puritans' conception of their wilderness condition is dramatized by Milton's choice of a similar situation and imagery.

Rowlandson is hardly a fair young virgin, nor is her chastity ever at stake, but the wildwood scene, the pagan "crew," and the proferred drug are all homespun equivalents to features in Milton's tapestry-like masque. Held prisoner by that meta-Comus, Metacomet, "fixed" like the Lady Alice in a pagan seat, Mary Rowlandson resists temptation while her errant Brothers, the bumbling militia, wander about the mazy woods. Mary's protecting Spirit is no Ariel, but God Himself, and if her chastity is not the issue, grace under pressure is, and in neither masque of virtue is the outcome ever in doubt. The terms of Mary's rescue, however, are very much dictated by the circumstances that separate the reality of the American woods from Milton's fairyland forest, for no personified Connecticutus emerges to succor the Puritan prisoner. Indeed, that savage stream serves as an instrument of further suffering: "Instead of going toward the Bay, which was what I desired, I must go with them five or six miles down the river . . . where we abode almost a fortnight" (140). In the end, Mrs. Rowlandson is rescued by "Mr. John Hoar," a transformation effected with hard English shillings, not on the bank of the Connecticut, but in the shadow of Wachusett mountain, at the end of a long and painful walk toward home (155-56).

Given this terminal landmark, we can read Mrs. Rowlandson's narrative as conforming to the theocratic metaphor, a parable in which wilderness rivers provide scenes of hardship, not vistas of plenty, a desert terrain emphasizing the limited but undeniable felicity of home and hearth. On the metaphysical level, similarly, Mary Rowlandson's experience asserts the protective power of faith and the comforting assurances of hope, the both reinforced by Scripture, to which she adds her own testament. For with the Psalmist she declares "the works of the Lord and His wonderful power in carrying us along, preserving us in the wilderness, while under the enemy's hand, and returning us in safety again" (134). And with Jeremiah she draws a salutary lesson from her sufferings, which epitomize New England's punishment for "our perverse and evil carriages in the sight of the Lord" (160). But in her piety Mary Rowlandson comes dangerously close to the pietism for which Anne Hutchinson was excommunicated and exiled, a proximity which adds yet another dimension to her narrative.

As wife and mother, Mary can be seen as a figuration of the female center to all communities, whether in New Israel or Old, her attitude throughout a traditionally feminine one of passive forbearance in the face of adversity. She is a female Christ and a Puritan Una, type of the Church in the Wilderness, surrounded by "roaring lions and savage bears that feared neither God, nor man, nor the Devil, by night and day, alone and in company: sleeping all sorts together, and yet not one of them ever offered me the least abuse of unchastity to me, in word or action" (161). Yet this is, after all, Mary Rowlandson of Lancaster, Massachusetts, and though she denies speaking it "for my own credit," which "some are ready to say," and ascribes her safety rather to the "presence of God, and to His glory," to do so implicitly enrolls her among the Elect, her chastity an equivalent to Major Mason's victory over the Pequots. As victim, that is, Mary emerges as heroine, her immaculateness among hazards evidence of her sainthood, and to take the emphasis of her narrative to its logical conclusion is to read the entire war as a demonstration of her sanctity. A shipload of sailors goes down so that Robinson Crusoe may be brought to his senses and New England is burned over so that Mary Rowlandson may have her ordeal.

Her experience, moreover, gives Mary a singular blessedness, for as she points out, only suffering like hers can elucidate certain "scriptures which we do not take notice of or understand till we are afflicted" (147). In her descent to the level of Indian life, starved to the point where she was able to eat that "which another time would have been an abomination," Mary Rowlandson has in effect taken a special wilderness communion, not exactly a Black Mass, but something perilously close to it (149). Refusing temptation in the obvious form of Philip's pipe of tobacco, she has succumbed to a much more subtle bait, not unlike the apple held out to Eve, granting her knowledge denied Adam. It is significant in this regard that Rowlandson adopts male biblical personae throughout her narrative, assuming the voices of prophets and patriarchs as she wanders through the woods until she has gathered a goodly company about her, enforcing the metaphoric guise of Captive Israel. Losing her children, she becomes not Rachel bereft, but Jacob bereaved of Joseph and Simeon, and the references to lions and bears may connote Una's condition, but the reference is to Daniel. Mary crosses the Baquaug twice and twice echoes the words of Isaiah, and in the interval having assumed the *personae* of (among others) the Psalmist, Jonathan, Jeremiah, and Job, she ends her narration with the triumphant words of David and Moses. Only once does she drop a reference to a woman's name from the Bible, and then it is "Lot's wife," a masculine predominance that lends a definitive rigor to her story, which is high on faith and hope but low on charity (132).

The increasing dependence on the ferocious voices of the Old Testament is an obvious aspect of the transformation of the Puritan errand, and we may attribute Mary's sexual bias to the influence of sermonic types made familiar by her husband and his fellow ministers. But the undeniable effect is to cast her in the role of Prophet-Psalmist, which is in New as in Old Israel a priest's and hence a male part. Increase Mather in his sermonic history of King Philip's War is a case in point, the minister's wife from Lancaster having a certain advantage over Boston's foremost preacher: though she lacked the requisite Harvard degree, Mary underwent a version of ordainment denied her male counterpart, and is licensed to speak therefore concerning the meaning of "certain scriptures," texts containing mysteries closed to the prying Mather eye. In considering the subversiveness of this inadvertently sibylline strand, let us recall how unimportant the incident of the Wethersfield Maids was to John Winthrop and Edward Johnson, how the only male who saw its meaning was an ardent supporter of Anne Hutchinson, the woman who was Winthrop's nemesis and hence Johnson's "Jezebel," not a Jael but a female "Sisera" (121). Symbolically as well as chronologically, Mary Rowlandson is a transitional figure through whom Anne is transformed into Hannah, the heroic prototype of frontier womanhood. Anne is banished and murdered by God's satanic agents, Mary is captured by same and suffers but triumphs, and Hannah (the name implies God's favor) inflicts the judgment of Jael upon her Indian captors.

Rowlandson's narrative looks forward therefore to a time when the woman in the wilderness landscape will play a much more active role as defender of home and hearth—indeed, it survived to serve subsequent occasions. By the time it was reprinted in 1773, the pious title and accompanying jeremiad had been cropped off along the way—a utilitarian stripping much like that by which the German *Jäger* became the Kentucky rifle—and the title page was decorated with a picture of a woman shooting at four men. It is an image hardly justified by the contents of the book, yet as a heroic, male (albeit tragic) action lies concealed in Mrs. Rowlandson's married name, so in her narrative there is curled a fierce embryo, an Ishmaelite theme which only long wilderness passage would bring forth. The Jeremian frame drops away like a husk to reveal a muscular Christian Deborah / Diana, evidence of the transforming power of the American woods, where is found the mystic source giving forth Indian streams.

291

iii. Captivity Thence Captive, Us To Win

Given the place and implication of Mrs. Rowlandson's great temptation scene, it is fitting that Mary and Joseph (and presumably a babe
or two) removed soon after her ordeal to Wethersfield, by 1680 well
within the pacified precincts of the Connecticut Valley. But the upper
regions of the great river remained a hazardous territory, an elongated
zone of conflict which, with the Merrimack Valley, would slowly re-
align New England's geopolitics, no longer marking the farthest
bounds of civilization's reach but becoming arms of settlement that
moved inexorably northward. Still, what permits upward mobility also
allows for downward descent, and the Connecticut river increasingly
served as a conduit of French and Indian aggression, much of which
by the end of the century was visited on Deerfield and her neighboring towns. This was the scene of the epochal attack that resulted in
the ordeal of Quentin Stockwell and the adventure of Wait and Jennings, but a quarter-century of experience suggested that the sufferings
of the former would prove the rule, the trail along the upper Connecticut, then across to Lake Chaplain and on to the St. Lawrence becoming a veritable valley of the shadow of death.

Deerfield's people appear in Mather's *"Decennium Luctuosum"* as
an "extraordinary instance of courage in keeping their *station . . .*
and their worthy pastor, Mr. John Williams, deserves the thanks of all
this province for his encouraging them all the ways imaginable to
stand their ground" (II: 640). Williams's congregation is the theocratic
ideal, a "praying and valiant little flock," fortified against wilderness
wolves by the Hedge of grace—a sanctified hamlet on a frontier well-
defended. The essential fallacy of Mather's pious strategy was revealed
in 1704, when Williams's stalwart sheep were taken by surprise attack,
providing the minister with an extended opportunity to demonstrate
his hardihood while under prolonged personal seige, keeping his sta-

292

tion even on the trail and in the midst of papists and pagans in Canada. His account of that ordeal, *The Redeemed Captive Returning to Zion* (1707), is a version of spiritual autobiography that provides a perfect complement to Mary Rowlandson's narrative, converting to metaphor the covert dimension of her experience. Mary as Mother is the Puritan Community incarnate, but John as Pastor is the Church, a personification of the sacred ring of grace which symbolized sanctity for the Puritans. John-the-Congregationalist in the Wilderness is a citadel of zeal, a little bit of Harvard Yardage borne like the Ark of the Covenant to Canada and back, intact.

Williams and his fellow Deerfield captives were taken along the same route followed by Quentin Stockwell nearly thirty years before, likewise a winter-time trek through snow and over ice, and Williams's sufferings were if anything more severe. Two of his children were killed during the attack on Deerfield, and his wife was murdered soon after, being weak from childbirth and unable to keep up. Yet Williams turns his individual woes to the service of the general good, Deerfield's case serving to illustrate the familiar theocratic adage, "that days of fasting and prayer, without reformation, will not avail to turn away the anger of God" (7). As spiritual autobiography, then, Williams's narrative is a pointed extension of Mather's *"Decennium Luctuosum,"* the captive himself a miniature *"Hecatompolis,"* protected because of his prayerful, pious state. Where Mary Rowlandson emerges from her narrative a female Christ, John Williams is rather a feminine one, dressing himself in glory with a somewhat womanly grace, as Deerfield Captive and Massachusetts Martyr a Joan of the Boston Ark.

There is less wilderness in Williams's account, but much more Babylon, for his journey north occupies only some thirty out of nearly one hundred and fifty pages, as the minister, along with his Indian captors, hastens to Canada. There his important ordeal begins, not his great suffering from grief, hunger, and bloody feet, but the seige laid on his Puritan faith by wily Jesuits and their Indian dupes. Williams has good words for the French Governor of Quebec, who tried to get his captive children returned to him, but for the Jesuits he has nothing but angry contempt. Though the circumstances of his stay at Chateau Riche, near Quebec, were hardly cruel, the threats by priests and Indians being mostly gestures without substance, Williams is at pains to present himself as under constant duress. Where Mrs. Rowlandson refused to take tobacco with Metacomet, Williams resists overtures of conversion, even to the point of struggling against the efforts of priests who attempt to bring him (literally) into their church.

Such episodes, as when his Indian captor tries to force him to make the sign of the cross, have an effect much like Mrs. Rowlandson's knitting-work, being quite different from what was intended. In the end, the Reverend Williams emerges from his story of Christian courage as an intolerable prig, filled with a Cotton-Matherish stuffing: "And almost always before any remarkable favor, I was brought to lie down at the foot of God, and made to be willing that God should govern the world so as might be most for His own honor, and brought to resign all to His holy sovereignty: A frame of spirit, when wrought in me by the grace of God, giving the greatest content and satisfaction; and very often a forerunner of the mercy asked of God, or a plain demonstration that the not obtaining my request was best for me" (76-77). Like a steeple-cock on a church spire, Williams celebrates the blowing of the wind from any direction with a silent crow of triumph, for whether it blows north, south, east, or west, it never blows ill for him.

While other prisoners were kept by the Indians from praying, Williams found frequent opportunities for his favorite exercise, petitioning God for His "protecting presence," not only for himself and his fellow captives but for Massachusetts also, "that God would be a little sanctuary to us in a land of captivity, and that our friends in New England might have grace to make a more thankful and fruitful improvement of the means of grace than we had done; who, by our neglects, find ourselves out of God's sanctuary" (69-70). This idea of *sanctum ex sanctuarium* dominates his narrative, a strategic metaphor that is but another version of the Puritan's Wall of Grace, being a traveling Camp of Israel "in the land of strangers" (162). Throughout his ordeal, Williams presents himself as a prayerful stronghold of watch and ward, for whose benefit God stages occasional demonstrations of His dislike of Catholics, as when He burns down "the seminary, a very famous building," and then, as if to emphasize His point, later hurls a lightning bolt at "the very place" where the fire had started (78-79).

These Matherish touches are not coincidental. Williams was related to the son of Increase by marriage, and Cotton, while his kinsman was still in Canada, collected some of Williams's captivity compositions for his *Good Fetch'd Out of Evil* (1706). Having thereby given Williams an opportunity to do "service, even when confined from serviceableness," Mather hastened to sit down with his kinsman when he returned from captivity shortly thereafter, "and studied and contrived and united counsels with him," as he noted in his *Diary*, "how the Lord might have revenues of glory from his experiences" (I: 568, 575). As with certain politicians, proximity to Cotton Mather tended toward propinquity, and if John Williams did indeed compose *The Redeemed Captive*, it was under the heady influence of the Boston divine. Like the "Lecture" which Mather wrote but "employ'd" his kinsman to read "unto a great auditory," and which was duly appended to the first edition of Williams's book, the narrative itself was a captive performance in a double sense, being a wilderness experience with a Boston bias. "It is certain," Williams observes toward the end, "that the charity of the whole country of Canada, though moved with the doctrines of merit, does not come up to the charity of Boston alone, where notions of merit are rejected; but acts of charity performed out of right Christian spirit" (142-43).

Despite the title of his book, Williams nowhere makes reference to Canada as Babylon, but the association appears in Mather's sermon, a celebration of the captive's return which is decorated with numerous quotations from Exodus and the Psalms testifying to God's protection of His Chosen People both in the wilderness and captivity, but which ends with the usual threatening note concerning "the briars and thorns of the wilderness" and tears shed by "the rivers of Babylon" (165). There is, in this regard, an interesting shadow metaphor in John Williams's "Dedication" to *The Redeemed Captive*, which praises Governor Joseph Dudley for his "uncommon sagacity and prudence, in contriving to loose the bonds of your captivated children" (4). God redeems His children, but the Governor of Massachusetts provides the wherewithal, resulting in a most unusual slip of the pen by Williams (or whomever): "Nothing was thought too difficult by you to effect this design, in that you readily sent your own son, Mr. William Dudley, to undergo the hazards and hardships of a tedious voyage, that this affair might be transacted with success, which must not be forgotten, as an expression of your great solicitude and zeal to recover us from the tyranny and oppression of our captivity" (4-5). By such means, William, Son of Joseph, becomes the Redeemer, and though the blasphemy is hardly intentional, the irony was cast in Boston.

Let us add a third figure to this drama of redemption, a haunting and worrisome presence in the annals of Puritan New England whose story is told by only a few meager entries in diaries and chronicles. For among the Deerfield captives was Williams's little daughter, Eunice, named for her Mather mother, a child of seven whom the Indians refused to ransom back, causing her father much anguish concerning the state of her soul. Bringing his narrative to a close, he referred to the children left in Canada "among the savages," and who, "having lost the English tongue, will be lost and turn savages in a little time, unless something extraordinary prevent" (141). Williams asked for "prayers to God" that Eunice and others like her might be gathered back to New England, "being outcasts ready to perish" (142). Mather's diary reveals that he, at least, heeded the request, praying for his cousin's little daughter "in the hands of the French Popish Indians," though his prayers were not made "with such a frequency and fervency of supplication as I should have" (II: 92-93). Mather compensated for this deficiency by making "her condition an argument in discourses with my own children, for thankfulness and piety," thereby displaying his usual willingness to make good use of his kinsman—and other people's suffering (104).

In 1713 John Williams returned to Canada with a commission to arrange for the return of English captives, but Eunice, who had by then not only forgotten her native language but married an Indian, refused to leave. She is thenceforth missing from the ranks of distinguished kinsmen regularly mustered in Mather's diary, being assigned, presumably, to that Puritan Limbo, "the dark dispensations of Providence," the usual way of disposing of troublesome Canadian matters (191). Before the news of Eunice's refusal to return reached Boston, Samuel Danforth Junior expressed a hope to Samuel Sewall that it might be with her "as when Samson married a Philistine," and Sewall noted in *his* diary that he likewise saw a good omen in her name— which he read as "Happy Victory" (II: 708). But the victory was not this time for God and Massachusetts, Eunice having been "captivated" by the Indians in a sense not meant by her father, her wilderness condition leading to a loathsome transformation.

The silence in Cotton Mather's diary concerning Eunice's further fate has an audible clang to it, excluding her evermore from Christian care. A Puritan Eurydice without a Boston Orpheus, Eunice remains a potent wildwood symbol, both witch- and wraith-like, a fearsome waif flitting through the northern forests, a Lady Alice running with her Canadian Comus. That she was the daughter of Eunice Mather, and that her grandson was Eleazar Williams—the half-breed Hiawatha and crackpot Dauphin—does not diminish her importance as a wilderness symbol of Ovidian changes. Eunice's story is a mythic alternative to the metamorphosis of Jezebel into Jael begun by Anne Hutchinson, who also had a daughter captured by savages, a child who, according to John Winthrop, "continued with them about four years until she had forgot her own language, and all her friends, and was loath to have come from the Indians" (II: 277). Thomas Morton was dying in Agamenticus even as the Governor wrote this, but his laughter continued to ring in western wilds.

iv. Plain Russet-coated Captain

An alternative version of the year 1704 is found in the memoirs of Captain Benjamin Church, the hero of Hubbard's history of King Philip's War, and a veteran of several later campaigns. Despite his advanced age and avoirdupois, Church was so exercised by "the miserable devastations made on Deerfield . . . especially their cruelties towards that worthy gentlewoman, Mrs. Williams" that he vowed to "fight and destroy those savages as they did our poor neighbors" (243-44). The (by then) Major heaved his (by then) ponderous weight onto a luckless horse and rode off to do his duty by his countrymen once again, his "Fifth and Last Expedition East" lying not toward Quebec, but along the (by then) well-beaten waterway to Nova Scotia. This was the route first charted by General Phips, whose attitude toward Canada Church fully shared, though his tactics in that regard were entirely different. Indeed, soldier Church emerges from his memoirs as Phips's counterpart, a homespun hero to match Mather's iron-clad monument, for both his experience and his Plymouth birth gave him a perspective on American matters quite dissimilar to the line propagated in Boston.

Though Church's *Entertaining Passages Relating to King Philip's War* (1716) promises to render "Some Account of the Divine Providence" in his adventures, the total "some" is not excessive, most "passages" being chiefly "entertaining." Like Smith, a soldier of his own fortune—both providential and public—Captain Church is a distinctly New England *miles,* a militiaman, the Cincinnatus from Little Compton sharing his time between the plow and the sword. At the outbreak of King Philip's War he was something of a frontiersman as well, having removed from Duxbury to a new plantation perilously close to Indian territory, a neck of woods which would become part of Rhode Island. In the midst of clearing land and protecting himself from pesky savages, Church received his first "commission from the government to engage in their defense: And with my commission I received another heart, inclining me to put forth my strength in military service: And through the grace of God I was spirited for that work, and direction in it was renewed to me day by day" (ix).

This is one of the few times Church associates his military exploits with God's grace, but it is a significant exception, for notably it is his commission which, like a covenant, acts to fill the newly appointed Captain with a new "heart." Throughout his narrative Church cites his other "commissions," even printing them verbatim, an old soldier displaying his medals. They seem to have had something other than a civil power for him, being associated with the preservational power of "the overruling hand of the Almighty." Again, this initial emphasis is not borne out by subsequent allusions to providence—the militant Church being anything but the Church Militant—but it does put into perspective the Captain's ambivalence concerning the civil source of his commissions. For the chief tension which emerges from Church's narrative is between civilian authority and military necessity, the stress (and strain) which give shape to the narratives of Captains Smith, Gardiner, and Mason.

Cotton Mather regarded Boston as the chief jewel in the New England diadem, but Church tends to regard it as a carbuncle of a different order, and the Governor Dudley praised by John Williams is portrayed as a sycophant of the British Crown. Moreover, the Captain has a way of using the word "gentlemen" which expresses his sublime contempt for those privileged Boston citizens who refused to take his advice and often failed to pay him for his services. The Boston antagonism is a Plymouth institution as old as the Rock, but there is latent in Church's version a democratic bias, illustrated by the story he tells of being refused by the "gentlemen in Boston" the money for his passage home after he returned, in 1690, from his second campaign against the French and Indians. For a Rhode Island drover, whom the penniless Captain met in a Roxbury tavern, was more generous, meeting his request for forty shillings with an offer of " 'forty pounds if he wanted it' " (197).

Another kind of democracy informs Church's narrative, also, the fellowship of arms, a true commonwealth of perils which, unlike Winthrop's, opened to receive the Indian, the Captain being instrumental in recruiting native troops—including the renegade savage who shot the rebel Wampanoag—to fight against King Philip. Moreover, having "inquired of some of the Indians that were become his soldiers, how they got such advantage often of the English in their marches through the woods," Church thenceforth used Indian tactics, keeping his forces "divided and scattered" (108-9). William Hubbard also advocated using Indians to fight Indians, but only after finding biblical sanction for the practice, and he could not bring himself to the point of adapting heathen tactics to Christian warfare (II: 228, I: 113-16). Church was never bothered by such nice theological distinctions, and for him "the better side of the hedge" was always the winning one (131). Making a typically Yankee virtue out of necessity, he continued to employ Indians and their ways of warfare throughout his long career of killing them. As with the similar practice of Captain Smith, Church's wilderness strategy was not a matter of acculturation, but of martial expediency, ever the cutting edge of technological advance, beat out on Smith's anvil, "experience." Yet as with the frontier woman, long experience tends to have a reciprocal effect, and toward the end of his narrative Church becomes somewhat Indianized, like so many native-born Yankees, having a distinctly Algonquin profile.

The sum of Captain Church's wilderness ways is epitomized by his campaign of 1704, providing the occasion for the full display of not only his tactical knowledge, but also his thorough dislike for General Courts, which had likewise accumulated over the years. Along with a request to attack Port Royal once again, Church submitted to Governor Joseph Dudley a list of required troops and materiél for his expedition, and though he never got permission to sack the Nova Scotia town—Dudley having referred that matter to the "Lords commissioners" in London, on whose "board" it remained (253)—Church did get the men and supplies he asked for, a list which provides a sum of his military know-how. Along with the usual "three hundred Indians at least," and "four or five hundred pairs of Indian shoes" for his English soldiers, Church requested fifty whaleboats especially equipped for portaging, and whalemen to row them into Canadian waters (245-47). During a quarter-century of fighting along the rivers and bays from Hubbard's Piscataqua to Pemaquid and beyond, Church had learned the efficacy of whaleboats to amphibious warfare. Light and speedy craft, indigenous inventions of Yankees who used them to hunt whales in coastal waters, they were effective in other kinds of hunting also, their rapid approach throwing the enemy into consternation.

Ranging the northeast coast, and penetrating into Canadian territory by means of rivers, Major Church and his whaleboat flotilla revenged New England for the depredations of Quebec by attacking the Nova Scotians with Indian ways and means. Gracing his activities at the last with divine intention, Church gives the narratives of Underhill and Mason a thrust into a succeeding century, and his view of providence, like theirs, has both a Judaic and Indian look: "Some few of our cruel and bloody enemies were made sensible of their bloody cruelties, perpetrated on my dear and loving friends and countrymen," revenge administered in such a fashion "as they had been guilty of, in a barbarous manner at Deerfield; and, I hope, justly" (268). Church was forbidden by his orders from harming any French settlers, but he took care to rattle his saber so hard his prisoners' teeth chattered, warning them that "if ever hereafter any of our frontiers, east or west, were molested by them, as formerly, that he would (if God spared his life) and they might depend upon it, return upon them with a thousand of his savages (if he wanted them), all volunteers, with our whaleboats, and pursue them to the last extremity" (279).

By accident, however, a few French Canadians were killed during his campaign, and the Boston halter slipped perilously close to the Major's neck upon his return. So also was Captain Smith nearly hanged when he came back to Jamestown from the Pamunkey in 1608, and like Smith (and Lion Gardiner), Church received slim recompense for his "great expenses, fatigues, and hardships" (286). Yet another captain's narrative engendered by the American experience, Church's account of his Indian campaigns is one more apologia-complaint, addressed in his case to his fellow citizens of New England—his "neighbors." Where the Reverend John Williams returned from his ordeal of 1704 to sing the praises of Boston, Church ends his last campaign by once again turning his very broad back to the Bay, for the "real" enemy, finally, is found in Mather's town, where gentlemen and their Governor wait on the pleasure of the Crown.

Cotton Mather's version of King Philip's War in the *Magnalia* gives the Little Compton Captain a full theocratic treatment, making him over (like Phips) into "another *Shamgar* . . . employed by the providence of Heaven," his "very *name*" suggesting "unto the miserable savages *what* they must be undone by fighting against" (II: 562, 574). But Church in his own account assumes a native, democratic dress, a difference further illustrated by his attitude toward Fort William Henry, whose erection by Sir William Phips at Pemaquid is celebrated by Mather as "the finest thing that had been seen in these parts of America" (619). Being built entirely of stone, the fort was hardly the example of *"prudence, industry,* and *thriftiness"* advertised by Mather, but was an exercise in conspicuous construction expressing the General's megalomania and the author's concomitant love of grandiose architectonics. Like Phips's Canadian campaign (and the *Magnalia*), it was a monument of misconceived strategy, whose cost of maintenance was "continually complained of as one of the 'country's grievances,'" and it was eventually surrendered to the enemy (620).

For his part, Major Church preferred whaleboats and scattered troops, and when asked by General Phips for his opinion on the matter, he answered "that his genius did not incline that way, he never had any value for forts, being only nests for destruction" (210). It is best, as Simon Suggs observes, to remain shifty in a new country, and Suggs is the Voice of the Border, that perilous Ovidian zone. In Church's Indian ways and means we have a major departure from English usage in America, and as Phips's defeat at Quebec looks forward to Braddock's fall, so Major Church is a forecast of that hero of western waters, Robert Rogers, a far-ranging Yankee Indian born in Methuen on the north bank of the Merrimack, a town once part of Hannah Dustin's Haverhill.

v. Faith, Sir, We Are Here Today and Gone Tomorrow

Like the convergence of the Spanish and French adventures in 1542, that grand year of illusion, the events of 1704 in New England provide a marvelous coincidence, a miracle of meaning, one of those amazing reticulations of event which contribute to the literary aspect of the emerging design. Moreover, we may add to the adventures of the Reverend Williams and Major Church the travels of Madam Sarah Kemble Knight, who set out from Boston to New York even as the one was enjoying the dubious felicity of Quebec and the other was cruising the coast of Nova Scotia. Her journey to the Hudson and back provides a humorous third to their perilous voyages, for Madam Knight on the road, like Mrs. Rowlandson in the woods, resembles Chaucer's more than Milton's Alice. A stalwart woman of the New World, she also shares with the wandering wilderness wife of Lancaster a married name with chivalric resonance, but there the resemblance stops. For hers like the Reverend Williams's is a tale of two cities, and though her pilgrimage was a secular, not a saintly errand, it certainly acted to reinforce her conviction that Boston was a very good place indeed.

Boston and New York were separated by wilderness enough in 1704, and the route between was bisected by a number of treacherous streams to be crossed at hazard—whether by bridge, ferry, canoe, or on horseback. The folk of colonial New England seldom longed to go on pilgrimages, but when overland travel was mandatory, they set out not in the spring, but the fall of the year, when rivers were lowest and roads as passable as they might be. It is a wonder that Madam Knight went at all, curious that she chose to go by horseback and not by boat, but understandable that she departed Boston in early October, "to New Haven," as she thought, one of those American plans that tended to go awry on the road. Since her journey parallels in direction the perennial Hudson-bound push of westering Puritans, and since her *Journal* takes definition and pattern from the ubiquitous presence of rivers along the way, the element of inadvertency adds a final and characteristic touch, an irony which subsequent events would reveal.

1704 was also the year in which Boston's first newspaper was published, an event which, like Madam Knight's journey, is symptomatic of the lack of communication between and within the New England colonies. But both are prophetic also of improvements soon to come, and Madam was the sort of person who would make them: like Benjamin Church she is a combination of traits which are typical of an emerging American temper, not only personal independence and enterprise, but a detectable regional pride. In most other respects, Sarah is Benjamin's antithesis, in matters of setting as well as sex, being firmly fixed in Boston, where she was at various times a schoolteacher, legal scrivener, and a keeper of shops and boardinghouses, business careers occasioned at first by her husband's long absences in England and then by his death. It was a busy life and a town life, and Knight's was likewise a business trip, symbolic in its own way of the changing New England character. Sarah is supposed to have taught young Ben Franklin his penmanship, and certainly the same blue ink colored their veins, her trip to New York, like his subsequent exodus to Philadelphia, an expression of the burgeoning Yankee spirit.

But as a humorous traveler's tale, Madam Knight's *Journal* resembles a picaresque narrative by Smollett, taking its tension from the essential disparity between town and country life. With Smollett, Sarah Knight prefers the former, whose amenities are enhanced by the ordeal of life on the road. The comic tone is established early on, her first guide after leaving the comforts of Dedham being an uncouth bumpkin "resembling a globe on a gatepost" as he rides on before her in the gloom, a Hudibrastic "shade" and the presiding genius of her voyage out: "He entertained me with the adventures he had passed by late riding, and the imminent dangers he had escaped, so that, remembering the heroes in *Parismus* and the *Knight of the Oracle,* I didn't know but I had met with a prince disguised" (2-3). Despite her satirical tone, the Boston traveler is grateful for her guide's "universal knowledge in the woods," a wilderness necessity which will provide a thematic paradox throughout. Sarah's backwoods Virgil is only the first of several conductors through a dark and dangerous terrain, and he leads her safely to lodgings in Billings, the first of many rustic "Stages" where Madam will spend a night of dubious felicity, a series of advances into and out of the wilderness equivalent to Mrs. Rowlandson's "Removes."

Stages there are along the way, but no stagecoaches, and some hint of the primitive level of communications at the turn of the century is given by the fact that her guides during the next leg of the journey are post riders, the eastern post turning Madam Knight over to the western post at midday. Picking her up at the western terminus of the Providence Ferry, he leads her through Rhode Island to the eastern bank of the Pawtucket, "which they generally ride through. But I dared not venture" (5). Taking passage instead in a small and shallow canoe manned by a boy, Madam Knight, like Mrs. Rowlandson crossing the Baquaug, is at pains to avoid a soaking, "very circumspect, sitting with my hands fast on each side, my eyes steady, not daring so much as to lodge my tongue a hair's breadth more on one side than t'other," fearing that even "a wry thought would have overset our wherry." Like Mary in the wilderness, Sarah's perilous position brings to mind "Lot's wife," but Isaiah is not quoted and the closest Madam Knight comes to "Providence" while crossing over water is on the ferry of that name.

Warned by the post rider of yet another "bad river we were to ride through," Madam Knight's apprehensions are darkened by the approach of evening: "No thoughts but those of the dangerous river could entertain my imagination, and they were as formidable as various, still tormenting me with blackest ideas of my approaching fate—Sometimes seeing myself drowning, otherwhiles drowned, and at the best like a holy sister just come out of a spiritual bath in dripping garments" (6). The concluding image is baptismal, but that is not the implication, and "dying with the very thoughts of drowning," Sarah is further tormented by the transformations her lively imagination works on the forest around her: "Each lifeless trunk, with its shatter'd limbs, appear'd an armed enemy; and every little stump like a ravenous devourer." In this state of mind she is led to the bank of "the hazardous river he had told me of," and summoning "all the courage I was mistress of, knowing that I must either venture my fate of drowning, or be left like the Children of the Wood," Madam Knight "gave reins to my nag; and sitting as steady as just before in the canoe, in a few minutes got safe to the other side, which he told me was the Narragansett Country" (7).

Safe across is not safely through, and though divested of Indians by Captain Church and his courageous company, the area is wild enough still for a Boston lady, "the way being very narrow, and on each side the trees and bushes gave us very unpleasant welcomes with their branches and boughs, which we could not avoid, it being so exceeding dark." To her dismay, the post rider left the weary widow behind in "the dolesome woods, my company next to none, going I knew not whither, and encompassed with terrifying darkness; the least of which was to startle a more masculine courage." Doubting at this point the wisdom of her errand, Madam Knight borrows the language of the Puritan pulpit: "my call was very questionable." But at the darkest moment her prospects are suddenly irradiated by an approximation of grace, "the friendly appearance of the kind conductress of the night, just then advancing above the horizontal line. The raptures which the sight of that fair planet produced in me, caused me, for the moment, to forget my present weariness and past toils; and inspired me for most of the remaining way with very diverting thoughts" (7-8).

Lapsing (as is her wont) into verse, Madam Knight pays homage to "fair Cynthia," whose "light can dissipate fears," whose "bright aspect rescues from despair . . . And a bright joy does through my soul diffuse," poetic diction again evoking an experience of grace (8). That her conductress is the pagan goddess who protects imperiled women recalls again Milton's Sabrina fair, being likewise something of a good fairy, transforming the dismal forest into "the pleasant delusion of a sumptuous city, filled with famous buildings and churches, with their spiring steeples, balconies, galleries, and I know not what: grandeurs which I had heard of, and which the stories of foreign countries had given me the idea of" (8-9). The protective, transformational role of Cynthia, "the way being smooth and even, the night warm and serene," in effect turns the woods into a better Boston, and in the wilderness as in the town, Madam Knight lives on "Moon Street."

Two more "Stages" of discommodious accommodations brought Sarah to the Pawcatuck River, where she found the water high and her courage at its "lowest ebb." Stopping by "a little cottage just by the river, to wait the water's falling," Madam Knight, like Mrs. Rowlandson beside the Connecticut, sits herself down at an extreme remove from civilization. The cottage was a "little hut," "one of the wretch-edest I ever saw as a habitation for human creatures," with "clapboards . . . so much asunder, that the light come through everywhere" (13). This "picture of poverty," like Mary's experience of savagery, puts Sarah's distress into (poetic) perspective: "Their lodgings thin and hard, their Indian fare," reduces her "late fatigues" to a "notion or forgotten dream" (14). As Mary Rowlandson went on to meet King Philip, so Madam Knight next encounters an equivalent phenomenon, a backwoods American, "an Indian-like animal . . . who makes an awkward scratch with his Indian shoe, and a nod, sits on the block, fumbles out his black junk, dips it in the ashes, and . . . fell to suck-ing like a calf, without speaking, for near a quarter of an hour."

This is the abhorred Thing Itself, Cotton Mather's Indianized Eng-lishman, William Hubbard's borderland monster, gnawing his hunk of beef jerky in savage silence, yet "ugly as he was," Madame Knight was "glad to ask him to show me the way." Mary's interview with Philip marks the westernmost point of her many "Removes," and Sarah is taken by her "tattertailed guide" to Stonington, the first "Stage" on her journey where she is "very well accommodated both as to victuals and lodging," and the last stage of her wilderness passage (15). Within a day's ride of New London, Madam Knight has reentered the bounds of civilization. "Very handsomely and plentifully treated and lodged" in New London, she is likewise received in New Haven "with all pos-sible respects and civility" (16, 18). But it is New York, the western terminus of both New England and her journey, which provides her *Journal* its cosmopolitan ideal, antithesis to the varieties of backwoods and wilderness life encountered on the road.

Sarah Knight finding "my business lying unfinished by some con-cerns at New York depending thereupon, my kinsman, Mr. Thomas Trowbridge of New Haven, must needs take a journey there before it could be accomplished, so I resolved to go there in company with him" (25). In short, the traveler now becomes a tourist, and finds that the "City of New York is a pleasant, well compacted place, situated on a commodious river which is a fine harbor for shipping" (28). The orderly widow is also pleased by the "very stately and high" buildings of brick, variously colored "and laid in checkers," which, "being glazed, look very agreeable" (29). The interiors are "neat to admira-tion," the woodwork "kept very white scoured as so is all the partitions if made of boards," and "the hearth is of tiles and is as far out into the room at the ends as before the fire." Despite geopolitical differences, the Dutch and the English share certain tidy proclivities, and the mark of Holland remains on English Manhattan, in its architecture and the conduct of business and social affairs alike. Dealt with fairly and exactly, Madam was also "handsomely treated" wherever she went, and it was "with no little regret" that she left, "having transacted the affair I went upon and some other that fell in the way" (31).

By contrast to the checkerboard city, neighboring Connecticut is an irregular mix of moral rigidity and sloppy manners, a vast rural demonstration of "the great necessity and benefit both of education and conversation; for these people have as large a portion of mother wit, and sometimes a larger, than those who have been brought up in cities; but for want of improvements, they render themselves almost ridiculous" (24). Symbolic of the Connecticut condition is the tobacco-chewing "tall country fellow" who labors greatly at the purchase of little: "Spitting a large deal of aromatic tincture, he gave a scrape with his shovel-like shoe, leaving a small shovel full of dirt on the floor, made a full stop, hugging his own pretty body with his hands under his arms, stood staring round him, like a cat let out of a basket. At last, like the creature Balaam rode on, he opened his mouth and said: Have you any ribbon for hatbands to sell I pray?" (23). Uncouth but not uncivil, Connecticut is a middle ground in Sarah's travels, as roadway and landscape a contrast to wild Rhode Island on the one side and civilized New York on the other. Its ungainly marriage of moral strictness and commercial opportunism is not unlike the "pumpkin and Indian mixed bread" and "bare-legged punch" which had such a disagreeable "aspect" and "so awkward or rather awful a sound" for the genteel lady from Boston (25).

Connecticut's towns are often flawed, instance Stamford, "a well compacted town, but with a miserable meeting house," or Norwalk, where "the church and tavern are next neighbors," or Fairfield, which has a "spacious meeting-house and good buildings," but where the "inhabitants are litigious, nor do they well agree with their minister, who (they say) is a very worthy gentleman" (33-34). Still, it is "a plentiful country for provisions of all sorts, and it's generally healthy. No one that can and will be diligent in this place need fear poverty nor the want of food and raiment" (36-37). So John Smith wrote of Massachusetts nearly a century earlier, and Connecticut two generations after Hooker's arrival is still a place badly in need of improvement, its people lacking in social graces and its roads needing equivalent repairs: "As bridges which were exceeding high and very tottering and of vast length, steep and rocky hills and precipices (bugbears to a fearful female traveler)" (33). It is understandable, therefore, that Madam Knight arrived safely back in Boston with "joy and satisfaction," giving thanks to "my Great Benefactor for thus graciously carrying forth and returning in safety His unworthy handmaiden" (39).

Sarah's narrative thereby ends with an echo of Mary Rowlandson's, and though her prayer is a pro-forma performance, she would in due time follow her wilderness sister to Connecticut, again on a different errand. Madam Knight moved to New London in 1714, on the occasion of her daughter's marriage to Colonel John Livingston, a widower whose first wife had been the only child of Fitz-John Winthrop, "a gentleman of an ancient and honorable family, whose father was Governor here sometime before him, and his grandfather had been Governor of the Massachusetts . . . a very courteous and affable person, much given to hospitality, who has by his good services gained the affections of the people as much as any who had been before him in that post" (24-25). But amiable Fitz-John was the last Governor Winthrop, and the marriage of his son-in-law to Elizabeth Knight tied a knot signaling the changing character of New England.

Putting aside her Boston business for country matters, Madam Knight began buying up lands that had once been Winthrop property, and settled in Norwich, Major Mason's town on the Thames. She continued to keep shop, but she also operated mills and farms, and expanded her domain by acquiring lands once owned by Uncas. By such means did she assist in the metamorphosis of eastern Connecticut into a bustling paragon of industry, forecasting the time when the Thames and its two main tributaries would be strung like a necklace with towns given form and function no longer by a church, but a factory. What was earlier a territory of adversity was rendered georgic ground by the Boston Knight, huswifery which channeled rivers of peril into millstreams of profit, a mechanic spirit turning the wheels of mercantile conversion.

The record also reveals that Madam Knight kept a tavern, perhaps with the intention of ameliorating the lot of poor travelers, though the same record reveals only that she once sold liquor illegally to some lingering John Mohegan, the last of his tribe. For the Indians who were the personification of wilderness for John Williams in 1707 had already been reduced in Connecticut to helpless dependency on the English. Madam Sarah describes them in her *Journal* as "the most savage of all the savages of that kind I had ever seen," but the reference is to their moral, not their martial character, the Indian in Connecticut by the turn of the century having been diminished to the level of a pitiful joke. The true savage in Knight's adventure is the grum changeling in moccasins who escorts her across the river and out of the woods, a white man reduced to barbarism by his wilderness condition.

Along with the tobacco-chewing bumpkin of Connecticut, he is the prototype of backwoodsmen of a later period and a farther west, who will inspire similar contempt from another female traveler whose maiden name was also Kemble. But where the bumpkin is laughable in his grotesqueness, the brooding, junk-chewing specter has something frightening about him, a quality suggesting the raw silent force of primal nature, reflecting the power of the torrent over which he leads the trembling traveler. He is at once the Man of the Woods and the Man of Waters, the brown god who replaces the red Janus, guardian not of entrances but of crossings, a joint emblem of threat and safety, of apprehension and relief. He holds the secret of the place in his keeping, and to him you must apply for passage across.

XI

RETURN, ALPHEUS

Taylor, Sewall, Wolcott, and Company:
Some Poetic Fabrics from the
Linsey-woolsey
Loom

i. Dread Voices

Maps were the means by which the unfolding idea of the New World was graphically expressed, becoming thereby symbols of the unknown taking definitive shape, as massive white areas cohered into an outlined coast with rivers ranging inland, the blankness retreating before the advancing details of certainty. But maps also, as in the case of Michael Lok's contribution to Hakluyt's *Divers Voyages*, could promote myths, consummations of dreams devoutly desired, giving form to the formless, opening a gateway to a western paradise. For Renaissance Englishmen, therefore, the map of the New World is a complex diagram, the face of and a face upon mystery, yielding John Donne an erotic image and Thomas Hooker a spiritual application: "Meditation goes upon discovery, toucheth at every coast, observes every creek, maps out the daily course of a man's conversation and disposition" (X: 214). But the meditational is an inward voyage, and like the erotic exploration it is a closeted concern, "the traversing of a man's thoughts, the coasting of the mind and imagination into every crevice and corner" (213). Since poetry in Puritan New England is, for the most part, like the sermon, an adjunct, even an aid, to meditation, it is largely a record of interior voyaging which, despite Hooker's heroic figure, is seldom more than a garden walk, a stroll with God in Gethsemane.

Most Puritan poets were preachers, so this limitation and emphasis is not surprising, and the effect was to promote the combination of concentricity and transcendentalism which is endemic to sermon literature, resulting in a poetic walling-out of the New World landscape, metric masonry reinforcing the closed theocratic view. Edward Taylor is not only the most accomplished of New England Puritan poets, but the best example of their ecclesiastical bent. Mute, inglorious Grays may slumber in Massachusetts graveyards, but the Great Discovered

of Congregational poetry refreshed himself in the glimmering landscape of the Bible, or drew upon domestic and communal concerns for
his poetical materials. Having traveled overland in the winter from
Cambridge to his frontier parish—at Westfield on the western side of
the Connecticut—Taylor in 1671 chose for his first sermon a text from
Matthew, with Jacques Cartier adopting John the Baptist as his persona, but no such wilderness identity informs his verse. Though he
devoted the rest of his life to the problems of a frontier community,
including the outbreak of King Philip's War shortly after his arrival
there, Taylor seldom let those matters invade his poetry.

Academic even in ecstasy, Taylor constructed his poems from the
Puritans' favorite sermonic tropes and with sensual metaphors encoded
the mystery of Puritan communion, figures of enclosure and nurture
that have the intensity of personal investment but which are in reality
highly conventionalized expressions of devotion. Secure in his "nut-
meg garden," whose walls contained "the world's circumferential glory
vast," Taylor drank from no Connecticut, but from "Adam's typick
stream," the divine river that "runs through ages all" (193, 86, 189).
Taylor figures "Jordan's stream" as "the border," not of some New
England Canaan, but "of God's land," and though once (as through his
study window) we glimpse redeemed captives "Paddling in their canoes
apace with joys / Along this blood red sea," it is more often "the Ark
of Grace" that cruises his meditational shore (98, 96, 225). The "sweeping flood" of 1683 is rendered by Taylor in terms of revilement and disgust—purgatives and excrement—and though the imagery is consistent
with his conventional loathing of self-and-the-world ("Becrown'd with
filth! Oh! what vile thing am I?/ What cost, and charge to make me
meadow ground?/ To drain my bogs? to lay my frog-pits dry?"), still, it
also suggests one good reason for his immaculate garden of verses, watered by "golden gutters" and "golden pipes" of sweet communion (471,
73, 21).

So also Anne Bradstreet, whose heart "rose up" in rebellion against
the prospect which inspired William Wood to write his homely
eclogues, and who with Edward Taylor sought refuge in an inner
asylum. Her work is likewise influenced by the language and forms of
theocratic literature, the Tenth Muse in America springing up close
by the pulpit, her view through the church window more often than
not commanding a graveyard. Just such a scene informs Bradstreet's

"Contemplations," a poem which combines successfully the worlds of nature and spirit but in terms evoking a landscape of mind not Massachusetts. A "goodly river" is central to the scene, channelized into an emblem of Life's flow, a stylized " 'happy flood' " which holds its course toward the "longed-for ocean" of Death, " 'Thetis' house, where all embrace and greet' ": " 'Thou emblem true of what I count the best, / Oh could I lead my rivulets to rest! So may we press to that vast mansion, ever blest' " (210-11).

That Bradstreet might be describing the Charles or the Merrimack is possible, but her river along with her "stately oak" and "sweet-tongued Philomel," are borrowed from the garden of English poesy, literary types decorating an interior landscape irradiated by "Phoebus" and populated by a cast of biblical characters. Thomas Morton was equally guilty of converting the American wilderness into a classical vista, his Frocoise an Arendian source, a springing up in the New English Canaan of Alpheus, river sacred to pastoral poetry. But Anne's Alph runs through no pleasure dome, for her idyll has an elegiac tone, her river a somber *memento mori,* a reminder that Death, not Love, is the permanent resident of earthly Arcadias. Her poem ends with the engraved "white stone" of Revelation, but the context also suggests memorial marble (214). Where Morton celebrates a paradisiac interior, the source of four great rivers, unhappy Anne's happy (because forever dying" stream has an invisible origin, as if to repudiate the wilderness out of which New England rivers flowed. Morton's imagination takes wing westward, but Anne's moves seaward to maternal Thetis, and though that "best" emblem is figured as Heaven's threshold, it is also the way home to England.

The shrinking of poetic sensibilities from the harsh American scene transcends Puritan doctrine, being part and parcel of the Renaissance antipathy to inchoate, hence chaotic and therefore evil aspects of nature. Taylor's typological tracery asserts this larger frame of reference by forming a delicate bridge that carries the intellectualized images of Donne and Herbert to the American strand, and Bradstreet likewise embroidered the plain red flannel of her wilderness *Angst* with allegorical thread borrowed from the Fletcher brothers, Giles and Phineas, her baring more a burdening of her bosom. Puritans may have fled ecclesiastical tyranny in England, but their poems bend gladly to an imperial yoke, a pillory of traditional forms, and we may better appreciate the scarcity of landscapes in their verses by recalling that the topographical tradition is not only a minor aspect of seventeenth-century English verse, but one associated also with Sir John Denham's *Cooper's Hill*—a Royalist manifesto.

First published in the critical year 1642, Denham's poem gives a local as well as loyal cast to the Virgilian georgic mode, instilling the English scene with an intensely patriotic fervor, politicized poetics dominated by the great pastoral harmonies of the royal Thames. A celebration of Charles I, specifically, who figures as a facsimile of Saint George, *Cooper's Hill* more generally champions the English constitutional balance of King and Parliament, and takes its shape and meaning from the Renaissance idea of *concordia discors,* the harmony resulting from a tension of opposites. The emergence of Massachusetts' bicameral government was a similar process, but the Via Media understandably does not find overt expression in the works of her poets. Clio inspired William Hubbard to write a neoclassically balanced if not epic account of New England's history, but the Tenth Muse in America has a distinctly Calvinist look, and may be pictured with the *Bay Psalm Book* reclining on a tomb. "In Adam's fall," the *New England Primer* warned the rising generation, "we sinned all," the first letter in a grim alphabet well-suited to wall-writing, which was seldom the language of accommodation. Like the breasts of Puritan mothers, anointed with wormwood so as to wean their infants more quickly to harsh wilderness fare, the *Primer* was a nursery of adversity, from which children graduated to *The Day of Doom* (1662).

Hardly an epic in length (though tiresome enough to modern sensibilities), Wigglesworth's masterpiece takes the form of neither journey nor battle, but a trial—just such a painful, undue process as Thomas Morton experienced in New England. The popularity of the poem may be ascribed to its readers' faith that they were among the Sheep (though outnumbered in the poem by the Goats), and could therefore "behold with thankful wonderment" the fiery punishment of "all those that were their foes" (83). Whether his readers squirmed with anticipated pleasure or pain, Wigglesworth (as his name advertised) gave good value for money received. Still, despite the fact that his is indisputably a colorful scene, none of the color is local, and though Mrs. Rowlandson gives the outset of her wilderness drama a hellscape setting, Wigglesworth does not acknowledge the complement. Where the preacher's wife was drawn sufficiently out of doors so that she was forced to acknowledge the American scene, the preacher's poet remained in his study.

In terms of landscape, the poetry of Taylor, Bradstreet, and Wigglesworth could have been written in England, as the prose of John Bunyan could have been composed in America, for only the bias of the defining pattern is local: Bradstreet's nostalgia, Taylor's concentricity, Wigglesworth's punitive, and Bunyan's salvational emphasis. But Mather's *Magnalia* could only have been written in Boston, Massachusetts and the necessity which impels attention to landscape in Puritan histories also inspired a minor poetic tradition in New England, a slim shadow literature of equivalent verse. The authors were not preachers, but were members of the laity, not professional, but (even at the most ambitious) part-time poets, yet their works variously assume an identifiably American burden, evincing the kinds of "differences" which distinguish a later, national literature, not the least of which is the bubbling up of a subdued but recognizable Alpheus, the Ovidian reincarnation of Thomas Morton's Erocoise in a Canaan ever new.

ii. Discourse of Rivers, Fish, and Fishing

In genus as well as genius, Edward Taylor's poetic counterpart in New England was Benjamin Tompson, the two men sharing a Harvard education, but not much else. A schoolteacher not a minister, Tompson was another of those Benjamins with a strong Yankee profile, and throughout his long life he yearned to become a public poet, seeking the glare of fame while Taylor sought the purer (if less elusive) light of grace. Taylor establishes the recusant, reclusive, and rural muse in New England, but Tompson points the way to later Boston bards, and his is likewise an urban muse, despite his residence in Dedham. Like Virgil in that respect, like Dryden, he was keen to the winds of change, and by the end of the seventeenth century Tompson seems to have

317

sensed a quickening mood. Thus it was that when the Royal Governor, Lord Bellomont, arrived in Boston in 1699 he was greeted by the aging Dedham Dryden in a manner suggesting that the old age was indeed out, of fashion as well as time.

Though ambitious in verse, Tompson wrote mostly occasional poetry, the greatest of which was occasioned by King Philip's War, the most by someone's death, and he seems to have jumped to the new occasion provided by the Governor's arrival with a pen squeaking for joy. Since it was an event realizing John Winthrop's worst fears of "a general governor" being sent over by the King, this may seem like strange behavior on the part of the poet who a quarter-century earlier had pinned a lament to the hearse of Winthrop's son and namesake. But in fairness to Tompson, it must be said that his poem was but part of the general display of jubilance, for the mood of Massachusetts was one of willingness to hope for the best. Still, Tompson's performance was a remarkable display of agility, a gesture of courtesy approaching Flimnapian gymnastics, for he approached the Governor's coach in the guise of Nathaniel Ward, paying such homage as would have drawn the "country hobnails" from the Simple Cobbler's boots, the poem which he read being likewise a rustic suit.

At the heart of his lengthy ode lies a New England "Eden," no longer an arena of adversity, but a cornucopia of plenty, spilling her "rich presents" at the feet of the noble Earl. Mountains stand bareheaded before the royal Governor, mines tender their wealth, gardens their flowers, and fruitful vines conspire to make him bowers. This is hardly the Psalmist's Vine celebrated by three generations of theocrats, but rather a parasitic symbol of colonial eagerness to cling to Him from Whom all blessings flow, the Governor, a contributary vein symbolized the sacred, bordering rivers of Winthrop's Patent:

> *Charles River swoln with joys, o'er flows with thanks:*
> *And sends his golden trouts up winding banks.*
> *Old Merrimack was ne'er so glad before:*
> *And casts up salmon free cost on the shore.*
> *Deep conges drop the elm; tall cedars bow—*
> *And Corydon to gaze deserts the plough (166).*

Tompson's model seems to have been Ben Jonson's grateful tribute to Penshurst, the "high swolne Medway" now the Charles, for as there, "all come in, the farmer and the clown: / And no one empty-handed, to salute / Thy lord, and lady." Tompson's ode shares little with *Cooper's Hill,* the occasion being more specific and the setting more general, yet it provides a pastoral equivalent to Denham's Tory poem, affecting a radical change in the metaphorical landscape of New England. In 1648 an anonymous descriptive poem attributed to Edward Johnson, *Good News from New-England,* was published in celebration of the Cambridge Platform—counterpart to the prose propaganda written to impress Cromwell's England—which aligns the landscape to the traditional harbor view: "Boats may come up unto our doors, the creeks convenient lie, / Fish plenty taken in them are, plains plowable hard by" (204). But in Tompson's hands a half-century later this accommodating wilderness asylum becomes a contributory flow, type and symbol of colonial submission to royal rule.

And yet, as Bellomont soon discovered, Yankee hospitality is a version of an Indian gift, consisting of little offered in exchange for much, and those cost-free salmon came with hooks and line attached: Tompson's tribute, like any contract, demands close scrutiny. As a poet in search of preferment, Tompson undoubtedly had his own angle out, yet his is primarily a plea for Massachusetts: as fields need to be "washed with showers" to yield "rich presents," so to find the glad Eden hidden in New England, the Governor must "adopt" her people, the kind of covenantal arrangement which Israel in America preferred—whether with gods or governors. There is, moreover, a militant note at the end of Tompson's poem, adding to the homage of pastoral folk the heroic services of the militiamen of Massachusetts: under the generalship of their new Governor, "whose very sight might make Quebec your own," the "brisk sons of Mars, Valour's right heirs" stand ready to "storm that world" to the north. Bellomont spent his short stay in Lilliput wrangling with Increase Mather and the General Court about the terms of Harvard's Charter, and his death soon afterward precluded any realization of the bellicosity in his name. But Tompson's geopolitical sentiments were prophetic, and prescient also was his Toryish tone, for despite rumblings of rebellion in Boston, her bards would remain loyal to the throne. Even Cotton Mather was willing to bend his neck to gain admittance to the Royal Society, and his nephew, Mather Byles, was so sycophantic a poet as to style himself an American moon reflecting the sunlight of the divine Pope—the prelate of Augustan verse—as colonial a congé as one could wish from a Congregational cleric.

Yet Puritan life confounds even as it inspires generalities, and as the weightiest refutation of the notion that all was black and white in Calvinist New England is the colorful diary kept by Samuel Sewall, so that writer was responsible for a Whiggish counterpart to Tompson's Tory poem, a broadside to match the other man's salute. Unlike Tompson, Sewall seldom associated himself with the poetic muse— unless we can count his friendship with Edward Taylor at Harvard and afterward—but his occasional amateur flights are an important aspect of his versatility, that ambidexterity which is such a powerful refutation of the popular notion of the single-minded, slab-faced Puritan. Lawyer, judge, merchant, land-speculator, scholar, philanthropist, Sewall seems another forecast of Ben Franklin, yet he was perhaps more Brahmin than Yankee, with a speculative and transcendental cast of mind. No matter how you turn him, Sewall will not fit any convenient slot, and his poetic broadside, *Upon the Drying Up that Ancient River, the River Merrymak*, is similarly without genre or prototype, yet it manages to epitomize the role of the river in the landscape of Puritan New England.

First published in 1720, Sewall's poem is a regional, even a localized exercise, but unlike Denham's great georgic, it is a bit of bucolic fun, a bagatelle upon which not too much importance can be placed without doing harm to the author's intention. And yet the Chief Justice of Massachusetts—like the Dean of Dublin and the Philadelphia Printer— never set his hand to a *mere* bagatelle, and if his poem on the Merrimack provides a contrast in seriousness and scope as well as genre to his chiliastic tract, *Phaenomena Quaedam Apocalyptica* (1697), the more ambitious prose of the one provides an important gloss on the verse of the other. The *Phaenomena* is itself a singular document, a rambling, erudite, and often obscurely rendered treatise on the anticipated millennium, its optimism providing an obstacle to any easy conclusions about the mood of Massachusetts at century's end. That one of Boston's most prominent jurors would hold out hope for the West while the town's most promising preacher (and his friend) was threatening divine vengeance from the East is an undeniably paradoxical bi-polarity. Stranger still is Sewall's opinion that New Jerusalem might be located in Mexico, a latitudinarian view breaking free of Boston parochialism, and though Cotton Mather in his *Theopolis Americana* (1710) borrowed his friend's architectonics, it is notable that he returned the Holy City to Massachusetts.

Still, despite his magnanimous theopolitics, Sewall's phenomenological tract ends in Winthrop's Patent, concluding with a prose apostrophe to New England, a patriotic version of Merlin's Prophecy and the sort of thing which had its verse equivalents in the almanacs of the day (63). Two years before Benjamin Tompson emptied the rivers of Massachusetts into Governor Bellomont's lap, Sewall invoked the Merrimack's constant flow of salmon as one of many pastoral guarantees that "Saints of light" would continue to be born in New England, a chauvinist symphony second to none. Therefore, when nearly a quarter-century later the great bordering symbol of permanence seemed about to have its upper length taken away by the territorial claims of New Hampshire (thus reversing Governor Winthrop's widening of his bounds by a similar maneuver), the Merrimack became a symbol of quite a different order, keying a complex chain of associations by its first line, "Long did Euphrates make us glad" (973).

This apparently mock-heroic touch contains a number of possible connotations, for the Euphrates appears in the Old Testament not only as one of the four great rivers of Eden, but as the eastern border of Israel, and as the gateway to the infamous Babylon of the Captivity Psalms. In Revelation, moreover, the drying up of "the great river" Euphrates would make way for "the kings of the east," being associated with the pouring out of the Sixth Vial and Babylon's destruction. This particular prophecy amounted to an obsession with Sewall, who in his diary and his *Phaenomena* associated it with his own version of millennium, providing proof that it would occur in America. By means of a complex cat's cradle of authorities and historical instances, Sewall established to his own satisfaction a connection between the drying up of the Euphrates and the conversion of the Jews (including Indians), an apocalyptic event associated with the pouring out of the Seventh Vial, whose waters would run westward, toward the New World: "I believe, as certain, that they will never cease to run there: but will rise higher and higher, until they become a very long, and broad, and deep

RIVER. Because the People that are planted by them, begin to be placed under the influences of that *New* National Covenant" (41).

Sewall plays in jest upon these connotations in his Merrimack poem, which amounts to a private joke among friends, and begins his broadside as he ended his tract, using the Merrimack-Euphrates as a symbol of constancy, which has run for "thousands of years" from "his remote, and lofty head, / Until he with the ocean wed" (973). Like Denham's royal Thames, the noble Merrimack is a fertile stream, a river of plenty, and Sewall's poem is packed with a Hesiodic catalogue of New England's flora and fauna, all "refreshed by this goodly stream." As a symbol of permanence, moreover, the river is associated with images of stability, like the "dutiful salmon" who yearly visit their "parent dear," and with ideas of order, like the "allotments" of water the river provides: "Thus Merrimack kept house secure, / And hop'd for ages to endure; / Living in love, and union, / With every tributary son." In contrast to Tompson's tribute-bearing river, Sewall's Merrimack is a figuration of not colonial, but federal unity, a union of confluencies central to the integrity of Massachusetts.

But this happy convergence, this "pleasant, steady course," is ended when "an ambushment was laid / Near Powwow Hill, when none were afraid," for "unawares, at one huge sup, hydropic Hampshire drunk it up!" The terminal joke turns on an image familiar to New Englanders by 1721, one long associated with the disruption of domestic tranquillity in Massachusetts and with the dangers of living beyond the Merrimack—that native American "phenomenon," the Indian ambush and captivity. A broadside Sewall wrote in 1701 couples the spread of God's "impartial light" with "the transplanted English Vine," praying that Indians (and Jews) might be given "eyes to see," thus asserting in small the original Puritan errand. But his poem of 1721 places the Indian in the more familiar framework of the jeremiad, warranting a mock warning equivalent to the sermon with which the *Magnalia* closes: "Look to thyself! Wachusett Hill; / And bold Monadnock, fear some ill! / Envy'd earth knows no certain bound; / In HEAV'N alone, CONTENT is found" (973; *cf.* 441).

Denham similarly ends his ode to order with a catastrophe: Comparing parliamentary restriction of royal power to a river forced into "a new, or narrow course" by farmers greedy for land, Denham gives figure to the tyrannical reassertion of imperial prerogative as a flood:

"No longer then within his banks he dwells, / First to a torrent, then a deluge swells: / Stronger, and fiercer by restraint he roars, / And knows no bound, but makes his power his shores" (162). Both poems therefore emphasize the lesson of "bounds," but Sewall's drought is antithetical to Denham's flood, for where the Tory's disaster enforces the neoclassical maxim—never so well expressed than by Pope—"Whatever is, is right," Sewall's ambush suggests that Horatian balance is hard to achieve in a new country. In America, "the poor Indian" often lurks "behind the cloud-topped hill," which is named "Powwow," not "Cooper's"—though a Cooper would a century thence make that perilous peak his own. Powwow Hill was not in Winthrop's prospect, either, but by Sewall's day it had become a trinitarian third to Wachusett and Monadnock, a geopoetical landmark commemorating the transformation of the Macedonian Indian to a menacing presence. Like the river, the red man is a ubiquitous reminder that boundaries are uncertain, even treacherous, that pastoral contentment is an illusion, that there is no asylum this side Jordan, no Pisgah view obtainable in Massachusetts.

In 1725 the lesson of Sewall's broadside was dramatically demonstrated by Captain John Lovewell, who marched his men from Dunstable against the Indians of Maine. Lovewell had earlier led a similar expedition up the Merrimack to its source, Lake Winnepesaukee, and from there to the headwaters of the Saco, where he surprised and massacred a war party. He unwisely chose to repeat his route a second time, and marched past the scene of his late victory into an ambush, a blunder which, like Custer's, elevated the dead Captain to the stature of folk hero, inspiring a popular ballad and a jeremiad by the Reverend Thomas Symmes. The latter was less celebratory than the former, for Symmes saw Lovewell's defeat as the work of "the finger of God," and went on to a Matherish finger-shake of his own: "NEW ENGLAND must reform, or . . . anyone that observes the signs of the times, may I think, evidently foresee, that in one twenty years more, the glory of *New England* as *New England,* will be much more than hitherto, if not TOTALLY eclipsed, GOD *in His infinite, sovereign mercy prevent it!*" (27-28). Wherever the New Canaan was, it was not in New Hampshire.

iii. Silent Touches of Time

The people of Connecticut, as they approached their centennial, may well have thought that Canaan lay in their direction, for events since the Pequot War suggested that their Seal, like the Bay Colony's, was a prophetic sign. A second-hand symbol, absorbed along with Warwick's Patent at Saybrook, it showed a vineyard with a sheltering hand overhead displaying a label with the motto *"Sustinet Qui Translutit,"* a Latin version of John Cotton's dockside promise concerning divine protection of transplanted vines. Despite Lion Gardiner's growlings, Connecticut remained relatively untouched by Indian attack during King Philip's War, even as the wild boar was ravaging the Massachusetts Vine, and in the fifty years that followed, violence moved ever farther afield. Governor John Winthrop Senior had reconciled himself to Hooker's defection by regarding his new neighbor as a buffer zone against his enemies, and so it worked out in 1637, but afterward the relationship was reversed, Massachusetts protecting her daughter from Indian attacks along the upper reaches of the Connecticut River Valley. Moreover, John Winthrop Junior, long the Governor of the western colony, obtained the kind of generous charter from Charles II which Increase Mather had labored in vain to get from James II, establishing a reign of peace and prosperity (and Winthrops) that extended well into the eighteenth century.

Nothing, as Sewall reflected, lasts on this earth forever, and as Madam Knight observed, by the turn of the century the inhabitants of Connecticut were not a peaceful, but a restless, litigious lot, the spirit of liberty engendering more contentiousness than gratitude. The scene in church and courtroom often resembled the Fairfield full of contentious folk through which the Boston Traveler passed, for if the Connecticut Vine grew tender grapes, there could be heard the insistent barking of little foxes. A victim of that discontent was the sometime pastor of Westchester, the Reverend Joseph Morgan, a Connecticut native and self-educated minister, who was forced by troubles with his free-born congregations to remove to Freehold, New Jersey. There he wrote *The Kingdom of Basaruah* (1715), a fable of the fall of man in which the Bunyanesque vein becomes apoplectically swollen, evincing not only characteristic American differences, but the changes obtaining in regions west of Boston.

Morgan's mythical land of Basaruah ("Flesh-Spirit") is bisected by a Jordan-like river called Paligenesia ("Regeneration"), and the object of his allegorical action is to get Anthropos (Mankind) out of the Wilderness (the World) and into Shamajim ("Paradise"). Morgan clearly prefigures the evangelism which will spring forth in more sophisticated Connecticut form as Jonathan Edwards, and it is worth noting in this respect that where Boston theocrats labored for a century to keep saints from crossing terrestrial Jordans, the western fundamentalist was chiefly concerned with getting them across the heavenly one. More important, in both instances Mankind maintains a Yahoo-like fondness for "Wilderness Pleasures," and where eager to cross over the Connecticut and the Hudson to "a *better country*," Morgan's parishioners seem to have been reluctant to seek his paradisiac strand. "Our country perishes for want of the Gospel," moaned Morgan in a letter to Cotton Mather in 1722—rather a one-sided correspondence—and he labeled Arminianism "the most effectual and mischievious of all the engines yet ever the Devil formed against the salvation of men" (166). Ironically, however, it is Morgan's fervent anti-sectarianism which works against the strategy of his allegory, his evangelical errand becoming bogged down in attacks on doctrinal errors.

This eschatological legalism finds expression also in Morgan's pervading sense of *process*, his epic figured in terms of Old and New Charters, guarantees, securities, warrants, proclamations, and prohibitions, the mass of paperwork needed to get people into Paradise. That Death is personified as a sheriff is a typical touch, Morgan's allegory betraying a law-and-order platform below the salvational burden. In these terms, at least, it has a counterpart in another example of Connecticut handicraft, the longest poem in Roger Wolcott's *Poetical Meditations* (1725), if anything an even more virtuoso display of home manufacture: "A Brief Account of the Agency of the Honorable John Winthrop, Esq. in the Court of King Charles the Second, Anno Dom.

1662; when he obtained for the Colony of Connecticut His Majesty's Gracious Charter." The strongest link between the works of Morgan and Wolcott is the matter of the Charter, but there is a detectable resonance shared in general by both, resulting in another one of those ill-assorted but undeniable pairs that characterize the literature and history of early New England.

Like Taylor and Tompson, Wolcott and Morgan go oddly hand in hand, both having been born in Connecticut within five years (and forty miles) of one another, each being forced to earn and learn his own way in the world, neither sharing Sir William Phips's magical good fortune. Of the two, Wolcott was by far the most successful (and worldly), for starting out as an apprentice to a clothier, by 1625 he was a lawyer, judge, and a regularly elected Magistrate, and he would go on to become Governor of Connecticut and the founder of a prominent political family—his life a Frankliniad that parts company with Morgan's westward path into poverty early on. Moreover, where Morgan was a zealot, Wolcott was a politician, and though no turncoat, a tailor who knew how to trim a garment to his own advantage. At mid-point in his rise in 1725, Wolcott may have hoped that his muse would elevate him in the estimation of college-educated gentlemen, but his epic has a more pointed if equally pragmatic end, and lurks among the conventional, devotional flowers in Wolcott's book like a cannon set up in Edward Taylor's poetical garden. Advertised in its sub-title as "Being the Improvement of Some Vacant Hours," Wolcott's verse resembles Yankee whittle-work, some of which was useful, some ornamental, and most of it tricky as a trap. The very title of his epic, like that of the volume which contains it, is misleading, for the account of Winthrop's "agency" is indeed short, but only because most of the poem is taken up with a description of the initial settlement of Connecticut and the consequent Pequot War.

Massachusetts' poems concerned with Indian wars, from Tompson's *Crisis* to Philip Walker's *Captan Perse & His Coragios Company* (c. 1675), were written under conditions inimical to epic composition. Connecticut's Wolcott, by contrast, had the advantage of almost a century of historical distance, enabling him to construct an action in the Virgilian mode. Still, his poem is no less responsive to his times, like the revisionist chronicles of New England anticipating the historical romance by making a political fiction out of past events, and his perspective is similarly nostalgic. Yet this, too, is in the Virgilian tradition, and, like the Roman poet, the Yankee bard set out to underwrite authority by celebrating ancient accomplishments. So also Cotton Mather, and Wolcott's epic, likewise, contains that disjunctiveness which plagues Clio in Massachusetts, a deep cleavage which, as in Morgan's *Kingdom,* is identified with a regenerative river, not a baptismal, but a rejuvenating stream, a genial flow not to be crossed, but to be followed into a flowering land. Like Major Mason's original narrative, Wolcott's poetic version of the Pequot War is a refutation of the Massachusetts metaphor, a springing up in Connecticut of Denham's Thames, a New-English Alph accompanied by a prophetic voice.

iv. The Noblest Motive

Something of the political climate in Connecticut in 1725 may be gathered from a paragraph in the Preface to Wolcott's book, a contribution by the Reverend John Bulkley of Colchester:

I presume there are not many in this popular, levelling day who will not . . . say that in lawful governments that are founded in compact, the more general error is that too much power is given up by the community, and vested in their rulers; *I am very sure among us at least, there are not many, who (Pardon me if what I say be amiss) generally speaking are a people trained up, but too much, in* principles of rebellion and opposition to government; *and who as to the Constitution obtaining among us, as popular as it is, yet think it* defective by error on the other extreme. *Yet all this notwithstanding, certain it is despotic forms are not the only that are prejudicial to the ends of government, but those erring on the other extreme are perhaps as inconsistent with them, and of this, besides their but too often exemplifying the condition of Ephesus at a certain time when Paul was there. . . . (xiv).*

Through the tortured, circumambient syntax there can be heard the sarcastic grinding of teeth and the hiss of expletive spittle which is the sound of the exercised Tory. It is not surprising to find St. Paul's name dropped from the mouth of the son of Gershom Bulkley, but what a wonder it is to find "the words of that great man Mr. Locke, who well understood the true origin of all lawful authority" cited in support of arguments against "a matter which has been the occasion of much debate and contention as well as many other evils among us . . . the matter of Native Right as it's commonly called . . . in the vulgar phrase" (xv-xvi). "Native Right" seems to echo "natural rights," but as that "vulgar phrase" suggests, something different is meant.

Roger Williams seems to have been responsible for putting the idea of "Native Right" in motion, insisting that the Indians owned the land they lived on by virtue of living on it, an opinion which ran counter to the Puritan concept of "Lord's Waste," which turned on the necessity for land to be put to good (i.e. profitable) use before it was properly owned. The latter idea had seen good service during the first century of Puritan presence in New England, but by 1725 the native rights' theory had a number of advocates, few of whom shared the idealism of its first proponent and the most of whom had bought land from James Fitch Junior. Son of the missionary minister of Norwich, the Reverend James Fitch—who had contributed a chapter to Increase Mather's *Remarkable Providences* and a wife to Edward Taylor—James Secundus was another Junior with a somewhat different errand in America from his father's. He was, as it were, a truer son to his grandfather, Major John Mason, his heritage involving land holdings based on ambiguous deeds of conveyance signed by Uncas and his sons over the years, an instrument which assumed the shape of a political weapon in Fitch's hands.

Because of the Indian's vague notion of tribal boundaries and his concommitant eagerness to please his white friends and get as good a price as possible for something he held valueless, the land in Fitch's control overlapped property which the sons of John Winthrop Junior—Wait and Fitz-John—considered theirs. The result was an early manifestation of the classic American antagonism between old wealth and new, a power struggle dignified on both sides by appeals to high principle, the Bible, and law. On Fitch's side were the people who had bought parcels of his land and others who hoped to do so, and on the other side were the Proprietors, men of high (and extensive) estate in whose care the disposal of remaining unclaimed wilderness resided. Fitch's struggle long outlived him, associating his name with forces for expansion, in Connecticut as in Massachusetts identified with revolt against centralized, duly constituted authority. So it is that for John Bulkley the proposition that "all men are and ever were *born free, equal and independent*" is equated with a *"State of Nature,"* an anarchy without "any *common, establish'd, positive law*" (xix, xxi). The Indian, therefore, cannot lay claim to any more land than what he has cultivated, and the "bigots" who claim otherwise are enemies of law and order.

Roger Wolcott's position on native right was as befits a rising man—unclear. If, upon occasion, he supported the claims of Fitch's party, in his epic poem he came out for the Proprietors, a stand that has a sloping shadow in the fact that Wolcott by 1720 had speculated in lands abutting the property in dispute. So despite its neoclassical shape, Wolcott's epic is something less than Homeric in disinterestedness, being a Yankee *Aeneid,* sandwiched between Bulkley's attack on native right and a lengthy advertisement by Joseph Dewey, the Connecticut clothier who paid for the book's publication. Wolcott's is a political production, based like the Republic a half-century thence on the sacredness of property, and though Bulkley claims that his Preface was inspired "by some passages in the ensuing muse," the effect probably preceded the cause, Bulkley calling Calliope's tune (xv).

Besides marshaling arguments against native rights, Bulkley discusses the poet as historian, citing Sidney's *Apology* and listing the Ancients "who have taken that way to raise up monuments to, and eternize the names and actions of their admired heroes" (viii). Certainly Mather's statue of Sir William Phips was just such an erection, but where the Boston embalmer made claims for a true likeness, Bulkley admits that Wolcott of Windsor has "mingled a great deal of *mythology*" with fact. Considering the poem's purpose, this is not surprising, but it is a strange recipe for the son of the author of *Will and Doom* to recommend, the House of Fiction in New England being in the neighborhood of Hell. But as with Morgan's *Basaruah,* overwhelming necessity overrules fine distinctions, and Bulkley's Preface grants Wolcott poetic license on behalf of law and order, his epic "design" being "no other than to pay a just debt to the memory and procure due regards to the family of one, who not only being view'd in his own *personal accomplishments* was a person of distinguished worth, but many ways *highly deserved of the public"* (x-xi).

The last is the definitive phrase, for to honor John Winthrop Junior is in effect to give sanction to the Proprietorship system for which he stands. For Bulkley, God is "the Great Proprietor of the World," a provincial metaphor but a sign of the times in Connecticut at the start of the eighteenth century. And Roger Wolcott, who knew the shape of the elephant, aimed his epic at the desired end, honoring both Winthrop and the Proprietor God—whose secret name was "Land." Still, Wolcott's poem does not form a seamless whole with Bulkley's Preface, and much as Joseph Morgan's Puritan love of disputation got in the way of his evangelical errand, so Wolcott's neoclassical motive disrupts his political design. An apparently simple exercise in the service of the general good, Wolcott's poem breaks down in its particulars.

v. The Soldier and the Saint

The fiction begins, with all epic actions, at the start, where Wolcott presents Charles II as a good-natured and generous ruler, aching to promote the colonies' welfare: *"What news, my lords? How go affairs abroad? | What more remains to do for England's good? | Do distant parts of our dominion | Want farther help or favor from the throne?"* (21). Why Wolcott has his merry monarch speak in italics is not readily apparent, but perhaps it suits his notion of deference due, setting the tone for the subsequent interview between the sons of Charles I and John Winthrop Senior. For in answer to the royal request, *"What has been done, and what's a doing there?,"* the "agent from Connecticut" obligingly turns the question to his own ends. "Prostrating himself with reverence," in dogged couplets he paraphrases the spaniel terms of Connecticut's original petition, an agile exercise that forever removes the notion of the Puritans' stiff necks, managing to beg pardon for Connecticut's twenty-year delay in advancing the cause of royalty without explaining it.

Ever well-mannered, Charles does not press the point, but before granting the New Charter, asks Winthrop for an account of how *"Your patriarchs . . . led your tribes from hence,"* his chosen metaphor providing a lead which Winthrop tactfully ignores. " 'RELIGION was the cause,' " begins the Congregationalist from Connecticut, not escape from persecution, but a matter of pure " *'Divinity,'* " the Puritans heeding the call that the light of the Gospel should be " 'Extensive as the sun's diurnal shine' " (24). Silent on the westward course of the Gospel light, Winthrop instead stresses the Puritans' sadness at leaving " 'their parent isle / Their whilome happy scat,' " a patchwork of fact and fiction which soon becomes the whole cloth of fable. Like Winthrop's Fleet, the voyage to America runs into stormy weather, but it-is the " 'Reverend Warham' " who calms the seas with prayer, ecclesiastical prominence explained by the fact that John Warham—notable in the *Magnalia* only for being "the first preacher that ever preached with notes in our New England"—was the founding minister of Wolcott's Windsor. For similar reasons, the ship bearing " 'Holy Warham' " does not even put in at Massachusetts Bay, but keeps " 'further westward' " to the Connecticut River (26).

At the river's mouth they are met by an accommodating Indian named "Soheage," who tells the English that " 'The garden of America did lie / Further up stream, near fifty miles from hence, / Part of which country he himself was prince" (27). Wolcott's Indian realtor was named for the river Sachem who sold the land on which Wethersfield was planted—later returning injury for insult by betraying the town to the Pequots—and the Indians of Connecticut were certainly eager (at first) to attract English settlers to their valley. But the encounter at the entrance suggests the Virginian, not the New England experience, and in the manner of Newport's ship, the Puritan ark stands " 'northward for th' expected country,' " sailing straight up the river, blown by " 'fresh southern gales . . . upon the smiling pavement of the flood.' " Passing next through " 'awful straits, / Where the stream runs through adamantine gates,' " they are rewarded with the Virginian prospect of a New World Garden: " 'A glorious country opens to their view, / Cloth'd all in green, and to the eye presents /

Nature's best fruits and richest ornaments' " (27). Like sailors landing on a tropic isle, " 'Brave youths, with eager strokes, bend knotty
oars,' " and the happy land responds in kind: " 'Glad shouts bring
cheerful echoes from the shores.' "

Such is hardly the conventional Puritan manner of taking possession
of even the most promising land, and Wolcott's green muse expands in
an epic simile taken from the field of love, not war, Donne done over
to suit American needs:

> "*As when the wounded amorous doth spy*
> *His smiling fortune in his lady's eye,*
> *O how his veins and breast swell with a flood*
> *Of pleasing raptures, that revive his blood!*
> *And grown impatient now of all delays,*
> *No longer he deliberating stays;*
> *But through the force of her resistless charms,*
> *He throws him, soul and body in her arms.*
> "*So we, amazed at these seen delights,*
> *Which to fruition every sense invites,*
> *Our eager mind, already captive made,*
> *Grew most impatient now to be delay'd,*
> *This most delightful country to possess;*
> *And forward, with industrious speed, we press*
> *Upon the virgin stream who had as yet,*
> *Never been violated with a ship*" (28).*

No slip of the pen is this, but a third evocation of the landed virgin
conceived by Hakluyt and further tricked out by Morton, now at last
associated with a pulchritudinous river uterine, once again enforcing
the resemblance to Newport's passage, not Hooker's crossing.

As Captain Newport was greeted at the head of the James by "Powhatan," so " 'Upon the banks king Aramamet stood, / And round about
his wondring multitude.' " The historic Aramamet was a shrewd dealer
in lands, responsible for luring the English to Windsor, but in Wolcott's account he is every inch a mile-high king, " 'Majestic Aramamet,
with his lords' " being type and symbol of noble savagery. Like Percy's

Little Powhatan, he gives fair words for fair: " 'What you propose (quoth he) is just and good, / And I shall e'er respect your neighborhood; / Land you may have, *we value not the soil,* / *Accounting tillage too severe a toil*' " (30). These last are not royal italics, but imperial emphases, reminding the reader of the prefatory argument concerning native rights. Yet Wolcott, by elevating Aramamet to epic majesty, has in effect trampled Bulkley's argument with a heroic foot, for one of the minister's main points was that Indian sachems were neither hereditary nor constitutional monarchs, and had therefore no legal authority to dispose of tribal lands to John Fitch.

The logic of Wolcott's poem seems to suffer a version of time lag, implying a distinction between land deals (and Indians) of the seventeenth and eighteenth centuries, a disjunctiveness enhanced by his elevated treatment of the Pequot War. No longer a satanic savage, the Indian is now a noble enemy cast in a classical mold—cruel, over-proud, but brave—a worthy adversary in an epic action. The speech by the Pequot sachem Sasacus to his " 'noble captains and wise counsellors' " provides absolute contrast to the address by Tompson's "bacon-rind" Philip, even though it turns on the same argument: " 'You know how that of old our ancestors, / By their known liberties and ancient laws, / Were well allowed to marry many squaws' " (39). The rhyme remains but gone is the pidgin English. Still, Sasacus may be " 'great in glory' " but he is " 'greater still in pride,' " being " 'Much by himself and others magnified,' " and against the advice of a wise old "Paynim" he declares " 'War with the English nation' " (37, 41-42).

What follows is so patent an imitation of the *Aeneid* that placenames like "Saybrook," "Wethersfield," and "Hartford" have a strange and uncouth ring, and though the burning fort at Mystic is described as a " 'dreadful emblem of the flames of Hell,' " " 'Mystic-town' " more closely resembles Troy-town than an Indian palisade, as " 'its wealth, high battlements, and spires, / Now sinketh, weltring in conjoining fires' " (67, 69). This tendency is further revealed by Wolcott's concluding page of "Errata," all of which are from his epic poem and many of which are not corrections but revisions, whereby "bows and arrows" become "bright armor" and "sagamore" becomes "a prince" (referring to Uncas), a movement from vernacular to "poetic" terms. Freely mingling classical and biblical allusions with patriotic references to Cressy and Agincourt, Wolcott inflates Major Mason's exploits with an epic efflatus extending to his unwieldy (in terms of diction) " 'blunderbusses,' " made over into Miltonic machines whose " 'Thick sulphurous smoke makes the sky look black, / And heaven's high galleries thunder with the crack. / Earth groans and trembles, and from underneath, / Deep vaulted caverns horrid echoes breathe' " (71). Such bloat has a certain flatulence, being rather more mocking than truly heroic, but Wolcott's intention is otherwise, and his weight of emphasis on Mason's war, like his elevation of Mohegans and Pequots to Incan stature, works against the presumed purpose of his poem.

For if Mason's victory " 'America for the English won,' " then surely his descendants—which included James Fitch—are as worthy of "due regards" as the Winthrop heirs, successors, and assignees. Yet what holds in Connecticut for the sons of Winthrop does not necessarily hold for the son of a Fitch, political like religious matters proceeding not by logical steps but by leaps of faith. We are here in the presence, as Bulkley reminds us, of a myth, Winthrop a proprietor god made over in the image of the great God Proprietor, like the King of Basaruah associated with the granting of a New (and better) Charter. Whatever the effect of the Pequot War on the logic of his poem, Wolcott seems to have regarded it as an expanded parallel to the stag hunt in the 1655 version of *Cooper's Hill,* a complex series of associations turning on the scene of the royal stag's death, which is Runnymede, the "Charter" this time sealed "in blood." Pointedly, the royal stag is Charles I, and in moving from the victory over the Pequots back to Winthrop's interview with Charles II and the obtaining of Connecticut's Magna Carta, Wolcott rings in a reference to that " 'blessed martyr' " himself, " 'a victim to the popular rage' " (74). Denham figures Charles I as an emblematic St. George, being both "Soldier and Saint," but Puritan does Cavalier one better by intimating that the monarch was a type of Christ, " 'being thus conformed to the King of Kings,' " God taking him " 'from his kingdom transitory,' " and setting him " 'on a throne of endless glory' " (75).

A further manifestation of God's design to do good was His placing Charles II " 'safely on your father's throne,' " or so Wolcott's Winthrop reads events, thereby associating the quelling of Pequot rebellion in America with the " 'happy restoration' " of " 'that blessed martyr's line' " in Merry England (76, 74). And Charles II, for his part, instructs Winthrop as to how a permanent peace may be kept in Connecticut, for in order that " 'the people of that happy place' " may remain " 'blest with happy English privileges,' " they must beware of malcontents who have such an " 'admiration' " for freedom " 'That every act of order or restraint / They'll represent as matter of complaint,' " for such is " 'Satan's masterpiece,' " identified by Joseph Morgan with Arminianism, but by Wolcott with Democracy (77-78). His final Tory touch is to have Charles instruct Winthrop to " 'Let your New English multitude / Remember well a bond of gratitude / Will lie on them, and their posterity, / To keep in mind their freedom came by thee' " (78). For he thereby lends proprietorship royal sanction, driving an imperial bias through the whole fabric of his poem, turning on the paradoxical rhyme "multitude / gratitude," the one historically (in Israel and New England) showing precious little of the other. As Yankee epic, Wolcott's poem is distinctly an establishmentarian exercise, in which the emphasis on peace and harmony through law and order is fastened by colonial chains, "bonds of gratitude" which ensure that the status of the Winthrop dynasty is very much quo.

But in celebrating the agency of the Son, Wolcott reneges on the errand of the Father, and where Sewall's broadside acts to enforce the theocratic metaphor, Wolcott's epic asserts a Connecticut peace surpassing even Tompson's poetic undertaking, thereby rejecting William Hubbard's reading of Hooker's wilderness exodus for a distinctly heroic, paradisiac version. Reflecting the metamorphosis of Puritan life during New England's first century, Wolcott's poem bends the linear and progressive dimension of the Puritan errand to a geopolitical not millennial end, in which the river proves to be an inland thrust to empire and where the Golden Age is not in the past or future, but now— and forever and ever, amen. Wolcott's poem in this regard has another and even more prophetic disjunctiveness, for royal rule is evoked chiefly to strengthen local authority, his Connecticut Valley assuming the independent shape of American domain, the words on the label in the hand over the vineyard on Hooker's Great Seal revised to read "OUR CHARTER."

vi. Search Not His Bottom, but Survey His Shore

Moses Coit Tyler found Wolcott's epic laughable, and so it is, having that inadvertent humor that haunts the Puritan errand, but we must give the poet credit for his design, even where it subverted his intention. For Wolcott framed an action which brings together the most dramatic aspects of American life in the seventeenth century, both in Virginia and New England: the perilous ocean crossing, the up-river, inland voyage, the entrance to a garden world, peaceable dealings with Indians erupting in warfare, and an English victory signalling righteous as well as rightful possession of the land. As Bulkley promised, it is a myth, but it would in time become *the* myth, as Wolcott's Romanized Mohegan would become the Romanticized Mohican of James Fenimore Cooper, much as the elevated neo-classical Captain who marched against the Pequots is a prefiguration of the hyperbolean Captain of the *Pequod*.

Central to Wolcott's Tory epic is the Connecticut River, an eighteenth-century equivalent of the Romantics' Mississippi, being not a symbol of sublime power but, like Denham's Thames, a hieroglyph of imperial harmony. Yet certain differences obtain in America, not the least of which is the paradisiac theme, and in answer to King Charles's inquiry concerning " 'this new-found river,' " Wolcott's Winthrop reaches for an analogy which his father carefully avoided: " 'I think our land is near as good / As that which was unto Moses shew'd,' " thereby making a Jordan of the Connecticut (31-32). But unlike Joseph Morgan's "Paligenesia," Wolcott's regenerative river lends unity, not divisiveness to the landscape:

> *"This gallant stream keeps running from the head,*
> *Four hundred miles ere it with Neptune bed,*

Passing along hundreds of rivulets,
From either bank its crystal waves beset,
Freely to pay their tributes to this stream,
As being chief and sovereign unto them;
It bears no torrent nor impetuous course,
As if 'twere driven to the sea by force,
But calmly on a gentle wave doth move,
As if 'twere drawn to Thetis' house by love.
    "The water's fresh and sweet; and he that swims
In it, recruits and cures his surfeit limbs.
The fisherman the fry with pleasure gets,
With seines, pots, angles, and his trammel-nets.
In it swim salmon, sturgeon, carp and eels;
Above fly cranes, geese, duck, herons and teals;
And swans, which take such pleasure as they fly,
They sing their hymns oft long before they die" (32-33).

Though there is a couplet assigned " 'The husbandman,' " who " 'for his diligence, / Receives an ample, liberal recompence,' " the scene is much more reminiscent of Morton's Erocoise than of Denham's georgic, agrarian Thames, a hunter's paradise where " 'The fatted roebuck and the fallow deer / Yield venison as good as that which won / The patriarchal benediction' " (33, 35). Figured like Denham's river in royal terms, flowing with neoclassic " 'majestic grace' " between " 'equidistant' " ranges of mountains, " 'a vast interspace, pleasant and fair,' " the waters of the New World river have magical restorative powers, suggesting the fabulous fountain of youth, and the animals round about live in a virtual Peaceable Kingdom: " 'At the cool brooks, the beavers and the minks / Keep house, and here the hart and panther drinks' " (35, 34).

Among Wolcott's partridges and moose there sings a "philomel," but Roger's neoclassical grouping has most definitely a Connecticut cast. Moreover, his secondhand poetic furniture serves a purpose different from the equivalents in the pastoral verse of Bradstreet and Morton, for like the Puritan mentality, his heroic couplets are well suited to the conversion of wilderness into tidy plots of land. Secured by the Soldier's victory over the Pequots, protected by the Saint's royal Charter, Connecticut rests secure between guardian mountains, enjoying the peace that only order and balance can bring. Though a radical departure from the terms of Winthrop's errand, Wolcott's poem asserts in Augustan dress the familiar Puritan faith in bounds, walling in the Happy Valley with a Yankee version of a Roman Peace, sealed with the symbolic Vine.

Still, if we peer beyond Wolcott's river to his mountains, where eagles "bring their young ones forth out of those crags, / And force them to behold Sol's majesty, / In mid-noon glory, with a steady eye," we catch a prophetic glimpse of yet another Great Seal and hear the sound of distant fife and drum (36). The valley, like the mountains, hatched a glorious brood for whom Freedom, Equality, and Independence had a meaning somewhat different from that assigned by the Reverend John Bulkley. Herein lies the final paradox of Wolcott's poem, for the paradise he paints is associated with the early days of Connecticut, not the putative Golden Age of gratitude assigned to the present time. It is a perfection of virginity long since departed, and even as Wolcott's poem was published, the residents of his Happy Valley were looking for greener fields, hence the dispute between the heirs of the Soldier and the Saint over Indian lands. And in 1738, a century after the Pequots were defeated, Connecticut settlers from Winthrop's New London on the New England Thames moved westward to the Housatonic, a river with an Indian name meaning "beyond the mountain," there to found a town called "Canaan." And it was from James Fitch's Windham County that migrating Yankees departed for the Susquehanna on the eve of the Revolution, founding the town and county of Westmoreland—named for a place in England but prophetic, surely, in terms of coincidental morphology.

The myth to which Wolcott gave prescient form is restless within neoclassic bonds, whether forged by charters or couplets, and seeks like Alpheus to renew itself ever again. So it was that in 1745 Major General Roger Wolcott found himself in John Mason's boots, marching against the Canadian stronghold of Louisbourg, a prelude to the storming of Quebec and the crushing of the Canadian Carthage, winning (in the words of his Major Mason) "America for the English" at last. In his journal of the victorious campaign, the older and more conventionally pious Wolcott credited the victory to God, echoing the historic Mason (and Psalm 118) by acknowledging "it is the Lord's doing and it was marvelous in our eyes" (158). But as early American literature it is the heroic shape of his epic which tells, carrying the expansive spirit beyond Quebec, in a western flight that with an eagle's eye takes in a promising land across the mountains, a valley defined by a great confederated system of rivers which would be transformed into the Palladian shape of an always expanding, yet orderly Republic. The presiding genius of that emerging design would be an American version of St. George, a champion in whom the qualities of Wolcott's Good Governor and Stalwart Soldier are combined, his exploits celebrated by a Connecticut poet as *The Conquest of Canaan*, thus sealing for all time the differences generated by the West. Upon that seal, as on his prophetic maps of New England and Virginia, may be detected the crest of the American Aeneus, Captain John Smith, and his motto, "To Conquer Is To Live."

XII

ON HIS MAJESTY'S SERVICE

Robert Beverley,
William Byrd,
and the Palladian Version
of American Pastoral.

i. Ill Fares the Land

Meanwhile, back in Jamestown, not much had happened since 1624—
not much, that is, so far as literature was concerned. Something of the
disparity between the cultures of Virginia and Massachusetts is suggested by the fact that Mather's *Magnalia* was the last in a long line
of Puritan chronicles, while Robert Beverley's *History of the Present
State of Virginia*, published three years later, was the first general account of that colony's past to appear since John Smith's epic effort.
Though the course of empire along Chesapeake Bay had hardly been
untroubled, Virginia suffering her share of Indian wars and tensions
between Crown and Colony, the various conflicts did not engender an
outpouring of pamphlets equivalent to the blackletter flood released
from time to time by the Boston theoctopus. The "literature" of Virginia is largely confined to records of state and the correspondence,
official and otherwise, exchanged between colony and mother country.

If there was a literary tradition in colonial Virginia, it was the writing of promotional tracts, which did not stop with the death of Captain Smith. There is a continuity of euphoric efflorescence associated
with Chesapeake Bay which spread north by east during the latter part
of the seventeenth century, the ridiculous excesses of Maryland's Muse
resulting finally in the satire of Ebenezer Cooke's *The Sot-Weed Factor* (1708), indeed approximating self-parody in George Alsop's eccentric prose rhapsody, *A Character of the Province of Maryland* (1666).
Where Cooke stresses the dreary reality of golden prospects, Alsop gives
his own game away, concluding his preposterous paean to the New
World paradise with a shocking image of urinating Indian women,
who stand "bolt upright with their arms akimbo, performing the action, in so confident and obscene a posture, as if they had taken their
Degrees of Entrance at Venice, and commenced Bawds of Art at Leg-
horn" (86). Rather more promiscuous than promising, Alsop's Indian

343

woman is a revised version of Pocahontas, the Virginian virgin become a Maryland whore, an image in harmony with Thomas Morton's Merry Mount consort.

It is a symbolic icon, for if Clio in Massachusetts sustained the Puritan's orthodoxy, in the South she was the toast of the Cavaliers, a propagandistic and self-serving tradition epitomized by Captain Smith's *Generall Historie,* a book to which Beverley was in debt, in terms of substance and spirit, if not style. Little more than a tricked-out promotional tract, Beverley's *History* testifies on several levels that the colony's present state was pretty much her past condition, and while attacking the spirit of heedless opportunism that continued to shape events on Chesapeake Bay, Beverley's book took its own form from a similarly self-interested motive. Mather's monumental tome most certainly has its determining bias and is swollen with manneristic stuffing, yet it is still considered relatively trustworthy where matters of record are concerned. But the relative slimness and clean lines of Beverley's volume are deceiving, for his account of Virginia's past is entirely in the service of the present moment, a propagandistic impulse abetted by sheer ignorance, resulting in clumsy errors innocent of intention but testifying that in the South the past is a very relative matter, in terms of kinship as well as accountings of fact.

The promotional emphasis of Beverley's *History* is keyed by his use of the past in the service of the future, a point of view which promises much, turning from old losses to new gains by means of a pivotal *if*: "This part of Virginia now inhabited, if we consider the improvements in the hands of the English, it cannot upon that score be commended; but if we consider its natural aptitude to be improved, it may with justice be accounted one of the finest countries in the world" (118-19). Preserving the cadences and figures of earlier promoters, Beverley depicts Virginia as a terrestrial paradise, a New World Canaan, an Eden of "delicious fruits, which without art, they have in great variety and perfection" (298). But therein lies the Edenic trap, for, as in Morgan's mythical Basaruah, "the goodness of the fruit leads people into many temptations," the paradox of plenty being that "where God Almighty is so merciful as to work for people, they never work for themselves" (297).

Despite its Arcadian colors, therefore, Beverley's *History* has a Jeremian emphasis, the laziness of Virginian planters being a southern counterpart to Puritan backsliding. Where propagandists of a century earlier proposed the conversion of Indians to useful, civilized ways, Beverley attacks the "slothful indolence of my countrymen" in the "hope it will rouse them out of their lethargy, and excite them to make the most of all those happy advantages which nature has given them" (319). As for the hope of Hariot and Hakluyt, the Indians have been harmed, not helped, by association with Englishmen, degenerating through "drunkenness and luxury" from their "simple state of nature," losing not only their land, but their "felicity" and "innocence" as well (233). By placing this satiric reality in the midst of an idealized pastoral landscape, Beverley creates a disjunctive dimension equivalent to that of the Massachusetts historians. Where the Puritans' wilderness opens to a paradisiac prospect, however, Beverley's Eden gives way to georgic ground, yet, as in New England, the river is central to Virginia's ambiguous terrain.

First of all, the River, like the Garden, is an essential component of Beverley's Canaanite conceit: "As Judaea was full of rivers, and branches of rivers, so is Virginia; as that was seated upon a great bay and sea, wherein were all the conveniences for shipping and trade, so is Virginia" (296). And as with the fertility of the garden, so with the commodiousness of the river, whose convenience carries a curse, a paradox of plenty foreseen by Captain John Smith in 1624: "This liberty of taking up land," complains Beverley, in a virtual paraphrase of Smith's lament, "and the ambition each man had of being lord of a vast, though uninhabited territory, together with the advantage of many rivers, which afforded a commodious road for shipping at every man's door, has made the country fall into such an unhappy settlement and course of trade, that to this day they have not any one place of cohabitation among them, that may reasonably bear the name of a town" (57-58). Promoting an incipient anarchy of self-interest, Virginia's rivers also facilitate the spread of "the disease of planting tobacco," and Beverley's hostility to this geopolitical malaise, his emphasis on the importance to future prosperity of developing towns, manufactures, and diversified agriculture, not only echoes John Smith's recommendations but mirrors the perpetually consolidational Boston viewpoint.

Rivers in New England likewise exerted a powerful pull, but where in the North the theocratic scheme of settlement by townships provided counterpoise, in Virginia the fluvial force held full sway. County boundaries, established at first according to parish circuits and a well-ordered "propinquity of the extremes to one common center," were later transferred to the necks of land separating waterways, "with respect to the convenience of having each county limited to one single river, for its trade and shipping" (243). Beverley deplores the weak condition of the Church in Virginia, but his attack is chiefly on the abandonment of regular, neoclassically designed political divisions for the organic unities determined by geographical and commercial necessity, a point of view closer to William Hubbard's than to that of the Mathers. But with his contemporaries in New England, the Virginian historian shares a sense of decline and a concomitant faith in the power of centralized authority to set things aright. He likewise posits a Golden Age and a Good Governor, the both identified with Sir William Berkeley, Beverley's counterpart to Cotton Mather's Sir William Phips, the knight in each case championed by a son whose father was intimately associated with the fortunes of the former incumbent.

Still, Beverley's cosmetic portraiture—*his* Sir William—is enlisted in the service of a cause far different from Congregationalism, and it is notable in this regard that where Sir Edmund Andros is for Mather an example of colonial tyranny, a symbol of the arbitrariness of governors appointed by the Crown, the same man when transferred to Beverley's Virginia becomes "a great lover of method, and dispatch in all sorts of business," administrative efficiency which struck the independent Puritans as a willful abrogation of their Old Charter rights (102). Andros hardly went down the Virginian throat as easily as Beverley implies, for what was hot grease in Boston was not all gravy in Jamestown, but Andros qualifies for Beverley's approval because he used his power to promote towns and industries, thereby continuing the great (and futile) efforts of Governor Berkeley. Nor was Berkeley himself in his later years the benevolent, unselfish administrator portrayed by Beverley, who rids his man of dross so as to create a *Vir Bonum* designed to display the faults of Governor Francis Nicholson to worst advantage. For Beverley's Nicholson, like Mather's Andros, is a type of arbitrary despot, neglecting Virginia's well-being (towns and manufactures) for the whimsical exercise of power, thereby dividing "the most friendly, and most united people in the world, into very unhappy factions" (106). As in the matter of the Garden and the River, Beverley's account of Virginia's Governors posits a neoclassical antagonism, geo-political decline figured in terms of order versus misrule.

Where Governor Berkeley was somewhat less than the ideal *magister* portrayed by Beverley, Governor Nicholson deserved better than he got, having done as much as any before him to develop commercial centers. Berkeley's career in Virginia was long, Nicholson's short, but both men commenced as fair-minded administrators and ended as self-centered tyrants, facts which Beverley shapes into satiric abstractions. Undoubtedly his portrait of Berkeley benefited from nostalgia and his attack on Nicholson most certainly reflects Virginia's mounting anger over that governor's increasingly arbitrary and fractious rule. And yet, some measure of Beverley's self-interest is revealed by his account of the creation of the one town whose growth Nicholson did indeed encourage—Williamsburg. Dismissing the practical and sym-bolic reasons for relocating the seat of government near the groves of learning in Virginia as mere "pretext," Beverley presents the abandon-ment of Jamestown as a whimsical and retrograde step, leaving out of his stated reasons the fact that he owned land in the town in question. It is a lacuna with a dark, Matherine look, and with Cotton Mather, moreover, Beverley enlists Clio in the service of a larger truth, his de-piction of Nicholson as a captious tyrant transcending the matter of local real estate. As Mather's Sir William serves to illustrate a proto-nationalistic cause—the invasion of Canada—so Beverley's Sir Francis provides the occasion for an indirect attack on colonial rule.

Among Nicholson's arbitrary acts was his use of a law intended "to suppress rebellion and to pacify and reconcile the people one towards another" for the implementation of injustice, digging up "in revenge of personal injuries, and for support of the heavy mismanagements which the country now groans under" a law that imposed a heavy fine and imprisonment "upon any man that shall presume to speak disre-spectfully of the Governor" (88). In Nicholson's hands equivocal laws become instruments of repression, misrule given particular point by the causes of the "rebellion" which gave rise to the law—the revolt against Berkeley's regime led by Nathaniel Bacon in 1675—an episode which is central to the carefully covert argument of Beverley's *History*. For Beverley uses the figure of anarchy in arms as a dramatic demon-stration that colonial rule, even under the best of governors, can be-come an *agent provocateur*, that the planter's independent spirit is galled rather than harnessed by arbitrary taxes and ill-considered laws. Contemporary with King Philip's War, Bacon's Rebellion was its counterpart, the result of tensions created by a half-century of slow expansion, and with William Hubbard, Beverley imposes a neoclassical frame on the outbreak of violence, a perspective of law and order which is not without a subvert, disjunctive dimension.

ii. Dire Effects from Civil Discord Flow

Bacon's Rebellion, like King Philip's War, involved troubles with regional Indians—indeed, news of the conflict in Virginia aroused rumors in New England (according to William Hubbard) of "a design of a general rising of the Indians against the English all over the country" (II: 92-93). The rebellion in the South was more complex, involving not only the antagonism between red men and white resulting from the conflicts engendered by expansion, but an equivalent hostility among the white settlers themselves. Virginia had suffered from much greater Indian attacks in earlier years, the massacre of 1644 serving as a close counterpart to the issues and outcome of King Philip's War, and there had been collisions of interest between the Burgesses, the General Council, and the Governor which were equivalent to similar struggles in New England. But Bacon's Rebellion was a combination of conflicts, a complicated interrelationship of divisions which exemplify the pains of Virginia's transformation from a colony to an embryonic nation-state.

Following the creation of the House of Burgesses and General Council in 1617 and (in 1625) the substitution of a Royal Governor for the authority of the Virginia Company, politics in Virginia, as in Massachusetts, tended to assume a pattern of opposition between oligarchical and popular forces. Where the Council was an appointive body, filled by men of considerable education and landed wealth, the Burgesses were likely to be men of the middling classes, who (in time) were identified with the newer sections of the tidewater region. The Governor and his Council, like their counterparts in Massachusetts, most certainly had their differences over the years (as in the "mutiny" of 1635), but during Sir William Berkeley's first administration (1642-52), the Governor, his General Council, and the Burgesses worked in harmony, a bicameral unity enjoying the same benign neglect that allowed Puritanism to gain a foothold in the New World during the previous decade. The outbreak of Civil War in England inspired in Virginia fierce declarations of loyalty to the throne, nor was the squirearchy silent when Charles I lost his head, but for the most part it was tobacco as usual, and having had their occasional say, the planters quietly submitted in 1652 to Cromwell's governance. During the interregnum, as New England fought for her Way, Virginia underwent quiet but profound change, the House of Burgesses exercising political supremacy dictated by Parliament, and though the old system was reestablished with the Restoration, the ascendancy of Governor and Council was more symbol than fact.

It was, however, a symbol enjoying very real powers extending deep into the fabric of local government, and Governor Berkeley—following his return to office from grand isolation on his plantation—began increasingly to manipulate country matters in favor of centralized authority at Jamestown. Sir William's attempts to heave the balance of power in his own direction were perhaps (from his point of view) a necessary reaction to a decade of popular rule, but his efforts were not so much on the King's behalf as on his own, a signal difference dictated by motions in London following the arrival of Charles II from *his* grand isolation in France. Berkeley, along with sundry Cavalier exiles and planters of high degree, welcomed the return of the Stuart monarchy, but the Restoration soon became to Virginia what the Commonwealth had been to New England, a something less than celebratory occasion. Virginia, like Massachusetts under her New Charter, began to feel the irksome tug of royal reins, curbs that had a particularly bitter taste in Royalist mouths, and the man trapped in the saddle, as always, was the Governor. Stiff with age and pride, Sir William bargained for time, restraining popular and ignoring royal will by appointing friends to the General Council and packing the House of Burgesses, afterward refusing to call for new elections.

One predictable result was the creation of a junta, a ruling elite of wealthy planters with whose well-being the Governor, after two decades of residence on his own large plantation, was much more concerned than he was with the arbitrary dictates of that meretricious monarch, Charles II. Another perhaps less foreseeable result was a growing antagonism between the majority of smaller planters—many of whom had settled in the up-river regions of the tidewater zone—and the Governor's cabalistic rule. In both instances, grievances (between Council and Crown, Commoners and Council) were acerbated by the unstable economy of the monolithic plantation system, and the Governor, hoping to diversify and increase the colony's productivity, made efforts to encourage the fur trade, measures which produced a surprising result indeed. The consequent explosion of popular resentment assumed insurrectionary shape, taking its name as it took its spark from a young counterpart to the cold, aging Governor, Nathaniel Bacon himself a man caught in the middle, as much a victim as a promoter of a fiery summer of discontent, central figure in a masque of anarchy played out along the rivers of the Bay.

iii. Think How Bacon Shined

Following the massacre of 1644, Governor Berkeley proved more successful than his Cavalier counterparts in England at clearing the land of evil, and drove the Indians beyond the Fall Line. He further secured the Virginian peace by building forts at the heads of navigation on major rivers, a martial equivalent to Winthrop's Wall, which, in the manner of Sir William Phips's fort at Pemaquid, became a focus of discontent. More expensive than useful, Berkeley's forts were chiefly of value as strongholds from which to launch exploratory expeditions in search of passage to the Pacific and increase the volume of fur trade with the Indians. Since up-river planters, like William Byrd the Elder, engaged in the fur trade themselves, the competitive presence of Berkeley's forts was resented, and when realignment of Indian territorial imperatives resulted in attacks on isolated plantations along the frontier, Berkeley's reluctance to retaliate appeared to be protective chiefly of the Governor's own interests.

The result was a situation along the Fall Line which resembled by 1675 the classic frontier antagonism, with the Indians on one side and the down-river squirearchy on the other, a volatile mixture to which Nathaniel Bacon provided the fuse. Sent as a scapegrace to the plantations in 1674 by his father, Bacon belonged to the educated and wealthy class of emigrant who usually rose quickly to the top—if not killed by the fever—and he was appointed by Berkeley to the General Council soon after his arrival. But Bacon's "Quarter" was located close to the headwaters of the James, a proximity to the Fall Line which allied him with up-river planters like his neighbor William Byrd, and it was under Bacon's banner that unauthorized border warfare spread into insurrection. For Indian attacks were but a final jackstraw heaped on an intolerable burden of taxes and unjust policies, not all in Berkeley's power to remedy, but associated nonetheless with his insulated administration. Young Bacon, as a member of the educated elite, was welcomed as a spokesman and leader by the rebels, and he seems to have had considerable magnetism, serving as a cohesive (if not always consistent) center of the rebellion until he succumbed to fatigue and fever.

Figured in terms of misrule, Bacon was anathema to the chroniclers of his day, but a later generation of Virginians would celebrate him as an early champion of democracy. We may in this case credit the version of his contemporaries: ruthlessly effective in the field, and useful as a figurehead, as a true revolutionary Bacon was more a flash in the pan than a shot heard round the world. The laws passed by the Burgesses elected during his meteoric ascendancy have been graced by his name, but, as with his tenancy of "Bacon's Castle," the connection is tenuous. Moreover, though Bacon's Laws most certainly provide hard evidence of widespread discontent, they are not aimed at colonial rule in general but at the specific injustices of Berkeley's reign. In form, Bacon's Rebellion only resembles a revolution, and in substance Bacon's Laws were largely reformatory, an attempt to redistribute the burden of the colonial yoke more equitably.

Still, those would also be the characteristics of revolt in 1773-74, and as the provincial patriots a century later were forced by their own rhetoric and British obdurateness into severing the colonial tie, so Rob-

ert Beverley's account of Bacon's Rebellion is an accidental prolegomenon to that circumstance, coincidental prophecy resulting from his
nostalgic perspective. Beverley's loyalties, like his father's during the
event, were with Governor Berkeley, a strategic alliance necessitating
a certain shaping of facts, as in his account of Bacon's Laws, the particulars of which he avoids by an abstract summation, thereby placing
the onus of blame not on Berkeley, but on misguided home rule, safely
identified (in 1705) with Charles II. Wholly protective of the Governor,
Beverley's strategy likewise dictates a certain sympathy with the Rebel,
his Bacon a much more complex figure of misrule than either Hubbard's wild-boar or Benjamin Tompson's pork-rind Philip, being no
mere satanic caricature, but an ambiguous portrait of discontent. Part
Absolom, part Achitophel, Bacon is "young, bold, active, of an inviting
aspect, and powerful elocution," but is ruled by a "seditious humor,"
and is thereby qualified to "head a giddy and unthinking multitude"
(78). This last phrase tips Beverley's essential conservatism, and by his
account the winds of change in Virginia have a flatulent note, an expansion on Hobbes's anatomical conceit: Bacon's Rebellion is an
"intestine commotion," internal disorder from which emerges a populist champion of "the poorer sort," and if Hubbard's Philip is cast as a
traitor to the English King, Beverley's Bacon is an even more fearsome
specter, a betrayer of his class, being a "gentleman" who gave "countenance to a riotous mob" (74, 78).

Beverley, like Hubbard, concentrates on the rebel's rise and fall, the
Governor remaining off stage during most of the action, but Sir William is no Captain Church. The scenario is arranged instead to avoid
more embarrassing truths, for Berkeley was unable to rally the Colony's support behind (or before) him. Thus, according to Beverley, the
rebellion was put down not by the civil sword but by providential intervention, God being "pleased, after some months' confusion, to put
an end to Virginia's misfortunes, as well as to Bacon's designs, by his
natural death" (84). Beverley does not enlarge in the Puritan manner
on this providential note, but he exercises a Matherine pen concerning
subsequent events, blotting from the record Governor Berkeley's campaign of retribution against the leaders of the rebellion and their associates: confiscatory as well as condemnatory, Sir William's reconstruc-
tion of fortunes along the rivers of Chesapeake Bay is consigned to the

Cavalier equivalent of the Puritan limbo for bankrupt Canadian business.

Berkeley's repressive, bloody course of vengeance, like Phips's career of stupid malfeasance, was ended by his recall to England, and he also was saved from disgrace by death. Beverley scants this matter, and further rearranges history by attributing the law against speech disrespectful of the Governor—which Nicholson would turn to tyrannical ends—to Governor Lord Culpeper, Berkeley's successor, who arrived in Virginia with "the advantage of restoring peace to a troubled nation," when it was in fact one of Sir William's dicatorial devices (86-87). Still, Beverley's filial piety, like Cotton Mather's, is difficult to extricate from his patriotic bias, revealed by the phrase, "troubled nation." His *History* is aligned along vectors of discontent not much different from those which in time would lead to revolutionary conclusions, and despite his conservative, nostalgic burden, Beverley's alterations of fact are a sheath putting forth the outline of a sword, a carefully couched warning to England concerning the incendiary possibilities of bad laws and worse governors.

Beverley's jeremiad, therefore, is aimed against both the indolence of Virginia and the ignorance (and arrogance) of England, implying that the "mob," having once been driven to "hazard their necks by rebellion," may be counted upon to repeat the performance under similar circumstances (74). "I am an Indian," announces Beverley in his Preface, assuming in the manner of Benjamin Tompson a rustic guise—not, however, that of a shoemaker or shepherd. It is distinctly an American and a wildwood costume, connoting simplicity with something of a latent threat, identical to the disguise with which Boston's Sam Adams—himself no mean writer of Philippic—gave a native character to the forces of rebellion in 1773, thereby transforming William Hubbard's "Sons of Violence" to "Sons of Liberty." In Virginia as in Massachusetts, the Indian became increasingly identified with the purposes of an embryonic nation, nursed in a womb of empire fed by blue veins bearing Indian names. Providing harbors of nurture, they elongate inland, becoming conduits stretching toward greater rivers beyond.

iv. Alps on Alps Arise

Sympathetic identification with Indians, whether in New England in 1773 or Virginia in 1705, depended upon a certain period of relative peace between the colonial and aboriginal populations in those disparate parts of America. As Roger Wolcott in 1725 was able to grant the Pequots heroic stature, so Beverley in his *History* promotes an image of the Indian which is the antithesis of Mather's satanic savage, a fit inhabitant for his paradisiac landscape and witness to the longevity of Arthur Barlowe's Golden Age vision. The hostile view of the Indian is associated by Beverley with the rebels of 1675, "minds full of discontent" who vented their "resentment" of colonial rule on "poor Indians" before burning Jamestown to the ground (78). Devoting a quarter of his book to an account of "the native Indians," Beverley depicts them as naturally virtuous, even loving creatures—rather feminized savages in the Pocahontas mold. It is a melioristic portrait expressing the author's stated hope that the natives could best be accommodated to the colonial presence by intermarriage, and is thereby an expansionist profile however dulcet, since savagery in Virginian promotional literature tends from Barlowe on to put forth a friendly face from the woods.

The Southern consistency in this regard is borne out by the career of a Virginia-bred Puritan, Daniel Gookin the Younger, who, having departed that den of roaring Cavaliers when the Act of Conformity was passed, became henceforth something of a nonconformist in Massachusetts, enlisting himself in Apostle John Eliot's missionary work among the Indians. Gookin was also a militia officer, civil official, land speculator and coastal trader, substantial Yankee callings which seem ill-suited to his evangelical activities. Yet Gookin's unfinished history of New England provides a unifying key, for all that the Captain undertook has a mercantile cast, from encouraging local manufactures to urging that Eliot's "Praying Indians" engage in remunerative activities betimes: while the Apostle was fishing for pagan souls, the Captain was trying to convince them they should peddle their Merrimack salmon in Boston. This combination of mercantile and missionary zeal took a more militant cast when Gookin faced toward the west, expanding to the epical dimensions of his Great Plan for assembling an army of soldiers, artisans, and missionaries to search out and secure the fabled great "sea, or lake, or some navigable river running into it" (29).

Citing Captain Smith's account in *The Generall Historie of Virginia* as his authority, Captain Gookin declared the "undoubted truth, upon clear demonstration, that there is such a lake, or arm of the south sea," within four hundred miles of Boston, and while admitting that his project was costly, he insisted that it would be "greatly advantageous unto the discoverers, not only in . . . conveying and communicating the Christian religion unto so many poor, ignorant souls . . . but also in accumulating external riches, as well as honor, unto the first undertakers and perfecters of this discovery" (158). Gookin also noted that the French in Canada were "very jealous lest the English discover and settle this place first," thereby anticipating a century of competition for control of the Great Lakes (159). But as Gookin's work among the Indians of Massachusetts was discredited by the outbreak of King Philip's War, so his proposal remained buried in the manuscript of his unfinished history, a prophetic Merlin under a stone of neglect.

Gookin's mercantile like his missionary projects ran counter to the main current of New England enterprise, and bear the geopolitical marks of the imperial Virginian quest. Yet his projecting enthusiasm is essentially Puritan even proto-Yankee in its mingling of profit-seeking and middle-class piety, industriousness that transplants the early Virginian expectation of finding the Northwest Passage into New England once again, recalling the millennial vision of Edward Howes and reinstating Thomas Morton's wildwood dream. If Gookin's westering urge provides a paradoxical ligature between enterprise north and south, it suggests also that if the Puritan settlement on the Nansemond River had prospered, Captain Smith's version of Virginia's future might have been realized. Certainly something more than mere opportunism was needed to get civilization moving beyond the tidewaters of Chesapeake Bay, and if Gookin was the only New Englander to look

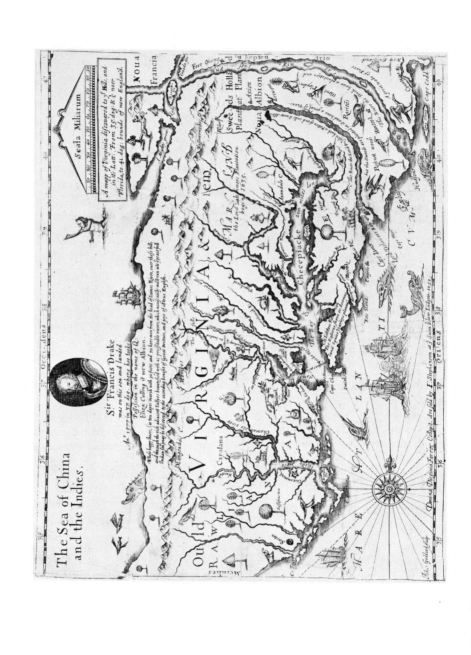

John Farrar's Map of Virginia (1651). Courtesy I. N. Phelps Stokes Collection, Addenda Map IX, New York Public Library.

Farrar's Virginia. In effect *Hakluytus Redivivus*, Farrar (or Ferrer) propagates the old myth of China across from Chesapeake Bay, conjuring up the spirit of Sir Francis Drake and letting Triton blow an imperial horn. But the "New" Virginians, like the "Ould," were slow to obey the summons. See Cumming *et al.*, *Discovery of North America*, 268-69.

longingly west, he was one of a very few Virginians to do so as well. A century of uncertainty about the proximity of the Pacific to the headwaters of Virginia's rivers resulted in a hundred years of indifference, a reluctance to search out prospects beyond the falls so long as the land below remained plentiful and fertile. Nor were the Indians of the interior as friendly as Beverley's melioristic portrait suggests, and when traders rode inland their horses wore tinkling bells to advertise their pacific intentions. William Byrd the Elder was careful, likewise, to build his trading post no farther upstream than the falls of the James, near the spot where Captain Newport was turned back by word of the fierce Indians beyond and in line with the circle of forts built by Beverley's ideal Governor.

Sir William Berkeley himself proposed in 1648 to lead an expedition in search of the truth of rumors which had not much changed since John Smith's face was reflected in Virginia's waters, but nothing came of it. And in 1650, a party of explorers got only as far west as the Roanoke falls, from Fort Henry on the falls of the Appomattox, where the Occaneechee Indians had built a fort of their own, effectively blocking further progress along the trading path to the south. Until Bacon's forces removed that barrier by butchering the inhabitants in the manner of Major Mason, it remained an effective door against discovery. Still, the promotional impulse is willing to make peace with the harshest realities, and the rebuffed travelers upon their return had printed an enthusiastic account by Edward Bland of the "rich, red, fat marl land" along the rivers of "New Brittaine" (129). In 1651, also, John Farrar gave visible proof to theory by printing a map of Virginia which incorporated every territorial fiction associated with the interior. However, the fact remains that though no one seems to have challenged Farrar's iconographic assertions, nobody rushed to verify them either. That exploration and expansion was a minority issue at midcentury and afterward is testified to by the silence on the matter during the period of the Burgesses' great power, and something of the difficulty experienced by Berkeley in encouraging voyages of discovery beyond the falls is suggested by the fact that the first man to render an account of the regions to the south and west was no Virginian, but a German physician, John Lederer.

In the service of Sir William, Doctor Lederer undertook three journeys into the interior between 1669 and 1670, the first and last of

which carried him to the Blue Ridge. But in terms of mythic metamorphoses, his second voyage was the most important, laying a lateral
southwestern line in search of the Northwest Passage that became in
time a major trading route, for Lederer's was another metaphysical errand with mercantile results. As literature, moreover, *The Discoveries
of John Lederer* (1672) contains a certain creative reach, the narrative
of his second journey being, like John Smith's *True Relation,* an account of interior regions that opens to vast stretches of the imagination.
Fearing Indian attack, Lederer's Virginian companions stopped at the
Roanoke, content to identify one of the northward-swinging bends of
that serpentine river as "an arm of the Lake of Canada" (150). Scoffing
at that notion, Lederer proceeded on with an Indian guide, and saw
and heard enough of the western territory to convince him that it was
considerably more than "eight or ten days' journey" from sea to shining sea, that no navigable rivers fell from the far side of the Appalachians into the Pacific (166). And yet in exploding one myth, Lederer
set others in motion, for he described and gave shape by his map to a
large but nonexistent lake in the west, a body of water which he was
sure gave way to distant mines of gold and silver. He also drew on his
map with a generous hand a "barren sandy desert" and a "continuous
marsh" taking three days to cross, thereby providing his narrative the
perilous passages familiar to romance literature (161, 159).

Published in England, Lederer's mixture of fact and fancy was dedicated to Lord Ashley, who as Shaftesbury would soon turn his attention
from colonial to local affairs, and the subsequent course of exploration
of the western regions was likewise cut short in Virginia by the rebellion to which it in part gave rise. Symbolic in that regard was the death
in 1680 of Colonel Abraham Wood, a man whose obscure origins and
rise to prominence is connected from first to last with the exploration
of the lands beyond the falls. Perhaps the Abraham Wood who arrived
in 1620 as an indentured servant, by 1640 he owned considerable property in the up-river counties, and in 1644 Wood entered the political
life of the colony, first as a member of the House of Burgesses, then as
a member of the Council. In 1646 he was commissioned captain of
militia at Fort Henry, and was one of the seven men who made the
journey to the forks of the Roanoke in 1650. In 1671, presumably under orders from Governor Berkeley, the by then Colonel Wood sent
out from Fort Henry the first of several parties of exploration which

A MAP OF THE WHOLE TERRITORY TRAVERSED BY IOHN LEDERER IN HIS THREE MARCHES.

1. the first March
2. the second March to Mahock
3. the place where the English left him, and his March alone to Ushery
4. His March home again.

5. The third March
6. a quick sand at the head of Rapahanock river
7. The Lake of Ushery
8. A great Marish.

Pars

Leagues

Cross Sculpsit

John Lederer's Map of his Travels in Virginia. From *The Discoveries of John Lederer* (1672). Courtesy New York Public Library.

Lederer's Travels. Drawn to illustrate his book of *Discoveries*, in which Lederer tried to lay to rest the old myth concerning the proximity of the Pacific Ocean to the Appalachians, this map contributes an equally fictitious lake (borrowed from the Virginia of Mercator-Hondius [1606]) and added "a great marsh" as well to the southern range. For a detailed account of Lederer's mistaken topography, see W. P. Cumming (ed.), *The Discoveries of John Lederer* (1958), 69-95.

continued the work begun by Lederer. The reports of Wood's men provided more facts than Lederer's account, and their efforts opened a trading path to the Cherokees through the mountains, but as literature concerning the western regions they are not much.

All such adventures—or at least the written record of them—stopped with Bacon's Rebellion, and Wood's death put a symbolic seal on the second phase of expansion in Virginia, which never, during his lifetime, did more than inscribe tentative lines on the blank surface of the interior beyond the falls. Robert Beverley mentions Berkeley's sponsorship of "new discoveries abroad amongst the Indians," but his account is both perfunctory and erroneous, and he evinces little apparent interest in such matters (72-74). Whatever his reasons, the historian's emphasis on the importance of establishing new centers of trade on the Bay rather than on the necessity of exploration reflects the Virginian mood in 1705. But if Beverley's book had any effect on the shape of Virginia's future, then its proportions miscarried his message, for while Beverley's encouragement of towns and industries was ignored, his paradisiac view was perpetuated, as planters continued to move inexorably inland along the multitudinous rivers of the Bay, and it was not long after he wrote his *History* that the future unhappiness of the Virginian nation was dictated by the opening of a farther range. The result was a realignment of forces creating a zone of geopolitical conflict prefigured by the frontier antagonisms that resulted in Bacon's Rebellion, but it was a future consequence of present acts to which Virginia's historian was blind. Indeed, as that inland thrust of empire gathered momentum, Robert Beverley was of the party that lead the way.

v. Wide the Limits Stand

The prime mover behind the third phase of expansion was the need for land to implement the wasteful plantation system, and its chief instrument was Alexander Spotswood, just the kind of good governor as Robert Beverley had described. Governor Spotswood set to work briskly on the colony's behalf as soon as he arrived, in 1710, but though his efforts seem to have met with Beverley's approval, they were not always in accord with the General Council's wishes. Nor was Spotswood as concerned with encouraging the growth of towns as in advancing Virginia's frontier—and increasing his own acreage thereby—and it was therefore an imperial impulse which inspired the Williamsburg Alexander to cross the Blue Ridge in 1716 and seize what was on the other side. Proceeding on horseback to the source of the James River and beyond, Spotswood, something more than a century after the founding of Jamestown, fulfilled Captain Newport's desire, and in a manner which the old pirate would have enjoyed. For the expedition was a jolly picnickiad in which good drink and plenty of game made up the epic menu, festive complement to the catalogue of Virginia's worthies who went along, at the head of which appears the name of Robert Beverley.

The historian of Virginia was not, however, the chronicler of Spotswood's grand outing, the casualness of which is attested to by the fact that the only surviving record was kept not by a native Virginian, but by a young Huguenot émigré, John Fontaine, who had come over from Great Britain in 1715 to buy land for his two brothers and a married sister. In the course of his travels about Virginia, Fontaine experienced a curious version of southern hospitality at Beverley's plantation, where he was detained for a week while his host plied him with home-made wine and proposed land deals involving 999-year leases, neither of which appealed to the shrewd if pious Frenchman (265-67). Indeed,

Fontaine's journal is throughout an interesting gloss on Virginia's pastoral myth, Spotswood himself emerging as something of a real estate developer, laying out "an avenue about half a mile long" through the wilderness near his fort on the Meherrin River (280). If Fontaine's observations help to explain the economic pitch and literary moment of Beverley's *History,* they also attest that new energies were set in motion by a new century, a mood of optimism and opportunism perfectly expressed by the Governor's expedition over the mountains. The river discovered on the other side was the Shenandoah, which Spotswood named "Euphrates," evoking not an apocalyptic but an agrarian stream, and despite Beverley's animadversions against taking up land, the historian was seen by Fontaine to cast a covetous eye on a large, fertile tract beside the Rapidan, on whose banks the Governor and his jolly planters camped during their return trip (288, 290).

This mixture of gaiety and greed characterizes Virginian enterprise from the beginning, which is from first to last the story of a brotherly band of laughing Cavaliers, and the increase in industriousness observable during the early years of the eighteenth century did not diminish the Virginian comedy. No planter was more ambitious for empire than William Byrd of Westover and none wore his wig with a looser buckle, and his account of running the Dividing Line between Virginia and North Carolina is a literary epitome of the Cavalier spirit. Byrd, in London at the time of Spotswood's expedition—on business that did not endear him to the Governor—never belonged to the Order of the Golden Horseshoe that was "instituted to encourage gentlemen to venture backwards, and make discoveries and new settlements" (288-89). But he was no less an advocate of backwards ventures in the hope of future profit, his journey westward in 1728 continuing the thrust—albeit in a different direction—begun by Spotswood. It is a continuity, moreover, that is reinforced by the Fontaine connection, for though John returned to England after securing property on Spotswood's Meherrin River, his brother, Peter, became the pastor of Westover Parish, on the James, gaining thereby a certain immortality, not as the keeper of but as an occasional figure in another man's diary, always good for conversation or cards. Yet Peter Fontaine figures most prominently in Byrd's account of his western voyage, the preacher having been pressed into service as a chaplain, caring for the souls of surveyors and marrying and baptizing settlers along the way.

Fontaine's was a spiritual errand, but in Byrd's narrative of the expedition the spirit of fun prevails, nor was the Reverend Peter immune from the general jest.

Byrd's experience inspired not one, but two narratives: his *History of the Dividing Line*, which was intended for publication but did not see print for more than a century, and his *Secret History of the Line*, meant for private circulation but preserved nonetheless. The both as an organic whole give literary shape to the essential dichotomy of the Virginian adventure, accommodating paradisiac myth as well as the picaresque reality. Imposing an imperial—indeed, literal—line upon the land, Byrd's twin testaments provide a heroic and a satiric complement to Beverley's *History*, an aesthetic kinship carrying colonial enterprise beyond the falls. As the disjunctive dimension of Beverley's book is the difference between wise and foolish Virginians, so Byrd's narrative twins project that dichotomy into a further range, drawing a line not only between Virginia and North Carolina, but between two ways of life.

Byrd on the disparity between Virginians and North Carolinians resembles Madam Knight on the state of manners in Connecticut, and his observations are given added asperity by the geopolitical dispute which gave rise to the line. As with Winthrop's Great Wall, it was a matter of boundaries between sister colonies, territorial imperatives which were centered in the physical fact and symbolic role of rivers. There was, moreover, not one border in question, but two, each colony insisting on observing the boundary giving it the most terrain and hence the widest jurisdiction, resulting in an uncertain division of authority not unlike the problems created by the Pope at Avignon. The quarrel in the South (as that between Massachusetts and Plymouth) turned on a tributary creek, the Nottaway, for the acquisition of that otherwise not notable waterway would give North Carolina a route to Albemarle Sound, enabling her planters to get around the Virginian prohibition against shipping their tobacco from Chesapeake ports.

Not surprisingly, Byrd's account in his *Secret History* of the North Carolina Commissioners resembles Winthrop's disparaging remarks concerning the delegates from Connecticut, Williamsburg concurring with Boston that character declined with the sun. The public version of events takes a somewhat higher road, avoiding personal attacks, but Byrd's Virginia emerges still as a true avatar of the Cavalier spirit, while North Carolina is portrayed as a backwoods anarchy, a "Lubber-land" resembling Hubbard's New Hampshire. With Hubbard, Byrd hews to a neoclassical as well as a geopolitical line, and in the South as in the North, once again the issue is law and order versus misrule. Whatever their sectarian and social differences, the Cavalier and Yankee ride side by side into the wildwood, revealing a common set of Anglo-American attitudes as they go. Yet the landscape has a distinctly Virginian coloration, for Byrd's motive, like Beverley's, is decidedly promotional, placing Garden and River in familiar juxtaposition. His wilderness passage finally ends with a paradisiac prospect, thereby bringing together the dominant motifs (as well as motives) of earlier Virginian literature, his twin history of driving the Line a late but gorgeous flowering of the laughing, opulent, winking Southern Muse, who shares with Morton's virginal New Canaan a distinctly Indian look.

vi. Treading Classic Ground

In another of his travel narratives, *A Progress to the Mines,* Byrd describes a "facetious widow who was so kind as to let me into all the secret history" of a neighboring parson and his wife, and the book entitled *Secret History of the Line* is likewise largely gossip (344). It is, therefore, a prose equivalent to *The Rape of the Lock,* being a mocking epic whose main drive is provided by prying in the name of Peace, a version of closet entertainment testifying that life in the colonies shared with life at court a boredom that was a starveling for bad news of friends and acquaintances. Gossip lies on the far side of satire from the jeremiad, for it is based on the assumption that the confidants are themselves free of the vices, follies, and misfortunes which make up the burden of their stories, and rather than speaking in thunder, gossip denounces by means of a whisper and a smirk.

Gossip is likewise a parasite, feeding fullest on familiar hosts, and it is Virginia's Richard Fitzwilliam who is the chief butt of Byrd's ridicule. As "Firebrand," he is characterized as a perpetual malcontent, a fomenter of discontent and a creature of appetites, a figure of misrule and a traitor to his class and colony. In the literature of colonial America, Firebrand is assigned a place similar to that of Morton, Metacomet, and Nathaniel Bacon, a provincial approximation of a familiar type in English satire. His antithesis (and antagonist) is Byrd's flattering self-portrait, "Steddy," who remains level-headed throughout, holding fast to dead center and thereby providing the *Vir Bonum* essential to the Augustan mode. Where Firebrand is a pimp to opportunity, animated by selfishness, Steddy is in "His Majesty's Service," identifying his wilderness mission with the royal will, remaining loyal to the terms of his commission, his purpose as straightforward and pure as the Line itself.

Still, though gossip may share with satire a bigoted bite, the woof is often not much worse than the warp of circumstance, and Byrd's *Secret History* is patterned after the course of real events, his caricatured Firebrand licensed by Fitzwilliam's personal deficiencies and his continual siding with the North Carolina Commissioners. As a journey, the *Secret History,* like Madam Knight's *Journal,* resembles one of Smollett's trips, being a picaresque progress by an ill-assorted band of wayfarers thrown together for a time. It is a genre in which Firebrand is an essential ingredient—indeed, he is a fellow traveler recognizable to us all, for there is no test of character like a prolonged episode of discomfort on the road. Firebrand, quite clearly, fails to make the grade; instead he drops out along the way, defecting with the defaulting Carolinians, providing a major transition in the tone and trajectory of the outward voyage.

For in the manner of the captain's and captivity narratives, Byrd's *Secret History* assumes a series of stages, carrying the surveying party into the wilderness and back. As Madam Knight's journey was determined by rainfall, so the danger of rattlesnakes made it necessary that Byrd's expedition be undertaken in two parts, the survey through the settled regions taking place in the spring, the remainder of the line driven to the mountains in the fall. This development is common to both versions of the event, but the seasonal dimension is much more clearly marked in the *Secret History.* During the spring voyage, Venus is clearly in ascendancy, "Firebrand and his faction" taking fullest advantage of their hosts along the way, for the "Knights of the Rum Cask" are upon occasion Knights of the Burning Pestle, breaking "the rules of hospitality by several gross freedoms they offered to take" with women encountered en route (59). But during the autumn phase of the expedition, Mars takes dominance, as the line progresses into an untenanted wilderness, and the narrative begins to assume the shape of adventure, comedy becoming a matter of belly and bowels. Firebrand and his "gang" do not last long in this more difficult terrain, where his achievement as a hunter (like his record as a lover) is mostly a matter of boasting.

Steddy, by contrast, is not only chaste during the journey through the settlements, but provides a model of patient, good-humored leadership in the wilderness beyond, following his own order given at the start of the expedition, that the Virginians set "the Carolina men a constant pattern of order, industry, and obedience" (48). Throughout, Steddy tries to enforce the traveler's rule that "when people are joined together in a troublesome commission, they should endeavor to sweeten by complacency and good humor all the hazards and hardships they are bound to encounter, and not, like married people, make their condition worse by everlasting discord" (72). But the "evil genius" of the expedition, Firebrand, is assisted by his "shadow," the incompetent Virginia surveyor "Orion," in making trouble by complaining about lodgings and arguing over prerogatives, creating tension which at the last breaks out in an episode of sudden violence. For in the course of an argument, Firebrand falls on "Honest Meanwell," one of the Virginia Commissioners, with "a limb of our table, big enough to knock down an ox," a blow prevented only by the quick action of Steddy (106). Soon afterward Firebrand and the Carolina Commissioners depart, and "a general joy discovered itself through all the camp when these gentlemen turned their backs upon us" (112-13).

The dispute which occasioned Firebrand's violent attack was over whether to continue the line on to the mountains or, having determined "the grand debate" about the Nottaway River to Carolina's satisfaction, return back home. The Carolina Commissioners (and Firebrand) were of the latter opinion, but Steddy intends to "finish the dividing line," with or without Carolina's help, "lest His Majesty's service might suffer by any neglect or mismanagement on his part" (112). Where the Carolina faction felt that the line would not need to be extended to the mountains for "an age or two," Steddy maintains that "the west line should be carried as near to them as may be, that both the land of the King and of the Lords may be taken up the faster, and that His Majesty's subjects may as soon as possible extend themselves to that natural barrier" (110-11). The Line, therefore, is not only a regulatory device determining jurisdiction over settled regions, but it is a symbol of progress, pointing the way for future plantations. In leaving Firebrand and the Carolina Commissioners behind, the Virginian surveyors in effect strip themselves of the encumbrance of faction, the line becoming a pure instrument of unanimity, a mean to which all things refer. Moreover, because of increasing hardships encountered in the wilderness, the Line promotes a Spartan necessity, evoking the martial spirit associated with linear penetration of the American interior.

As a result, Steddy's "command" begins to take on a distinctly paramilitary appearance, and to promote "good humor" and esprit de corps, Steddy creates a facetious "Order of Maosti," a wildwood version of Spotswood's Order of the Golden Horseshoe, he and his men sporting a "turkey beard in our hats by way of cockade" (139). Making the health of his men a personal concern, Steddy doses them with various medicines for their ailments—which include an epic case of constipation. But the most important aid to good humor on the march is plenty of food, and where the comedy on the first leg of the expedition was largely derived from Firebrand's love of liquor and lechery, it soon becomes a matter of diet—in specific, bear meat—and in particular, the craving for it by the Chaplain. John Fontaine noted in his account of Spotswood's Blue Ridge expedition that bear "tasted very well, and would be good, and might pass for veal, if one did not know what it was" (290). His brother the Reverend Peter knew very well what he was eating, but seems to have got past his brother's Old World squeamishness, developing a voracious appetite for that particular article of wilderness diet.

The joke of Chaplain "Humdrum's" inordinate fondness for bear meat depended upon the popular belief that it was an aphrodisiac, bawdy humor turning on Humdrum's prudery. During the first leg of the expedition, the Chaplain was dubbed "Dean Pip" because the "maidenly" preacher had objected to the surveyor's term, "pricked line," insisting on "pipped line" instead (80). And on the second voyage, having been relieved of his baptismal duties in the wilderness, Humdrum replaces Firebrand as the central object of fun, promoted "from the Deanery of Pip to the Bishoprick of Beardom," a phallic joke typical of the rough humor of camp life (133). Humdrum's Huguenot sensibilities were also "disturbed" by *Hudibras* being read aloud, and "he gabbled an old almanac three times over to drown one noise with another," but the Hudibrastic spirit continues to reign in the Virginian wilds (130). As with the jokes at the Chaplain's expense, much of the humor derives from the increasing ubiquitousness of the American Bruin, and depends upon the attempts of Steddy's men to try their hand at hunting. Whatever their skills with the transit, the surveyors had difficulty drawing an accurate bead on a moving target, and the job of supplying the camp with meat is assigned to an Indian— appropriately named "Bearskin." But a good many of the laughs result from the anthropomorphic shape of the bear, who leaves a very human footprint and seems at times to be a man in a fur suit. Or a woman, rather, since the chief anecdote is a "romantic adventure" involving a would-be hunter and an "old gentlewoman" with a cub, a story with distinctly Rabelaisian overtones (136).

As a source of fun and feasting, the Bear is a central symbol in a wilderness which presents some dangers but which is also "a theater of plenty," a paradise of game resembling Morton's New English Canaan, being an epic terrain that is a hunting- not a battle-ground, establishing the basis for an emerging Southern tradition (137). Byrd tacitly asserts the difference between Cavalier and Puritan by his use of the Mosaic analogy, wherein much meat for the eaters brings "great content in Israel" (103). In devising a badge for his Order of Maosti, "a wild turkey in gold with the wings expanded," Byrd hits upon the motto *"Vice Coturnicum,"* a reference to the quail that sustained the Jews in the wilderness, and while testifying once again that New England had no patent on the Exodus idea, the motto also serves notice that the Virginian emphasis is not on adversity, that the wilderness itself is "a land of plenty both for man and beast" (122). Byrd's Providence likewise is no punitive force but a kindly patron, averting "sickness of any consequence" and supplying "food convenient for us in the barren wilderness" (143).

As in Exodus, moreover, Byrd's "bounty of Providence" is a trail of manna leading to a valley of superabundance, and though the line is driven through many "dirty places and uneven grounds," it leads at last to "the most beautiful river that I ever saw" (79, 116). At one end of Steddy's passage lies the Dismal Swamp, a "dreadful place," but at the other is the "beautiful river" which he names for the region of Canaan settled by the tribe of Dan after the coast became "too little for them." Like Wolcott's Connecticut, therefore, Byrd's Dan is a paradisiac stream, a central feature in a park-like scene, "gently flowing and murmuring among the rocks, which were thinly scattered here and there to make up the variety of the prospect" (116-17). By such means is Byrd's biblical river given a picturesque frame, an aesthetic in which variety has a distinctly profitable hue, the Dan being "paved with gravel, which was everywhere spangled with small flakes of mother-of-pearl that almost dazzled our eyes" (116). A Jordan writ small, the Dan is "a most charming river" running through "a charming piece of ground," lending promise to a land commanded from "a mount, which we called Mount Pleasant for the beauty of the prospect from thence" (121).

The picaresque dimension of the landscape is preserved by mountains named "Pimple," "Wart," and "Maiden's Breast," but the land which Steddy claims for himself along the Dan he calls the "Land of Eden," a paradisiac plot at the heart of the western wilderness. We may assume that Byrd's enthusiasm for the region is honest enough, but we cannot discount an element of propaganda, reflected in a river "the sand of which is full of shining particles" and having "no falls over which a canoe might not pass" (121-23). The line, that is to say, having been associated at the start with King and Commission, leads finally to the rich lands to which Byrd made personal claim, Duty becoming a matter of Domain, promoting the very self-interestedness condemned in Firebrand and the Carolina Commissioners. Steddy finds it needless to mention his personal hopes for the land he has so enthusiastically described, but it is a silence like that attending Mather's description of Sir William Phips's Canadian campaign or Wolcott's epic bias, a tacit motive which gives additional meaning to his stated hope that "His Majesty's subjects may as soon as possible extend themselves" along the vector that provides a northern boundary to Byrd's Edenic tract. Like the line itself, it promotes an essential disjunctiveness, a cleavage cutting through the heart of his promised land.

371

Byrd's Lands on the Carolina Frontier

William Byrd's Map of his Land of Eden (1733). From William K. Boyd (ed.), *William Byrd's Histories of the Dividing Line* (1929). Courtesy Louis Round Wilson Library, University of North Carolina.

Byrd's Eden. Dependant from the great line he surveyed, Byrd's triangular section of North Carolina lands is located at its farther end, being a slice from the tenderloin that suggests the private advantage to be gained from public service while testifying to the primacy of rivers in settling the regions above the tidewater plantations.

vii. Another Yet the Same

Byrd's subterranean motive and hence his disjunctive dimension is expanded in the public version of his expedition, *The History of the Dividing Line,* which, like the histories of Virginia by Smith and Beverley, serves as chronicle and propaganda, promoting both the general good of Virginia and the author's particular profit. Byrd's enlarged account of driving the line increases the paradisiac element while excising much of the picaresque humor and gossip, a process which intentionally promotes an epical elevation and size. Not that Byrd loses his sense of humor, only that his pitch and proportion change, the comedy attaining a transcendent plane, endowing the fine prospects obtainable in the West with a golden aura, Virginian equivalent to New England's millennial glow. Avoiding the personal quarrels which provide tension and laughter in the *Secret History,* Byrd instead derives humor from the geopolitical necessity which warranted the driving of the line, setting both tone and theme in a brief, prefatory history of Virginia. By "showing how the other British colonies have, one after another, been carved out of" Raleigh's original patent, Byrd establishes a comedy of progressive dismemberment and diminution, a Hobbesian conceit that comes down at last to the specific dispute with North Carolina, which Byrd reduces (in the manner of William Bradford) to the mock-epical "difficulty" of determining ownership of the Nottaway River by "finding out which was truly Weyanoke Creek" (157-69).

This wry tone holds thenceforth, as does the theme of divisiveness, the dividing line enforcing a distinction between the two colonies between which it passes. Byrd's comparisons are uniformly favorable to Virginia, as in his descriptions of Norfolk and Edenton: the one town evinces "the two cardinal virtues that make a place thrive, industry and frugality," while the other is an epitome of backwater sloth, where "a citizen is counted extravagant if he has ambition enough to aspire to a brick chimney" (173, 207). Norfolk is located on the commodious Elizabeth River, "the banks whereof are neither so high as to make the landing of goods troublesome or so low as to be in danger of overflowing," but Edenton is sandwiched between Albemarle Sound and "a dirty slash . . . which in the summer is a foul annoyance and furnishes abundance of that Carolina plague, mosquitoes" (173, 207). Justice in Edenton "is but indifferently lodged, the courthouse having much the air of a common tobacco house," nor is there any public place of worship, the people being "much more private" in their devotions "than in their vices."

Byrd is sarcastic likewise concerning the "excesses of freedom and familiarity" with which the townspeople treat their Governor, less an expression of democracy than penuriousness, for "they are of the opinion their rulers would be apt to grow insolent if they grew rich, and for that reason take care to keep them poorer and more dependent, if possible, than the saints in New England used to do their governors" (208). Byrd also pokes fun at the "Saints" as canting hypocrites who seek to profit from illegal tobacco traffic with North Carolina, but he admires them for their frugality and industriousness, virtues to which he directs Virginia's eyes and to which he would like to bend Carolina's back. Save for a few cornfields, Byrd finds not many "tokens of husbandry or improvement" in North Carolina, where "indolent wretches" live after the easy manner of "lazy Indians," the men doing nothing while the women work, and though the region is so fertile that it "might with a little care and pains be brought to rival that of Egypt, yet the men are here so intolerably lazy they seldom take the trouble to propagate it" (184, 204, 192). By Byrd's accounting, North Carolina is a veritable "Lubberland," the laziness of its inhabitants due both to the "great felicity of the climate and the easiness of raising provisions" and to "the foul and pernicious effects of eating swine's flesh in a hot country" (204, 185).

In sum, Byrd's Carolina is but Beverley's Virginia writ gross, and if laziness there is a matter of climate and diet, it also results from an innate Virginian inclination, "a thorough aversion to labor that makes people file off to North Carolina, where plenty and a warm sun confirm them in their disposition to laziness" (204-5). Like Hubbard's New Hampshire a backwoods drain for all manner of deviants, North Carolina is also a border haven for outlaws, not only "runaway slaves, but debtors and criminals," a happy anarchy which is threatened by the dividing line (186). As with Massachusetts so with Virginia, for whomsoever is taken within her borders "must submit to some sort of order and government, whereas, in North Carolina, everyone does what seems best in his own eyes" (196). Serving as a great regulator, the line is driven along by men whose industry likewise points up the sloth of the borderers, a contrast given particular point by the Dismal Swamp, which becomes in Byrd's *History of the Dividing Line* a symbolic feature of the backwoods landscape. As most of the "slashes" in the vicinity of Edenton "seem all to have a tendency toward the Dismal," so the Swamp itself is a vast "filthy circumference," a "mass of mud and dirt," a miasmic wasteland: "not even a turkey buzzard will venture to fly over it, no more than the Italian vultures will over the filthy Lake Avernus, or the birds in the Holy Land over the Salt Sea where Sodom and Gomorrah formerly stood" (207, 209, 194). "Dismalites," is what Byrd calls the surveyors, "the first of mankind that ventured through . . . this *Terra Incognita*," comparing their labors to Hercules and the Augean stables, a heroic analogy which, with several tall tales told about the great swamp, elevates their ordeal to an American version of epic action (187-88).

While emphasizing the unknown vastness of the Great Dismal, Byrd proposes that this "source of no less than five several rivers" be drained, a project which would make the area more healthy "and at the same time render so great a tract of swamp very profitable, besides the advantage of making a channel to transport by water carriage goods from Albemarle Sound into Nansemond and Elizabeth rivers in Virginia" (202). This was one of Byrd's favorite schemes, to which he devoted a subsequent pamphlet, and like the line itself it is both a progressive and technological project (and Herculean as well), and its espousal by Surveyor General Washington in later days further weds the georgian aesthetic to civil engineering in America. Imposing a linear order on wilderness anarchy, Byrd's Palladian program is a Horatian recipe for orderly progress which stresses the value of utility. So, it might be added, was the Puritan ideal, and where William Wood proposed putting harness on the moose, a century later William Byrd regarded the buffalo as less a wilderness curiosity than a potential source of wool, milk, and—most particularly—power, being capable of "drawing vast and cumbersome weights by their prodigious strength" (301-2). The bear continues to dominate the wilderness landscape, the humorous anecdotes carried over from the *Secret History,* but in the process Bruin is rendered into oil—"used by the Indians as a general defense against every species of vermin"—and dung, which "will make linen white, being tolerable good soap, without any preparation but only drying" (294, 296).

The Horatian view of America presupposes a benign wilderness, easily domesticated, and Wood's accommodating system of circles becomes in Byrd's *History* a glorification of the ways of God to man. There are rattlesnakes in Byrd's neck of the woods, but there is also "rattlesnake root," a remedy for the snake's poison, and most of the ailments to which the settlers are prone may be cured by remedies found growing in the region, including the rattlesnake itself, the oil of which eases "the pain and shortens the fits" of gout (272). So it is that "in what part of the woods soever anything mischievous or troublesome is found, kind Providence is sure to provide a remedy. And 'tis probably one reason why God was pleased to create these and many other vexatious animals, that men should exercise their wits and industry to guard against them" (293). Unlike the Mathers' harsh God, Byrd's is a benign mechanic, an Enlightenment engineer who has disposed all things to man's propositions, and his ameliorative formula expresses Samuel Purchas's faith in "the mutual supply one country receives from another which creates a mutual traffic and intercourse among men," a doctrine of corresponding "wants" which holds out the prospect of a mercantile millennium (291). While in harmony with Wood's wilderness, Byrd's is rather more a pantheistic territory in close proximity to Pope's Windsor Forest, for its reigning spirit—"the gracious guardian of the woods"—is a benevolent Omnipresence, like the author a promoter of good works and water works as well.

viii. Allur'd to Brighter Worlds He Led the Way

Byrd's expansiveness characterizes the view at the farther end of the line, as well, the neoclassical beauties and economic potential of the region "from the river Irvin to Sable Creek" being described as "fertile as the lands were said to be about Babylon," having the added advantage of "being a higher and consequently a much healthier situation than that" (290). Commencing with an assurance that "a colony of one thousand families might, with the help of moderate industry, pass their time very happily there," Byrd indulges in a string of "mights" concerning crops yet to be planted in fertile plains unfurrowed by a plow, the chronic euphoria of Virginian propagandists which insists that "everything will grow plentifully to supply either the wants or wantonness of man" (290). Here again, also, is the Virginian paradox, Byrd calling for "moderate industry" while encouraging "wantonness," an irony enforced by the location of the tract in question, Byrd's Eden like Edenton being on the North Carolina side of the line, its inhabitants liable therefore to the laxity and laziness which he described at the eastern end of his path.

Still, Byrd distinguishes between his own inland garden and the lowland region, with its "malignant fevers" and "one dull and constant succession of warm weather diversified only by rain and sunshine." For inland, "brisk northwest winds purge the air," and the soil benefits from "the advantages of frost and snow, which by their nitrous particles contribute not a little to its fertility," to say nothing of producing delight by "the variety and sweet vicissitude of the seasons" (290). Byrd's "sweet vicissitude" is the Virginian version of New England adversity, a benevolent stress which warps all things to man's "convenience." In harmony with this divinely ordered mechanism of variety is Byrd's pastoral prospect at the farthest end of his line, obtained from "an eminence which overlooked a wide piece of low

378

grounds, covered with reeds and watered by a crystal stream gliding through the middle of it. On the other side of this delightful valley, which was about half a mile wide, rose a hill that terminated the view and in the figure of a semicircle closed in upon the opposite side of the valley. This had a most agreeable effect upon the eye and wanted nothing but cattle grazing in the meadow and sheep and goats feeding on the hill to make it a complete rural landscape" (306). Ignoring the surrounding wilderness, Byrd places his pastoral scene in a neoclassical frame, an absolute imposition of aesthetics on the far western range, dominated by the unifying semicircular form.

Looking to the distant mountains, Byrd finds a somewhat different composition, a peak "so vastly high it seemed to hide its head in the clouds, and the west end of it terminated in a horrible precipice" (266). A veritable Doctor Syntax where scenery is concerned, Byrd names it "the Despairing Lover's Leap," perhaps not the first but positively not the last time this sentimental commonplace will be scrawled across blank spaces that appall. Byrd similarly converts the barrier mountains that blocked further passage of the line into "a natural amphitheater," the Burkean sublime once again curbed by the benign shape of an enclosing curve, a picturesque mixture of orderly wildness. But this "romantic scene" is made possible only by the rainfall which dispersed an ominous haze that had concealed the mountains, a most un-Mosaic "cloud of smoke" threatening to produce a savage presence: "As we went along we were alarmed at the sight of a great fire which showed itself to the northward. This made our small corps march in closer order than we used to do, lest perchance we might be waylaid by Indians" (267, 264).

Keeping a sharp eye out for "any track or any other token of these insidious foresters," Byrd and his men find only "the track of bears, which can't without some skill be distinguished from that of human creatures made with naked feet." Merging with the even more human but no less bestial outlines of the "insidious forester," the bear leaves a mystic trail marking the stepping-off place into absolute wildness. Here again is the disjunctive note, the dark threat marring a pastoral prospect, as through the center of Byrd's Land of Eden there winds a Kishon Creek, tributary to his paradisiac Dan. Yet it is the Dan that dominates both map and book, and Byrd draws a distinction between the character of the Indians who live beyond the mountains and those on the eastern side, a demarcation resembling William Wood's circles of "shires." And like his kinsman, Robert Beverley, he proposes matrimony, not genocide, as a solution to the problem of the races, being a pleasant and loving way of presenting "opportunities of improvement" to the Indian (221).

Civilizing through marriage is a dominant theme in Byrd's *History*, and here too the Dan dominates, being a potential waterway linking the wilderness region to the settlements on Albemarle Sound. Thus the canoe passage in the *Secret History* now opens to admit "even a moderate flat-bottomed boat," along with the observation that in the Virginian Canaan (as in Johnson's Concord) obstructions to navigation can be removed by "the blowing up of a few rocks," access to the Sound being an "unspeakable convenience to the inhabitants" not yet arrived (255). Unspoken also is the tacit relationship between opening navigation on the Dan and the digging of a canal through the Dismal Swamp, an artificial confluency that would in effect provide waterway from Westover to the west. For the Dan "runs away" toward the southwest "with a very flush and plentiful stream, the description whereof must be left to future discoveries, though we are well assured by the Indians that it runs through the mountains" (252-53). This again is the imperial perspective, for in terms of actual current the Dan flows out of the mountains and from the southwest, but in expansionist figures Byrd's royal river is a progenitive thrust into "exceeding rich land, full of large trees with vines married to them, if I may be allowed to speak so poetically" (253). As a poet, Byrd wrote mostly light verse concerning females of his acquaintance, but his prose paean to the Dan is a Virginian equivalent of Roger Wolcott's Connecticut idyll, dominated by the erotic metaphor that characterizes southern landscapes from the start.

As Wolcott's celebration of the Connecticut Valley serves as an inadvertent prelude to the French and Indian Wars, so Byrd's Alpheus penetrates the mountains which block his line. He is certain that "Potomac passes in a large stream through the main ledge and then divides itself into two considerable rivers," and Byrd reports stories by woodsmen that the Roanoke, Shenandoah, and a "wide branch of Mississippi all head in one and the same mountain" (271). Thus Hakluyt's hope of a great divide survives into another century, Byrd's "conjectural geography" no longer involving a vast inland sea, but the mountains themselves, a "natural fortification before the French," and like the forts on the falls the Alleghenies will eventually prove a means of gaining a farther west. Having earlier compared the difficulties of running the line to the labors of Hercules, at the end of his *History of the Dividing Line*, Byrd gives his narrative a final epic turn, anchoring the heroic enterprise in "the shadow of the Cherokee mountains," where he and his men "were obliged to set up our pillars, like Hercules, and return home" (320). The original Herculean pillars marked the limits of the heroic sphere for the ancient world, but in Virginia they are a gateway to yet another epic terrain, Byrd proposing at the end of his narrative that the discovery of "a shorter cut" to the Cherokee Nation would "certainly prove an unspeakable advantage to his colony by facilitating trade" (274-75).

Columbus it was who broke the great circle of the classical world, sailing through the Herculean gate along the path of the sun, laying an imperial and Apollonian line which would become a parallel determining the tangent for adventurers to come. As Byrd's dividing line continued the trajectory of Ralph Lane and John Smith inland, so it was an extension of Hakluyt's mythic vector, pointing no longer toward a great "back sea" but an immense interior valley. For if we extend Byrd's line beyond the mountains, it intersects the Mississippi near that mystical confluence with the Ohio which would provide the heart and arteries for an emerging American empire. In setting up his pillars Byrd set in motion yet another cycle, completing an earlier while projecting a later line, that diagram of empire in America which is a perpetually unfinished plan. His is a landscape given shape by an imperial aesthetic and a colonial necessity, yet it evokes republican themes and genres yet to come, a neoclassical vista of perspective lines drawn to a vanishing point in the west, beyond which a detectable glory arises with the setting sun.

EPILOGUE

Stretch Thy Reign, Fair Peace!
from Shore to Shore

In the opening pages of Byrd's *Secret History,* Steddy strikes a pose on Currituck Inlet looking out to sea, no Cortez in Darien but more a Gulliver in Brobdingnag, casting "a longing eye" toward England before commencing his wilderness errand (55). But where Ann Bradstreet's nostalgia gave added force to her yearning for Heaven, Byrd sought to duplicate the Old World in the New, and on a subsequent trip to his Land of Eden, in 1733, he sat down in camp one night to lay out "the foundation of two large cities" in Virginia, giving the name "Richmond" to the town located on his land near the falls of the James. He thereby evoked not only the place of palaces and parks within view of England's Thames, but gave expression to his dreams of New World wealth, for he predicted that the heads of navigation on Virginia's rivers were "naturally intended for marts where the traffic of the outer inhabitants must center" (388). What Nature provided, Byrd was quick to dispose of to his own profit, and his city on the falls is an urban complement both to his georgic plantation nearer the sea and to the Arcadia on the Edenic river in the west, geopolitical equivalents to the three literary parts of the Virgilian scheme—the idea of *super-urb* being central to the epic design.

Byrd's Richmond is also a worldly counterpart of the Holy City which gave center and purpose to enterprise on Massachusetts Bay, and along with his dividing Line and interior Canaan, it expresses an aesthetic held in common with Wall-girt New England. Virginia was slow to heed the advice of Captain John Smith, but William Byrd could not have chosen a more symbolic location for his colonial emporium, built near the spot where Captain Newport planted his cross, commencing the process of supplantation, and whence Bacon marched forth to complete it. Richmond moreover rose up on the site of Byrd's trading post, thereby compounding the military with a mercantile necessity, a process in all ways dialectical: from Captain Smith's adventures to Captain Johnson's millennial epic and on to Cavalier Byrd's western journey, commercial progress in colonial America takes a linear, martial, and technological shape, imposing an advancing, regulating Line on the map. The differences that obtain between North and South are largely a matter of overt versus covert expression, the Virginian search for paradise being sanctioned, even exploited, by the ruling *aristos,* while the oligarchy in New England imposes a ban on the popular urge, promoting instead a landscape of wilderness adversity. But North and South the pastoral urge prevails, a mythic Alpheus that forever springs up anew in regions to the west, a subterranean current beneath wilderness terrain.

Thomas Morton's vision of New England asserts this underground force in very strong terms, an upwelling of the Cavalier spirit in the midst of the Puritan desert, but though Morton portrayed himself as a loyal agent of the Crown, a champion of orderly exploitation harassed by anarchic Separatists, he was in truth an outlaw. It is in William Byrd that a kind of synthesis is achieved, the pastoral impulse figured in linear terms, and if Morton suggests an American Proteus, Byrd, like Captain Smith, has most definitely a Mercurial outline, his surveying rod and chains a technological version of Caduceus, that badge with complex cosmic and comic associations. The Caduceus is the emblem of a trickster deity who is also the guardian of travelers, a god of commerce and a peacemaker, bearing a symbol that is the sign of the Healer and the scepter of Authority. Behind Roman Mercury, moreover, stands Hermes, associated with borders and highways, and like the Herm, Byrd's dividing Line has a certain phallic dimension. At the start of his *Secret History,* Steddy observes that Mercury is in conjunction with the Moon, and the narrative which follows is among other things a pursuit of Diana's nymphs by Jove's messengers, a genteel geopornography in which the narrator-hero leads a pack of randy dandies into the underwood world, the surveying rod following the *élan* of the Commissioners' loins.

In the public version of events the phallic element takes a more decorous form, a progenitive thrust of civilization into fertile lands: Byrd's *History of the Dividing Line* is informed throughout by his official errand, undertaken in His Majesty's Service. Like John Smith's exploration of Chesapeake Bay, Byrd's Line provides both roadway and boundary, symbol of stability and progress, a long, thin, westward shadow cast by the eastern glow of regnant Authority. But Mercury is also the protecting deity of mercantile enterprise, a god of the marketplace as well as the road, of the city as well as the countryside, associated with good luck and the discovery of treasure. And so is William Byrd, a trickster figure withal, his own interests (like Smith's) lending wings to his epic assignment, and thus the picaresque dimension holds throughout, given further complexity by the characteristic Virginian projection of golden expectations on a virgin land. Don Quixote rides again into the American woods, his lean silhouette accompanied by a fat shade, the Man of Lines and the Man of Loins giving definition to the landscape through which they pass, the Visionary transforming the view as his companion Appetite eats his way through the wilderness of plenty.

In Byrd's mocking version of Exodus it is Aaron the Priest who is the hungry man, and the Cavalier vision of millennium has a correspondingly earth-bound horizon, an equivalent to the dead level celebrated by Handel in his *Messiah,* not proposing a future moment when the valleys will be exalted, the mountains lowered, and the crooked made straight, but a little bit of Piedmont in the here and now. Byrd's river is not a perennial distant Jordan but a present and promising Dan, with the Irvin forming a twin, serpentine shape twining about the Line, a fructive confluency and a Euclidean configuration providing a sign for the great Virginian Surveyor General and National Messiah to follow in years to come. For much as Wolcott's celebration of Puritan Soldier and Saint paves a watery way for the saintly soldier whose advent will glorify a revolution, so even as Byrd wrote his *History of the Dividing Line* the George was born who would replace the King whose commission was the will and way of the westering Cavaliers. Thus the Mercurial Byrd heralds the Apollonian Washington, who was first prefigured by the American Aeneas, Captain John Smith.

"The symmetry of form attainable in pure fiction," observes Herman Melville at the close of *Billy Budd,* "cannot so readily be achieved in a narration essentially having less to do with fable than with fact. Truth uncompromisingly told will always have its ragged edges; hence the conclusion of such a narration is apt to be less finished than an architectural finial." But as *Billy Budd* is a fable shaped to unfinished perfection, so America as a series of ragged facts sometimes assumes the bare linear beauty of fiction, for one lambent moment holding absolute pitch and proportion before collapsing in the onward rush of event. And yet when it does, "like smooth white marble in the polished block not yet removed from the marble-dealer's yard," the glory enhances a terrible bare beauty, a revelation of the clean sharp edges of imperial design.

Ex Libris

If American studies can be said to have a tradition, it is that continuity which begins with Frederick Jackson Turner's *The Frontier in American History* (1920), the powerful trajectory of which was given new impetus (if with somewhat delayed results) by D. H. Lawrence's idiosyncratic *Studies in Classic American Literature* (1923) and William Carlos Williams's derivative *In the American Grain* (1925). The idea that the American frontier was a special place, a zone of not only geopolitical but psychological transformation, is most certainly a complex and therefore elusive proposition, one which, like Melville's (not unrelated) Whale, has attracted its share of monomaniacs and doubters. But the idea of the frontier remains a powerful force, a metamorphic quantity which continues to shape and be shaped by our literature, including the writings of scholars presumed to be objective. It is no coincidence that the subtitle of the book which has, more than any other, directed the course of American studies over the past quarter-century, is *The American West as Symbol and Myth.* For despite its objective tone and apparatus, Henry Nash Smith's *The Virgin Land* (1950) is as much a promulgation as an investigation of the frontier idea.

Avoiding Lawrence's apocalyptic Freudianism and tempering Turner's equivalent piety with the saving grace of ironic realism, Smith still evinces a certain religiosity, a neo-Jeffersonian bias revealed in his willingness to detect transcendent meaning in the artifacts of our capitalist culture, whether geopolitical tracts or dime novels. Stressing the inherent—even archetypal—antagonism between the "myth" of the "Garden" and its often barren reality, Smith at the same time mounts untested assumptions about the paradigmatic nature of "popular" culture, a methodology that is mythic to the core. A much different tack has been taken by Charles L. Sanford in *The Quest for Paradise:*

Europe and the American Moral Imagination (1961), which approaches the Edenic idea in America from the European tradition, giving much more attention than Smith to its primacy among intellectuals—whether philosophers, poets, or novelists—and much less to its prevalence as a popular myth. Sanford's is more properly the *history* of an idea, not its promulgation, a study complementary to R. W. B. Lewis's *The American Adam* (1955), stressing (in Sanford's words) "story" instead of "hero," but taking the same high road out of Eden. Edwin Fussell's *Frontier: American Literature and the American West* (1965) follows the same route, providing an exhaustive demonstration of the extent to which metaphoric frontiers permeate our national letters.

A somewhat different direction has been taken by Roderick Nash in *Wilderness and the American Mind* (1967; rev. ed., 1973), which, though it traces the religiosity (and politics) of primitivism from the Puritans' wilderness condition down to Woodstock Nation, is basically a study of the American parks movement. With Sanford, moreover, Nash casts a wide and inclusive net in terms of chronology and materials, avoiding Smith's paradigmatic method. The subjective, selective, "mythic" continuity is best represented by Leo Marx's *The Machine in the Garden: Technology and the Pastoral Ideal in America* (1964), which, after a preliminary survey of pastoral attitudes in Virgil, Shakespeare, and colonial propaganda for settlement in Virginia, extends Smith's paradigmatic reach to almost poetic lengths in an examination of the imperfect dialectic generated by the conflict between Jeffersonian agrarianism and Hamiltonian industrialism. Where Smith is concerned chiefly with the West, Marx concentrates on what he calls the "Middle Landscape," and yet a third area on the mythic map, the "City," has been filled in by Allan Trachtenberg, whose *Brooklyn Bridge: Fact and Symbol* (1965) presents an alternative fact to Marx's railroad as a transcendent symbol of technology. But the conjunction in Trachtenberg's subtitle expresses a bothersome distinction, revealing the dichotomy inherent to the mythic approach, and he has subsequently expressed serious reservations about what Marx has defended as an "unscientific method."

Still, the ongoing work in American studies has been if anything more rather than less arbitrary, pleading from ever more special cases. Thus Roy Harvey Pearce's scholarly *The Savages of America* (1953; rev. ed. entitled *Savagism and Civilization*, 1965) was followed by

Leslie A. Fiedler's interpretive *The Return of the Vanishing American* (1968), a study in the Lawrentian vein which gave an erotic cast to the frontier, making way for Richard Slotkin's *Regeneration through Violence* (1973), most appropriately published on the fiftieth anniversary of Lawrence's *Studies*. Slotkin's book is both Dionysian in sympathies and Procrustean in execution, employing an indiscriminate, even free-wheeling use of Jungian and Freudian terms that results in a bias against the Puritans reminiscent of H. L. Mencken's slab-minded animadversions. More balanced (though less comprehensive) is Annette Kolodny's *The Lay of the Land* (1975), which renders a decidedly feminist view of the wildwood congress discerned in the American landscape by both herself and Slotkin.

Sharing a psycho-linguistic approach, the studies by Slotkin and Kolodny are highly politicized as well, along with Fiedler's *Return* obeying the call of the wild 1960's. The primitivistic, populist undercurrent in Smith's *Virgin Land* and Marx's *Garden* at last surfaces, and though Slotkin provides a lengthy introductory definition of "myth," by drawing heavily on Jung's theory of archetypes he in effect has recourse to merely another system of assumptions, lending the dubious blessing of jargon to the method initiated by Henry Nash Smith. Slotkin's book appeared as I was beginning work on my own, Kolodny's after my final revision, and if her findings concerning a dominant metaphor in colonial literature provide a gratifying parallel, Slotkin's reductive approach increased my determination to demonstrate the pluralistic nature of the American experience from its beginnings. I had already, in 1972, published an essay which serves as a prolegomenon to this present study, "Some Green Thoughts on a Green Theme" (in *Literature in Revolution*, ed. by George Abbott White and Charles Newman), in an attempt to compensate for Leo Marx's intentional avoidance of pastoralism's political implications. In that essay, as here, "myth" is used in the conventional sense of actions resonant with belief, employing a retroactive perspective which endows metaphors with the sanctity of historical continuity, isolating parabolic patterns which reduplicate Ovid's not Joseph Campbell's metamorphoses.

In the manner of a novelist I have tried to accommodate complexity, to demonstrate, even diagram, the counterplay of forces, human and natural, which determined the course of empire that is the American epic. Accepting the necessity of subjectivity inherent in interpretation,

I have followed Aristotle, not pursued some *anima* into the New World wilderness, and while presuming to detect revelatory metaphors, I have attempted to demonstrate their political, not their psychological origins. Finally, so as to give due stress to chance and circumstance, I have emphasized the literariness of literal events, the coincidental *figura* that often lends significance to human endeavor. Since the chief artifacts of record are narratives of personal encounter and formal histories, those genres dominate the primary materials used, and I should like in this regard to state my indebtedness to David Levin's *History as Romantic Art* (1959) which, though concerned with a later period, is not only a singular example of how the language of literary criticism may be applied to nonfiction, but is a foremost demonstration of the extent to which historical perspectives are shaped by individual and generational conditions.

Because the present study, unlike those listed above, is limited entirely to the colonial period and therefore is necessarily devoted to the literature engendered by the New England experience, I conclude this bibliographical note by relating my own point of view concerning the Puritan accomplishment to the present course of scholarship in that tangled, even thorny field. Much as American studies is dominated by the figure of Henry Nash Smith, Puritan scholarship remains in the shadow of Perry Miller, continuing to concentrate on what he defined as the dual contribution to our institutions and literature of the wilderness errand, one aspect being political, the other ideational in character. Thus the theological concept of Covenant combined with the joint-stock arrangement of primitive capitalism to provide the democratic basis of our Constitution, while the idea of election, with its potential for a mystical emphasis on self, contributed to the rampant individualism of the American character.

Yet Miller was also sensitive to the tragic implications of the Puritan experiment, the failure of which is inadvertently symbolized by the unfinished state of his own magnum opus, *The New England Mind.* Beginning with the original errand in *The Seventeenth Century* (1939), Miller never got past the transformation *From Colony to Province* (1953). Various manifestations of decline were further charted by Edmund Morgan, in *The Puritan Family* (1944; rev. ed., 1966) and *The Puritan Dilemma* (1958), a biography of John Winthrop. Since the Winthrops were in a sense *the* founding family, their dynastic degeneration as traced by Richard S. Dunn in *Puritans and Yankees* (1962) is synoptic, and Darrett B. Rutman has provided a tragic frame for the emergence of *Winthrop's Boston* (1965) from his utopian City on a Hill. Kenneth Murdock's *Literature & Theology in Colonial New England* (1949) emphasizes the limitations of Puritan literature, and the sense of failure that permeates their chronicles is the subject of Peter Gay's *Loss of Mastery* (1966).

During the past decade, however, scholars have tended to stress the positive (in the sense of prevailing) aspects of the change *From Puritan to Yankee* (1967), as in Richard L. Bushman's study of Connecticut's metamorphosis. Robert Middlekauff's *The Mathers* (1971) proposes that the second generation of Puritans defined their errand more accurately than did the first, and Robert Vaughn's *New England Frontier* (1965) provides a useful antidote to Slotkin's genocidal views regarding the relationship between Puritans and Indians. Still, Vaughn stops short of King Philip's War, which provides Slotkin his strongest case, and Peter N. Carroll's *The Puritans and the Wilderness* (1969) demonstrates the rhetorical changes that lent an increasingly hostile shape to the landscape, part of the Mathers' campaign to affect reformation. But Carroll's is not a self-righteous stance, and one effect of his study is to convey the complexity and changing dimensions of the Puritan presence in America, providing a literary counterpart to the sociological approach of Kai T. Erikson's *Wayward Puritans* (1966) and John Demos's *A Little Commonwealth* (1970).

The most thorough study of pluralism in early American culture is Michael Kammen's *People of Paradox* (1972), a discourse whose direction my own narrative follows, in that Kammen conveys a strong sense of continuity, the forward reach (for better or worse) of our colonial civilization. I take further strength from his assertion that "the 'American studies' movement . . . has belletristic origins, has largely located its manifestations in the literary culture, and has been almost exclusively preoccupied with nineteenth- and twentieth-century situations, to the neglect of colonial origins." For those are precisely the emphases which this present volume is in part intended to correct, while staying within the bounds of aestheticism—as opposed to historicism. Thus Kammen's objective stance compels a discontinuous approach to our multifaceted culture, a series of essays which isolate and identify phenomenal clusters illustrating his various categories, "legitimacy," "biformity," etc., a method resembling Smith's use of paradigms but with a statistical, not "belletristic" emphasis. My aim, by contrast, has been to approximate the confluent flow of signal events, including books, while demonstrating disjunctiveness throughout.

Recent studies in Puritan literature share in common a stress on the positive or prevailing drift of early American letters, the legacy derived from the liabilities of Puritanism in the New World. One major development has been the isolation and definition of distinctive genres, whether Slotkin's concern with captivity narratives, Daniel B. Shea, Jr.'s *Spiritual Autobiography in Early America* (1968), or Sacvan Bercovitch's monograph on the jeremiad, *Horologicals to Chronometricals* (1970). Bercovitch is also chief among a number of younger scholars who have been developing the connection between Puritan hermeneutics and the symbolic modes of American romantic writers, articles gathered in his *Typology and Early American Literature* (1972) and contributing to his *The Puritan Origins of the American Self* (1975). This last is the most important study to date of the "differences" obtaining on the American strand, a detailed explication of the complex union between literature and locale which makes straight Perry Miller's wandering way through the wilderness from Winthrop's Boston to Emerson's Concord. Moreover, by delineating the Puritan origins of what would become Manifest Destiny, Bercovitch fills in a large blank in Ernest Tuveson's *Redeemer Nation: The Idea of America's Millennial Role* (1968). Had his study been available I would have had a much easier task coming to terms with the apocalyptic theme in New England. Still, our conclusions are often similar, though several definitive differences remain, mostly concerning Mather's *Magnalia* and the Puritans' landscape art.

The most ambitious attempt in recent years to render a full account of "A New Culture in a New World" is Larzer Ziff's *Puritanism in America* (1973). Influenced by the work of Raymond Williams, Ziff's concept of culture is largely a matter of economic and political currents, and though he provides a long needed correction of Perry Miller's theological emphasis, where detailed analysis of Puritan literature is concerned Ziff leaves wide margins, which I have gladly appropriated to myself. He is particularly scant in his treatment of Puritan histories and personal narratives, and does not concern himself with the definitive role of typology in the transformation of the original errand. But despite their differences in these regards, Ziff shares with Bercovitch (and Miller) a preoccupation with the intellectual history of early New England, and since my own inclination is toward people animated by ideas rather than the reverse, I prefer to align myself with another tradition associated with Cambridge, Mass., one which has been neglected since Samuel Eliot Morison went to sea.

Written in the great tradition of Francis Parkman, and with the drama (while countering the bias) of Charles Francis Adams, Jr.'s *Three Episodes of Massachusetts History* (1892), Morison's *The Builders of the Bay Colony* (1930) and his three-volume history of Harvard (1935, 1936) lend a literary shape to often unlikely materials. The historian's vigorous hand found a more suitable subject, surely, in his *Admiral of the Ocean Sea* (1942) and, more recently, *The European Discovery of America: The Northern Voyages* (1971) and *The Southern Voyages* (1974), though Morison's strenuous, even imperial empiricism precluded a favorable opinion of Edmundo O'Gorman's *The Invention of America* (1961). If I am indebted to Morison for innumerable clarifications, O'Gorman drove home to me with the force of revelation the inherent fiction (and folly) to be found in the earliest literature of American encounter. Bernard DeVoto's *The Course of Empire* (1952), Howard Mumford Jones's *O Strange New World* (1964), and Louis B. Wright's *The Dream of Prosperity in Colonial America* (1965) likewise contain in varied compass demonstrations of how expectation may warp reports of actions undertaken in the service of mistaken ideas, a questing continuity from Columbus to Captain John Smith that supplies Evelyn Page her *American Genesis* (1973). Graphic delineations of illusion may be found in W. P. Cumming *et al.*, *The Discovery of North America* and in Hugh Honour's *The New Golden Land* (1976), complementary exhibits of American icons created by European hands.

Honour's book also drives home another of our historical ironies, for while New World images engendered by the Old World tend to stress the Southern and therefore the most exotic aspects of America, in the English colonies themselves few works of art were produced outside the Northern region, in literature no less than in the graphic arts. Louis B. Wright's *The Cultural Life of the American Colonies* (1957) tends to blur the issue by avoiding the regional distinctions established in his *The Atlantic Frontier: Colonial American Civilization* (1951), but until recently he has had the Southern range pretty much to himself, ascendancy in a waste wilderness not unlike that of William Byrd. As in his *The First Gentleman of Virginia* (1940), moreover, Wright has had to define "intellectual qualities" in a very broad sense, and to write rather large in other respects besides, so as to derive a literature from some pamphlets, several books, and a fugitive diary or two. Howard Mumford Jones, in *The Literature of Virginia in the Seventeenth Century* (1968) produced a slim volume that is perfectly in keeping with his subject, but which without an informative discussion of Captain John Smith would have been thinner by far. The most considerable treatment of Southern colonial literature to date, J. A. Leo Lemay's *Men of Letters in Colonial Maryland* (1971), achieves its bulk by abandoning Virginia for her sister colony and by extending its inquiry up to the Revolutionary period, which lies beyond the area covered here. Still, in his opening chapters on the relationship between propaganda for settlement and the Maryland Muse (whether Alsop or Cook), Lemay provides a treatment of the comic tradition in the colonial South that has helped me greatly in coming to terms with the other side of the pastoral mode in Virginia.

The distinction between satire and pastoral in the South is equivalent to the difference in the North between epic and sermonic modes, the reality contained in the one often outstripping the ideals borrowed from the other, literature North and South testifying that in terms of primary creation it is finally the transformed landscape which is the premier artifact, providing a text often contradictory to the published word and a more definitive shape than any carved on stone. That is why George R. Stewart's collection of imprints in *American Place-names* (1970) is as important as R. W. G. Vail's indispensable *The Voice of the Old Frontier* (1949), why Ellen Churchill Semple's *American History and its Geographical Conditions* (1903) and Ralph H. Brown's *Historical Geography of the United States* (1948) should be read by students of American culture more often than they are. With Smith's *Virgin Land,* they are indebted to Turner's thesis, and provide flow charts for the process Ziff calls "a culture of expansion," introducing to the symbolic landscape those topographical barriers and avenues which play such an important if silent role in my own account, monumental dimensions of adversity and accommodation that were instrumental in determining America's imperial design.

Bibliography of Primary Sources

What follows is a short-title list of works limited to those from which quotations are taken in the body of this book, and to which reference is occasionally made by means of the abbreviations below. It is not intended as anything more than a guide for readers wishing to place a quotation in context, but I have attempted to cite the most accurate editions available and the most available editions accurately. In cases of multiple authorship the book has been for the sake of convenience entered in full under the editor's name. Entries marked with an asterisk will be included in a companion volume to this study.

CFP: Young, ed., *Chronicles of the First Planters.*
CPF: Young, ed., *Chronicles of the Pilgrim Fathers.*
HPP: Bradford, *History of Plymouth Plantation.*
RM: Shurtleff, ed., *Records of Massachusetts.*
T&W: Smith, *Travels and Works.*
WJ: *Winthrop's Journal.*
WP: Ford and Forbes, eds., *Winthrop Papers.*

Alsop, George. *A Character of . . . Maryland* (1666). Ed. Newton D. Mereness. Cleveland: 1902.

Alvord, Clarence W., and Lee Bidgood. *The First Explorations of the Trans-Allegheny Region.* Cleveland: 1912.

Anon. *The Summons to Newe England.* In *An American Garland.* Ed. C. H. Firth. Oxford: 1915.

Anon. *New Englands First Fruits* (1643). In S. E. Morison, *The Founding of Harvard.* Cambridge, Mass.: 1935.

*[Archer, Gabriel]. "A Relatyon of the Discovery of our River." In Barbour, *Jamestown Voyages.*

Barbour, Philip L., ed. *The Jamestown Voyages.* 2 vols. Hakluyt Society, 2nd ser., vols. 136, 137. Cambridge, Eng.: 1969.

*Barlowe, Arthur. "Discourse of the First Voyage." In Quinn, *Roanoke Voyages.*

Beverley, Robert. *The History . . . of Virginia* (1705). Ed. Louis B. Wright. Chapel Hill: 1947.

Bland, Edward. *The Discovery of New Brittaine* (1651). In Alvord, *First Explorations.*

Bradford, William. *Of Plimoth Plantation.* Printed as *History of Plymouth Plantation.* Ed. W. C. Ford. 2 vols. Boston: 1912.

———. "Some Observations of God's Merciful Dealing." In *Proc. Mass. Hist. Soc.,* 1st ser., vol. 11 (1871).

Bradstreet, Anne. *Works.* Ed. Jeannine Hensley. Cambridge, Mass.: 1967.

Burrage, Henry S., ed. *Early English and French Voyages.* New York: 1906.

Byrd, William. *The Prose Works.* Ed. Louis B. Wright. Cambridge, Mass.: 1966.

*Cartier, Jacques. "The First Relation," "A Shorte and Briefe Narration," and "The Third Voyage." In Burrage, *English and French Voyages.*

Church, [Benjamin and] Thomas. *Entertaining Passages* (1716). Printed as *The History of King Philip's War.* Ed. S. G. Drake. Exeter, N.H.: 1829.

Cotton, John. *Gods Promise* (1630). In *Old South Leaflets,* vol. 3, no. 53. Boston: n.d.

Cushman, Robert. *A Sermon, Describing . . . Self-Love* (1621). Stockbridge, Mass.: 1822.

Danforth, Samuel. *Errand into the Wilderness* (1670). In Plumstead, *Wall and Garden.*

Denham, Sir John. *Expans'd Heiroglyphicks: A Critical Edition of . . . Cooper's Hill.* By Brendan O Hehir. Berkeley: 1969.

Denton, Daniel. *A Brief Description* (1670). Ed. Felix Neumann. Cleveland: 1902.

Drayton, Michael. "To the Virginian Voyage" (1606). In Wright, *The Elizabethans' America.*

Fontaine, John. "Journal of Travels." In *Memoirs of a Huguenot Family.* Ed. Ann Maury. New York: 1852.

Force, Peter, comp. *Tracts and Other Papers.* Vols. 1 and 2. Washington, D.C.: 1836-38.

Ford, Worthington C., and Allyn B. Forbes, eds. *The Winthrop Papers*. 5 vols. Boston: 1925-47.

Gardener, Lion. *Relation*. Ed. W. N. Chattin Charlton. Hartford: 1901.

Gilbert, Sir Humphrey. *A Discourse of a . . . Passage to Cataia* (1576). In Quinn, *Voyages and Enterprises*.

Gookin, Daniel, *Historical Collections of the Indians in New England* In *Coll. Mass. Hist. Soc.*, 1st ser., vol. 1 (1792).

Gorges, Sir Ferdinando. *A Brief Narration* (1658). In *Coll. Mass. Hist. Soc.*, 3rd ser., vol. 6 (1837).

Hakluyt, Richard (the Younger). "A Discourse of Western Planting." In Taylor, *Original Writings*.

———. *Divers Voyages* (1582). Ed. John Winter Jones. Hakluyt Society. London: 1850.

———. "Epistle Dedicatory to . . . Ralegh," from *De Orbe Novo Petri Martyris* (1587). In Taylor, *Original Writings*.

———. "Epistle Dedicatory To . . . Ralegh," from *A Notable Historie Containing Foure Voyages . . . unto Florida* (1587). In Taylor, *Original Writings*.

———, et al. "Instructions given by way of advice." In Barbour, *Jamestown Voyages*.

*Hariot, Thomas. *A Briefe and True Report* (1588). In Quinn, *Roanoke Voyages*.

Higginson, Francis. *New-Englands Plantation* (1630). In Young, *CPF*.

Hooker, Thomas. *The Application of Redemption . . . Ninth and Tenth Books*. London: 1657.

Hubbard, William. *A General History*. Ed. William T. Harris. Boston, 1848. With *The Recently Recovered Pages of Hubbard's History*. Ed. Charles Deane. Boston: 1878.

———. *The Present State of New-England* (1677). Reprinted as *The History of the Indian Wars*. Ed. S. G. Drake. 2 vols. Roxbury, Mass.: 1865.

[Johnson, Edward]. *Good News from New-England* (1648). In *Coll. Mass. Hist. Soc.*, 4th ser., vol. 1 (1852).

[———]. *A History of New England* (1654). Reprinted as *Johnson's Wonder-Working Providence*. Ed. J. Franklin Jameson. New York: 1910.

[Johnson, Robert]. *Nova Britannia* (1609). In Force, *Tracts*.

Knight, Sarah Kemble. *The Journal*. Ed. Malcolm Freiberg. Boston: 1972.

*Lane, Ralph. "Discourse on the First Colony." In Quinn, *Roanoke Voyages*.

Lederer, John. *The Discoveries* (1672). In Alvord, *First Explorations*.

Mason, John. *A Brief History* (Thomas Prince's edition, 1736), In *Coll. Mass. Hist. Soc.*, 2nd ser., vol. 8 (1819).

Mather, Cotton. *Diary*. Ed. W. C. Ford. 2 vols. *Coll. Mass. Hist. Soc.*, 7th ser., vols. 7-8. Boston: 1911, 1912.

———. *Magnalia Christi Americana* (1702). Ed. Thomas Robbins. 2 vols. Hartford: 1852.

———. "Reports of Divine Kindness." In Williams, *Redeemed Captive*.

———. *The Short History*. Boston: 1694.

———. *The Way to Prosperity* (1690). In Plumstead, *Wall and Garden*.

Mather, Increase. *A Brief History of the War* (1676). Reprinted as *The History of King Philip's War*. Ed. S. G. Drake. Boston: 1862. (This text does not include the *Serious Exhortation* issued with the original edition.)

———. *An Essay for the Recordings of Illustrious Providences* (1684). Reprinted as *Remarkable Providences*. Ed. George Offor. London: 1890.

———. *A Relation of the Troubles* (1677). Reprinted as *Early History of New England*. Ed. S. G. Drake. Boston: 1864.

Morgan, Joseph. *The History of . . . Basaruah* (1715). Ed. Richard Schlatter. Cambridge, Mass.: 1946. (Contains three letters from Morgan to Cotton Mather).

Morton, Thomas. *New English Canaan* (1637). Ed. C. F. Adams, Jr. Boston: 1883.

*"Mourt, George" [George Morton], ed. *A Relation or Journall* (1622). In Young, *CPF*. (Commonly called *Mourt's Relation*.)

Peckham, Sir George. *A True Report of . . . Discoveries . . . by Sir Humfrey Gilbert* (1583). In Quinn, *Voyages and Enterprises*.

Percy, George. "Observations . . . out of a Discourse." In Barbour, *Jamestown Voyages*.

Plumstead, A. W., ed. *The Wall and the Garden*. Minneapolis: 1968.

Prince, Thomas. *The People of New England* (1730). In Plumstead, *Wall and Garden*.

————, ed. Williams, *The Redeemed Captive*. Boston, Mass.: 1758. Reprinted, Springfield, Mass.: 1908. (Contains a lengthy afterword by Prince.)

Purchas, Samuel. *Hakluytus Posthumus, or Purchas His Pilgrimes* (1625). 20 vols. Hakluyt Society, Extra Series. Glasgow: 1905-7.

Quinn, David Beers, ed. *The Roanoke Voyages*. 2 vols. Hakluyt Society, 2nd ser., vols. 104, 105. London: 1952.

————, ed. *The Voyages and Colonising Enterprises of Sir Humphrey Gilbert*. Hakluyt Society, 2nd ser., vols. 83, 84. London: 1940.

Rolfe, John. "Letter to Sir Thomas Dale," from Ralph Hamor's *A True Discourse of . . . Virginia* (1615). In Wright, *Elizabethans' America*.

*Rosier, James. *A Brief and True Relation* (1605). In Burrage, *Early Voyages*.

Rowlandson, Mary. *The Sovereignty and Goodness of God* (1682). Reprinted as "The Captivity of Mrs. Mary Rowlandson," in *Narratives of the Indian Wars*. Ed. Charles H. Lincoln. New York: 1913. (This text does not include Joseph Rowlandson's *The Possibility of Gods forsaking a People* issued with the original edition.)

[Scottow, Joshua]. *A Narrative of the Planting of . . . Massachusets* (1694). In *Coll. Mass. Hist. Soc.*, 4th ser., vol. 4 (1858).

Sewall, Samuel. *The Diary*. Ed. M. Halsey Thomas. New York: 1973.

————. *Phaenomena quaedam Apocalyptica*. 2nd ed. Boston: 1727.

————. *Upon the Drying Up . . . the River Merrymak* (1720). In Sewall, *Diary*.

————. *Wednesday, January 1, 1701*. In Sewall, *Diary*.

Shepard, Thomas. *God's Plot . . . Being the Autobiography and Journal*. Ed. Michael McGiffert. Amherst: 1972.

Shurtleff, Nathaniel P., ed. *Records of the . . . Company of the Massachusetts Bay*. 5 vols. Boston: 1853-54.

————. *Advertisements for . . . Unexperienced Planters* (1631). In Smith, *T&W*.

Smith, Captain John. *Advertisements for . . . Unexperienced Planters* (1631). In Smith, *T&W*.

————. *A Description of New England* (1616). In Smith, *T&W*.

————. *The Generall Historie* (1624). In Smith, *T&W*.

*————. *A Map of Virginia* (1612). In Barbour, *Jamestown Voyages*.

————. *New Englands Trials* (1622). In Smith, *T&W*.

————. *The Travels and Works*. Eds. Edward Arber and A. G. Bradley. 2 vols. Edinburgh: 1910.

*————. *A True Relation* (1608). In Barbour, *Jamestown Voyages*.

————. *The True Travels* (1630). In Smith, *T&W*.

Strachey, William. *The Historie of Travell into Virginia* (1612). Eds. Louis B. Wright and Virginia Freund. Hakluyt Society, 2nd ser., vol. 103. London: 1953.

Symmes, Thomas. *Lovewell Lamented . . . A Sermon*. Boston: 1725.

Taylor, Edward. *The Poems*. Ed. Donald E. Stanford. New Haven: 1960.

Taylor, E. G. R., ed. *The Original Writings . . . of the . . . Hakluyts*. 2 vols. Hakluyt Society, 2nd ser., vols. 76, 77.

Tompson, Benjamin. . . . *His Poems*. Ed. Howard Judson Hall. Boston: 1924.

————. "To Lord Bellamont." In *The First Century of New England Verse*. Ed. Harold S. Jantz. New York: 1962.

Underhill, John. *Newes from America* (1638). In *Coll. Mass. Hist. Soc.*, 3rd ser., vol. 6 (1837).

Verrazzano, Giovanni da. "The Relation . . . of the land by him discovered." In Hakluyt, *Divers Voyages.*

White, John. "Narrative of the 1590 Voyage." In Quinn, *Roanoke Voyages.*

[White, John, of Dorchester]. *The Planters Plea* (1630). In Force, *Tracts.*

Wigglesworth, Michael. *The Day of Doom* (1662). Ed. William Henry Burr. New York: 1867.

Williams, John. *The Redeemed Captive* (1707). Thomas Prince edition (1758). Springfield, Mass.: 1908.

Williams, Roger. *The Complete Writings.* 7 vols. New York: 1963.

Winslow, Edward. *Good Newes from New-England* (1624). In Young, *CPF.*

Winthrop, John. "A Modell of Christian Charity." In Ford, *Winthrop Papers.*

———. *Journal.* Ed. James Kendall Hosmer. 2 vols. New York: 1908.

Wolcott, Roger. "Journal at . . . Louisbourg." In *Coll. Conn. Hist. Soc.,* vol. 1 (1860).

———. *Poetical Meditations* (1725). Reprinted as *The Poems.* Ed. James F. Hunnewell. Boston: 1898. (This text does not include John Bulkley's "Preface.")

Wood, William. *New Englands Prospect* (1634). Ed. E. M. Boynton. Boston: 1898.

Wright, Louis B., ed. *The Elizabethans' America.* Cambridge, Mass.: 1966.

Young, Alexander, ed. *Chronicles of the First Planters . . . of Massachusetts.* Boston: 1846.

———, ed. *Chronicles of the Pilgrim Fathers.* Boston: 1841.

———. *The Humble Request* (1630). In Young, *CP.*

INDEX

A Mighty Maze,
But Not Without a Plan

Byrd, William, of Westover *(Cont.)*
Eden, 371, 372-73, 381; *Progress to the
Mines,* 366; *Secret History, 365-71,*
374, 377, 380, 385, 386

Caesar, Augustus, 15, 25
Caesar, Julius, 20, 60
Cain, 248, and Abel, 273
Cambridge (Mass.), 195, 314
Cambridge Platform, 153, 222, 231, 250,
319
Camoens, Luis de, *Lusiad,* 15
Canaan, 15, 101; as American metaphor,
42-43; New England as, 123, 146, 150,
167, 171-74, 385; Connecticut as, 196,
212-13, 245, 249, 251, 324, 325, 336,
338, as not, 197-98; Hudson Valley as,
128, 250-51, 252, 325; New Hampshire
as not, 323; Virginia as, 43, 121, 122,
149, 344, 345, 380, 385; Kentucky as,
252
———— and Puritan literature, 101, 121-
22, 145-46, 385; history, 105, 197-98,
206, 212-13, 224, 225, 229, 236, 238,
245, 249, 250-51, 268; jeremiad, 127,
236, 322-23; poetry, 314, 315, 317, 336;
propaganda, 122-23, 150
———— and Virginian literature, 43, 121,
122, 244-45, 371, 380, 385
(see also Exodus; Jordan R.; Promised
Land)
Canada: Cartier explores, 13-14, 17-21;
Champlain explores, 84, 89; La Salle
and, 21-22; as Puritan Babylon, 282,
293, 295; as Puritan Carthage, 252,
267, 282; as Puritan Canaan, 268, 338-
39; Sir Wm. Phips's invasion of, 267-
69, 274, 296
Canada (town), *see* Quebec
Cape Cod, 91-95, 105-6, 115, 135, 157, 223
Cap Rouge River, 20
Captain's narrative: as genre, 13, 14, 15,
17, 38-39, 51, 55, 63-66, 69, 80, 106-7,
300; cf. captivity narrative, 70,
208, 273, 281; and Puritan history,
281; and Virginian history, 367
Captivity narrative: as genre, 80, 209,
281-84, 316-17; cf. captain's narrative,
70, 208, 273, 281; and jeremiad, 282;
and American metamorphoses, 70,
283-84, 291; and Israel in bondage,
209, 285, 290
Carthage, 34, 252, 267, 282, 338
Cartier, Jacques: name as prophecy, 13;

explores St. Lawrence, 13-14, 18-21;
voyage as prophecy, 14, 20; and American epic, 13-14, 16-17, 21; and Indians, 13-14, 18-20; and Northwest
Passage, 13, 20; and imperial aesthetic, 17; and Verrazzano, 17-18; influences Hakluyt, 29-34 (map, 32-33);
as American hero, 13, 16-17, 21, cf.
Columbus, 13, 19-20, cf. R. Lane, 37-
38, 39, 40, cf. Newport, 51, cf. Rosier,
45, cf. Smith, 55, 66, 69, 70, 72, 75, cf.
Standish, 95, 110, cf. Taylor, 314, cf.
Winthrop, 138; "Brief Narration," 18-
20, 34, as epic, 13, 14, 16-17; "First Re-
lation," 18; "Third Voyage," 20-21
Castaway narrative, see *Robinsonade*
Cervantes, Saavedra Miguel de, *Don
Quixote,* 25 *(see also* Don Quixote)
Champlain, Samuel de, 21, 110; cf.
Capt. J. Smith, 84, 89; map of New
France, 183
Charles I, 93, 316, 330, 334, 349
Charles II, 219, 324, 349-50, 352; in Wol-
cott's "Brief Account," 330-35, 336
Charles River: J. Smith describes, 88-89,
and maps, 93, 119; Pilgrims and, 119;
Winthrop's symbolic journey on, 134-
35, 161, 181, 216; as border, 134, 146,
155, 191, 214, 227, 318; and expansion,
140, 190, 192, 195; and Puritan poetry,
315, 318
Charter, The Royal (Massachusetts' Old
Charter), 134, 142, 143, 214, 230, 235,
236, 269, 325, 346 *(see also* Puritan errand; Winthrop's Patent)
Chaucer, Geoffrey, *Canterbury Tales,*
127, 302
Chaunis Temoatan, 39, 41
Cheese Rock, 161, 162, 177
Chesapeake Bay, 63, 357, 365; Ralph
Lane concerning, 39, 41; J. Smith explores rivers of, 67, 81, 84-85, 386; and
maps, 81-83, 94; and Northwest Passage, 81-85; and shape of Va. settlement, 158, 179; as Va. Mediterranean,
81; as river, 84; as symbolic center, 81-
84, 343, 344, 350, 352-53, 355, 362
Chickahominy River: and Northwest
Passage, 68-69; J. Smith's exploration
of, 68-70, 73, 78, 273; as symbolic
stream, 68-69, 78; and American literature, 273
Chowan River, 39-41, 44, 56, 63, 65 *(see
also* Roanoke R.)
Christ: militant, as heroic archetype, 17,

Index

Index

Smollett, Tobias, 303, 367
Solomon (Ecclesiastes), 66, 239, 255
Solomon, King, 99
Spenser, Edmund, 25, 29, 42, 45, 54; *Colin Clout*, 25; *Faerie Queene*, 25-26, 27, 37, 53-54, 61, 80, 289, 290
Spiritual autobiography, as Puritan genre, 223, 281, 293
Spotswood, Gov. Alexander, 363-64, 369
Squanto, 94, 107, 117
Standish, Captain Miles: symbolic name, 95; symbolic exploration of Cape Cod, 95, 108-15, 134; encounters with Indians, 108, 116; as American hero, 95, 108-9; and American epic, 95, 118-19, 121; and Mosaic metaphor, 110, 118; a comic figure, 95, 108, 109, 111; cf. J. Smith, 95, 108; cf. B. Church, 118, 120, 123; attacks Merry Mount, 166-67; satirized by T. Morton, 108, 176
Stewart, George, 6, 11-12
Stockwell, Quentin (story of), 283, 292, 293
Strachey, William, *Historie of Travell*, 47
Styx River, 241
Summons to Newe England, 150
Supplantation: rivers and, 13, 52-53, 54, 189-90, 101, 117, 154, 213, 226, 274, 385; in Virginia, 52-53, 54, 79-80, 385; in New England, 117, 154; as drama, 94, 189-90, 213, 226, 274; as epic, 198; as comedy, 226 (*see also* Jacob; Lord's Waste)
Susquehanna River, 338
Swift, Jonathan, 233, 320; *Gulliver's Travels*, 18, 179, 202, 318, 319, 325, 385
Symmes, Thomas, *Lovewell Lamented*, 323

Tasso, Torquato, *Jerusalem Delivered*, 14
Taylor, Edward, 315, 317, 320, 326, 328; as poet, 313-14
Thames River (Eng.), 7, 26, 45, 46, 316, 322, 327, 336, 337, 385
Thames River (New Eng.), 183, 201, 202, 207, 213, 215, 308, 338
Thoreau, Henry David, 184
Tilley, John, 208, 232

Timothy, 269
Tindall, Robert, 50
Tobacco; as article of trade, 26, 76, 85-87; as symbol of Virginia, 26, 54, 76, 87, cf. corn, 94; as symbol in New Eng., 205, 288
Tompson, Benjamin, 317-18, 320, 326; *Funeral Tribute to . . . John Winthrop* (Junior), 318; *New-Englands Crisis, 241-44, 256*, 326, 333, 352; *New-Englands Tears,* 241; "To Lord Bellamont," *318-19,* 320, 321, 322, 335, 353; "Upon the Elaborate Survey . . . by William Hubbard," 241
Town Brook, 91, 227
Tragedy: on Kennebeck R., 226-27; beyond Merrimack R., 247-48; King Philip's War as redemptive t., 244-45, cf. Bacon's Rebellion, 352
Troy, 12, 333
Two Brothers, 181, 182, 215
Tyler, Moses Coit, 336

Ulysses, 84
Uncas, 117, 202, 208, 214, 219, 232, 308, 328, 333
Underhill, Captain John, 202, 203-6, 212, 215, 224, 231, 248, 249, 258; as American hero, 205-6, 211, and as anti-h., 203-6; *Newes from America, 206-11,* 212, 232-33, 282, 300

Vane, Gov. Sir Henry, 202
Van Twiller, Gov. Wouter, 191-92
Vaughan, Robert, 63, 64-65, 83
Verrazzano, Giovanni da: and Northwest Passage, 17, 20; *Relation,* 17-18 (*see also* Verrazzano's Sea)
Verrazzano's Sea, 17, 20, 21, 22, 29, 31, 33, 34, 69 (*see also* Northwest Passage)
Vine, as Puritan symbol: 120, 147-48, 150, 235, 238, 318, 322, 324, 335, 338
Virgil, 85, 91, 261, 317; Dante's, 274, 303; *Aeneid,* 15-16, 27, 81, 222, 270, 326-27, 329, 333; *Ecologues,* 25, 59; *Georgics,* 25, 59, 150, 178, 316 (*see also* Pastoral)
Virginia: symbolic name, 37, 43, 50; as pastoral terrain, 26, 35-36, 45-46, 50, 54, 55, 344-45; as Canaan, 43, 345-46, 370-71; as epic, 25-27, 34, 41-42, 60,

421421

quoted, 135-36, 144, 161-62, 163, 168,
181, 189-95 passim, 199-205 passim,
210, 214-15, 220, 227, 297; his map,
136-38, 151, 157; letter to his wife,
143; "Modell of Christian Charity,"
139-140, 145, 148, 152, 197, 221, 228,
235, 246, 271n.
Winthrop's Patent, 134, 136-38 (map),
146, 155, 180, 207, 252, 321
Winthrop's Wall, 140, 141, 148, 151,
184, 191, 192, 193, 194, 195, 198, 213,
214, 220, 224, 249, 250, 251, 252, 259,
350, 365 *(see also* Border; Hedge)
Winthrop, Wait, 328
Wituamet, 108, 116, 118
Wolcott, Roger, 326, 329, 338-39; as
American hero, 338-39; "Brief Account," 325-26, *326-27, 330-30, 354,*

371, 380, 387, as epic, 326-27, 336;
Poetical Meditations, 325-39 *passim*
Wood, Colonel Abraham, 359-62
Wood, William, 151-52, 193, 314; *New
Englands Prospect, 151-58,* 170-71,
175, 178-79, 180, 200, 207, 376, 377,
380; map of New England, *155-57,*
240, 243, 249

York River (Pamunkey), 53, 68, 71-79
passim, 288, 301

Zechariah, 215, 221
Zion, 273, 288